The Illusion of "Truth"

The Real Jesus Behind the Grand Myth

The Illusion of "Truth"

The Real Jesus Behind the Grand Myth

Thomas Daniel Nehrer

CHRISTIAN
ALTERNATIVE

Winchester, UK
Washington, USA

First published by Christian Alternative Books, 2014
Christian Alternative Books is an imprint of John Hunt Publishing Ltd.,
Laurel House, Station Approach,
Alresford, Hants, SO24 9JH, UK
office1@jhpbooks.net
www.johnhuntpublishing.com
www.christian-alternative.com

For distributor details and how to order please visit the 'Ordering' section on our website.

Text copyright: Thomas Daniel Nehrer 2013

ISBN: 978 1 78279 548 3

A CIP catalogue record for this book is available from the British Library.

Design: Lee Nash

Printed and bound by CPI Group (UK) Ltd, Croydon, CR0 4YY

We operate a distinctive and ethical publishing philosophy in all areas of our business, from our global network of authors to production and worldwide distribution.

CONTENTS

A Note to the Reader

If you want to understand what Jesus of Nazareth was all about, you'd better not ask a Christian. You'll get a fantasy-based, sterilized figure of a perfect, divine, inerrant superman. The Christian caricature emerges from ancient lore and medieval paintings replete with halo and ever-smiling countenance, that Anglo-Saxon-featured portrait, god-imbued myth, idealized wonderment, suffering Savior – and all other shared notions of an *übermensch*. These will only inhibit your search.

If you want to understand the real Jesus, you must – from the outset – flush from memory an extensive array of culturally iconic but fully deceiving mind images.

If you really want to understand Jesus, his message and meaning, you'd better not ask a scholar. You'll get a logical conclusion – scientifically and hermetically extracted from crumbling Greek papyrus manuscripts, rationally reconstructed to prove unquestionably that he was a wise teacher, itinerant healer, apocalyptic doomsayer, standard period rabbi, charismatic fraud, traveling comedian or didn't actually exist. You'll find some fascinating, historical accounts – and a lot more useful information than Christianity will supply – but not the real Jesus.

If you absolutely want to understand the "real" Yeshua, the visionary who roamed the dusty roadways of first-century Roman Judea, you'd better find a grounded mystic to ask, one who is aware of Reality and its integrated functionality with the Consciousness that experiences it – but who isn't lost in cryptic, vague spirituality and occult grandiosity. Your source needs to take Jesus' metaphorical illustrations of a Kingdom "within" and translate them into comprehensible English.

That particular quest will be remarkably easy for you to accomplish. You already found him. All you have to do is keep reading.

But...

You'll need an open mind. Without that, stuck in either "true believer" devotee mode or "analysis only" scholarly framework, you won't get it. And you'll need considerable background on Jesus' context – his culture and its historical setting. I'll supply the latter. If you don't have the former, the open mind, you'd better go read something else consistent with your preconceived "Truths". You won't ever understand the *real* Jesus.

For years now, Biblical scholars, archeologists and historians have been reconstructing a "historical" Jesus. Through extensive research into ancient manuscripts and thorough analysis of writing styles, cultural conditions, changes introduced by copying and distortion via translation, scholars have painted a fascinating picture of Jesus of Nazareth. Indeed, I rely heavily on scholarly accounts for context. But, while his life and times – what he likely said and did – can be deduced from ancient accounts with reasonable probability, conclusions as to what he *meant*, and thus, what he *was* remain elusive to such overt analysis.

People – devotional, scholarly and you included – see life through a veil of personal beliefs and accepted definitions, interpreting reality and descriptions thereto based on a deep-seeded world view firmly solidified during early childhood. This integral bias in really understanding life stems from an innate human propensity: the mind wraps itself around its accepted tenets, predisposed to confirm held beliefs.

Thus, any observer, *however objective*, will only ever glean a tainted view of Jesus' nature, unconsciously distorted to conform to personal expectations. Where the Jesus devotee sees a divine super-human, the scholar interprets a wandering teacher or healer. Each will find a man shaded in hues that stem from his/her own world view. And the search remains like a hall of mirrors in a carnival, with seekers ultimately observing no more than a distorted image comprising, in essence, their own preset bias.

My perspective, however, and my interpretation of Jesus' nature – a "real" Jesus vs. an aggrandized or historical one – differs from both "true" believers' icons or objective academicians' reconstructions. While I will first illustrate the historical setting and reconstruct Jesus' place within that context based on extensive research into scholarly publications, when I explain Jesus' message and its substance, the perspective will emerge from a unique, unobstructed angle.

Through time, through man's ages of development from nomadic to agricultural and on to technological, occasional individuals have perceived Reality and their own conscious engagement of it more clearly than their peers. Jesus was certainly such a visionary, as his parables and occasional other statements indicate a clear and unique awareness for life's functionality.

However, clouding the picture – thus opening Jesus' perceived nature to diverse misconceptions – are other comments and deeds attributed to him of a more mundane nature, traditional in essence, even superstitious in nature. As myth and lore accrued on accounts of Jesus' life after his early demise (and appended even later), his message muddled toward many potential interpretations.

My trek through life, detailed later, has provided a viewpoint explicitly freed of distorting beliefs and definitions common to the traditional western mindset. When I regard statements and parables attributed to Jesus, I can separate points voiced originally by a visionary source aware of life's flow from those which reflect notions common to his and subsequent times, *because* I am aware of life's subtle, interactive function, as he was.

Focus... Cultural Context: Overview

To clarify Jesus' "real" nature and message, it is vital to enhance the historically derived picture with a thorough illustration of the mindset of Jesus' contemporaries: how they saw their world and how he would have learned to see things. Equally necessary to explore for valid sense to be drawn from his parables is the general mindset of the common man as it has evolved over two millennia to our time. That evolution led to common western ideas *you inherited*, as woven into the beliefs and assumptions that color your engagement of daily life and underlie literature, history, story-telling and even language itself.

If you do not understand how **you** see Reality and your own Self within it, you will assume you understand life fully from this haughtily modern standpoint, presuming your default cultural complex of notions to be accurate and valid. But *all people in all times* fallaciously assume they understand life as they interpret experience consistent with their belief structure. Views shared by peers through common thinking, literature and arts seem always to be corroborated, thus becoming reinforced.

Until you begin to recognize that life functions in subtle ways that elude common perception and supersede the standard modern religion-and-science mindset, you will *never* grasp Jesus' illustrations of a "Kingdom" to be found *within* – a message deep and profound, cryptic to common thinking, yet blatantly obvious to one who perceives life's real function.

Oh, and...

One other point here: I don't employ mushy New-Age generalities or glowing, light-headed spiritual claims. I don't cower daintily in awe of cultural "Truths", which aren't. Not only do I disdain political correctness, but I abhor its more insidious cousin: spiritual correctness – reverence typically accorded popular but invalid doctrines. If you aren't prepared for an in-depth, unfettered, intellectual view of Consciousness and Reality, ready with an open mind to have the grand distortion of religion exposed, you've opened – or downloaded – the wrong book.

This account will clarify *precisely* what Jesus meant in his teachings and quite accurately what he was – the "real" person. Beyond that even, it will clarify for you precisely *what you are*.

Without the latter, you'll never comprehend the former.

Without understanding your place as a conscious entity manifesting and engaging an experiential Reality, you will only be able to perceive Jesus within the confines of your belief structure. And that would present that hall-of-mirrors Jesus caricature comprising a divine myth or a deduced, amenable stick figure – either of which may perhaps satisfy your own needs, but have nothing to do with the real man.

Communicating New Vision: Hurdles Galore

Moving man's view of himself and life past common thinking, the true visionary faces great difficulty: exactly that deluded mindset the sage would have listeners outgrow is the very filter *through which any new perspective must pass.*

Most people, solidly frozen into long-held, common notions, are unable to grasp clearer views. But another factor further hinders any movement: established views have invariably attracted practitioners who make their living off their fields. These have a vested interest in maintaining adherents: new approaches could render religions and various healing practices obsolete; they could displace various spiritual disciplines. Each of those fields features many who make their entire living from the genre, accepted experts in the field of explaining life – those preachers, priests, healers, gurus, scientists, self-help experts, holistic practitioners, rabbis, psychologists, philosophers, imams, physicians, etc. With titles and degrees, broad respect and high status in society, will such professed experts be open to ideas that question their expertise, thus threatening their cozy niches?

For years now, I've encountered such a situation.

Already having jettisoned religion as a valid explanation for *anything* as a 10-year-old, thereabouts, I came to see science as an incomplete (thus faulty) account of real life by my thirties. Regarding other genres, I could detect flaws – along with occasional insights into Reality – in eastern mystical traditions, holistic health, core spirituality, modern philosophy and every other established explanation out there. Ultimately, aided by a mystic experience and facilitated by a long inner journey and fierce personal independence, I came to see, personally and intimately, the interactive nature of Consciousness/Reality – far more clearly than standard, popular and even advanced esoteric explanations did or could depict.

In short, I consciously, explicitly scoured my subconscious store of absorbed notions, layered there from childhood, and deleted *any and all definitions and beliefs* I held. Concurrently, recognizing the innate connection between mind and body – and subsequently between Consciousness and Reality – I cleared away a plethora of inner roots that were leading to outer health, relationship and success issues, a gesture that always spurred improvement in real life. That inner journey, spread over 30 years or so, led to personal *Clear Awareness*, a state of cognition equivalent to the mystic experience I'd had during my twenties – only now it is ongoing, not periodic and fleeting.

Trying to explain Clear Awareness – through a website, books and talks across the English-speaking realm – has been an adventure steeped in the above condition: some get it and benefit greatly, many others *kind of* get it, but don't pursue the requisite inner journey, while most just don't get it. And the preponderant horde *doesn't even listen*.

Visionaries of the past faced precisely the same effect. For them however, it was worse, often much worse. Socrates, blamed for aggravating gods (which, of course, didn't exist, but were widely believed in), was forced to commit suicide. Lao Tzu, tired of dealing with the blockheads of his day, wandered off, never to be seen again. Jesus of Nazareth, engaging dogmatic forces of his time, was summarily crucified. Meister Eckhart was hounded by the church over his penetrating teachings until his death, and Galileo relegated to house arrest by the same fixed thinkers.

For my part, though, complications resulting from such a gesture have eased up a bit. First, this timeframe and setting are more placid. Modern America and European-based cultures allow a freedom of expression not available earlier.

Second, modern English, flexible, concise, yet illustrative, allows fuller expression than ancient Greek, Chinese, Aramaic, Middle German or Italian of those mentioned seers. English has acquired a vocabulary allowing pointed illustration of mind elements and psychological processes adequate to illustrate inner structures that correspond to outer effects.

Third, far more people have begun to look deeply into life. The potential audience for profound insights is not only considerably larger than ever before, but also more educated, more exposed to alternate proposals and often open to considering even more advanced perspectives than they've heard. (The only down side here is that fancy new esoteric explanations abound: vaunted spiritual teachers still not quite perceiving life's functional Oneness often create new, more mystical-sounding "truths" – which, indeed, are only the same old misconceptions rephrased – providing more adorned illusions to get caught up in.)

And fourth, reaching people through advanced communication facilities in this timeframe is much easier. (With a similar drawback – lots of goofy, fallacious voices out there.)

As for any threat from irate Islamists or dull-witted fundamentalist Christians, I have come to shed the inner conflict and struggle that would entice backlash from aggressive sources. This alone should mitigate the long tradition in many creative fields that, in order to succeed, one must already be dead.

I have no more interest in martyrdom than in attracting followers or supplicants.

To Make the Point

Visionaries have two principal means to immediately communicate insights beyond people's mundane, common mindset. They can liken awareness to equivalent situations in life to which the listener can relate – using metaphor, analogy and other grammatical tools to picture points. Or they can illustrate how listeners can *gain* such awareness – a path to proceed on, techniques to engage, what to look for within. Both of these gestures are much more precise and expansive now than earlier visionaries had at their disposal, given reasons just listed.

Lao Tzu relished use of allusion and interconnected illustration to picture reality's flow as the *Tao*, an essence not explicitly describable. Gautama, the Buddha, however, was pretty good at doing just that, for he described various aspects of reality exceptionally concisely – if not always accurately. Additionally, the Buddha provided applicable techniques meant to propel the seeker toward greater awareness – meditation and corrected thinking.

Jesus of Nazareth – as we will see in great depth – relied heavily on simile with his parables, likening his "Kingdom of God" concept to various aspects of daily life for Galilean peasants he addressed. His principal gesture was simple teaching.

By comparison, for communicating means to enhance awareness, I illustrate techniques of self-hypnosis, dream analysis and other means to explore explicit information in the subconscious, then relate it to real-life meaning. Perceiving the connection between Self and experienced reality – Jesus'

Kingdom – requires enhanced focus both inward and outward. While scarcely able to get there by simply reading Jesus' wisdom, one can certainly relish that wisdom having already gotten there.

Brand New Word

Before proceeding, I need to augment the English language.

Noncept. That's it: created by revising the "con-" (together, jointly) in *concept* (a general notion or idea) into a neutralizing "non-", and combining that with the retained "-cept" root (from Latin – *cipere* or *capere*, meaning *to seize*). A *noncept* – henceforth – is a word for something **that doesn't really exist**, but is formulated in the imagination with whatever characteristics are assigned to it.

That renders, in my terminology, the word *"concept"* as referring to a real thing – something demonstrably in existence in reality, either tangible (desk, foot) or intangible (pain, hope).

Some examples of noncepts are unicorns, fairies, the government, headaches and colds. None of these exist as understood. But each of them generates *an illusion* of existence based on definitions (often absorbed early in life) and commonly shared references.

(What you think of as government is actually a collection of big buildings and people carrying out tasks. Headaches and colds are conditions of the body, perceived and experienced only in the physical context. The word *noncept*, by the way, is not a noncept itself. I'll let you figure that out.)

Many notions of highly cherished, sacred things don't actually exist in reality, making them *pure* noncepts. I may rattle your contentment by exposing flawed definitions deeply embedded within your mindset by pointing that out.

In order to outgrow fallacy, it is vital – and exceptionally beneficial – to shed illusions of "Truth" embedded in cultural fallacies, however widely accepted and deeply honored they are. Let's angle right into Jesus' life with a look at essential background points.

Slant In:
Jesus' Real Life – Background and Context Freed of Myth

Christianity has coexisted for so long with evolving western culture that it has become tightly woven into the common mindset, permeating not only its world view and literature, but even language itself. However religious you might be – or might have ever been – Christianity's values (many quite negative), inferences and myths form a subtle but significant part of your "understanding".

Should you consider yourself Christian, your religious tenets may be welded so firmly to your self-image and world view that the following in-depth look at the history and myth of Christianity could prove disturbing to your equilibrium, for many "Truths" you've been handed on golden platters are, at their core, anything *but*.

Should "true believers" have made it even this far, recognize that I feel no need to ever sugar-coat any perspective for easier consumption. Your convictions may be shaken, but your understanding of reality can only improve.

All others will *want* the unbridled, unmitigated facts about the real man whose teachings and deeds led to Christian theology, spiritual dominance – or rather, imposing societal dominance based on a spiritual façade – and the structured paradigm that grew out of that unique, early first-century life of Yeshua, the man from Nazareth.

But there aren't any.

Facts, that is.

Even his name, "Yeshua" – likely pronounced ye-*shew*-a, a very common name in his day – was corrupted through language translations and transliterations through the Latin "Iesus" (yay-zoos) to the westernized "Jesus" we know him as. However, as we will see, this phonetic alteration is nothing compared to the plethora of changes applied to his message from the outset and continued over two millennia. A tradition that garbled his name has much more thoroughly mangled the meaning to his legacy and originally simple, yet profound message.

As to "facts" as a basis of understanding things in this investigative age: if there is anything greatly preferred to valid, reliable information in our culture, it is the *appearance* of facts – nice, tidy story lines that seem complete and perfunctory, stories that can be widely circulated in mutual agreement, despite lacking validity. And, as there are **absolutely no** historical facts concerning the life of Jesus of Nazareth – not a single word about him recorded during his lifetime – Christianity provides such a wonderful substitute appearance.

Views of Jesus

There are some 1.2 to 1.3 billion people in the world who consider themselves Christian. Yet, if you queried each of them for a description of god's nature and the spirituality they believed in, you would get 1.2 to 1.3 billion different answers – that is, to the extent that many of them could actually formulate an answer. Many don't really know what they believe enough to explain it. Others, if not simply parroting stock Christian jargon, would utter inconsistent, divergent accounts and outright impossibilities – yet each explanation would be perfectly believable to the person holding the religious tenets.

That is not surprising: the mind judges "Truth" *based on* accepted beliefs – whatever they are, they seem valid. The shock would be the vast difference among Christians as to understanding.

Beyond those billion variations on the theme of redemption, three main views of Christianity and life will be regarded here:

1. The Orthodox: stated tenets of the Roman Catholic Church and offshoots as to:

- What life is all about, as construed through theology and tradition,
- What Jesus was and did, reconstructed consistent with the gospel accounts (less myth and accrued lore), and
- What that means, not only in itself, but to you and modern society.

2. The Scholarly: results of research and analysis of ancient manuscripts, leading to:
   - An evaluation as to what the ancient writers meant,
   - Who they actually were,
   - How things changed all along the way, and
   - How many different conclusions can be drawn from the evidence.

3. Mine: how an ancient visionary's perspectives, woven into sketchy accounts, appear to another visionary who explicitly sees reality beyond commonly held, fallacious notions.

The Orthodox view has grown, evolved and morphed considerably across two millennia. It was invented early on by people who never saw, heard or knew Jesus, based on vague accounts passed along by those who had, but who themselves had basically failed to understand his message – and by Paul based on his own vision. It was revised all along the way in response to political expediency, weak logic, popular mores, whim and church organizations' agendas – including a propensity toward maintaining control, enhancing wealth and perpetuating church organizations and priesthoods.

It is vital to see not only what Christianity asserts, but *where its precepts came from* – how they evolved from primitive, superstitious metaphysical claims into "Gospel Truth". In that pursuit, it is pertinent to note that, what is now considered *orthodox*, as established and correct theology, was once only *one of many varying views*. What made it main-stream orthodoxy wasn't its inherent rectitude, but that holders of this view had the political clout to stamp out other views, thus bludgeoning them into the isolated, derided category of *heresy*.

Scholars have long attempted to cut through church claims, Biblical accounts and tradition to discern what the historical Jesus would have been like. They've dissected ancient manuscripts, comparing early and later versions of New Testament (henceforth, "NT") books to extract a more impartial understanding than could ever be gleaned by simply reading English NT accounts. Documents include some 5700 remnants in the original Greek, thousands more in other languages, ranging from fragments to the four, rather complete uncial works – including the Codex Vaticanus and Codex Sinaiticus from the mid-fourth century. (*Uncial* means very old style Greek script, all upper case, no punctuation, no spaces between words.)

Able to read the original text in surviving manuscripts, researchers compare writing styles and varying content, the motivation of scribes along the way to change things, the meaning of ancient phrases and claims, etc. – analyzing the ancient Greek text in light of historical situations and cultural values.

So, much of this book relies for context on scholarly research into what the "Historical Jesus" was all about.

However, scholars attempting to swoosh away the haze of distortion clouding what Jesus really said and did, can only reach conclusions based on *their own world views* and under-standing of life. But the exceptionally diverse viewpoints expressed across the New Testament – reflecting changing perceptions of Jesus' nature through time as NT books were written – provide evidence to reach many different conclusions. And scholars do just that! Indeed, one can find some noted researcher or other who has reached *just about any* variation of possible conclusion – interpreting Jesus as anything from main-line Jewish rabbi to rebellious creator of a new religion, from stand-up comedian to wise teacher, from itinerant metaphysical healer to fake magician!

It's a fairly lucrative field – writing articles and books about the historic Jesus. Scholars, it seems, are actually *motivated* to reach different conclusions than their peers, otherwise they couldn't write yet another book about Jesus!

My take will be different. While scholarly research provides extensive information, the *real* Jesus, the man who voiced various timeless insights on life, can only be revealed when life is understood better than the common mindset of our time allows. Having clarified his historic setting and the political situation of first-century Judea, Galilee and the Roman Empire, I won't be looking for a sterile historic character, one deduced from shreds of his comments and reports of his deeds passed along for decades before being recorded.

Rather, having spent much of my life clearing from my own mindset the debris of flawed ideas – religious notions (a controlling god), pagan impressions (luck, fate) and scientific tenets (chance, probability, external causality) – I see *clearly* a direct relationship of consciousness with encountered reality. This "Clear Awareness" of a functional Oneness of Self with Reality is a standpoint approached, if not fully arrived at, by great visionaries of the past.

Thus, my stance provides a twofold advantage in reconstructing the real Jesus: first, I recognize perception of this integral Oneness when it is expressed by other visionaries. And second, I don't "form an opinion", i.e., draw conclusions based on complex underlying impressions, common to cultural "Truths" and riding typical beliefs and assumptions. Instead, having dismantled those synthetic mind elements through which most impressions are construed, I perceive the essence of situations directly, undisturbed by familiar cultural bias, trendiness, political pressure and favored interpretation. So I see clearly what Jesus meant with his parables, and have unique insight on how he would have arrived at his level of awareness.

He wasn't alone among our predecessors in seeing life more clearly than his peers.

Lao Tzu termed life's encountered flow the *Tao* – loosely translated: "The Way". To promote awareness of this Tao, he illustrated in the Tao de Ching how rational manipulation, that is, concocted action, would only interfere with that flow. Gautama termed such a state of consciousness *Nirvana* – pictured slightly different from, but in effect equivalent to, the Hindu *Moksha*. Plotinus, in his Enneads of the third century, spoke of the "One" without division or multiplicity.

Doubtless many others – Heraclitus, Plato and possibly Aristotle, Jacob Böhme, Honoré de Balzac, Bartolomé de las Casas, Meister Eckhart, Benedict Spinoza, Blaise Pascal, Dante, and Shakespeare of earlier times, Walt Whitman, Krishnamurti, Alan Watts, Sri Aurobindo, Gurdjieff and many others of more recent times – glimpsed or fully comprehended life's interactive Oneness as well, relating their vision in some fashion to others.

Jesus' insight took form in his expression, "Kingdom of God", a status he was illustrating as being "within", i.e., a state of mind.

Following background on Jesus' life and times in this segment, the **Upright** section reviews all the caveats to accepting gospels at face value. **Straight** then traces the real Jesus' life, exploring encounters he must have had, lessons he must have learned and realizations he must have reached in order to outgrow the standard Jewish world view to reach his level of perception. **Diagonal** extracts Jesus' perceptive insights in parables and other sayings. Then **Slant Out** illustrates how his vision evolved in the hands of subsequent generations of people who failed to comprehend his message.

The Point of All This

Keep in mind this *most fundamental point* as the guiding principle for this endeavor: **the purpose of the pursuit is to understand how life works**. Any philosophy purports to explain reality's function – and religion is only a specialized philo-sophical statement claiming to garner, often exclusively, **THE** "Truth" concerning the human engagement of reality.

The principal inhibiting factor in the pursuit of under-standing is the utter gullibility of the mind – this over-riding tendency for the psyche, once having accepted a set of beliefs and definitions, to interpret reality in a way that confirms them. Religions take hold and dominate a culture, not because they accurately portray reality, but because *they appear to*, once having been accepted – such that succeeding generations are heavily indoctrinated into the shared cultural mindset from birth.

People compare their experience to the complex set of rules and definitions they absorbed since very early childhood. They find "Truth" in situations and explanations – often full of noncepts – that coincide with pre-accepted notions or judge as fallacy anything outside accepted tenets.

Yet, reality operates in a consistent way – the same physical, interactive functions are in play for every conscious human in existence. If religion reflected reality as it actually works, all religions would be the same: accurate rendering in words depicting life's real flow. But they certainly aren't! Indeed, not only are religions radically different, but any single religion – e.g., Christianity – displays broad differences in detail claimed by various denominations and countless variations off those theologies held by individual believers!

Life has a clearly discernible, easily recognizable integrated flow to it. It can be perceived and made good use of for each alert human to promote practical benefit within daily life. But implanted ideas easily distort that perception, infusing artificial, fallacious notions – particularly as to causality – into personal cognition in place of direct observation. The mind simply embraces accepted ideas as base "Truth", so that they take on a veneer of validity that the believer can scarcely avoid because all subsequently encountered phenomena and explanation is compared back to them for acceptance.

Remember: *Whatever you believe in appears true.*

Reality's functional flow can never be debated: reality manifests as it does regardless of individual recognition of its value-based inter-active function. Only simulated notions about reality – creeds, definitions, assumptions, paradigms – can be argued over. And that debate knows neither end nor resolution, as each arguing party hosts a personally customized fantasy – with each appearing unwaveringly valid to the holder.

Religions, from initiation through organization phases, invariably morph subtly from attempting to *describe reality,* i.e., depicting how life actually works, to reconfirming their invented, synthetic elements – and keeping their priesthoods employed.

This work provides an exposé of the concocted ideas that grew from the spurious admixture of archaic traditions, Jesus' insights into life's flow, misperceptions and misattributions of his peers and subsequent generations as to his meaning – and eventually to a critical examination of evolving Christian sects.

But regard of such theology and dogma must always be kept in perspective: the degree to which Christianity fails to depict reality is the extent to which it will be exposed as fallacious.

The Setting – Historical and Philosophical

I have absolutely no doubt that Jesus of Nazareth was a real person of first-century Judea, by then a Roman province on the eastern shores of the Mediterranean. He certainly was conceived and born, then grew up as all of us did/do, eating and drinking, learning and interacting with contemporaries. And I have no doubt he joked, discovered and enjoyed sex, had his successes and frustrations – and that he was crucified to end that life.

With some research, one can cut through romantic and mythical attributes heaped on that once real person to perceive what his life and times must have been like, and in surprising detail.

So let's set the stage for the timely arrival of a peasant Galilean whose near anonymous lifetime would revise the trajectory of western civilization.

The Jewish Culture – in Traditional Context

The traditional Judean society into which Jesus was born about 4 BCE (Before Common Era = BC) had a long and firmly defined cultural heritage. From earliest times, Israelite tribes evolved into historical Judeans, emerging from a Semitic people of nomadic, herding and early agricultural ways. These Hebrew peoples stemmed, as per tradition, from forefather Jacob – the son of Isaac and grandson of Abraham, "Patriarchs" in the early second millennium BCE. Separated from their neighbors ethnically *not at all*, but culturally by their clannish attitude and functionally via religious fervor – believing themselves to be favored by their regarded god – they experienced a rocky history due ostensibly to their geographical homeland.

As a spawning ground of early civilization, the warm and sunny Middle East nurtured some of man's earliest cultures – from Sumer, Akkad, Assyria and Babylonia of the Fertile Crescent, Persia and Media farther east, to Egypt at the south and the Phoenicians, Hittites and ultimately Greeks to the north. The smaller numbers of Israelites – with intense tribal identity and unique, unyielding religious traditions – only rarely held their own to maintain an independent kingdom in the face of powerful neighbors.

By the time of Jesus' birth, Rome had controlled Palestine for some 60 years. But in a historical context, Roman domination followed tumultuous centuries of mostly foreign supremacy.

From David and Solomon's United Monarchy a millennium before Jesus, a split led to conflict and the eventual absorption of the northern part, Israel, into Assyria under Tiglath-Pileser III about 730 BCE. By the sixth century BCE, Babylon had conquered the southern division, the Kingdom of Judah and, having destroyed its beloved Temple, seat of its revered Yahweh-god, removed much of its population back to their own Tigris-Euphrates center. Nearly fifty years later, Cyrus the Great's Median/Persian Empire, following its conquest of Babylon, allowed return of many (mostly younger generations) to the homeland, even helping them rebuild. But foreign dominance continued under the Achaemenid Empire during this "Second" Temple period.

Persian regional control ceased with their defeat in 332 BCE by Alexander the Great. The ensuing era ushered in strong Greek influence throughout the Middle East, now cultural as well as political/military. Alexander, as his Macedonian army gained control of vast swaths of land stretching on to India, left colonies with organized control of conquered lands. Upon his early death – Alexander had not quite mastered his self-proclaimed godhood to the degree of functional immortality – his vast empire became partitioned, each region falling under control of various of Alexander's generals. Seleucus gained control over Babylonia, launching the Seleucid Empire, while Ptolemy garnered Egypt, founding the Ptolemaic dynasty. Their successors maintained – with varying levels of competence – the lofty status and conflictual attitude of those former generals.

Caught right in the middle? Yes, the Hebrew people found themselves dissolved from the Macedonian Empire only to be dominated by the Ptolemaic for a century, then the Seleucids until 141 BCE. By then, the latter empire having deteriorated, a period of independence emerged under the Hasmoneans following the Maccabean Revolt.

That period of self-rule was anything but placid, however. Intrigue and conflict ultimately led to a virtual invitation for the Romans to invade. Pompey obliged, establishing control in about 63 BCE. The Romans first kept Hasmoneans in tacit control under Hyrcanus II as nominal High Priest – but real political power rested from then on with increasingly Imperial Rome, whose interests were initially overseen by Antipater.

Antipater the Idumaean, quite a manipulator, wrangled himself efficiently into Roman graces, becoming the first Procurator of Judea, so named as a Roman province. His career was shortened by poison in 43 BCE (not an uncommon early retirement plan in coming times of the Roman Empire). By 36 BCE, his son, Herod (the Great), had emerged as client king of Judea, serving at the pleasure of Rome.

Herod, despite extensive building and reasonably prosperous times, was despised by his people. Ostensibly Jewish – Idumaeans from that southernmost province of the region had been forcibly converted – he was deemed illegitimate as ruler. His propensity for doing away with priests and family members, a lavish lifestyle and heavy taxes all added to common contempt. Herod died about the time of Jesus' birth, leaving his son, Herod Antipas in control of Galilee as tetrarch. (Antipas received that honor due to his father's penchant for executing most other eligible heirs. Tetrarch was less than king, in that Antipas only ruled over a quarter of Judea, including Galilee and Perea, a district east of the Jordan River and Dead Sea.)

Significant to note in that overview was the hard-headed, fervent mindset that was part of the Jewish tradition and religion. Rome, during its expansion from Republic into Empire, encountered, tolerated and even absorbed many regional religions. But, nowhere did it face the ardent encapsulation of religious traditions and mores into society as with the Jews. Most other religions at the time – in many variations – imagined gods in pantheons of some configuration or other, but typically acknowledged other groups' deities and cults. Not so the Jews: in their minds, their god was exclusive.

Laying the Foundation – Onto the Footer

Understanding points Jesus presented to his peers requires exploring how Jews, local Greeks, Romans and other ethnic mixes inhabiting the region perceived reality. Without a clear recognition of the common ancient mindset, regard for precepts presented in the Gospels and Christian tradition becomes distorted by a default – yet *highly flawed* – impression that people back then thought and acted like people today, that their daily interaction with neighbors and family was similar to modern man's. This defective assumption unavoidably distorts perception of Jesus and his message. It's a pit trap devotional adherents to Christianity have occupied for ages – and one that the scholarly critic, seeking to reconstruct a historical Nazarene, can scarcely and only dimly peek out of.

Indeed, to understand the mindset of Judea's common man and the more sophisticated – priests, scribes, prophets, Pharisees, philosophers, etc. – it is correspondingly vital to understand the common, *modern* mindset: how *contemporary humans* understand reality to function. Without recognizing how we each attribute causality to life's engaged flow – and that certainly includes you and any school of thought to which you ascribe – any explorer of Jesus' nature will join the devoted Christian, astute Jew and "objective" scholar, trapped in blissful ignorance in that spacious pit of misunderstanding.

However, resolving how minds of the first and twenty-first centuries (plus those intervening ages) worked is still not enough to determine Jesus' viewpoint and meaning. The reader must also begin to recognize *how life actually works*.

The psyche's *functionality* and common capability in earlier versions of our species, including those several millennia ago, was roughly equivalent to ours. But their foundation of assumptions – interwoven beliefs as to life's qualitative source and manifesting mechanism – differed considerably. Without seeing how Jesus' contemporaries thought, without seeing how "modern" man thinks *AND* without seeing how life really works, all three, any evaluator (including you) will chip, carve and conveniently shape Jesus and his deep insights into a form that fits neatly into that perceiver's mindset.

Jesus, as a handful of other true visionaries through time, could see how reality works in ways imperceptible to others. He tried to explain that clarity of vision to peers using simple aphorisms and parables to liken life's flow to various aspects of their simple agrarian lives.

But the body of his teaching and actions was grossly misinterpreted in his day. His succinct illustrations became mixed with common thinking of the time, misunderstood as they were by unschooled peasants who heard them. Because he didn't compose anything personally, this resultant mishmash was passed along in oral traditions for decades before anything was recorded – and even then, that convoluted, often internally conflictual account continued to be revised for centuries. As generations passed, the grossly mythologized theology that resulted grew and sprouted ever new shoots off the fallacious bundle until orthodoxy has all but covered over the gems of wisdom that still remain to be seen in Gospel accounts.

My purpose here is to expose the fallacy and highlight the wisdom.

Reality functions in an invariable, inviolable way. Ancients, tied up with rigid notions of gods and spirits as forces, couldn't see that functionality. Moderns, adding to those noncepts many external forces and sources, can't see life's flow either. Jesus *could* – to some degree. My intention is to reveal his insights, stripped of their original distortion and two millennia of added philosophical and theological tarnish.

The Ancients and Their Way of Thinking

Two thousand years ago, with customs well rooted in longstanding, heavily superstitious traditions, mankind attributed causality to the mystical realm of spirits and supernatural forces, headed up by gods. While the pantheon of specialized gods under Zeus/Jupiter of the Greco-Roman world had grown tired and less vivid in the common mindset, still gods, Fates – the Moirai, that personified trio inflicting destiny on man by spinning the thread of life, then measuring and cutting it based on their own agenda – and other good and evil daemons were seen to dictate events in one's life. They were deemed exclusively *causal*; they were regarded as holding the power to make real events happen, good or bad, according to their own plans.

That acquiescence to unseen spirit forces in ancient, common cognition of life held by the average person *cannot be overstated*. Most people then – certainly including the Galilean peasantry Jesus encountered – were illiterate and uneducated. They had no exposure to science (which didn't yet exist) and mathematics – little even to philosophy, save for some minor Greek influence, with that restricted to intellectuals. Geography consisted of vague impressions of powerful empires off to the east and west, with much of the world dim, distant and unspecified.

Had the common man in Palestine thought about it at all, he would have considered the world flat, with land riding on and surrounded by water below and above. Keeping water up there was the "firmament" – a great, canopy-like dome not too far beyond where birds could fly. Indeed, the firmament had gates for the sun and moon to go through, and through which water fell as rain from the waters above. Stars were loosely attached to this dome and sometimes fell off. The heavens, abode of gods – or Yahweh and his angels, as other original gods slowly got demoted – was up there in the sky even beyond the firmament.

Medical science – the interactive function of the body, its organs, nerves, etc. – was basically unknown. History was recorded in a biased fashion, but not studied commonly: there were *no schools* as we know them (only scholarly enclaves, such as the Library at Alexandria and other Hellenistic facilities). Only the very wealthy educated their offspring. And even they had no recognition of health sciences, anthropological differences

24

between cultures, nutritional values of foods, law (beyond the unquestioned dictates of rulers), human rights or many of the other frameworks of modern cross-cultural understanding we hold as assumptions.

Children of the large lower classes not only weren't educated, but were routinely exploited if not abused – made to work, sold off in marriage, treated as property. (They certainly didn't sit endlessly watching TV, playing video games or texting one another, but had to work from early in life.) They would have been handed common cultural conjecture as **fact**, as revealed and accepted truth as to *how things were* – not as a religion, such as we regard common belief structures. With no alternative ideas available and likely punishment – imagined from the gods, exacted by parents and society – for any questioning of popular tenets, children then, as most do now and have done through all time, simply accepted explanations they were handed.

Humans of the first century not only didn't think independently, they didn't even *want* to: the ancient was highly motivated to fit anonymously into society, to share the common mindset and *not* stand out. Each, having grown through that childhood indoctrination period, looked at traditional explanations not as a religion, as an explanation with options. Rather, each bought into prevailing notions *without question* as to how life worked – having had local cultural "Truths" hammered into their mindset since childhood with no alternatives available, duly fearful of divine retribution for evil thoughts. They might question certain interpretations, but not core tenets.

Indeed, Latin, the language of the Romans during centuries of ascendance and decline, didn't even have a word for religion until late in its run; religion wasn't deemed a creed or set of convictions to be switched or dabbled in, but the *standard way of life,* self-evident, unquestionable.

This psychological adherence to religion was even more pronounced within the Jewish culture, given its ages-long identification with its exclusive god and his laws as identified by prophets and refined by long traditions.

But universally, common man didn't understand astronomy – had no recognition whatsoever of the earth with atmosphere and oceans orbiting the sun along with other planets.

More generally, wandering regularly through the night sky, the planets were associated with local gods, named after them. Even days of the week became associated with – and named after – gods (Woden's Day, Thor's Day, Saturn's Day) – inventing a 7-day week precisely because, along with sun and moon, five planets were visible moving through the "heavens". Eventually, these planets/gods were attributed causality based on slowly established astrological relationships of stellar and planetary positions – orientations that seemed to correspond to real events, even *cause* them. Likewise, omens were read into appearances of comets and eclipses. (Some of these occult practices persist today, nurtured by ever-gullible minds, ready to interpret reality through held beliefs and always preordained to reconfirm them.)

Aristotle's cosmic model featured earth surrounded by concentric crystalline spheres with sun and planets, etc., attached, each rotating at different velocities over a static earth. This model evolved complexity by the second century BCE needed to explain complicated, sometimes retrograde, planetary movement. But little of even that primitive model, shared by scholars, dispersed into common understanding.

Without newspapers or anything approaching objectivity in accounts passed along, people had no information on current events elsewhere – knowing only what they heard of distant lands from hearsay and rumor, perhaps delivered by caravan drivers or wandering minstrels, stories rife with fear and exaggeration. In cities, rumors spread rapidly – and changed with each telling!

Biology hadn't emerged, leaving people ignorant of microscopic life forms, infection, cause of fermentation, need for fertilization of crops, etc. Nor had geology. Lacking background in reliable history, common folk held correspondingly little orientation towards reporting events impartially.

Peasants hated their aloof, excessively wealthy rulers, but didn't understand why the elite held power or even *how*, beyond force of arms. Common folk not only had no understanding of climate or weather patterns, they didn't even recognize that *air* existed. They thought drought was punishment from the gods, believing prophets could elicit rain through incantations or entreaties. (When it worked, it was proven true; when not, apparently the entreaty wasn't adequate or the god angry. Any outcome fulfilled common convictions!)

They had little regard for individual expression and personal fortitude: believing gods and spirits to be dominant (what that word comes from!) in human affairs, they thought that configurations of animals' entrails could foretell the future. Indeed, they slaughtered an animal as sacrifice to appease appropriate gods before battle and killed a bigger one as thanks afterwards if successful.

Throughout the Greco-Roman realm, in order to detect what the gods had in store, divination was long practiced. Oracles were deemed the conduits to the spirit realm, able to directly scrutinize their god's will. Lesser-connected seers were thought able to read the intent of the gods, generally by examining those animal entrails to predict upcoming events by interpreting liver, lung or other conditions. Other such means of predicting upcoming events spanned man's cultures – from oracle bones and the *I Ching* in China to common occult gestures of reading palms, the stars, numbers, crystal balls, tarot cards, melting or dripping wax or even tea leaves.

Many of those, too, survive in some form or other to this day – save tea leaf reading, a practice sharply diminished by the invention of tea bags.

Libation was common – pouring out a few drops of wine (or

whatever) before drinking as offering to the gods. And of course, special notation was used to even *address* any particular god – lest that deity be offended. A key means of influencing gods had been giving them offerings and sacrifices – from ritually slaughtered animals (Jewish "shechita" is still practiced) to grain and virgins.

Omens, portents and signs were sought as indications of the gods' intentions, curses and jinxes highly feared.

The point to all of these observations is that, to the ancient mind and to **far too many even today**, *a specific, dictated destiny* is currently in store – about to happen, or "in the cards" – for each of us to encounter as set there by the force of some external, i.e., spiritual, source.

To ancient minds, **gods and spirits were causal**; *man wasn't*. It behooved the interested party, so implied, to predetermine just what exactly is in store so decisions could be made whether or not to proceed with current undertakings. And in the interests of divine cajoling, urging positive events to happen certainly required reverence and offerings to the gods – or atonement, fasting, self-inflicted pain, etc. – to elicit from them desirable events.

Overlaid within common, functional paradigms for local groups sharing pantheons and mythical world views was the hierarchical character of imagined gods, their roles, powers and interactive propensities. This was the case virtually everywhere two thousand years ago.

A good example to illustrate that is Ahura Mazda, the wise and beneficent god in Old Persian lore.

Zoroaster, in reconstructing Persian traditions centuries before Jesus, had promoted Ahura Mazda from the chorus to soloist, picturing him as primary creator god. But, as a force of good and promoter of truth in the world, he was locked in ongoing conflict with the negative Angra Mainyu. Ahura Mazda (personifying words meaning light and wisdom) came complete with his entourage of Amesha Spenta – "Bounteous Immortals", angelic sorts of entities that in turn personified positive qualities of wholeness, devotion, etc. Later on these Immortals, as such things evolve, became attributed to domains (again, what that word comes from) of life, such as water, fire, cattle, etc.

Jewish lore isn't so straightforward. From the time of David, the prevailing god was named "El" or variations thereof: El-Shaddai (god of the mountain), Elohim (plural, the gods). El was rooted in Canaanite belief and not uncommon in various Middle Eastern groups in times one to two thousand years BCE. He was paired with Asherah as wife or consort and father to other gods – e.g., Mot (Ugaritic death god) and Yam (Sea god of Canaan) – and figured prominently in regional myth.

But Yahweh (or YHWH, the four-lettered "tetragrammaton" – without vowels, as per that time) was the name most often attributed to the Jewish creator god, particularly later, approaching the time of Jesus. Yahweh's roots are more obscure, but it, too, was associated with Asherah in early times – according to clear archeological indications. At some point it either paralleled El, or eclipsed him after Israel (the northern part of the original kingdom where El was more firmly rooted) fell to the Assyrians and Yahweh took center stage in the Jerusalem temple (located in Judah to the south, where YHWH was imagined).

Clouding the exact evolution of El and Yahweh as concepts (and any other aspect of belief, for neither El nor Yahweh ever existed as anything except mind images of fervent believers) is the invariable propensity of associated religions to *revise their history* along the way according to subsequently popular interests. Judaism, for example, presents itself as monotheistic and retrofits that claim on its history by revising its lore. But in ancient times, Judaism was much more accurately Henotheism, wherein people (particularly common folk) worshipped a principal god while accepting the existence of other deities, or

Monolatrism, where many gods were acknowledged, but only one worshipped.

In religions where dogma and definition passed through the ages via oral traditions as personal exchange and generational indoctrination, change was inevitable and easy: the past was simply revised to suit present whim. Yahweh's peer gods became lesser in rank, ultimately relegated to mere angels. Hallowed accounts were updated – simply changed by the priesthood as needed to fit current interpretations. Even as writing made recording of traditions possible, for ages written materials had to be regularly recopied as old manuscripts wore out. Changes were easy and common as pious scribes would make revisions consistent with current conceptions (immaculate or not) – or simply not copy documents with accounts that differed from preferred interpretations.

Many a Jewish (and certainly later, Christian) tenet has passed into oblivion upon being rendered unpopular. With each revision, the past was simply reconstructed to fit current belief – a policy of deception inherited by its progeny, Christianity.

Fear and Powerlessness

So common peasant farmers, fishermen, housewives, laborers or basket weavers Jesus would have encountered were very super-stitious. Totally unfamiliar with modern sciences and means of communication, unaware of history and current events beyond word-of-mouth accounts from caravan merchants or rumor, unable to read and with no access to objective news sources, peasants of Roman Judea were isolated, very credulous, fearful people. They attributed creative power to a remote, aloof, yet potent god and feared the impact of demons and spirits, any of which could inflict pain, illness, insanity or failure without warning or effective recourse.

This idea – perpetuated overtly or subtly to this day – held that the spiritual realm was good and powerful whereas the mundane, physical realm was flawed and weak; the spiritual desirable, the material disdained. Man's "soul" element was thought trapped here in the world of pain and toil – prompting yearning toward the spiritual, resulting in efforts to appease the deity. Thus, burnt and animal offerings strictly followed revealed Law: complex rituals specified exactly how to slaughter animals and prepare food, how to conduct relationships, etc., to satisfy Yahweh. The process – the expertise required to deal with Yahweh correctly – had been revealed by prophets of old and was known only to priests of current times. That "expertise" and common fear that elevated it, promoted the priesthood into special societal classes – for *they* alone had the inside track to Yahweh's attention. *They* alone could interpret signs and dreams, could administer rituals properly so as not to anger Yahweh-god and bring punishment, opening the way for surreptitious demons to gain control.

Where we look to medication prescribed by a doctor to counter symptoms of illness, they would have recoiled in shame, thinking themselves inflicted as impure sinners or taken over by evil spirits. And their neighbors would have judged them so, too. The only recourse was repentance and purification – again via ritual.

The priesthood's driving authority was "Truth" as revealed in scriptures – insights gleaned by holy men of old and passed along through, by the time of Jesus, written accounts. Sense was made of a cruel and dangerous world by hearing and debating the meaning of scriptural passages – the dictates of the Psalms, words of Isaiah and Micah, accounts of Moses – then trying to relate those words to current, daily situations.

Common folk would have applied wine or oil to cleanse a wound – not to kill bacteria or soothe the skin, but rather to counter the *evil* that the lesion symbolized. To deal with illness, mental or physical, they might receive lashes or fast to appease Yahweh through personal suffering, or repent for sins they obviously *must* have committed to receive such illness as punishment.

But their principal means to accomplish intent – to erase the sin and impurity, thus assuaging Yahweh and eliciting favorable events – was to atone through sacrifice for sins inflicted on others. Distinct rituals specified exactly how to carry out such atonement: burnt offerings of perfect bulls, lambs, goats or doves, were required (couldn't dump your deformed lambs on ol' Yahweh), specifically chosen according to the negative act. Explicit peace, sin and grain offerings were carried out with exacting rituals performed by the priests.

By Jesus' time, large-scale sacrificial procedures had become institutionalized, with the Temple hierarchy and many suppliers of goats, lambs and doves reaping great profits from dictated procedures set into place earlier by Major Prophets.

Beyond that, the common peer of Jesus had more negatives to overcome.

The Class Structure

Filling out the picture of Jesus' cultural environment brings up an aspect of man's tradition that is much less rigid in western society currently than in other regions and in the world in general of earlier eras. The United States comprises a populace whose ancestors left Europe and other areas often enough to escape rigid societal *class* structures in place there. The mix prizes the flexibility of a system, wherein the possibility exists to better oneself – through education, hustle, training, imagination, etc., to improve one's lot in life. American class implications divide out based on wealth and education – both of which are attainable.

That flexibility can be taken for granted, by presuming other cultures in other times, featured upward mobility, too. Such was *not the case* in first-century Judea – or anywhere else on this planet at that time.

People by birth were virtually fixed into rigidly defined,

inflexible classes offering scant possibility of upward mobility.

At the top was royalty and the privileged class – landowners, high government officials and their families, whose children would learn to read and write, whose status and wealth passed on to those offspring. This small sliver of the population, perhaps 5 percent, controlled probably two thirds of the wealth.

In first-century Judea, *they* certainly didn't rock the boat. These people – along with the aristocratic temple priesthood, the Sadducees, also enjoying status, power and wealth from taxation – weren't about to fight or even offend the Romans and thus threaten their own good lifestyle.

Just under that upper class were scribes, those literate who wrote out legal forms, hand-copied documents and interpreted writings. There were no manufacturing operations, however, no "corporations" and little real industry, but there were merchants and artisans – smiths and potters, etc. They could make a living, despite the tax burden to the Romans and local ruler, plus another tithe to the temple. But that class was relatively small.

Below that were tenant farmers working the fields, vineyards and olive orchards, fishermen and laborers – basically construction people, involved in Antipas' building projects. The farmer owed a cut of profits or crop yield to landowners, while all owed taxes to the Romans, the local hierarchy *and* the temple cult. Indeed, most people would have been farmers to a degree. They grew whatever edibles they could in their own gardens and kept their own animals – typically right in the same small, dirt-floored houses they lived in.

Jesus' occupation, referred to in the gospels by the (Greek) word "*tekton*" would have been a general construction worker – laboring with his father on building projects. The romantic image of carpenter, building furniture or frame houses, is a romantic myth. The simple, mud-brick or stone houses of the time lacked amenities such as furniture and commercially crafted cabinets, wood being scarce and expensive anyway. And

Nazareth wasn't near the Sea of Galilee for boat-building operations. But building was plentiful, so masons and general-
purpose construction workers were certainly feasible lines of
employment. (Nazareth sat within an hour's walk of Sepphoris,
a regional center that was undergoing major building in Jesus'
time – due to heavy damage from an uprising following Herod's
death. Construction jobs would have been plentiful there during
Jesus' youth.)

With no social programs available, everybody had to earn
their "daily bread" somehow. Most worked hard throughout
their short lifetimes, following lines of work their fathers had.

Soldiers were needed, guards, etc. But while Rome drafted
many locals for its legions, Jews weren't sought for this line of
work: they wouldn't fight on the Sabbath, and wars couldn't be so
conveniently scheduled.

In comparison to much of the Roman Empire, slaves were
uncommon in Judea, it seems, so that bottom-end cultural
stratum was largely relegated to the peasantry for low pay or
food.

Cultural Standards

Framing the mindset of common people in Jesus' setting was the
traditional promotion of *purity*, tied in with the primitive spirit-
world-based standards of thinking. Imagining a god that
meddled continuously in human affairs from mass events down
to a personal level, the positive gesture to elicit favorable conditions via burnt and grain offerings – so considered – was *purity*,
i.e., cleanliness, in a defined sense more than physical, though
material cleanliness was a part of the equation.

Daily life in a village would have been pretty smelly. Without
running water and sewage systems, people had to fetch water
from the town well – hardly pristine to begin with – and carry it
home (a menial task often assigned to children) for all purposes.
For an extended family with an older generation and numerous

children (lacking other diversions, sex would have been a frequent evening pastime, with headaches likely not yet a good excuse for overworked females to decline it – however, many babies died early, tempering the household numbers somewhat) there was a lot of daily poop to deal with. And no bathroom, no outhouse in which to sequester it. Plus, goats, cattle and any other animals stayed right there *in the same house* – adding to the ambient stench. Outside the house, donkey dung and urine would have graced the streets, added to by men and dogs.

So conceptually, purity did include some recognition of sanitary values: anointing people, the principal gesture of purification, would have served to cover over ambient malodors with sweet fragrance. That symbolized good overcoming evil.

However, being pure involved more in a spiritual sense: following accepted traditional dictates as prescribed by the prophets – what to eat, exactly what to offer for sacrifice, how to prepare food, not working on the Sabbath, etc. Indications of higher purity – that is, as reflected in the reality Yahweh was deemed to manifest – included wealth, health, being Jewish and being male.

Being female entailed, *by definition*, impurity, owing to menstruation and long, primitive traditions featuring women as property in this male-dominant Patriarchal Society. Add seductive guile and its twofold negativity: temptation to physical pleasures (worldly, as opposed to high-minded spirituality) and control over men. Also *defined* as impure, and deemed lower class, were the diseased, lame, poor, non-Jews, outcasts, etc. Down there, too, were robbers, prostitutes, bar owners, herdsmen, tax collectors, those who ducked Temple taxes and those who didn't follow set rituals and observations.

So stratified, the culture Jesus grew up in was rigid and unyielding. Seemingly immersed in foul-smelling evil, it strived for the good, however out of reach it seemed.

Personal Engagement

As across the Roman Empire, the common man of first-century Palestine spent his day *not* driving off to his office or workplace in the morning (no such thing as regular pay with extensive benefits), *not* shopping at the store with all manner of food and household products available (town bazaars would have offered local produce and grain in season, perhaps expensive spices), *not* playing with the kids (no time for that) or helping them with homework in the evening (no schools) *nor* watching a movie (entertainment wasn't available), but trying to eke out a living.

A workday was as long as the season's daylight hours provided – and in Palestine, there were six of them wrapped around the non-working Sabbath. Active life took place during the daytime. With lighting only by oil lamp and fire (candles didn't appear in the Middle East until four centuries later), night activity was limited – and discouraged by the cost of olive oil or wood. Venturing out at night risked encountering thieves without police for security.

The typical man dominated his small home, likely treating his family with the same overlord authority that he faced from his government, his landlord and his imagined god. His effort was spent trying to follow traditional rituals to appease and not anger spirit sources of pain and hunger.

In his own mind, the average peasant was powerless; he faced real forces of cultural suppression and imagined forces of evil spirits out to get him and his family. Tolerance, fairness and empathy for the ill and less well off (all of whom, at least in Palestine, were deemed impure and thus eliciting their own fate) was unlikely. Social programs to help anybody were not part of the Roman agenda – nor of either Antipas or the Temple elite.

So, outside restricted, privileged groups – ruling and administrative classes, some merchants and the temple hierarchy – the average man had no upward mobility, no power and no hope. And the common woman, impure by definition, was worse off *yet*, both politically and socially inferior, particularly in the male-dominant Middle East. For sure, there would have been joking and social interaction, relationships between neighbors and friends, talk and gossip, and various festivals. Human nature survives despite conditions. But on a personal scale, daily living for Jesus' contemporaries was a tough undertaking.

The Bigger Picture

Adding to the bleakness of life for the Judean realm was an overriding negativity of tradition. For more than a millennium, generation after generation, Hebrew lore featured Yahweh's standing promise that the Jews would be independent, ruled by a descendant of David, free of outside oppression and control. That self-rule had been the guarantee of the covenant forged in ancient times, promised by a god who, in turn, expected his chosen people to honor him and him alone as sole deity-in-chief.

But for centuries, since the capitulation of Judah, the Jewish peoples had been almost continuously under foreign control. So, where was Yahweh all this time while his people suffered, toiling endlessly under the yoke of outside authority? Why would he allow the Babylonians, Seleucids and Romans to dominate his chosen people?

Far from ever questioning the very being of such an inept deity, the conclusion was invariably reached – likely promoted by religious authorities living privileged lifestyles – that the people had sinned, had worshipped other gods, had somehow failed their side of the bargain. And thought grew through time that any day now, people would have adequately atoned for their sins, and Yahweh would smite the enemies and restore the Jewish state to its rightful prominence. Leading that charge would be a grand hero, anointed as king and savior – a Messiah.

Ritually significant to Jewish tradition was that a priest, king or prophet be duly *anointed* with scented olive oil. This had to do with that orientation to purity: the sweet oil was cleansing and purifying, signifying goodness in opposition to foul-smelling, evil things. The Aramaic word, "Messiah" simply meant *Anointed One*, a person deemed special religiously or politically, consecrated by proper authorities using that time-honored gesture. ("Christ", of course, is Greek for *Messiah*. Subsequently, though, *Christ* took on vaunted meaning well beyond being anointed as head of state or holy man.)

So hope and yearning built over time that some great leader, a Messiah, duly selected by Yahweh from available stock if not supplied directly from above, would emerge to lead Israel to independence.

People in any time or place, when faced with austere realities, very often retreat into the safe confines of their own imaginations. When rejected by a lover or society, they'll imagine a more desirable setting, visualizing in the unhindered bounds of thought an alternate reality, more pleasing, more satisfying. Surely that's how it *should* be, how it **will be** one day...

So, it would have been then: if oppression and discontentment dominate life *now*, surely Yahweh will intervene to improve things *soon*. We need only follow the prescribed dictates – the Law and Prophets – to appease his requirements and unleash his mighty force. This had been promised by the covenant, foreseen by the prophets of old, foretold in the scriptures – all cornerstones of the undergirding Jewish world-view of the day.

Thus the comprehensive mindset Jesus would have encountered in his Galilee environs was a primitive one indeed. People projected power to the spirit realm, ultimately to Yahweh god, and looked to divining means and prophecy to foretell what would come. Hopeful but wary, trusting in imagined power sources to counter imagined evil, they faced a daily grind to feed themselves and their families and pay their heavy taxes.

The Western Version

We, too, inherited variations of these same elements of mind: concepts that project power to gods and intangible metaphysical sources. But the western mindset grew from *European* root notions – conceptually removed from Middle Eastern variations and only later overlaid with them.

European traditions at their core stem from ancient Germanic, Greek, Celtic, Slavic and South European peoples, most of whom emerged from the same Indo-European roots.

Before Abraham migrated from Babylon towards the southern Levant, before pyramid building began in Egypt, even before Sumer coalesced into civilization in southeast Mesopotamia, advanced inhabitants of the Black Sea region began to expand outwards. Having mastered agriculture and experienced its accompanying population growth, having developed the wheel and domesticated horses, various tribes began to migrate into surrounding, lesser populated regions. In time, they absorbed or displaced native groups, differentiating their language (as well as culture and ethnic identity) as they split regionally to become major European peoples: Greeks, Celts, Slavs, Germans, Scandinavians, various Latins, etc. (Basques remain today as a carryover indigenous people, where Finns and Hungarians represent a later incursion.)

Attitudes and the prevailing mindset of these early Indo-European peoples are reflected by their myths and gods. From Greek and Roman *Zeus/Jupiter* to the Celtic *Taranis* and Germanic *Odin/Wotan* and *Thor*, each with accompanying pantheons of specialized deities – sun, war, vegetation, love, fertility, harvest, fire, wind, etc., gods – specific projections of source causality can be seen.

Our western ancestors perceived a world ruled over and *directly influenced* by pantheons rather than predominant single deities, as in eventual Yahweh characterizations. Ancient Europeans projected their gods onto apparent star formations –

the constellations – and saw the planets, sun and moon, as well as comets and an occasional nova, as indicators of the gods' intent. As noted, they would fervently seek to portend the future by determining godly intent through various means of divination, and adjust plans accordingly. And they tried to influence their deities through animal sacrifice, prayer/entreaty and other means.

Interactive gods and goddesses imagined by our ancestors incorporated several features that passed to succeeding generations even as the gods themselves died out following the introduction of Christianity.

First, the Fates, mythical entities initially spinning the thread of personal life, evolved into a force unto itself that would dictate life's track: Fate, Kismet (Persian roots) or Destiny (Latin roots) all allude to a subtle power, a seemingly external agent, that is setting the course of events in one's life. Fate, generally, as the thought has come down to us, regards the present and future as events unfold. It indicates a prescribed outcome, hidden and not specifically sourced to a god or other explicit agent. Destiny tends to look backward, interpreting an inevitable line to life that led to the current outcome or to one's final status in life – as though, seen in retrospect, it were fixed in place and unavoidable.

Related to these, but separate and *in addition* – for **all such notions accumulate within the mindset** – is *fortune*. The Roman Goddess, Fortuna – cognate to the Greek Tyche – was deemed to capriciously inflict good or bad outcomes into life events. She lives still in the common words "fortunate" and its adverbial cousin, "fortunately". Notice how often you or others use those words – and recognize that doing so reveals a subtle attribution of causality, active within your own subconscious, that projects the underlying source of the event explained to some external force.

Two Key Points necessary to recognize concerning **Theism:**

1. The only difference between holding one god as exclusive or supreme and believing in many gods specialized in function is the number.
   - Gods exist only in the imagination of believers – however real they seem to those holders.
   - Projecting creative causality to one source as opposed to many is merely arithmetic.
   - In terms of idols which represented various gods: worshipping an idol or star cluster is no different than worshipping a concept.

2. As cultures evolved in their understanding, absorbing alternate impressions from surrounding or conquering groups or integrating more accurate perspectives from visionaries within their own midst, old ideas were never fully eradicated. All such cultural conjecture simply accumulates, covered over with new layers of definition, with the mix passed on to subsequent generations.
   - The mind can host numerous, diverse notions as to causality – how life works – that are inconsistent, even conflicting. Yet, it won't detect any contradiction, as all definitions, absorbed during early learning, are held as truths.
     - ✓ E.g., if a god created the world and drives it by instigating all events according to a divine plan, then luck can't be a valid mechanism driving events, as all causality would default back to the god. But a mind primed from early childhood with both of these common definitions won't

notice the exclusive dichotomy to those notions.

- ✓ Likewise, Science, attributing causality to real world forces and sources is absolutely inconsistent with religions that deem gods as instigators. Yet many people blindly accept both Christianity and Science, which are actually mutually exclusive paradigmatically.

- Elements pertaining to understanding how life works, shared across cultures, are built into the mindset in many subtle ways.
  - ✓ Not only are religion and likely science absorbed as explicit belief structures during childhood, but these common notions are subtly embedded in literature and entertainment. They are thus communicated and reinforced in every mode of value expression from childhood stories to cartoons to movies.
  - ✓ Indeed, language itself carries specific implications for the nature of reality – and different languages, in diverse tone and varying detail for describing experienced phenomena, incorporate substantially different world-views.
  - ✓ Common cultural behavior and personal interaction also reflect shared values and pass them on to subsequent generations.

- The religious and scholarly alike arrive at conclusions as to Jesus' nature based on the world-view they hold, the belief structure that shapes their interpretation. Inaccurate views of the function of reality can only lead to erroneous conclusions.

Also related functionally and bundled as well into standard

thinking is the impression of *luck*. The Indian goddess Lakshmi, presiding over wealth, beauty and, (you guessed it) fortune, weaseled her way into western thinking, likely through old German or Slavic connections. Luck, functionally, is more short term and immediate than related notions of fortune or fate. But the good/bad outcome impelled by some determining force *out there*, some subtle driver, seems insurmountable in comparison to personal will, planning and execution: hence the common sports idiom, *I'd rather be lucky than good*.

Luck, Fate and Fortune all slink stealthily within common western thinking. All are carryovers from ancient thoughts that undergird traditional European thinking. All predate Christianity in their roots. And all impact the holder's confidence and thus his/her life flow.

From the fourth century onward, as Christianity became the state religion of the Roman Empire – thanks to Constantine – the single god notion spread through various continental cultures. But importantly, *monotheism never really displaced older concepts*; it simply got piled on top of common cultural understanding. And it willingly adopted older pagan lore to promote acceptance. Easter, rooted in spring rebirth and fertility rites (Jesus rising from the dead, bunny rabbits and eggs) was a facelift of German rites to Eostre. Christmas borrowed gift-giving from year-end Saturnalia, its date from winter solstice celebrations (when the sun's trek, as rebirth, began to head northwards) and much lore from other pagan roots.

So European Late Antiquity and Middle Ages were dominated by common thinking that projected creative, effective power outwards to various imagined sources. Indeed, the lack of literary output and philosophical advancement of the often-termed "Dark Age", with a general cultural decline (in comparison to the preceding Roman Empire) that characterized Europe then **resulted directly** from the powerlessness of the shared mindset of superstitious, fearful people. With a dominating church riding fear and its own authoritative, self-serving attitude, stultification was the only possible outcome.

But by about 1600, some thinkers began to nudge man's point of view past the strictly religious.

Understand that religion, at least western versions of it, rests on a type of thinking called **Revelation**. This mode holds that truths concerning the workings of reality are hidden, masked by, through or behind a deity such that only a few privileged souls are able to see through the veil and "reveal" those truths. Long traditions of Judaism were compiled from prophets' revelations over centuries. Christianity's emergence rested solely on revealed word as put forth by Jesus, Paul and subsequent enhancers like Tertullian (inventor of the Trinity), Irenaeus, and Augustine on to Thomas Aquinas.

(Of course, such revelation wasn't actually revealing anything new or insightful about a god who didn't really exist. But rather it only added slight permutations of already accepted definitions – principally grander and more glorious versions of the same myth. Religious establishments and common people *never* accept valid, visionary perspectives as "revealed". Real insight into how life actually works, which always exposes the flaws of accepted "Truth", would seem *blasphemy*. Only notions in line with pre-accepted bunk are regarded as *revelation*.)

But revelation as a means of understanding began to be challenged by two other methods of differentiating truth from fallacy: **Reason** and **Empiricism**.

Reason, as rooted in ancient Greek thinking, was refined by Descartes, Hobbes and others to allow for considered arguments based on experienced reality as opposed to spouted, unques-tioned, exposure of supposedly divine secrets. Truth, i.e., veracity, had to be supported by rational argument.

Empiricism, while also rooted in Greek philosophical implica-tions, came of age through early efforts of Francis Bacon and John Locke from the seventeenth century onward. The gist of this line of thinking was that, if you want to understand reality, you must examine, explore and test propositions concerning real, physical aspects according to defined rules.

From empiricism, argued through reason, has resulted Science – a widespread system of regard that in the intervening four centuries has become a standard mode of thinking roughly on par with revelation still promoted by religion. Science as a paradigm considers only the "real" world, the micro- and macrocosm of particles and objects encountered daily. It attributes causality *only* to real agents – not to any sort of metaphysical source: gods, demons or fate. Science finds mathematical values in objects and their movement, not spiritual values in esthetics or derived meaning. Just as movement requires physical impetus, so accomplishment requires manipulation – if you want something to happen, *you must make it happen* through planning and execution. To science, the self and the world of objects are separate, the material realm only responding to force and manipulation.

Science's paradigm implies a flow through time of self-contained, isolated objects in a universe of space. These interact based on rules of momentum, gravity, etc., and change in movement upon applied force. To science, all **effects** have a real-world **cause**. And to science, since the real universe is the only thing that exists, consciousness is a fleeting, insubstantial result of brain function. *Human-level* consciousness thus results from long evolution of brain complexity based on natural selection. By this model, your capability to think, love, create, remember, emote, care and reason all result from synapses firing in the physical organ, the brain – for your consciousness must rest on brain function. Science, in essence, reduces meaning in life to mechanical functionality of a brain-generated consciousness that experiences it. Self-recognition, according to science's paradigm, must cease to exist upon cessation of physical viability, taking memory, value, accomplishment – and love – with it into oblivion.

Along with its physical-only model, science introduced "probabilities" into the common mindset as *Chance* – the percentage likelihood that an event might take place, based on known vs. unknown factors and influences.

Mankind, via propagation of scientific thinking, absorbed a more reasoned, logical approach to life. Science-based orientation impelled western culture toward an age of industry and, later, technology and communications.

However, just as earlier, when Christianity was introduced it didn't eliminate pagan conceptualizations, but layered new beliefs on top of them, so science simply added to the western mindset. It didn't fully displace religion, luck, fate, etc. Science *just heaped other definitions* onto the average person's already conglomerated psychic truckload.

Thus, common modern thinking incorporates *three* modes of intertwined understanding, customized in weight according to the individual:

1. Attribution of life experience to metaphysical forces (as per religion):
    *   A creator god out there making things happen.
    *   Luck, Fate and/or Fortune as independent functions driving events.
2. Acknowledgment of real-world power sources (thanks to science).
    *   The weather, government, conditions, rich people, earthquakes, bacteria and viruses, hiring practices, the economy, one's enemies, others' whims and priorities, laws, the police or crooks, one's own weaknesses – all these and more are deemed *causal,* needing to be counteracted personally through planned action and manipulation.
    *   Accidents and coincidences, unknowns, etc., combine for *chance* – even "random" – events. These might be

counteracted with insurance, strength, weapons, wealth and fortitude.

3. Use of Reason to manipulate any of those external forces and sources.

- We learn to get education, out-think, out-argue, work hard, pray, bully, cheat, use money as leverage, steal, etc., to overcome factors deemed causes to our lives.
- Effectively, we each learn to manipulate our parents while children, and apply those rules throughout life, regardless of efficacy.

So, modern man, unlike his ancient predecessor of Jesus' time, carries a *much more* complicated mindset. Instead of just offering sacrifices and maintaining purity to appease gods, we hold complex notions for how to influence perceived forces in our lives.

Even worse, by inheriting that complex of forces, modern man picked up supplemental *inner conflict* in the bargain. Conflict is inherent when gods *out there*, with other agendas, are deemed to make things happen. And struggle results within the mindset when imagined mechanisms of causality are inherently, by definition, unconcerned – as per science.

So instead of just imagining *gods* running the show, worrying about them and spurious demons, we modern individuals – and *collectively as cultures* – strive to contend with a plethora of real-world sources and forces. We spend much time, minds muddled in planning how to overcome all the factors aligned against us, executing complex procedures to manipulate a world seeming invariably opposed or uncaring.

How Life Works

As I explain the functionality of Consciousness engaging an interactive Reality, you will naturally compare my illustration with your own personal view of existence, perhaps "agreeing" with some points, disagreeing with others. Religious convictions may undergird your world view; you may base your understanding on scientific principles. As noted, many variations of those two paradigms populate our shared understanding. You certainly have your own custom blend of components formulating your overall view.

Whatever they are, it is important for you to focus on them for a time and *stipulate* for yourself what they are – particularly in the terms I've presented above: do you think a god directly causes events? Or luck? Do you think all causality can be traced to real-world agents, as science holds? Do you think illness is caused by bacteria invading the body, triggered by conditions? Or does the body sometimes just spontaneously malfunction? Does your cognitive awareness result from complex brain function?

Thorough review of your current understanding is essential, because whatever I explain that doesn't fit into your accepted *viewpoint* you will question, perhaps reject. Possibly you hold to a more eastern slant, with meditation at the core of Buddhist leanings. Rigid scientific orientation, should you hold that, would not readily allow considering metaphysical connections wherein the mind affects the real world outside of direct manipulation.

Likely, *whatever* your take on life, you see yourself as one thing and a world of objects and people "out there" as something else, detached and remote from the isolated *self* enclosed within your body-shaped container. Science, religion and each of those older notions – luck, fortune, etc. – are all functionally dualist; they separate the *self* from experienced reality.

But you are connected, whether aware of it or not. Practically all beliefs compromise that awareness.

The conscious Self which you recognize is intimately and inviolably connected to the flow of events and relationships which you experience daily – in terms of *quality* and *meaning*, how they impact you in measured experience. This connection, this "Oneness" with which you engage life is most noticeable in the patterns you tend to weave into your life...

Looking back into memories of your lifetime, you'll notice that you attract particular types of people – while individual relationships form, grow and fade through life's stages, *types* of people you engage and roles they play persist. Friends and intimate relationships now (or lack of them) replicate earlier interaction in repeating patterns back into your childhood – reproducing how you related to parents and siblings. The extreme case illustrating this propensity is the classic abused woman, breaking away from her belligerent husband and moving elsewhere to start over. Men she finds there, attracting and being attracted to, will invariably *also* be abusive.

With many, diverse qualities and subtleties, we all do the same. We all create patterns in our relationships, attracting certain types of people based on nature, not on action taken, not necessarily in accord with intent.

But we also create patterns in other life aspects, each customized to our own core nature. Health issues, when regarded not on specific episodes and illnesses but in terms of *impact* on our lives, also emerge in patterns. Within the framework of the intimate body-mind connection, how your body functions *in all ways* echoes inner guidelines.

And very notably, we create patterns in success or failure in our undertakings. For some, anything they try – business ventures, investing, playing poker, gardening, whatever – works well. Others can't win no matter what they attempt. Most lie somewhere in between those extremes, but invariably their "fortune" unfolds, once again, in meaningful patterns.

The *key limitation* to recognizing this pattern-generating propensity: we all learn as children to attribute causality to external forces and sources. Having absorbed cultural "Truth" assigning life's impelling power to gods and luck, we don't see our own personal role in eliciting meaningful outcomes.

First Hand Look

My first glimpse of this Oneness, this interconnectedness with which each conscious Self engages a meaningful Reality, was that fleeting mystic experience I'd had while traveling through Europe as a 24-year-old. Peering out over the narrow Ionian straits that separate Corfu from mainland Greece and Albania, in a fleeting moment, I could see clearly that I wasn't one *thing*, separate and removed from the trees, water and distant hillsides, but that I was a *Oneness*, perceiving itself from *within* its own being.

While that direct perception – and the ebullient feeling that accompanied it (no, I hadn't been sipping retsina or ouzo!!) – passed in short order, it left a recognition of a mindset, a percep-tivity or cognitive state that was possible, even normal and natural. But I had no clue as to how to return to that state of awareness.

Regain it, though, I did. That process required years of a multi-faceted journey – principally inward, but including extensive exposure to other viewpoints, eastern and western, ancient and modern. The key element to my journey was twofold: views of the subconscious from the outside in *and* the inside out.

During my thirties, living in San Diego, I did a workshop in Self-Hypnosis. While honing my technique to explore the inner realm, I found Leslie LeCron's pioneering book, *Self-Hypnotism*, which laid out explicit inner mechanisms that corresponded to outer physical symptoms. LeCron pointed out that all health issues had inner roots: by delving inward to remove the inner component by auto-suggestion, one could heal troublesome ailments – or rather allow *the body* to heal them, which it will do if not inhibited by negative inner factors.

The point was that **body and mind are connected:** eliminating inner roots to outer issues alleviated the external symptoms. Applying that technique, I found it to be invariably the case and proceeded for many years to encounter, identify and eliminate many physical issues, from minor to significant. Along the way, I uncovered additional mechanisms to LeCron's basic set. And I expanded the connection: consciousness is not only intimately connected to the body, but to *all of life*. Relationship issues and success/failure in undertakings all hearken back to inner roots: all difficulties in life stem from within – and are changeable.

So in decades following that early mystic experience, having realized the innate power to revise my life, I scoured my inner realm, searching the subconscious to clear away elements that led to failure, illness and rejection. And it always worked – no prayer, no visualization, no medicine, no acupuncture, just inner change resulting in improvement in my health, life and freedom at each step.

Along the way, I also jettisoned fallacious mind elements that projected causality to illusory sources and forces "out there" – including ones listed above.

For a brief period while beginning my inner venture, I gave psychic readings. In that regard – the "outside in" angle just mentioned – I found it easy in the proper setting, facing total strangers who had come for a reading, to clear my mind and simply tune into information about them. For subjects open and sincerely seeking understanding, that connection was effortless: pertinent information just came to mind. Nothing vague or hokey, asking no questions from which to formulate stock replies, using no cards or other props, I could just "read" people, providing pertinent, deep information about them and their lives, their intent, their weaknesses.

I don't do that anymore, rather preferring to illustrate how people can much more effectively read *themselves*. But it was a unique experience during my budding, mystical journey, to be at the same time exploring my own inner strata of meaning and psychological mechanism and reading other people's psychic shells – discerning in each pertinent insights into the inner roots of real life.

Perceiving the Oneness with which Consciousness/Reality functions requires clarity of view: beliefs and accepted definitions *always* interfere with that perception, distorting understanding by assigning causality to believed in and defined sources, some "real", some purely illusionary. If you find yourself doubting my explanation, it's simply because you learned to see reality driven externally. And, interpreting my account through your preset beliefs, you would likely "disagree" with my insight.

One could, of course, simply accept interactive Oneness as a *belief* – not seeing it clearly, just buy into the notion; indeed, believing is much easier than spending years combing subconscious stores for alternate notions of source-causality and culling them out. But superficial acceptance only adds another stratum to the many listed above (gods, fate, chance, external agents, etc.) and confuses the mind with conflictual impressions.

The psyche readily releases its store of programmed, illusory sources only through conscious, specific discharge of held tenets.

Consciousness, the essence of individual being, *creates* its experienced Reality. On a personal level, *you manifest the reality you encounter* – in terms of unfolding meaning woven into daily events and relationships – based on your **total inner mindset**. If you hold fear, separation and conflict within, you will weave those elements into your health, relationships and failure. If you lack self-esteem, having projected power out to gods or superiors, and hold struggle as valued characteristic, you will weave those qualities into your unfolding life as personal powerlessness.

You encounter, at its core, a *subjective* Reality, one based on meaning and value reflective of your own Self, not an objective universe, cold, particle-based and indifferent as science projects. But *seeing* that subjective, value-based quality hinges on awareness: perceiving Reality directly, clearly, untainted by common dogma and definition that dominate the typical western mindset.

Other Seers

Various visionaries through time came to see with some degree of clarity that Oneness, that intrinsic connection between Self and experienced Reality. Indeed, "Clear Awareness" of one's innate connection to life's episodes is the ultimate goal of any visionary experience: seventh heavens, alternate realities, spirit encounters and such in whatever scenario are mere ramifications of expectation and held mythical imagery. The ultimate destination of an inner journey – and, significantly, of incarnated life itself – is coming to see clearly *your own causal nature* in the unfolding of your life.

In ancient times, Lao Tzu illustrated the "Tao", as he termed it, the flow of reality that the rational mind could only interfere with, not effectively manipulate. "Stand before it and there is no beginning; follow it and there is no end," he noted.

"The great Tao flows everywhere, both to the left and to the right. The ten thousand things depend upon it; it holds nothing back. It fulfills its purpose silently and makes no claim..." The ten thousand things, of course, is the real universe, which flows, in terms of encountered values, from the inner realm.

Gautama, the Buddha, also became aware of the Oneness, noting explicitly how all things exist as interdependent on all other things. Recognizing the impermanence of all elements of Reality, he illustrated means to revise the inner for the purpose of affecting the outer and changing the self in the process.

But more modern visionaries also distinguished the Self-Reality connection. Here three noted teachers express *in their own words* Reality's Oneness without translation hindering:

Jiddu Krishnamurti (1895 – 1986) wove awareness into many rich, graphic depictions of life:

- In oneself lies the whole world and if you know how to look and learn, the door is there and the key is in your hand. Nobody on earth can give you either the key or the door to open, except yourself.

- I maintain that Truth is a pathless land, and you cannot approach it by any path whatsoever, by any religion, by any sect.
- …that thing which is timeless cannot be experienced. There is no experience at all. There is only that which is not nameable.
- Freedom from the desire for an answer is essential to the understanding of a problem.

Allan Watts (1915-1973) put things succinctly:

- But at any rate, the point is that God is what nobody admits to being, and everybody really is.
- …I'll tell you what hermits realize. If you go off into a far, far forest and get very quiet, you'll come to understand that you're connected with everything.
- But we try to pretend, you see, that the external world exists altogether independently of us.
- And although our bodies are bounded with skin, and we can differentiate between outside and inside, they cannot exist except in a certain kind of natural environment.
- No valid plans for the future can be made by those who have no capacity for living now.

Ramana Maharshi (1879 – 1950):

- What is called mind is a wondrous power existing in Self. It projects all thoughts. If we set aside all thoughts and see, there will be no such thing as mind remaining separate; therefore, thought itself is the form of the mind. Other than thoughts, there is no such thing as the mind.
- The place where even the slightest trace of the 'I' does not

exist, alone is Self.

- The mind will subside only by means of the enquiry 'Who am I?' The thought 'Who am I?', destroying all other thoughts, will itself finally be destroyed like the stick used for stirring the funeral pyre.

Without question, Jesus had a unique awareness of the Oneness as well. But he left no writings, voiced from his own viewpoint, which can, without question as to origin, illustrate that perspective. So the degree to which he recognized the role of Self as instigator of experiential life – as opposed to an external driving force, a deity – is difficult to specify.

He did, though, say and do things passed on by contemporaries, both gestures of which left an unparalleled imprint on succeeding cultural development and world history, however distorted and misunderstood they became. For exactly *what* he said and did were misunderstood by his unsophisticated peers and followers. Accounts of Jesus became laced with more mundane expressions of his time, revised by overzealous, small-minded and superstitious adherents, distorted through translation several times over, impregnated with myth during, after and even *long* after his lifetime and otherwise converted into elementary-school-level fantasy.

Still, perspectives on life offered by *anybody* with Clear Awareness of life's Integrated Oneness, even to lesser degrees, are distinguishable and obvious, easily differentiated from statements reflecting traditional thinking and myth. So, following a review of what is known about Jesus' life – as reasoned and researched by scholars from extant documents – and a reconstruction of what must have happened during his youth, period of maturation and growth, brief ministry and early demise, Jesus' words will be explored. Given insight beyond academic, base thinking – restricted to standard western attribution of causality as illustrated above – Jesus' deep, penetrating insights will be lifted from the mire of traditional devotional thinking and more recent academic conclusion.

And illuminated now by *your understanding* of how standard western thinking superimposes illusion that camouflages awareness of how life actually works, we will discover a real, live Jesus that actually had something of great value to say.

Upright:
Scrutinizing the Source

When looking for reliable information on anything of interest, be it automobiles or refrigerators for purchase, politicians to vote for or possible employers to work for, you apply certain qualifications to "facts" you encounter.

For cars or fridges, you have to realize that a sales person *will tell you anything* he thinks will convince you to buy his model rather than competing ones. Typical politicians *will tell you anything* they can concoct to convince you to vote for them. The prospective employer, interested in your talents, will paint a rosy picture of the company and its benefits.

For real evaluation on which to base *wise* decisions, unbiased information is much more useful. You can study road tests of cars and compare analyses of various brands of refrigerators. Widely available consumer reports review commercial products, featuring product users who can recount their familiarity. Politicians' records are often covered in the press – as are voices for and against candidates. Likewise, most employers' reputations can be checked; current employees can relate their experience in working there.

What information, then, is available for the task of evaluating Jesus – who he was, his actions and sayings and their meaning?

First, without writings from Jesus of Nazareth, nothing exists of a direct nature.

That's puzzling enough from such a historically magnified figure. Why didn't Jesus, perhaps the most influential individual *ever* – particularly one not an emperor or general – preserve his message personally and explicitly to avoid distortion? Did he write things that were later lost? Did he deem his role one of action only in ushering in a new age – not philosophical promotion of set tenets? Was he sub-literate in a culture not oriented to writing so that that script just wasn't his means of expression? So busy with travels and crushing popular demand, did he not have time? Did his sudden trial and execution curtail planned writing?

No information exists to confirm any of those possibilities. The fact is: Jesus wrote not a solitary word that survives.

Equally astounding is historical silence: not a **single historical account** refers to him *during his lifetime* from any source whatsoever, Roman or Jewish, official or personal.

This should surprise any curious observer, because extensive first-century Roman and Jewish accounts do survive. When gospel writers claim – decades later – that Jesus attracted thousands of followers throughout the region, worked stunning wonders and raised the ire not only of the Judean religious hierarchy, but of Roman authorities and Herod Antipas himself, surely *some* contemporary would have made note of that.

The Gospel of Matthew (Mt 27:51-53) claims that, immediately after Jesus' crucifixion, the Temple curtain ripped in two, the earth shook, rocks split and many dead bodies revived, came out of tombs and went into Jerusalem. Given burial practices then – entombed bodies were allowed to desiccate down to bones which were then packed into stone boxes called ossuaries – it would have been well beyond miraculous to recompose bodies back into usefulness from dry, packed bones crammed into boxes. One would think *that* event might have made somebody's chronicles, Roman, Greek or Jewish, around 30 CE (Common Era = AD).

But it took over 20 years for *any written reference* to Jesus to appear. And even that, Paul's letter to devotees in Thessalonica, along with subsequent letters to proto-Christian communities dating to the fifties, scarcely refers to the historical character at all. Paul's Jesus was not the living, breathing human – the real man we seek who traversed the hills of Galilee – but a voice from the sky, a vision stemming not from the actual Jesus, but from the fervent imagination of someone steeping in his own religious zeal.

Sparse, Scant History

Philo of Alexandria, noted Jewish philosopher whose life (20 BCE – 50 CE) spans that of Jesus, seems unaware of him. Philo expressed the need to differentiate Biblical writings between the literal and the allegorical (an insight many fundamentalists would greatly benefit from today), holding a rather Stoic perspective in his outlook. He was well educated, astute, well connected in aristocratic circles of the Hasmonean and Herodian hierarchies – and is reputed to have traveled to Jerusalem during the life of Jesus. Yet, his writings reflect no awareness of Jesus' existence.

Josephus, though, was aware of both Philo and Jesus – but only later, by a generation or two.

Flavius Josephus (37 – c. 100 CE) had been a leader of Jewish forces in Galilee in the uprising against Rome (66 – 70) that eventually led to the destruction of the Temple and much of Jerusalem. Following the siege of his rebel outpost at Jotapata by Vespasian, Josephus surrendered to the Romans and ingratiated himself to that general – a great career move, it turned out, as Vespasian later became Emperor. Pensioned as client of the imperial Flavian family, based on familiarity with unfolding history as translator during the siege of Jerusalem, his military experience and educated, aristocratic background, Josephus recorded much of what is known about first-century events in Palestine.

Josephus' writings – *The Jewish War* (c. 75) and *Antiquities of the Jews* (c. 94) – recorded the period's activities. Although princi-pally slanted (always a caveat) to Roman readers, those books provide unique historical accounts of events otherwise undocu-mented. That first book, recounting the major siege of Jerusalem by Romans some years prior, makes no reference to Jesus of Nazareth. But *Antiquities* mentions several key personalities of the early first century: John the Baptist, James, the brother of Jesus – and Jesus himself.

So Josephus is the first historian to make note of Jesus *having even existed* – and that happened *six full decades after his death*. Two more decades would pass before Roman history first featured references to early Christians in comments by Pliny the Younger, Tacitus and Suetonius. None of these provide any information on Jesus himself, but do begin to acknowledge by inference an original focus on that man, the "Savior" of later followers.

Lack of historical accounts concerning Jesus independent of subsequent devotees may rest on three other bases. Possibly references to him by Judean authorities were simply lost during that First Jewish-Roman War of 66 – 70. When Jerusalem city fell and the Temple was burned out – and even during the lengthy siege – countless documents were destroyed. Perhaps records of Jesus' Galilean escapades, disturbance of Temple activities and/or subsequent crucifixion did exist, but perished in those ruins.

Second, perhaps even more likely, early writings depicting Jesus as less than a divine being, i.e., a real, historical character with human flaws, were later destroyed on purpose by early Christians. By the fourth century, after Constantine coerced divergent factions of early Christendom to agree on theology (Nicene Council of 325 CE), many manuscripts supporting alternate viewpoints (Ebionites, Gnostics, Marcionites, etc.) were destroyed.

And, third, initial accounts, notes conceivably compiled by rare, literate followers of Jesus in Aramaic, simply didn't survive.

Invariably, to reconstruct in any fashion the real Jesus, information must be gleaned from the only accounts that remain: five Gospels. Scarce hints of his nature might be inferred from Paul's letters, even less from peripheral works – the Apocalypse of Paul, the Didache, the Apocryphon of James, etc. But for a look at Jesus, the three Synoptic Gospels, Matthew, Mark (Mk) and Luke (Lk), of the canon and the Gospel of Thomas provide the only useful information. The Gospel of John (Jn) presents a Jesus overly constructed around the author's own ideas – supercharged with evolved Christology, not reflective of the real person – though it may contain some hints of peripheral conditions that the others don't.

But discerning a real, live character from those glorified accounts requires **analysis and perspective** – not blind acceptance of archaic accounts. As we will see, these gospels are not independent, objective descriptions of Jesus' life – as in owner/user reports on commercial products – but rather pointed accounts much more in line with *sales pitches*. Gospel writers attempted to convince their peers of Jesus' otherworldly nature, weaving lore and mythical stories into accounts meant to impress, not to inform those early listeners of historical events. (Gospels were read aloud to early illiterate, devotees.)

But clearly, Jesus was a character outside the scope of all other ancient teachers, wandering healers, apocalyptic doomsayers, philosophical proponents and charismatic preachers. Dozens of those types came and went, leaving scarce traces of ever having existed. Jesus was different. But to find out how and why, it is necessary to explore in depth the gospels, those few sketchy accounts hinting of his real nature.

Caveats to Early Writing

Any and all "publishing" in early centuries of our era consisted of writing things out on scrolls of papyrus or parchment (dried, stretched animal skin), with paper not introduced from China until somewhat later. No publishing houses existed to screen authors, proof works and make copies for wide distribution (book stores didn't exist and libraries were rare) – let alone to evaluate content for accuracy and validity in the first place.

If you wanted to publish your work, you had to write it out personally or pay a scribe to do so. And you or others had to finance hand-copying necessary to create duplicates for distribution. Then you had to somehow disperse those copies to people who might be interested. But most people were illiterate and no

schools or universities existed – nor did publicity agencies, distribution channels or magazines. If you could afford to print your
ideas, it didn't matter what fantasy you were putting to text, it
got printed.

But papyrus – made of pith from papyrus plants grown in
Egypt – was not very pliable; scrolls of papyrus soon started to
crack when rolled and unrolled frequently. Even when cut into
pages and sewn or glued into the newer codex arrangement (like
a book), and even when written on more durable parchment,
documents later wore out through repeated use. Thus, new
copies had to be made every few years. Somebody – a library or
dedicated follower – years later, perhaps long after the author
had died, had to care enough about passing the work along to
make copies. Otherwise documents produced in early centuries,
whatever the topic, would simply deteriorate, ultimately
decaying to dust. Indeed, when libraries burned, entire works
could be completely lost to mankind. (This was the case with the
grand Library of Alexandria when Julius Caesar's military action
sparked a fire there in 47 BCE and when Christians in 391
decided to destroy anything they didn't agree with.)

When new copies were made (of course again by hand) to
extend the life of a manuscript's text, not only were errors
frequently made but changes could be *purposely introduced* – a
process called "interpolation". Accidental and intentional
revisions happened *commonly* throughout ancient times, certainly
including when subsequent scribes copied gospels and other NT
documents to preserve and pass on their content. Scholars,
exploring extant manuscripts of early Christian writing in search
of original wording, have been able to trace many such changes.
Comparison of the same passages in various versions shows
where changes, not found in pre-revision variations, became
embedded in subsequent copies of altered text. Regardless of
changes and how they affected meaning, as further copies were
made, the revisions were absorbed such that future readers

would consider the altered version as the "true" one.

Subsequent copying of Josephus' *Antiquities* provides a good example of interpolation. Well funded by Roman royalty, this work originally would have been officially published by quality scribes. For preservation through the ages, though, it would have required subsequent copying just like any other work – at any point of which it was prone to interpolation. This apparently happened in connection to its reference to Jesus.

In *Antiquities*, Book 18, Chapter 3, Section 3, the noted *Testimonium Flavianum* – long claimed by the Christian apologists as an independent reference to Jesus – is widely regarded by scholars to have been revised during copying around the third century. Here, in mentioning Jesus' condemnation by Pilate, the text flatly *labels* Jesus as the "Christ", stating that he appeared to his followers alive following his crucifixion as foretold by divine prophets. These comments seem to be reported facts, not unlike other volumes of historical events he documents.

However, Josephus, a Pharisee – decidedly not a Christian – *would not have written* such a highly Christianized account. Scholars, noting – along with other reasoned points – that earlier church figures referenced Josephus without notice of this claim, conclude that Josephus' passage likely *did* acknowledge Jesus and his crucifixion, but without the later Christian embellishments. Additional references to Jesus' brother, James, in *Antiquities* are consistent with the conclusion that the Jesus reference includes interpolation – a falsification during copying meant to support subsequent Christian intentions.

A prime example of blatant interpolation within the gospels occurs in Mark, chronologically the first Synoptic gospel written (c. 70 CE). The final twelve verses of Mark (Mk 16: 9-20) do not appear in the earliest, most reliable manuscripts. Because the original ending of Mark (16:8) is so abrupt – perhaps the writer of Mark never finished it or the original ending was lost – someone a century or two later added a more acceptable (to him and his community) finish. To the believer, though, this add-on by some unknown scribe much later is as valid as the original account from year 70.

Interpolation is a very important caution against attaching too much veracity to the gospels and the NT in general. Because original versions of those writings no longer exist and because so many variations occur in text among surviving manuscripts, *knowing exactly what the original text actually said is impossible.* Gospels in the Codex Vaticanus and the Codex Sinaiticus, the two oldest near-complete versions, both dating from the early 300s, have over 3000 differences in their text.

But self-publishing and interpolation are just two of many caveats for trusting ancient writings. There are *many* more. Drawing firm conclusions from any ancient, written source – but particularly proto-Christian authors – is much like accepting that car or appliance sales person's pitch: the writer's purpose was not to pass along objective information, but to convince you of something. Often, and certainly in the case of the gospels, there are no objective evaluations to reference for comparison, only other similarly biased accounts, each with an agenda – often subtle, at that. Without such cross references, unrealistic claims are impossible to corroborate.

As a similar example of ancient writing in a secular vein, Julius Caesar's Commentaries on the Gallic Wars document his military ventures in securing Roman control of northwestern European regions. For many claims, though, concerning victories, exploits, numbers of soldiers, etc., no other sources of information exist. Did Caesar report things accurately, or did he exaggerate victories and revise actual events for the purpose of promoting himself? Who knows? The Gauls never recorded their side of events.

Likewise, critically evaluating New Testament assertions faces the same dearth of comparative, objective accounts. Ancient writings diverging from orthodox thinking were purposely destroyed in the fourth century. (A Coptic-language papyrus codex of The Gospel of Thomas only survived such purging by being hidden in a sealed jar about 367 CE and buried at Nag Hammadi, along the Nile River. This work, recovered in 1945, likely reflects first-century original writing, recording early on some of Jesus' comments without narrative.)

There are, however, multiple documents produced by different people that can be compared: four gospels in the canon (three of which, however, the "Synoptics", are closely related), plus that preserved account of Jesus' sayings (Gospel of Thomas) and numerous letters by Paul and other sources. These can shed light *on each other* when compared and analyzed critically – revealing contradictions, inconsistencies, problems, errors and concocted stories.

Part of that critical process includes considering factors that shed doubt on the veracity of the gospels and peripheral early Christian works. Two distinct types of problems the gospels exhibit as reliable sources will be summarized here: *Literary/Compositional* and *Rational*. I've boiled NT issues down to eight categories of each type problem.

Caveats Specific to Gospel Authority: Literary/Compositional Issues

Biblical scholars, exploring each step of Christian evolution, have thoroughly analyzed all available documents from the oldest Greek manuscripts to later Latin and King James translations. Historians along with archeologists have reconstructed the first-century setting, illuminating many details from political intrigues of royalty to daily life of paupers. All this work is well documented, diverse and readily available. The problems assessed here are commonly exposed by academic sources, so I'm passing along a summary of research here, not advancing my own perspectives – except where noted.

First L/C Issue: No Publisher to Qualify the Work

As touched upon earlier, no composition dating from early centuries – expressly including NT works – was ever subject to evaluative publishing judgment, critique or editing proof by a professional staff to oversee and verify original content. Writers could make *any* statement or claim, write it out or have it written, and, *by that virtue alone*, imply validity to the content. Many outlandish, unrealistic assertions are made in the gospels that a legitimate publisher or editor would balk at. But believers seem to accept any report, simply because *they are there*, forming within their view the default standard by which reality is subsequently judged.

Core of Issue #1: Without any objective oversight or independent judgment concerning content – as we would expect in modern literary works – **claims made in the gospels are simply conjecture of the authors based on unverifiable sources.**

Second L/C Issue: Murky Source Material

The authors of the gospels, like all writers in all time periods, either reference information they have at hand – including things they've heard or read – or they make things up. (Tapping into secret, revealed mystical truths from divine sources or the Holy Spirit, should that be claimed for gospel writers, realistically falls into the second category: made up material based on held beliefs and values.)

For reference material, the author of Mark relied not on Jesus himself or any writings from him. Nor, four decades after Jesus' death and living in another region, did he likely contact people who had known Jesus. His sole source: oral traditions passed along by word-of-mouth for four decades. Oral accounts and stories reaching him must have consisted not of second- or third-hand accounts, but likely repetitions much farther removed. Non-literate societies tend to rely on recall more than we do. Thus their memories for detail can be better. But stories repeated and passed over geographical and cultural divides change considerably, particularly over time stretching out to decades.

If Mark's author did reference any written documents, they no longer survive. By the composition date of Mark – about 70 CE – oral traditions in this uneducated, highly superstitious culture certainly evolved considerably during 40 volatile years following Jesus' death, accruing lore, exaggerated by fear, ignorance and despair such that myth and wishful fantasy became built into the message as "fact".

Authors of Matthew and Luke expanded on Mark's commentary: that earlier text was certainly being scrolled in front of each as they wrote. They each incorporated material from a subsequently lost source both had available (called "Q" by scholars, from the German word *Quelle*, meaning "source"). Both had other information available, too – independent of each other – for each offers accounts unique to their works.

But *all content* written into Matthew and Luke about the year 85 was either heard or read elsewhere or made up – by the authors or somebody previous. For certain they revised things they heard to fit their intended message, because both demonstrably revise material from both Mark and Q, each in his own way, while incorporating it into their gospels.

Birth stories, the Nativity accounts, provide a great example of invented narratives – or reiterated fictions somebody prior had made up. Comparing Matthew to Luke (see the Fifth Rational Caveat) in detail, one finds two stories that *could not both be true*. Featuring mutually exclusive sequences, one or the other was simply incorrect – probably both. Most likely, they were both invented: at the time, everybody knew that Jesus was from Nazareth, so both stories had to locate him there growing up. And scriptures, contemporary indicators of validity to the common Judean mindset, had indicated that a great leader would come from Bethlehem, so each gospel had to explain him being born there. The authors of Matthew and Luke, likely living in different Middle Eastern localities, either heard different stories referencing those locations – or else they independently made up two different accounts. Neither anticipated comparison to the other, almost certainly unaware of each other's work.

Almost all of Mark appears in Matthew, although many faulty elements (wrong scripture attributions, flawed logistics, etc.) have been corrected. Content otherwise was revised to conform to ideas accepted in the Matthean community and by the writer.

Whoever wrote Luke incorporated about half of Mark, revising the slant to subdue the apostles' cluelessness and Jesus' secrecy while promoting women in its stories.

The story of Mark in 3:20-30 presents a good example of this "revision to suit" of both seen in the later Synoptics. Here, Jesus' family wanted to "take charge of him," saying he was, "out of his mind." That's understandable, as he was saying things that didn't fit into common thinking – implying in their vernacular that Jesus was possessed by some demon. This leads to accusations by Jerusalem insiders that he was in league with Beelzebub. Jesus questions, quite rationally, "How can Satan drive out Satan?" Matthew (12:22-37) and Luke (11:14-28), copying Mark, both feature the Satan explanation and, indeed, expand on that story considerably. But both *edit out* Mark's reference to Jesus' family calling him crazy!

This significant story, likely a real event, indicated how Jesus was regarded by his family. But reality didn't fit into the aggrandized image the later evangelists wanted to present. Snip! Change it to suit.

Exactly where the author of John got his material is unknown. John incorporates few Synoptic stories, and those differ: gone are Kingdom of God references and insightful parables. The long-winded, self-focused Jesus presented in John, typically dated to 90 CE or even 100, is so radically different from the Synoptics' picture that the author must have gotten source information much more evolved in what is called "Christology" – or he made up a Jesus that suited his theological fancy.

Core of Issue #2: Stemming from hazy source material consisting of **oral accounts** well removed from Jesus, possible now-lost, equally unsubstantiated manuscripts and **stories likely made up** to illustrate a prefixed viewpoint, the **gospels appear highly suspect as reliable sources.**

Third L/C Issue: Anonymous Authors

No gospel author's identity is reliably known. Contemporary authors from Greek, Roman, Hebrew and Egyptian sources are often known from other works they wrote or from historical references. Their biases and agendas can thus be defined, allowing conclusions based on a diverse picture, a degree of trust based on cross reference.

But no ancient gospel manuscript contains an original byline. The names attached were all applied much later; Mark and Matthew, for example, were attributed by Eusebius in the early fourth century based on claims by Papias dating from the second century but later lost. (Papias was apparently so unreliable his works were destroyed or simply not copied as they decayed and disappeared.)

The writer of Mark, supposedly once a companion of Peter, was a literate Greek speaker, educated and likely living in a Christian community in Syria or Asia Minor. But Peter's companions, indeed most likely all Jesus' apostles and other followers stemming from society's bottom class, were illiterate (see Acts 4:13) speakers of Aramaic, peasant fishermen and hand workers – not educated scribes. Doubtless Galilean followers of Jesus could converse somewhat in Greek – common in that multi-cultural region – but writing cohesive, structured accounts as appear in Mark is highly unlikely for any original, close associate of Jesus.

In terms of content, it is even more unlikely that Mark's author was closely associated with Peter when he depicts that apostle – indeed, all of them – so negatively.

Also, this first gospel written includes errors in geography and Jewish law – often corrected when the stories were reused in Matthew and Luke. It appears much more likely to have been written by a Greek unschooled in Jewish traditions than a Jew who learned Greek.

According to scholars, the style, grammar and word usage in Matthew, Luke and John are superior to that of Mark. The authors of those books likely lived in Cilicia, Syria or Egypt – formulating a message about Jesus consistent with accepted notions from their proto-Christian communities. But their real identity – names, bios, backgrounds, intent (other than that derived from their writing) and education are *totally unknown*.

But these points are obvious: Matthew, had he been the tax-collector disciple of Jesus, wouldn't have had to rely on Mark's account and other sources (like Q). With first-hand knowledge of Jesus, he would have been able to tell the story himself from personal experience. Likewise, if Luke were the physician known to Paul and accompanying him, his accounts of Paul's deeds and outlook would be more consistent with Paul's own statements from his letters. But they often contradict the real Paul's writings (the only such original works from a known author that survived).

And the writers of John (scholars note several different styles abruptly changing between sections), presenting a character totally unlike the Synoptic Jesus, were very unlikely – any of them – to actually be one of the disciples. By 90 or 95 CE, a surviving contemporary of Jesus would have been very old indeed – at least 90 in a society lacking health care, good nutrition and hygiene, where 40 or 50 was already quite aged. And that illiterate Galilean fisherman, John, son of Zebedee, would have had to take on a sophisticated Greek writing style and compe-tence – replete with Greek philosophical references to the Logos, or *"Word"*, depicted by Heraclitus and Plato to drive reality –

well beyond a peasant's level.

So, who wrote the NT gospels? Actually, technically, that's simple: *nobody* wrote the New Testament Gospels Matthew, Mark, Luke and John. Some anonymous figures in early church communities *did* assemble accounts of their regional religion's figurehead character from oral lore and written compilations of sayings, then *did* formulate bits and pieces of info into accounts depicting Jesus consistent with their community's credence. Only later, much later, indeed *centuries* later, did these primitive works – originally meant to be read aloud during meetings to small, illiterate assemblies of believers in the writer's locale – get turned into the Bible.

At first, the Jewish Scriptures (Torah plus Prophets – pretty much fixed in content by 200 BCE) were used by proto-Christians in their meetings. But it took centuries of wrangling among regional supporters of various versions of "Truth", extreme political pressure by Constantine and even more decades to reach agreement on the NT Canon, including various letters and Revelation. The point is significant: no writer of any of the 27 NT books was *actually writing the Bible* when he composed his work.

Outside of Paul, seven or eight of whose 13 attributed letters are considered to have actually been written by him, no author is known. That means 19 or 20 of the books of the NT are anonymous. Many are blatantly pseudepigraphic (forgeries, see next section), with famous names applied to artificially promote veracity.

Core of Issue #3: Not knowing who wrote NT works – including not only names but authors' purposes, backgrounds and qualifications – **elicits significant doubt as to veracity and believability** of content.

Fourth L/C Issue: False Attribution
Given unsophisticated literary and publishing standards in

ancient times, quite often, to impress readers, writers would attribute their work to some noted authority. While gospels were simply misattributed later to add authority, many of the NT letters were effectively forgeries: works written by unknown authors but attributed to, e.g., one of the apostles. This ruse, termed Pseudepigrapha, would make the author's expressed viewpoint seem more valid – and who's to know? Without printing and publication standards, copyright laws, etc., few could detect phony credits. The writer's own viewpoint in a document with the name of Peter or James on it, made into multiple copies and circulated to other unwitting communities would get the anonymous writer's opinion established much more effectively than using his own name. Under the circumstances, few figures in the early church had the knowledge and expertise to detect such deception.

Modern scholars, however, using sophisticated techniques to analyze surviving manuscripts, often expose such efforts. Based on writing style and content, letters outside those 7 or 8 by Paul are deemed Pseudepigrapha – not written by James, Peter, John or Jude (disciples or brothers of Jesus) whose names adorn them. The Gospel of John, letters attributed to John and Revelation may all have been written by *somebody* named John – a common name then as now – but not the disciple John, son of Zebedee. (That practice is called homonymous writing. It deceives only in so far as the church propagates the falsity that the disciple authored the work.)

As one branch of early Christendom emerged to become "orthodox" – fourth century – and progressed towards nailing down an acceptable canon of works, it did place value on apparent sources, but failed to identify valid writings of real apostles.

Core of Issue #4: The gospels and most NT books, not composed by the authors whose names are attributed to them, **present core scripture under a false guise.**

Fifth L/C Issue: Material is Neither Biographical nor Objective

In the first-century timeframe when the gospels were written, biography as a literary form hadn't been invented. Most accounts of famous people then were unmitigated praise, not in any way objective, researched reports. The gospels followed a Greek literary form that listed major accomplishments and noteworthy events from Jesus' life, but weren't truly biographical in style – though they do, almost in passing, illustrate some aspects of Jesus' life by fleshing out events in a physical setting. However, details in this regard, hazy enough, often vary from one gospel to another – even when one drew from the other.

In modern times, we are used to some degree of objectivity in reporting. Serious biographers conduct detailed research on the target person, finding documentation about that individual's life and accomplishments – perhaps even interviewing people who had known the subject. Newspaper, magazine, official political or business papers can all provide useful information.

But for gospel writers, no such information was available. No periodicals provided interviews of Jesus; no court records afforded details on Pilate's hearing; no libraries offered historical notes – only oral accounts originating from superstitious peasants long dead, repeated across years, distorted in untraceable ways, gave sketchy accounts of his deeds and sayings.

The gospels do incorporate fleeting glimpses of Jesus' personal life, but they were written with overriding intent to convince readers/listeners of the anonymous author's evaluation of Jesus' nature and status. Indeed, even *that* varied widely among the works – with John presenting a fundamentally different Jesus altogether from the Synoptics.

Core of Issue #5: The gospels, never meant to report, but rather to convince, **are in no sense objective and dispassionate biographies. They are glowing accounts meant to persuade people of the writers' convictions.**

Sixth L/C Issue: Later Revision by Subsequent Copiers

As mentioned but worth repeating: manuscripts, surviving copies of any ancient documents, Christian or otherwise, are copies of copies of copies many times over; they almost certainly don't contain the original content.

Scholars have detected literally multiple thousands of variations among extant gospel manuscripts even in original Greek versions, with no possible way to reliably reconstruct exactly what the originals said. The earliest surviving gospel manuscripts date to the third century, with a couple of fragments from the second. Two fairly complete NT codices, Vaticanus and Sinaiticus, both stem from *three centuries* after the originals were written. Those differ considerably.

Core of Issue #6: Given intervening revisions, it is difficult to pinpoint even in original Greek exactly what authors initially said.

Seventh L/C Issue: Ancient Greek Writing Conventions

Composition in ancient Greek was far less sophisticated than in modern languages – making it considerably less "user-friendly". Written Greek, even by the Hellenistic period, had yet to commonly utilize lower case letters or punctuation. Commas, set in place in a sentence to help clarify modifiers, regulate sentence flow and delineate meaningful phrases, simply hadn't been invented yet. Periods weren't used to end sentences, nor quotation marks to fully specify direct quotes. There were no paragraphs – and no dashes – to organize meaning, no hyphens to span words across lines and no question marks to clarify questions. Indeed, *there weren't even spaces between words!*

Try reading the following passage. This is generally how ancient manuscripts in Greek look to would-be translators fluent in that ancient tongue – except in hand written, less uniform characters:

IFYOUCANREADANDUNDERSTANDALLTHISTEXTW
RITTENWITHOUTPARAGRAPHBREAKSTOTALLYLAC
KINGPUNCTUATIONPARTICULARLYWITHOUTQUOT
ATIONMARKSHYPHENSCOMMASETCANDNOTEVEN
USINGSPACESBETWEENWORDSTHENYOUWOULDH
AVEBEENATHOMEINANCIENTGREEKTHEYHADNOS
UCHDELINEATINGMARKINGSJUSTABUNCHOFLETTE
RSSTUCKTOGETHERTHISMADECOPYINGPARTICULA
RLYBYPEOPLENOTTOOLITERATEDIFFICULTITLEDTO
MANYERRORSINCOPYINGTHEYDIDNTGETCORRECT
EDBUTJUSTPASSEDON

Actually, subsequent development of punctuation was driven in significant part by the need to read New Testament scriptures aloud in meetings. Reading jammed-together jumbles of characters aloud was difficult even for trained scribes who were used to it.

Several issues contributing to gospel unreliability stem from this convention:

One is: copying was difficult and prone to errors. Required every few years when manuscripts wore out or when they needed replication for distribution, copying was no easy task. Clumsy, exceedingly tedious and annoying at best – even when dictated – manual copying, often in dim lighting, was always prone to misspelling or omitting words – both nearly impossible to correct later.

Copying would have involved intense concentration. The process included looking up regularly to dip your reed pen into ink, with occasional pauses to reshape the hand-carved tip – or replace the pen and resume with a new one where you left off. This tedium demanded hours on end just to create a *single copy* of a short book like a gospel. Sometimes, particularly in the early church when typical proto-Christians were lower class peasants, copiers may not have been professional scribes and thus not really very literate. Copiers, perhaps slaves, didn't have to understand the text to mimic characters on another scroll, simply copy characters in order, one at a time. That practice, though, while much cheaper than hiring a scribe, led to even more errors. Hundreds of thousands of errors appear in the 5000+ extant Greek manuscripts.

A second distortion concerning Greek writing – one I haven't seen mentioned by scholars, but which is very obvious to me – is specifically **the lack of quotation marks**. In English, reporting somebody's comments can be expressed by informal reference: *Bill said he was going to the market.* In this statement, the reporter doesn't actually quote Bill, who could have said any number of things or nothing at all, simply nodding while pointing in a direction understood by the reporter.

Or, one can directly quote Bill: *"I'll be back soon – just running down to get some veggies," Bill yelled on his way out the door.*

In these two very different reports, a similar meaning is communicated. But in English, the quotation marks indicate a direct citation of Bill's words, implying that those were *exactly* the utterance that came out of Bill's mouth. If the source reporting this was reliable and truthful, had a good memory and didn't intend to deceive, it's very likely that Bill did indeed say what was quoted. In our time, people are fussy about that – not wanting to be misquoted and misunderstood.

But ancient Greek had no such indicators. John 7:45, in the original would have read in Greek something like this – with a few errors sprinkled in to make it more realistic:

FINALLYTHETEMPLEGUARDSWENTDACKTOTHECHIEF
PRIESTSANDPHAPISEESWHOASKEDTHEMWHYDIDNTY
OUBRINGHININNOONEEVERSPOKETHEWAYTHITMAN
DOESTHEGUARDSDECLAREDYOUMEANHEHASDE

CEIVEDYOUALSOTHEPHARISEESRETORTEDHASANY
OFHTERULERSOROFTHEPHARIESSBELIEVEDINHIM
NOBUTHISMOBTHATKNOW

But this exchange is rendered with direct quotations by whoever translated the gospel of John! And that presentation virtually declares that, "Why didn't you bring him in?" is *exactly* what the chief priests and Pharisees said – all assembled, word for word, even when *there was nobody present originally* who could have recorded it! Astoundingly some people believe these direct quotes that punctuate the gospels and the Acts are entirely accurate, accepting them as actual, historical discourse – *in English!*

This practice raises real issues, of course. John was composed a good 65 years after Jesus' death. With no traceable written connection over those 65 years for much of John's material, it is *absolutely impossible* to know exactly what Jesus had said way back two-thirds of a century previous. Yet, rendering those verses of long, rambling dialogue as verbatim quotes proclaims that Jesus said *exactly those words* John puts into his mouth. Of course, the original writer of John didn't use quotes – as they didn't exist in written Greek – but the translator/publisher of the modern Bible does. And that style strongly implies a validity that is pure illusion.

In general, people hearing oral presentations don't remember a whole lot accurately – particularly not details of long, rambling dissertations. But generally listeners do grasp the gist. Whatever Jesus said originally wasn't recorded on the scene by diligent note-takers (practically everybody in attendance was illiterate), but his words would have impressed listeners to some degree – particularly those vivid, short, colorful parables (missing from John). Disciples and close followers likely heard the same comments repeatedly as they followed Jesus around, so they could later recall his parables and repeated references – probably fairly accurately at first. These would have been rendered to writing perhaps not too long after spoken, but it may have been *years* later. (Remember, none of his followers knew he would be suddenly arrested and summarily executed. They would have sensed no immediate need to record his message.)

The three Synoptic gospels and the Gospel of Thomas most frequently repeat Jesus' short aphorisms and parables – doubtless all of them citing common oral traditions or written collections of sayings like Q. These may be fairly accurate, allowing for time and translation. But John has Jesus launching long-winded soliloquies mostly about himself. These lengthy passages clearly voiced opinions of the writer himself, not Jesus – a conclusion of the great majority of scholars, one with which I absolutely concur. But rendered as direct quotes by translators, they appear to be the precise words of Jesus.

And that is not only inaccurate, but highly deceptive.

All in all, the gospels are littered with direct quotes – sometimes when *nobody else is around* to even hear, let alone record and report later what would have been said! (This will be revisited as the Second Rational Caveat.) Even with listeners present, accounts of what was said would have passed across language barriers, been repeated word-of-mouth for decades before being written – then copied many times over and translated again. Regarding these quotes as explicit, real statements of Jesus and others is *total folly* – indeed, ***absolute nonsense!***

A third issue innate to this ancient writing convention **is lack of clarity**. Punctuation helps clarify meaning intended by the writer. Lack of it muddles meaning. Consider this sentence:

THECHIEFORGANIZINGSTRUCTUREIDENTIFIESREJECT
SANDCONTRACTSPROJECTSINSTOREFORTHEFUTURE

Or:

The chief organizing structure identifies rejects and contracts projects in store for the future.

As is, it indicates that a company's management team pinpoints undesirable ventures while establishing projects coming up. However, if commas are inserted after "chief" and "structure", the subject becomes the chief, the boss, whose actions lead to bringing structure to the whole process. If a single comma is placed after "identifies", the meaning changes again: the chief now does identifying, rejecting and contracting. If a hyphen is inserted between "in" and "store", the focus shifts to an in-house solution.

Eight possible meanings can be expressed with those words simply by revising the punctuation! Stated as in ancient Greek protocol, however, textual conventions cannot differentiate what is really meant.

For translation from ancient Greek manuscripts, the *translator himself* must creatively decide what the original writer meant in order to apply English punctuation properly to the final output. This can be very tricky when dealing with archaic expressions and words used current to the timeframe and specific dialect. It leads to decisions made on personal bias and impressions, which decrease reliability – the next problem.

Core of Issue #7: Primitive writing conventions in ancient Greek **lead to copying, quotation and clarity issues** – all casting doubt on reliability of content.

Eighth L/C Issue: Distortion by Translation

Major factors affecting reliability in early works must include the caveat of *translation*: things cannot be said precisely the same in different languages.

Languages color and flavor human statements concerning reality in diverse ways. Underlying concepts are expressed differently. Each language parses meaning and frames it into expression in distinctive ways. And characteristics of grammar and extent of vocabulary influence how each language allows formulation of meaning.

I speak fluent German along with my native American English, but in describing or explaining even a simple act or concept, the gist differs at least slightly when expressed in one as opposed to the other. Although English and German are very closely related, a similar description expressed in either tongue is simply *different* to a degree. Even similar root words have different shades and implications – and differing background knowledge slants meaning and compromises understanding.

Given that difference for simple, descriptive commentary, what about complex stories and explanations? Communicating deep philosophical and religious points, differences between languages are magnified, for then the expression rests on complex beliefs and understanding held not only by both writer/speaker and reader/listener, but by the translator sitting in between.

Jesus spoke Aramaic to his countrymen, a language common at that time, widespread in various dialects from Palestine through Syria and eastwards beyond Mesopotamia. That Semitic tongue was rich in metaphor and illustrative reference, poetic and evocative – one whose sounds themselves carried meaning. However, the gospels were written in Koine Greek, an Indo-European language slightly simplified from its parent, Attic Greek, but one more precise than Aramaic – honed by traditions of philosophy and business acumen, descriptive by nature. Whatever transitory process took Jesus' Aramaic phraseology for his parables out of Aramaic and into Greek, it could not easily and absolutely equate specifics of his message.

But that was just the first step. Centuries later, the original Greek – along with however much it still reflected Jesus' original Aramaic – was translated *yet again* into Latin. As the church grew, the version of Christianity – one of many that had sprung up from early communities – that came to dominate became centered in Rome. Latin slowly displaced the original works as Greek fell out of common use. But from which Greek manuscripts did early Latin ones derive? Versions close to the original, or ones that had been significantly changed? And how did meaning subtly reshape when translated to Latin?

As ages passed, the Bible was later translated into German and Middle English. Which version was used for that step: original, reliable Greek manuscripts or Latin ones? Good versions or sketchy, interpolated ones? And how much had Latin manuscripts evolved, revised over generations to reflect growing church dogma, politics and evolving theology?

When the printing press came into use by the mid-fifteenth century, the first work set to print was the Bible. But what version was used as source for printed versions in German? The best one that was, through exhaustive research, compiled from reliable, original Greek manuscripts – or one that was readily available in Latin?

When the King James Version was translated anew (1604 – 1611) and set to print in England, what version was used as source? How reliable were its Greek originals?

And in each step, who did the translating? Objective, fluent translators, dedicated to retaining original meaning, or heavily biased church functionaries oriented to slanting the translation towards his – or the prevailing, popular – viewpoint?

Actually, all along the way, these significant steps were taken using the most easily accessible manuscripts to go by, not the oldest, most reliable. And they were translated by church functionaries, aiming to weave currently accepted under-standing into the product, not original intent of the authors. (The 47 King James translators were all Church of England insiders.) In ancient and medieval times, scholarly thoroughness was *much less* a factor than domination by church officials wielding heavy political control.

Core of Issue #8: Translating literary works invariably distorts original meaning – even when done with objective care and sensitivity. **Alteration increases, however, and meaning is distorted when biased concerns oversee translation and influence the process.**

New Testament gospels are traditionally accorded a cultural sanctity and lofty regard completely out of line with their literary worth. That much is already indicated by the preceding eight points: if you would come across a document today concerning some topic of importance to you, yet it was:

- self-published without any neutral, objective recommendations,
- based on undefined and untraceable source information,
- written by anonymous sources, each of whom had an apparent agenda meant to convince you of something,
- falsely attributed to noted authorities of the field,
- highly colored to exaggerate positive attributes of principal characters,
- changed by unknown people on many occasions for a long time,
- translated from accounts written long ago in foreign text devoid of any punctuation, and
- distorted in unknown ways by several layers of translation,

would you find its substance to be dependable, believable such that you could rely on it to make vital decisions? I doubt it.

But that's the precise nature of the New Testament. So, should people bank their lives and well-being on the gospels and letters of that hallowed collection of old writings?

Hold on! Don't decide just yet. Several other difficulties loom beyond Literary and Compositional. Analyzing NT accounts critically against known historical accounts, other gospel texts and basic experiential reality reveals additional issues that affect believability.

Rational Caveats to Gospel Authority

Those eight caveats to NT explanations reveal structural and communication flaws – how they were compiled, written and preserved. The content itself has some real issues, too, that further detract from dependability:

Rational Problem #1: Incorrect Historical and Geographical References

The Gospels and the Acts aren't meant, actually, to be histories, i.e., accounts written with some degree of objectivity to explain what actually happened. Their authors' purpose was to pass along accumulated stories to members of their devoted community and other such groups to which these accounts would be circulated. But in describing events and situations, those authors, called *evangelists,* do refer to historical and geographical situations.

In questioning these, one can better understand the points raised in the gospels. If Jesus was indeed revered from Tyre on the Mediterranean through the Decapolis to the east and south to Jericho and Jerusalem, it says more than were he simply a local favorite in Nazareth. If historically verifiable statements are made – and prove accurate – it bolsters the author's reliability on other points that *can't* be verified.

On historicity, the NT is a mixed bag. Various historical references indicating rulers in place at the time of a depicted event are by and large credible: Herod the Great was still in control when Jesus was likely born (about 4 BCE), as reported in Matthew, Herod Antipas for the rest of Jesus' life as generally referenced.

But there are problems. Luke sets Jesus' birth at a time when Quirinius was governor of Syria – placing it after 6 CE, nine years later than Matthew. (There was no year "zero", so nine years passed between 4 BCE and 6 CE.) One of them had to be wrong. But, remembering that these accounts were assembled some 80 or 90 years after that birth, perhaps one of them was simply mistaken about the exact year.

Scholars and sleuths have compiled considerable historical and geographical inaccuracies in gospel notations – even more written into the Acts. You wouldn't, for example, go from "the vicinity of Tyre" (Mk 7:31) north through Sidon to reach the Sea of Galilee – it's the wrong direction (north vs. southeast), and archeology indicates no road back then going from Sidon toward that lake.

I'm inclined to overlook these bungled details: ancient gospel writers weren't researchers with access to libraries and maps. They were telling a story and they got some background details wrong. At most, Mark's errors in Palestinian geography only indicate that he lived somewhere else, not that he was completely unreliable. Luke's changes to Mark in material he incorporated from that earlier source don't negate the value of either writing, but show an interest in placing different emphasis on the dimly reported, principally undocumented situation from six decades previous.

Core of First Rational Problem: Logistical errors in gospel accounts indicate less than total expertise on the part of original authors, but only **emphasize the evangelical nature of the statement** over and above historical reporting.

Rational Problem #2: Impossible Reports

Much more critical in evaluating the veracity of gospel accounts is the stylistic expression of those works.

Writing a novel, you establish a narrative point of view. If that angle is strictly from the perspective of a particular character in the story, you only include information to which *that person* could be privy; things happening in remote locations and others' thoughts can only be introduced as that key player becomes aware of them. Stories with that "first-person" structure, unfolding exclusively to the perception of a single character, serve to pull the reader into the fictional reality, making it seem more experiential.

But you can just as well compose from a *universal* perspective in which all events are illustrated from a narrator angle – not a character in the story, the narrator is more a general observer. In that style (called *omniscient*), the narrator may be privy to *all* events, situations and even thoughts – or, at the author's whim, only to thoughts and experiences known to a single character (limited).

With many variations and options, those represent two principal styles of creative fiction writing.

Contrasted to that, *non-fiction* reporting is restricted in scope by the reality of reporting actual events – more like first-person fiction writing. Reliable authors, as functional narrators, can only report *what they are aware of.* Limited to what really took place, not knowing all factors contributing to the story and certainly unaware of the thoughts and feelings of most people involved, non-fiction journalists *can only report what is known* from reference material, observation, interviews, etc. – unless they make things up, which is then fiction.

Gospel authors had reference material – oral traditions, perhaps some written accounts – spanning the 40 to 60+ years from Jesus' death until their period of composition. None of them wrote with first-hand – or likely even second- or third-hand – connection to Jesus and real events they describe. But the gospel works are all presented as *omniscient, third-person accounts.* Gospel authors – expressing as narrators – seem to be aware of *everything* from remote events to people's dreams even from a century earlier, from thoughts and feelings to secret meetings behind locked doors. They know:

- What the woman, bleeding for 12 years, the one healed by simply touching Jesus' cloak, was thinking (Mt 9:21).

- Where the paralytic man went after being healed (Mt 9:7).
- What Pharisees were thinking (Lk 5:21 and 7:39).
- What went on behind closed doors as Pilate questioned Jesus (Jn 18:33-38) and exactly what was said during subsequent sessions between Pilate and "the Jews" and between Pilate and Jesus.
- What chief priests and Pharisees discussed with Pilate after the crucifixion (Mt 27:62-66).
- The type of plant whose stock was used (*hyssop,* Jn 19:29) to hoist up a vinegar-soaked sponge to Jesus while he was on the cross!
- Exactly, word for word, what angels said to Mary (Lk 1:26-37), to Zechariah (Lk 1:11-20), to Mary of Magdala and "the other" Mary (Mt 28:5-7) at the tomb, and to Joseph in his dreams (Mt 1:20-21, Mt 2:13).
- Verbatim, what the heavenly host and angel (Lk 2:13-14) said to the shepherds.
- Even which side of the altar the angel that appeared to Zechariah was standing on – when Zech was struck dumb (Lk 1:20) for the next year and *couldn't have reported that to anybody.*
- That angels attended Jesus during his time in the desert (Mk 1:13).
- What John the Baptist preached to the crowds (Lk 3:7-18) in remote locations.
- What was going on with the Logos and God *from the beginning of time* (Jn 1:1-5).
- What was discussed by John the Baptist, his disciples and "a certain Jew" (Jn 3:23-30) in a remote location removed from Jesus and his group.
- What the Samaritan woman told townspeople (Jn 4:28-30).
- What a voice from heaven said at Jesus' baptism (Mt 3:17, Mk 1:11 and Lk 3:22) – although the voice in Mark and Luke spoke only to Jesus.

Matthew and Luke even know, verbatim, what the devil said to Jesus and where he took him during the Temptation (Mt 4:1-11, Lk 4:2-13).

None of these could have feasibly been reported from a real event by any sort of witness through word of mouth on to an evangelist writing them down many decades later. These – and many more such stories – were fabricated by the writers based on stories they wanted to tell, or adapted from stories made up by others during the oral transmission stage.

The gospels (and the Acts) **are basically** *fiction,* constructed based on hazy old accounts of what generally happened decades before; they are meant to illustrate foregone points of view, not report with any degree of objectivity what really took place.

That is generally obvious from overall emphasis, but particularly clear from specific passages. For example, after the Last Supper (Mk 14:32-42, Mt 26:36-46, Lk 22:39-53), Jesus and the disciples – less Judas, who left to collude with chief priests – go to Gethsemane (Mount of Olives, as Luke has it – same location). Leaving the group in one place, then Peter, James and John to "keep watch", Jesus goes off some distance to pray. Here he's said to call on his heavenly father to relieve him of his coming ordeal. Upon returning to the three, he finds them asleep. The scene repeats twice more. Immediately thereafter, the group is accosted by Judas and priests, whereupon Jesus is carted off to trial.

With the disciples asleep, how does anybody know what Jesus prayed for each of those three times? Jesus was whisked away, never to walk free again. So who reported that event, including content of Jesus' silent prayer? How did it get recorded so that the evangelists could include the event decades later? Answer: it couldn't and didn't. The fictional story was made up to emphasize a point.

Core of Second Problem: The gospels and Acts are *creative* *fictions,* written from an omniscient narrative viewpoint, meant to convey a specific message – not objective reports composed for the purpose of reporting real events and situations.

Rational Problem #3: Functional Impossibilities

Where the gospels really reveal their unreliable nature is in reports that are totally unrealistic. For sure, these passages illustrate mystical, miraculous wonders intended by the writers to convince listeners of Jesus' grand and glorious nature. But they also reveal the myth-based, gullible mindset of listeners to whom the gospels (and Acts) were targeted – as well as that of initiating evangelist.

Sadly, that level of fantasy-mixed-with-reality has been propagated across many generations to the present day, holding many a true devotee locked within its primitive, unreal world-view.

It's one thing when the evangelists skew the geography of Tyre, Sidon and the Sea of Galilee. No big deal. But some events reported as facts are simply, flat out *impossible*. Include in that group a couple more blatant items that I could see through as a 10-year-old: *walking on water* and turning *water into wine*. Those things simply *did not happen!*

Nor did this: following Jesus' baptism by John (Mt 4:1-11 and Lk 4:1-13, copying from and expanding on Mk 1:12-13) the "spirit" led Jesus out to the wilderness, where the devil caught up with him to tempt him. Granted, 40 days in the desert without food might make you a bit woozy. (At least Mark has him attended by angels. Perhaps they slipped him a little manna.) But the encounters reported are pure fantasy.

In the second of three temptations, Satan led Jesus up to a high place (Lk 4:5, or "very high mountain" Mt 4:8) and showed him all the kingdoms of the world, offering him authority over all of them. (Jesus declined.) Of course, from no mountain anywhere – save the moon, given some patience to watch the world rotate for a day – can one see all the countries of the world, or even the whole Middle East. Does even the hardest-headed Evangelical

Christian think Satan whisked Jesus to Mons Huygens for a good view of earth?

Not to be overly nit-picky, as this passage clearly is meant to illustrate a point not report an event, but it reveals the primitive concept of the world held in the first century: a flat terra firma covered by a solid sort of shield, the firmament. If one sat on a mountain high enough, so the evangelists must have thought, one could see the whole flat disk of earth. That Eratosthenes of Cyrene had calculated the diameter of the huge sphere of the earth some three centuries prior – well, that source hadn't made it into gospel authors' bibliographies.

That devil then situated Jesus on top of the Temple in Jerusalem, suggesting he jump off so angels could save him. Another neat trick, though hardly very tempting. One might think – had it happened for real – that two figures perched on the Temple roof would have caught the attention of local priests and Roman troops. Did they levitate up there, with Satan clinging to Jesus' tunic? Did they climb up a pillar or conjure up a long ladder? Yea, another allegorical story, not an actual one. Fiction, as noted.

Have you heard the one about the Ascension? Only the author of Luke reports this (Lk 24:51) and reiterates it in his second volume (Acts 1:9). Jesus, reportedly having come back from the tomb to greet and intermingle with disciples on several occasions following his crucifixion, was taken before their very eyes right up into heaven, after which two men dressed in white appeared beside them assuring them he'd be back just like he left (something, by the way, that has yet to happen).

One key question: did authors of Mark and Matthew not receive this mythical story from oral lore or choose to ignore it – or did Luke's writer simply make it up? One of those.

And another: where do you suspect the resurrected Jesus went at that point? Into orbit?

In ancient times, the sky above, that *firmament* – pure noncept

– was deemed to be a solid dome, above which were waters, then above that, *heaven*. Its exact defined nature varied from region to region – but mostly was imagined to be a place where gods lived, whatever their local names. Elijah (2 Kings 2:11) was reputed to have been whisked up bodily to heaven by a whirlwind. Likely, the fantasy of Jesus following Elijah's exit scheme was fabricated (though only by Luke's author) to enhance Jesus' image as greater than that ninth-century BCE prophet. But the firmament doesn't really exist. Jesus couldn't have been transported bodily through it to a real physical location, heaven, above it, because that also doesn't exist. The story is absolute fiction – pure superstitious fantasy!

And *that* mythical invention leads to another: the Transfiguration of Jesus. He and three disciples were up on a mountain, praying. Jesus spontaneously (Mk 9:2-8, with Mt 17:1-9 and Lk 9:28-36 enhancing the story) started to radiate bright light as Moses and Elijah appeared "in glorious splendor" to talk things over with him. Then a cloud enveloped them all and a voice came out of the cloud – presumably Yahweh himself, praising Jesus and exhorting the disciples to "listen to him." Suddenly, poof! It was all over. (The disciples needed to be told to listen to Jesus at that late time point?)

Need I explain to you? That didn't happen! Perhaps *something* unusual happened – as will be seen in the reconstruction of Jesus' life – that was later exaggerated. But the Transfiguration as reported didn't happen in reality.

Core of Third Problem: Wild and crazy Hollywood-type special effects don't happen in Reality. But they can be reported by early writers and implemented by modern movie makers – in both instances of which they will be believed by naive people within whose belief systems such fantasies fit neatly.

Rational Problem #4: Ignorance of Reality
Completing the *Functional Impossibilities* theme, the gospel

writers' mindset must be noted. Reporting noncepts that didn't and couldn't ever happen divulges not hidden truths wispily revealed by a powerful but mystically elusive Deity, hinting vaguely to His mortal humans of His true nature.

Rather, it exposes primitive, superstitious thinking on the part of the writer and his audience – not only of first-century contemporaries, but of highly credulous peasants, farmers, workers, housewives, etc., down through time who, through fear and ignorance, accepted conjecture as truth. On their backs, a controlling and intolerant church built a pampered existence – riding the gullibility of common people through centuries, allowing no dissent.

At the moment of Jesus' baptism, heaven wasn't "torn open" (Mk 1:10), nor simply "opened" (Mt 3:16, Lk 3:21) so the Holy Spirit could descend on Jesus like a dove. Heaven, i.e., the sky, is an *illusion* – blue light diffracted when passing through the air, not the blue canopy shield believed in by the ancients. It couldn't be torn open – *there's nothing to tear!* Was this figurative speech? Okay. Poetic license? Alright. Allegorical illustration? Sure. Event? Nope.

Oh, and no voice boomed out from heaven, either.

The Ascension leaps from the previous category into Ignorance of Reality. Fear was rife in those ancient times, and death was at the top of the list of things to fear. With a judgmental deity lurking up there, ready to pick apart your every move during life, judging you negatively for every flaw, Satan on the sidelines waiting to get his evil mitts on you and the dark, metaphysical unknown hovering in the gap between, death intimidated and threatened superstitious minds. Much of the appeal of early Christianity was that it offered some loving respite from old, vindictive, oppressive, prudish, demanding and capricious gods, a dependable Heavenly Father in place of whimsical inflictions and punishment.

So the Ascension was basically a fabricated illustration of

Jesus rising intact, unharmed and not debilitated, into post life existence in God's heavenly lair – a satisfying wonder to the archaic, first-century mindset and to credulous rubes from that point on.

In Reality, people don't light up on mountain tops – as per the Transfiguration – and encounter speaking clouds. They don't tread water surface without sinking in, *however* much they believe in a mystical god. In Reality, lepers crippled with withered legs devoid of musculature don't get up and walk away.

Far too many accounts in the gospels simply overextend disbelief into areas of impossibility.

Feeding the multitude: Jesus conjures food out of thin air to miraculously feed groups of 4000 (Mk 8:1-9, Mt 15:32-39) and 5000 (Mt 14:13-21, Mk 6:31-44, Lk 9:10-17 and John 6:5-15). Believers accept that he did that while skeptics imagine that, if it happened at all, people were either spiritually fed, or simply shared food they had along as in pot luck, so that everybody ate until satisfied, with lots of leftovers.

Such stories doubtless evolved through time. Elisha of OT times (2 Kings 4:42-44) was reputed to feed a hundred people with twenty loaves. So *Feeding the Multitude* was either concocted or exaggerated to have Jesus outdo Elisha. Remember, these aren't historical accounts of actual events, but stories put up to convince the reader/listener of Jesus' exceptional status. That's pretty impressive stuff to a hungry peasant – a potential convert.

Imagine being there during the supposed feeding of the multitude. Look at a fish and a loaf next to it, about to be cut and served to the next hungry pauper in line. Does the fish expand lengthwise, so when you cut a piece off, the remaining piece expands to replace – before your very eyes – that chunk you just removed? When you cut the bread loaf or rip off a piece to give to the next person, does the hole grow back and fill in? Or do new loaves just appear on the table, poof, freshly baked and ready to serve with newly conjured fish, nicely browned and salted, popping into existence next to them? Did plates magically appear, too? Napkins? Why not wine?

Feeding the multitude didn't take place. The key to understanding life is to engage Reality, not blindly accept fantasy stories that never happened, but *seem* to have because anonymous writers two millennia ago reported them – and gullible, naïve children, taught these stories as facts generation after generation, grow up believing them.

Core of Fourth Problem: Reality works in certain reliable ways. Miracles don't happen, though real events may be construed as miracles within a given mindset – or be reported as otherworldly by ancient accounts offered by anonymous, superstitious sources.

Rational Problem #5: Irreconcilable Conflicts

The NT was written by many people – most, save one, of unknown identity – over the course of a few decades, then revised over centuries by intention, by translation and by reinterpretation. It isn't any wonder that there are viewpoints within the NT that differ and conjectural points established in some books that are in conflict with the message contained in other books.

However, the Bible is regarded – by many *absolutely*, by others to a degree – as fixed and perfect, the word of God, guided in revelation by the Holy Spirit, shaped into infallible truth as a final product. Given this rigidity, various religious voices go to great lengths to rationalize the many contradictions found from one NT writer to another, from one verse to another. Where these disagreements would normally serve to mitigate reliance on the NT as a viable source of any reliable info, much less a guideline for life, for the whitewashed, brain-washing message presented by churches, there simply is no discrepancy! For the true believer, each of these inherent conflicts can easily be rationalized away.

But for others, looking to shed childhood indoctrination into Biblical infallibility, a review of some of the more glaring conflicting points found in the NT will be very helpful:

Jesus vs. Paul: Numerous gospel references have Jesus focus his message exclusively on fellow Jews. He sends his disciples out to approach Jews (Mt 10:5-6) and says that he, himself, is "sent only to the lost sheep of Israel" (Mt 15:24). Elsewhere in Matthew, he emphasizes his purpose: fulfillment of the Law, not abolishment of it (Mt 5:17-18). Paul, on the other hand, as he moved to spread the word among all those interested in the region, is referenced repeatedly in Acts (e.g., Acts 13:47, Acts 22:21) and various letters (e.g., Romans 11:13) as extending his mission to Gentiles and that the Law was passé (e.g., Galatians 2:16) – that Jesus himself replaced the old way, such that acceptance of Jesus as savior sufficed.

Only with blinders firmly in place can these two gestures be reconciled. Obviously, Jesus focused on Jewish peers, trying to get them to see beyond restricted thinking based on concrete definitions. He apparently didn't appraise Samaritans or Greeks as reachable with this message. Now, wouldn't Jesus have known his own mission better?

Paul, however, with focus on his vision-in-the-sky Jesus, had no such qualms about planting seeds wherever they would grow – and they weren't sprouting so readily among the tradition-encrusted Jews. They, for the most part, already had their rules and beliefs. The *Messiah*, the *"Christ"* Paul was selling – one who had been executed as a common criminal – wasn't the hero they were looking for to lead the Jews against their oppressors.

The way to make sense of this discrepancy is to realize that both men, Jesus and Paul, were individuals with their personal points of view, presenting their impressions to peers as many others did then and now, not grandiose Supermen above and beyond mortals.

Knowing exactly what Jesus *did* feel about his mission is

nearly impossible, when the gospels are *expressing the viewpoints of their authors* and their communities, not necessarily reporting what Jesus really said and did. It is easier to comprehend Paul's message and his motivation clearly, because many of his letters survive. The Jesus depicted in the gospels, though, certainly contradicts Paul. And even Paul portrayed in the Acts differs significantly from impressions given by his own letters – which could fill its own Paul vs. Paul section here. To pretend otherwise is silly.

The Synoptic Gospels vs. John: Chronologically the last of the four gospels written, ascribed to "John", presents a Jesus so different from the Synoptic character that it seems to describe a different person. Again, this stunning divergence presents no problem to fixed believers. But one seeking understanding rather than confirmation of held convictions will benefit from exposure to differences, some direct contradictions.

1. **At Trial:** Quiet or talkative? *Can't be both!*
   - In Mark, Jesus says practically nothing to either chief priests or Pilate when facing their proceedings at his accusation. Authors of Matthew and Luke, copying Mark with some enhancements, follow suit – with Luke even having Jesus maintain total silence when facing Herod Antipas (a meeting the others aren't aware of.)
   - But, behold, in John, Jesus is fairly talkative with Pilate, explaining his motivations, his kingdom, why he was born.
2. **Performing miracles:** Signs or not signs, that is the question:
   - In the Synoptics, Jesus strongly refuses to perform miracles as signs (Mk 8:12-13, same story slightly revised in Mt 12:39, Lk 11:29) to the "wicked generation" proving his power.
   - Throughout John, though, Jesus is explicitly

performing supernatural acts *exactly for the purpose* of proving his exceptional nature.

3. **Jesus' Message:** Main gist of his spoken words radically different:

   - In the Synoptics, Jesus speaks primarily about the "Kingdom of God", repeatedly illustrating this state of being *within*, in many parables and aphorisms. These illustrations dominate, practically constituting his message.
   - But in John, the Kingdom of God is only mentioned once. John's Jesus lectures on end about the Father, proposing a nature certainly developed long after Jesus' lifetime.
   - The Synoptics' Jesus rarely talks about himself, referring to himself generally with the cryptic phrase, "the son of man". (Or son of Adam, as "Adam" means man/mankind in ancient Hebrew.)
   - John's Jesus elaborates on himself as main focus, describing his nature in many "I am" statements and long discourses aggrandizing his own nature.
   - In the earlier gospels, Jesus' key comments are short and to the point – crisp, clever parables with a surprising twist, pithy come-backs to leading questions.
   - The fourth gospel features long, rambling soliloquies from Jesus about himself, the Son and the Father.

4. **Different Nature of Jesus:** Actually, *each* gospel presents Jesus in a different light, slanting its message to emphasize a particular character. The Synoptics are roughly similar to each other – not surprising when Mark is reused and expanded upon by Matthew and Luke:

   - Mark illustrates a secretive, stoic Jesus, faced with a set of disciples who don't get it, quiet in agony at the end, seemingly deserted by his followers, his people and his Heavenly Father.
   - Matthew depicts Jesus for a Jewish proto-Christian community, emphasizing his Messiah nature as

fulfillment of scriptures as prophecies.

- Luke slants its Jesus toward a Greek/Gentile audience – showing him with a message for all, often with emphasis on the downtrodden and women.
- John expands Jesus into a full-blown parallel to God, a man aloof and lecturing on his own nature as model and glorification of all time.

Matthew vs. Luke: Jesus' birth as a miraculous event – his mother not having had the normally prerequisite sex – is depicted in divergent, mutually exclusive stories by the only two gospels whose creators seem to know anything about it. Notice how parallel features between Matthew and Luke cannot have both taken place.

- Matthew: Joseph and Mary live in Bethlehem at the time of Herod the Great (about 4 BCE)
- *Luke (in italics): the two live in Nazareth, but have to go to Bethlehem for a census at the time when Quirinius was governor of Syria (from 6 CE)*
- Joseph learns of Mary's pregnant state and considers calling the marriage off, but an angel assures him in a dream that the Holy Spirit did it. He relents and proceeds with things.
- *Mary gets a startling visit from the angel Gabriel, who explains to her amazement that she's about to become pregnant. (No explanation is given as to how she breaks the news to Joseph.)*
- After the birth at home, Magi visit from the east, amazingly finding them when a star hovers over their house. (How these astrologers arrive from the east following an eastern star isn't explained.)
- *After the birth, Shepherds visit from the fields, amazingly finding them despite sketchy directions from an angel, having somehow found their way into Bethlehem in the dark of night.*

This followed an appearance by heavenly host. (Why heaven would celebrate an event it had just instigated isn't explained.)

- After the astrologers depart, the couple, with baby, head off to Egypt to avoid Herod's wrath.
  - *A few days later, following circumcision and purification, they travel to Jerusalem for a sacrifice.*
- After Herod died, they returned from Egypt (as usual: to fulfill a prophecy), but not back to Bethlehem. They relocate to Nazareth **where they didn't live before** – of course, to fulfill another prophecy.
  - *After the rituals, they return home to Nazareth.*

As noted, these two accounts *cannot* be reconciled or conjoined. Either: one is right and the other wrong, or they're both incorrect. They appear to be just stories fabricated to have Jesus born in Bethlehem and raised in Nazareth – and cover for Jesus' known illegitimate birth.

It's certainly noteworthy that neither Paul, whose letters to early Christian communities predate these two gospels by some 30 years, nor the anonymous writers of other letters – nor the author of the wild-eyed symbolism that constitutes the book Revelation – ever reference the virgin birth. This mythological story seems to be based on some combination of three factors:

1. The presumed need of early Christians to keep up with other miraculous-conception origins for hero-type characters: Greek myth with gods siring children with human mothers (e.g., Hercules), Mithras, cults of Isis and Apollo.
2. The ultra prudish hang-up of early male-dominant cultures to avoid the unclean taint associated with sex.
3. Or the well-known mix-up of terminology associated with the prophecy that, in Matthew, the virgin birth is meant to fulfill. Matthew indicates that Isaiah (7:14) has prophesied

that, "A virgin will be with child." But the author of that work had apparently referenced the Septuagint the Greek language Old Testament (OT) translation available then for his hand-picked scriptural passage to rely on. The original Hebrew word in that passage of Isaiah meant "young woman", but got incorrectly translated into Greek as "virgin". Scholars point out as well that the Isaiah passage *wasn't a prognostication about a coming event in the first place* – as in predicting the birth of a Messiah – but a reference to a current event in its own timeframe, eighth century BCE.

It does astound me how nonceptual inventions like the virgin birth explode to such a hallowed state, yet are based on no substance and bring no theological, philosophical or practical value.

Jesus was not born of a virgin, any more than anybody else ever. Reality just doesn't work that way.

But early church founders were so hung up on the impurity of sex and sanctity of virginity that they would go to great lengths to keep Mary distanced from intercourse. By the second century, a doctrine had sprouted called the *Perpetual Virginity of Mary*; it was widely accepted by the fourth century. This declared that Mary, already hoisted up a high pedestal, was boosted even higher: she was declared *forever* a virgin. This required some additional fantasy, in that the gospels inconveniently mention Jesus' brothers and sisters. They had to be redefined as cousins or offspring of Joseph to a previous marriage. So Mary was declared a virgin *before* Jesus' birth, *after* it and *for all time*. This despite Matthew (Mt 1:25) explaining that Joseph hadn't had sex with Mary, "until she gave birth to a son," which implies he did *afterwards*. Perpetual Virginity? How utterly, unfathomably absurd!

That anti-sex fixation also produced the sheer nonsense of the

Immaculate Conception. Not to be confused with the Virgin Birth (of Jesus, which it often is as the public and the press are generally clueless), the Immaculate Conception dogma states that from the moment she was conceived (Mary, that is, through normal sex by her parents), she was freed by holy grace from the stain of "original sin" – the downbeat religious view traditionally held by the church of intercourse and normal human libido (which – noteworthy – both keep mankind going). This notion was concocted in the overwhelming piety of late antiquity thinking, but formalized by the Pope in 1854 in a papal bull – despite absolutely no implication from the gospels or original tradition from early times supporting it.

It can accurately be said, with exceeding lucidity, that a lot of bull has emanated from popes over the centuries, Immaculate Conception not the least within that category. I'll save *infallibility* for later.

In any case, Nativity stories in Matthew and Luke differ in ways that can't be reconciled.

One vs. The Others: There are so many inconsistencies among the gospels and Acts in describing events and statements of Jesus' time that details would fill numerous books. Scholarly works which *are* filled with such things are readily available for details, but here are a few as overview:

1. **The Last Supper:** variable stories contradict each other about key happenings.
   - Synoptics place event at Passover meal, John the day before (Day of Preparation) – a significant difference in Jewish ritual.
   - Communion established in Synoptics; feet are washed in John (no mention of communion).
   - Synoptics: quick meal, Judas exposed, off to Gethsemane for prayer. John: after Judas leaves, Jesus gives a long, long lecture.

2. **The Passion stories**: each gospel describes events leading up to the crucifixion and supposed resurrection differently, sometimes with details that contradict each other.

   - **Judas:** Matthew: Judas, remorseful, hangs himself. Acts: Judas buys a field, falls headlong, and, strangely, "his body burst open and all his intestines spilled out."
   - **Trial:** in Matthew, trial before Pilate egged on by chief priests and elders who are present. Pilate washes hands of affair, lets him be executed. Mark: before Pilate, Jesus admits he is "king of the Jews", says nothing more; Pilate lets him be taken. Luke: Pilate sends Jesus to Herod (Antipas, who, strangely, is in Jerusalem where he has no authority), who sends him back; Pilate lets him die anyway. John: long, segmented trial, with Pilate going out to talk with priests and crowd, back in to discuss with Jesus. Same outcome, different tale.
   - **Gospel accounts about post-trial events differ on all these points:** whose soldiers (Herod's or Pilate's?) mocked and put purple robe on Jesus; flogged or not; who carries cross (Jesus or Simon of Cyrene?); what was said on the way; taunting by soldiers; comments by thieves being executed; which associates of Jesus attended event; comments by soldiers; comments by Jesus; last words by Jesus; time of event; vinegar on sponge or not; time of death; timing of rip in temple curtain (before or after Jesus dies – and how would anybody know about this event happening elsewhere and when?); earthquake or not; tombs break open and old corpses come to life – or not.

3. **Matthew and Luke genealogies:** two family trees supplied by these two writers attempt to show Jesus was of the house of David, an important factor in "proving" he was really the Messiah: rational "proof" then amounted to showing something was predicted by the old scriptures.

However, the lineages differ considerably! Matthew lists 40 generations from Abraham to Joseph, while Luke, of the 74 generations he compiles the whole way from Adam, includes 54 from Abraham.

After David, they are *completely different.* Matthew has Joseph stemming from David via Solomon and his son Rehoboam. Luke says he comes from a line starting with David's son Nathan and his son Mattatha. Of course, you *can't be both*! Joseph's father according to Matthew was Jacob – not so, says Luke: it was Heli. (Two fathers would be more amazing than zero!)

But *neither one really matters!* In trying to picture Jesus' royal line – necessary to promote a heroic figure and fulfill scripture – they both forget that they *manufactured virgin birth stories!* So Jesus wasn't Joseph's son anyway, and thus not in the house of David. That makes both genealogies moot and House of David proof invalid.

Some would explain that Luke's genealogy actually traces Mary's line, not Joseph's, back to David, making Jesus of David's house through Mary. But Jewish "seed" passes along male lines. And anyway, *that's not what Luke says!*

4. **Resurrection stories:** these all differ considerably in relating what happened after the crucifixion – to whom Jesus appeared, when and what he did.

   - Paul (1 Cor 15:5-8) says: Jesus appeared to Peter, then to the twelve, then to 500, then to James, then to all the apostles, lastly to Paul, himself.

   - Mark: No account – Mk 16:9-20 was a later fabrication. Gospel ends when two Marys and Salome find the empty tomb and a young man in a white robe. They left and "said nothing to anyone."

   - Matthew (28:2-10): angel, having rolled back the seal stone, greets Mary Magdalene and "the other" Mary. Hurrying away, they encounter Jesus, who says he'll meet everybody in Galilee. The disciples go there and meet him. Jesus spoke and the story ends.

- Luke (24:1-53): Women (Mary Magdalene and others) go to tomb, find it empty, but encounter two men in gleaming clothes who say Jesus has risen. They report to disciples; Peter runs to grave, finds only strips of linen. Two others, seven miles away, encounter Jesus – but don't recognize him! They take him to dinner and just as they identify him, he vanishes. When the two report to the group, Jesus appears again, talks to them, opens their minds, then takes them out of town and is taken up into the sky.

- John (20:1-end): Mary of Magdala reports the empty tomb to Peter and another disciple, who run there to find burial cloth. Mary, returns to tomb, sees two angels, then Jesus – but doesn't recognize him at first. That evening, Jesus appears to disciples – behind locked doors. He appears again the following week inside locked house – and did "many other miraculous signs" for disciples. He appears later by Sea of Galilee, helps them catch fish and carries on an odd discussion.

- Acts (1:3-11): Jesus appears over about 40 days, telling the disciples to stay in Jerusalem, that they wouldn't know when the kingdom would be restored. Then he is taken up into heaven. Two mysterious men dressed in white, saying he would be back the same way he left.

5. **Technical Difficulties:** Numerous examples of small differences highlight the degree to which gospel writers revised stories at their whim.

- Mark (11:12) relates a story that a hungry Jesus, annoyed that a fig tree didn't have any fruit on it, cursed it. The next day, as they passed by, they saw it had withered (Mk 11:20). Matthew has to exaggerate that account. Mt 21:19-21 has the tree wither immediately.

- The Synoptics have Jesus "cleanse" the temple – aggressively break up the money changers, etc. – at the end of his ministry. Indeed, it immediately aggravates the authorities and leads directly to his accusation and crucifixion. John places that event at the beginning of his venture, completely changing the flow.

- Jesus' whole endeavor of teaching, travel, healing, etc., lasts about a year in the Synoptics. In John the duration is more like three years.

- In Mark (5:21-43) a synagogue leader approaches Jesus, asking him to come to heal his daughter who is dying. Luke (8:41-56) repeats the healing sequence. Matthew exaggerates the story (9:18) by having the girl already dead, requiring Jesus to revive a corpse.

- Matthew (8:5-13) and Luke (7:2-10) tell the same story, one absent from Mark, about a centurion's servant being ill and needing Jesus to heal him. Whatever the common source was and whatever it said, one evangelist revises it, or both did. In Matthew, the centurion approaches Jesus, in Luke "elders of the Jews" are sent.

- Mark (3:21) has Jesus' family, saying he was, "out of his mind," coming to take charge of him. Had Mary forgotten her discussion with Gabriel about Jesus being "great" and his "kingdom never ending"? Hadn't she informed the family about Jesus' miraculous birth, initiated by the Holy Spirit? Luke, in copying Mark's story about Beelzebub that follows Mk 3:21, conveniently has excised reference to Jesus' supposed craziness. Thus, a technical difficulty of meaning: Mark's report may be historically accurate and thus real. His family likely did find his teaching eccentric and troubling.

It is important to recognize how many differences, minor to major, permeate the NT. Many are understandable, having come from divergent sources. But many are critical – altering key components of the message itself, and damaging credence to the whole work.

Core of Fifth Problem: Many gospel accounts contradict each other. With such contradictions, **at least one has to be fallacious.** This extent of fallacy indicates the works are neither divinely inspired nor reliably credible.

Rational Problem #6: Myth Presented as Fact

The gospels and Acts seem straightforward, telling stories about Jesus and his aftermath by reporting incidents and deeds, interaction with other people, discussions with religious figures and disciples, etc. Intermingled with such events are many statements by Jesus and others presented as dialogue. Are these accounts myth or reflective of actual events?

"Myth" has come to equate with *falsity* in our culture of objectivity, old, impossible stories that couldn't have happened: Heracles capturing Cerberus without weapons, Gilgamesh seeking immortality from Utnapishtim, Thor battling the monster Jörmungandr. In ancient times, however, based on shared acknowledgement of influence by gods and demons, myth was a means to express, to illustrate, meaningful – to them – aspects of life that couldn't be simply stated. Myth appears commonly in the gospels and Acts: stories are generated to establish a point, typically emphasizing the special status and capabilities of Jesus.

But problems arise when, in our modern view, such myths are either summarily dismissed as unfeasible claims or blindly accepted as literal truths. In the literary track of the gospel writer, they were actually neither. Evangelists had stories to work with, passed along over decades, and favored within their communities as to what events in those accounts meant. So they creatively reshaped the stories to express a reality they were convinced of.

Skeptics will detail the many flaws, unbelievable miracles, revisions, etc., in the gospels – many of each exist, as indicated – and show them as grounds to doubt the whole story. That's a fairly easy case to make.

Believers will take the same material and rationalize it with often far-fetched, concocted explanations above and beyond the original text. Their explanations will satisfy believers preset to accept *any* reasoning, however weak, that supports their preconceived expectations. But to someone seeking understanding, such rationalizations only serve to expose weakness in original claims.

Both skeptics and believers err in rejecting and accepting, respectively, these accounts *per se*. As myth, mixed with teaching, literal reporting and other elements, more evaluation must be made of the canonical gospels, the Acts and Thomas in order to discriminate elements of value from flawed claims and extract them, while exposing and bypassing fallacies and exaggerations.

Elements of myth, even while carrying value believed by the writer to be important and useful, are ultimately *non-events*. For whatever the point evangelists would establish by reporting mythical elements as real events, unreal accounts don't propel the author's idealism into functional reality. One *can*, however, recognize the authors' excessive zeal in dispensing exaggerated elements without necessarily jettisoning the whole work.

Walking on water, feeding the multitude, incurring pregnancy by action of the Holy Spirit – these not only didn't happen, but reporting them as facts in line with and literarily indistinguishable from other believable events simply reduces viability of the whole work.

Raising Lazarus (Jn 11:17-44) and others from the dead, a key "sign" from John of Jesus' divine nature, makes a point about death, about Jesus and about his overall message and status. But to a twenty-first-century audience that sees reality more objectively, the story damages value; it doesn't enhance it. Was Lazarus only in a coma such that Jesus, by trusting himself and his own impulses, could confidently revive him with conviction that experience would bear him out? At some point not long after cessation of heartbeat and breathing, as known to a modern audience, the body starts to break down. Blood coagulates, bacteria in the gut start to consume body tissue, eyes and other parts dry out, brain and organ tissue break down.

Four days later, if really *dead*, Lazarus' corpse is no longer viable. For certain, Near Death Experiences are common now, given medical attention and greater documentation of real events wherein people return to life after clinical death. But they weren't dead too long, or nothing physically functional would remain for consciousness to re-inhabit. At some point revival, whether clinical via resuscitation or natural, *doesn't happen*.

Turning water to wine at a wedding festival would be a neat trick – certainly enhancing one's popularity at parties. But was it a trick, a sleight-of-hand substitution? Or did Jesus somehow hypnotize the group into thinking they were drinking wine? Or did the event get invented ten or twenty years later, growing from less miraculous claims reported just after the event? Or did the author of John just invent a good story to emphasize his point? One thing for absolute certain: Jesus did *not* take vats of water and turn it into wine. Reality doesn't work like that.

In any case, mythical events reported as facts, while perhaps impressing superstitious proto-Christians two millennia ago – and duping strong believers today – really serve to *detract* from NT value in the eyes of alert readers, not enhance it.

Core of Sixth Problem: Myth, presented as fact, **doesn't strengthen viability of the message, it detracts from it** for thinking people.

Rational Problem #7: Retroactive Prognostication

The Bible, NT or OT, is stellar at presenting future predictions that remarkably come true – except that the stories are actually far from prognostication: they were composed at a point in time where things reported as future predictions *had actually already happened*. Then the written account was passed off as having been written much earlier.

The prime case in point of this deception is the OT book of Daniel. The book's content is set in the time of Babylonian captivity and claims to have been written then. It lays out a set of dramatic predictions for the period from about the fifth century BCE onwards which all came true – up to a point about 165 BCE, after which they are all wrong. Scholars generally conclude, based on language usage and other sleuthing criteria that any original text was appended in a different style later, inserting predictions into old text so they would seem to be great revelations.

This happens in the NT as well. A manuscript produced in 85 CE can easily refer to Jesus as predicting back in the year 30 that all the temple's great stones would be "thrown down" (Mt 24:2) – when the writer knew that this *had already happened* during the Roman siege of Jerusalem by Titus in 70.

In ancient times, no fact checkers served to keep writers honest. Whoever wrote Matthew could make any claim he wanted to and credulous people who would hear his work read aloud had no means – and likely no inclination – to doubt anything he said! Gospel writers, drawing from oral traditions already handed along through many superstitious reporters from the 30s to the 70s – and across a cultural divide, Aramaic to Greek – could fabricate any story at all in order to express their inclination of understanding. Nobody would know. Their listeners weren't Athenian philosophers and sophisticated thinkers, educated in rhetoric and logic. They were common folk, mostly illiterate, fearful and downtrodden to begin with, looking for meaning in life and finding solace in shared stories of a mystical Savior who offered love instead of punishment or indifference.

Remember: Matthew's author, writing for a principally Jewish community of proto-Christians in which he lived, probably in

Syria, and that of Luke, perhaps from Antioch – or who knows where – **weren't writing the Bible** when they scripted their accounts. They had no vague inkling that their works would ultimately be added to the Bible they knew – the Greek version Old Testament, the Septuagint. And they had no awareness *of each other.* They did both know of the book we call Mark, however, as they drew heavily from its content – but wouldn't have called it "Mark", as that name wasn't applied for another century. Had they known of each other's efforts, perhaps they would have coordinated their fabricated stories of the Nativity and Passion to sync them up (or maybe just argued about them indefinitely, as per another tradition).

As to Prognostication...

Prediction of the future, of course, is a gesture long rooted in popular culture. It formed a critical part of daily life in ancient times and still rather dominates general focus – though means to do so may be more analytical and scientific (e.g., weather forecast), less intuitive, in our time. Still, a handy psychic or Tarot reader is likely to be found just about anywhere. To put prognostication into perspective, let's explore the inner-outer connection somewhat deeper:

Reality, unfolding in one's daily life, is not a collection of random events, nor is it driven by some external deity or forces called luck and fate. As illustrated, each individual attracts and encounters events and relationships that reflect his/her own nature. In this meaning-based Reality, information and related value sit at the core of being of consciousness. Meaning dominates the subconscious, drives dreams through the night, underlies emotional states and level of contentment during daily life and evolves constantly through further encounters within real life.

Information flow during this ongoing now moment, with value and meaning underneath that surface as substantial context, constitutes the exclusive flux-material of existence. *It's important to grasp that point:* understanding the consciousness-reality life experience depends on that perception!

Life in its essence is not an objective encounter, an engagement of real world remote objects and flesh-based people – separate and isolated from the Self – that one must reluctantly face daily. That's the illusory image science creates for the mind that accepts science as ultimate truth. Nor is life an ongoing test, created and inflicted by a creator deity – the paradigm concocted by western religions.

Life is a meaningful engagement of events and relationships that reflect the Self, that symbolize and materialize the complex store of value and significance held by the psyche within its mindset.

As such, constantly, within the intangible realm of psychic stores, of subconscious meaning, complex, interwoven threads of information reside, all interconnected. On a personal level, the mind accesses that information for every daily effort, for making choices, for interacting, for planning, for speech, for processing cognition, etc. The subconscious store of integrated under-standing is vast – but mostly invisible to conscious processes. The mind only digs out that which is needed at the moment from the vast repository of facts, beliefs, memory items, definitions, lessons learned, values held, self-image, world view, philo-sophical tenets held and disavowed, accumulated knowledge, etc.

That great store of content, intellectual in basis but emotional in consequence, is not only available to each individual via recall, but *is accessed by others*. That occurs unconsciously all the time throughout complex daily interaction, replete with shared meaning; it requires multifaceted coordination – all happening pretty much at a subconscious level. Convoluted encounters stem, not from random movement but from subconscious inter-action. "Accidents", indeed, aren't accidental at all, but are preset, initially coordinated at deeper psychic levels.

We all can consciously, purposely access our own deeper stores of psychic materials – it only requires focus inward, concentration, intent and practice. As noted earlier, the inward gesture of revising inner content constitutes *one's real lever* at affecting the external world – as patterned experience manifests directly from this inner realm.

But others have access as well to one's own inner store. This interchange is necessary for the daily flow of complex life, flow based on meaning and outcome.

But more than that, properly oriented individuals, if sensitive and allowed, can read other people's nature explicitly. Hence: psychics and character readers. The totality of one's inner mindset is available at all times; access to that store of information, however, is limited by belief, will and other inner elements. The open-minded, curious person approaching a psychic for information can have much revealed. The skeptic creates walls that inhibit access to meaning – and fulfill that person's overriding doubt.

At age 19, I encountered a perceptive psychic while traveling with friends. Posing as a handwriting expert – doubtless handy for business security in 1966 – this reader glanced at my signature (from which, even then, no perceptible information could be gleaned) and proceeded to read my life. She noted that I would travel extensively in life, accurately pinpointing a core feature of my many subsequent adventures. She said that I'd had major problems with my girlfriend that summer, but not to worry, as it would "all work out one day". Correct: we'd split up under trying conditions and did, later in life, have another brief go-round. But it wasn't the right relationship then, at 19, nor was it right much later at age 40 – so, indeed, it did all work out.

This psychic foretold in August of 1966 that I would only ever have one son: he would be born when I was 34. Abe indeed arrived in June of 1981 – ten days after my 34th birthday, 15 years after that prediction. All of her comments, of course, from the perspective of that moment lay in the future. They would all "come to pass", as the Book of Mormon might put it, but didn't impact me so much at that moment. That event might have been forgotten had she not added, as I left the room, a pinpoint description of the exact, complex situation that led me to that setting – reading a current situation of which she had no direct knowledge as though reading a paragraph.

Years later, during my mid-thirties as my personal journey unfolded, I encountered another psychic in San Diego. Under his tutelage, I gained clarity in accessing psychic info. In short order, I was also giving psychic readings. Never as explicit in laying out events as that lady had been, I could clearly read complex, meaningful elements of the nature of complete strangers. It wasn't a unique talent of mine, though, but rather a capability of all people – to varying degrees. Access to the subconscious store of information in others requires principally trust in oneself, an open mind – and a sincere subject (i.e., not a skeptic trying to test the reader).

In any case, predicting future events accurately is not only possible, but rather common. However, predicting the future inaccurately is also universal and probably even *more* common – and flawed voices of phonies can be much louder.

So, what to make of Biblical passages where the future is predicted by some agent and it comes to pass – in retrospect from the writer's standpoint? Jesus is presented by all accounts to be unquestioningly knowledgeable that he's about to be done in by his overzealous enemies, the chief priests and crew. Could that have been the case, and I mean, really? Or did the evangelists retrofit that doom and gloom onto the myth to emphasize their evaluation of him as divine, connected to the all-knowing almighty, and thus already informed of events to come?

There is one event reported at both ends – forecast to fruition – that reveals the thinking of the gospel writers:

When Jesus, presaging his own ministry, encounters John the

Baptist and is baptized by him, the latter seems to spontaneously recognize Jesus' lofty status (Mk 1:7-9, Mt 4:12-13, Lk 3:16-17). Immediately, the heavens open (whatever that means) and God himself speaks, announcing his pleasure at Jesus (Mk 1:9-11, Mt 4:16-17, Lk 3:21-22). The Gospel of John elaborates on the story (Jn 1:29-36). So, here is a prognostication, multiply attested, that the Baptist knows *right away* Jesus' elevated status.

However, later on John seems to forget all that! Later, the Baptist, at that point imprisoned, sends a couple of his followers to query Jesus as to whether he is *indeed* the one to come (Mt 11:2-3, Lk 7:22), or should they "expect somebody else". But wait! Hadn't John already revealed that – back at the baptism? Hadn't a divine voice boomed from above in recognition of Jesus' status?

Of the two episodes, the latter is plausible. The first, intuitive knowing of Jesus' elevated nature without any outward indication, is very likely fabricated, invented by evangelists to cover the rather embarrassing situation that Jesus came to John for baptism, which would indicate John was somehow spiritually superior. So stories had to be invented whereby John lowered his own status by his observation of Jesus' pre-eminence.

And that reveals the artificial tendencies of gospel passages, particularly in reports of foretelling the future. While such reading is possible, these gospel passages are much more likely constructs meant to glorify Jesus than reports of real prognostications.

Core of Seventh Problem: Claims of prognostication, retroactively fit into gospel accounts were almost certainly fabrications meant to exaggerate powers of Jesus.

Rational Problem #8: Messianic Prophecies from the Past – Misconstrued, Overly General and Falsely Applied

First-century people, as noted, were highly superstitious in their orientation to divine causality. For Judeans the reasoning was straightforward: if Yahweh and demons are the true power sources to life, you had better pay attention to great seers intimately attuned to divine dictation. Invariably, those were the vaunted prophets from the past, whose words were recorded in the scriptures. So OT passages were frequently referenced by gospel authors in connection to situations as confirmation, indeed, *proof*, that Jesus was Messiah – for past prophets had foretold his coming.

A clear example of reliance on prophetic attribution is seen in Acts 17:10-12. When Paul and Silas speak at a synagogue in Berea, the locals "examined the scriptures every day to see if what Paul said was true." It didn't matter if Paul's account reflected reality; the only important thing was that it fit in with scriptural "Truths" – i.e., accepted scriptural proof.

In a strange yet common twist of human nature, people of any generation are typically much more inclined to accept visionary perspectives from teachers of the past than those who are peers – regardless of how far advanced those current insights are over older ones. Most people are comfortable with tried-and-true explanations that fit within their accepted convictions, not with visionary ones that expose the falsity of their currently favored – though fallacious – notions.

Of course, in preferring earlier period visionaries, they're not really comparing current teachers to actual people from the past, but to *exalted mind-images* they hold of those earlier heroes. Being dead somehow adds a sheen of validity to characters: once dead and gone, politicians become statesmen, religious functionaries turn into saints. Likely prophets, the best of them, had their own problems gaining acceptance during their lifetimes.

So it was in Jesus' time. Jesus offered greater perspectives on reality, weaving his insights into digestible parables and illustrations, trying to move his peers' understanding forward. But people questioned him on the Law and Prophets – the standard of definition then – rigidly clinging to the past. To them, making sense of daily life required hearkening back to the divinely spurred prophecies, to entrenched truths of Isaiah and Proverbs, of Micah and Jeremiah – greater and lesser prophets of bygone days. If a situation in the current (first century) timeframe could be likened to those ancient "truths", shown how contemporary circumstances *now* were anticipated by past, precognitive declarations, then a certain rational support was established.

I have to think of my grandmother in this regard. She was a wonderful, old-fashioned person – hard working, unpretentious and totally without malice. But in making sense of the world, she would have an idiom, religious quote or colloquialism to cover anything. No matter what happened, she would liken it to some trustworthy phrase – imbibing meaning in the present by swishing it down with a gulp of the past.

Jesus' peers must have been like that: finding reinforcement for daily life in accepted wisdom – justifying real current events as fulfillment of prophetic "Truth". Certainly the evangelists were. The gospels are full of instances where OT scriptures are called up in connection with deeds of Jesus or unfolding situations. You don't get to the fifth chapter of Matthew, for example, before Isaiah, Micah, Hosea, Jeremiah, Deuteronomy and Psalms have all been referenced – some several times. This justification by reference to ancient prophecy was very important within their deity-dominated world-view to establishing veracity. Indeed, it remains so today for a certain dualistic mindset that, fully convinced of external causality, seeks assurance and thus security via reinforcement of prized tenets. And that can be the religionist, quoting the Bible, the philosopher, arguing Neo-Platonism or citing Kant, or the scientist revering Einstein and Bohr.

Following the logic that earlier visionaries were more advanced spiritually than modern ones, of course, doesn't work: the farther back one would look, the *more enlightened people would be!* Nomadic Shamans would trump the prophets. Neolithic cave painters would have to have been even loftier, symbolizing absolute truth in wooly rhinoceros depictions. Neanderthal magicians would have been outdone by Homo erectus philosophers and Australopithecine seers, in that order. Imagine how enlightened dinosaurs were!

Two questions arise concerning gospel reliability under this very important caveat: **who initiated the referenced OT passage** and **how well does the prophecy** (if it even is one!) **apply to the case in point**. It's easy to simply browse through gospels while scarcely glimpsing the many scripture referrals without delving into the OT reference to examine critical levels of meaning involved.

So, **firstly, whose references are they?** That is, who initiated the connection?

- Did Jesus and other characters – as depicted in gospel and Acts quotes and deeds with OT references noted – make the scriptural reference originally, coincident with the event?
- Or did the apostles sometime later, when recalling words and deeds of Jesus, add those justifications – which then got built into the story?
- Or did unknown transmitters of information about Jesus insert scriptural support later during decades of *oral tradition* story exchange?
- Or did the gospel authors, wanting to elevate authenticity (in the minds of early listeners) and prove the status of their Messiah, attach the OT references *much* later?

Scriptural attribution might have stemmed from any of those, or some combination, given the sketchiness of source material.

Indeed, one other possibility exists, with its own ramification: did Jesus take actions *solely for the purpose* of fulfilling prophecy – or seeming to? For example, in sending (Mk 11:1-7, Mt 21:2-5, Lk 19:29-35) disciples off to get a donkey's colt to ride into Jerusalem, did Jesus stage the entry *just to fulfill* the prophecy in Zechariah (Ze 9:9) stemming from about 500 BCE? It certainly looks like that is the case: why else would he go to all the fuss of riding the colt of an ass into town where his feet probably dragged the ground?

That, of course, begs the question: if you specifically do something to fulfill a previous "prophecy", is that valid evidence of anything? Accurate psychic predictions of events – with participants unaware of the prediction – are impressive prognostication. But, if somebody plans and carries out an event *just* to make a known prediction take place and thus *seem* visionary, the precognition becomes meaningless – a sham.

Quite a few entries by the evangelists appear to be just that type of fulfillment: planned and executed *just for the purpose of seeming to fulfill a prophecy* – and, by consequence, to look like the Messiah predicted way back when was your proposed one: Jesus. That is a pretty phony argument – not unlike a sales pitch. (Indeed, it must have worked to entice multitudes over the ages.)

Of course, maybe, Jesus didn't actually "stage" fulfillment, but, tired from the long Galilee trek, he happened to be riding a borrowed donkey into Jerusalem – but the disciples enhanced the story. Or that donkey story may have gotten elevated in significance years later, step by step, while being passed along as oral lore. Or perhaps the evangelist scoured the OT for suitable stories to affix to known Jesus actions, thus indicating fulfillment.

This **second question** about scriptural references actually raises **a double caveat:** not only **how well do the prophecies apply, but how accurate are they?** Again, reading the gospels casually, one tends to think that actions did fulfill prior prophecy – there must be something to it. But scholars have found that, quite often, the OT scripture listed *hadn't said what the NT writer claims or hadn't meant what the NT writer implied*. Many scriptural references aren't taken from prophecies aimed by the OT writer to his future, but simply *stories out of their own timeframe*.

Some are just phrases with no pointed reference at all! John 12:13 and Mark 11:9, quoting groups of people chanting, "Blessed is he who comes in the name of the Lord," from Psalm 118:26, pulled out of context, is so general it could apply *to any act at any time*.

As for scripture misapplied, some of that distortion may have to do with the evangelists being Greek-speaking Jews or Greeks. They may not have had the ingrained connection to OT lore that the native Judean or Galilean would have had. And their reference would have been the Septuagint (a translation into Greek, rife with its own flaws), not an original Hebrew text. Some of it may have to do with hastily selecting passages that seem, superficially, to support the main emphasis: to indicate Jesus' elevated status.

Whatever the grounds, the referential passages can be misleading and fallacious.

We've already seen (Fifth Rational Problem above) a major twist in meaning that the Greek OT introduced in translating the (Isaiah 7:14) Hebrew word *"almah"*, meaning maiden (or young woman or virgin) into the Greek word *"parthenos"*, which specifically means "virgin". Hebrew had its own explicit word for virgin, *bethulah*, which would have been used, had the early writer of Isaiah meant that.

But this word-selection distortion – inventing (Mt 1:22-23) a virgin birth out of a translation flaw – is actually secondary. The alluded Isaiah passage supposedly predicting Jesus' birth is *not a prognostication in the first place!* It refers to a child to be born *in Isaiah's own timeframe*, the eighth century BCE. It isn't predicting a future Messiah, but was originally written in Hebrew in the present tense. That child was to be a sign to King Ahaz as a precursor to an impending event – in Ahaz' frame of experience. The passage in Isaiah is originally *"is* born", not *"will be* born".

Thus, the claimed application to Jesus' birth is a total fabrication – but by whom? By Mary and Joseph back in 5 BCE, to cover up the scandal? By anonymous transmitters as exaggerated lore during the oral tradition phase, 30 to 70 CE? By the author of Matthew in 85 CE to aggrandize Markian accounts and further elevate Jesus? The source doesn't really matter. Vital is understanding the fabrication and consequent deception, *which is not uncommon* in the gospels given all the caveats.

By the way, to complete the disconnect: as per Mt 1:23, they didn't even name him Immanuel. They named him Yeshua.

So this Biblical reference is *both* inaccurate and doesn't really apply.

Matthew goes on to venerate Bethlehem as the birthplace of Jesus by quoting Micah (Mt 2:6 from Micah 5:2) that, "out of you will come a ruler." But when looked into, the Micah passage, in context, indicates something of a military leader who will indeed deliver the people – but not from the Romans in 30 CE, rather from an invasion of the Assyrians, again, about the eighth century BCE. It has absolutely, totally *nothing to do* with predicting a first-century Messiah, but rather indicates a contemporary leader to fight invaders centuries prior.

Next thing in Matthew (2:13-15), the author has Joseph and Mary head off to Egypt, then return – all that to fulfill Hosea 11:1, "out of Egypt I called my son." But a look at Hosea reveals that "son" refers to Israel, the people, exiting there under Moses thirteen centuries prior – not a prospective Messiah in 4 BCE. The author of Hosea wasn't predicting a savior, he was *reviewing the past*: Moses' trek out of Egypt.

Immediately thereafter (Mt 2:16-17) comes a passage from Jeremiah concerning the story about Herod, tipped off by the Magi, planning to kill Bethlehem babies in order to get Jesus. Why an aged king with dwindling health would care about a baby – particularly when he was busy executing family members he really had grounds to fear – is illogical to begin with. But the passage quoted from Jeremiah (31:15) is so generalized it could apply to anything at all!

I could go on and on with this, as there are many such flawed connections.

Some passages, of course, are indeed pertinent to the point they would support:

- Jesus, as quoted in Luke 22:37, referencing Isaiah 53:12, aptly reinforces his prediction of being captured and tried – but that presupposes that he actually knew what events were coming (highly questionable based on Rational Problem #7).
- The Malachi allusion (Mal 3:1) in Luke 7:27 is a correct reference – from the standpoint of the Jesus being illustrated – that the "Lord" would send a "messenger ahead", that being John the Baptist.
- Mark 9:48 references Isaiah 66:24 – where the "Lord" is ranting about punishments he would dish out (again, eighth-century BCE mindset) – and is loosely connected to the dire warnings Jesus is issuing (gruesome, but connected).

But for each such logical connection as those, stands an errant one elsewhere. Mark 10:19 has Jesus actually quote an incorrect Commandment: "do not defraud" – an error corrected when the passage is reused in Matthew and Luke. Matthew 8:17 claims that Jesus' healing was portended by Isaiah 53:4. But that passage of Isaiah is a long lament about afflictions, transgressions and iniquities. It isn't a prophecy about a coming healer.

So there are many flawed references scattered throughout the gospels and Acts – easy to find if you go looking. Passages are misconstrued – either taken out of context (from original scripture) and applied to situations not intended by the original voice – misquoted or somehow skewed to serve the purpose of the evangelist. There are passages so general that they could apply to anything, others so short that they support nothing.

And, of course, scriptural support as validation only has significance if one takes Biblical entries – writings from an earlier agrarian, superstitious, generally uneducated culture even more primitive than Jesus' first-century world – as somehow authoritative. Personally, I don't. And I think others do only because they were taught to do so as children.

Before abandoning problems associated with scriptural references, a very significant **third type of caveat** needs to be raised in regard to scriptural references: **the OT is so full of quotes, claims, prophecies and slants that practically any action can be connected to some scriptural passage**. So, no matter what was said or done by Jesus, the disciples or anybody else, *some phrase from old scriptures* could be found and attached to it, implying validity.

Let me illustrate that directly. I've written books and given many talks about the nature of reality. Now, I'm composing a book that looks in depth at Jesus, clarifying his viewpoint in the light of advanced perspectives. A quick search through the OT – or the New Testament for that matter – yields quotes that I could easily suggest foretell my doing these things. I *could* offer these, as the ancients did, as arguments supporting my validity. (Please note: *I'm not making that claim*, that my coming was foretold or that my teaching is a fulfillment of any Biblical prognostications! Not in *any way, shape or form*. I'm just showing how easy it is to make such connections.)

When I explain how each of us manifests reality from the depths of our consciousness, I could say, look, Psalms 104:5 presages that wisdom: "He set the earth on its foundations; it can never be moved." When you become aware of your interactive, causal essence within Reality, you become very secure. Doesn't Psalms foresee my perspectives as solidifying man's mental stance?

As I pass along visionary insights, I could assert that Psalms 49:3 validates me: "My mouth will speak words of wisdom; the utterance from my heart will give understanding." Doesn't that prove to the religionist that, sincere and insightful, I am right –

and fully supported by scripture?

When I tell you: there is nothing to fear when you recognize that you are behind the flow of your life. Well, Micah must have known I was coming, so I *could* claim, as per Micah 4:4. "Every man will sit under his own vine and under his own fig tree and no one will make them afraid." And, Micah 6:8, to boot: "He has showed you, O man, what is good." Don't you see, I could say – or my followers could if I had any, which I don't because I don't want any – that my coming was pre-ordained!

I could even point out where Jesus predicts *this very book*, meant to correct two millennia of gross distortion of his meaning. Referencing John 14:16, I could say Jesus anticipated my message: "And I will ask the Father, and he will give you another Counselor to be with you forever – the Spirit of truth." In an unabashed, self-aggrandizing gesture, well within the tradition of haughty church practices, I could claim to be that Counselor! Check out John 15:26, if you aren't convinced.

Of course, that's the kind of thing – claiming to align with ancient, venerated sources – that almost got Jesus chucked off a cliff (Lk 4:28-30), did get Paul flogged (Acts 16:23) and got Stephen (Acts 7:51-60) stoned. When you turn religious arguments on their heads in the face of rigid believers and stone-hard thinkers, they get really upset.

But I'm not claiming anything. To understand life clearly, you have to break away from archaic thinking, not reference it for validity. My point in this regard is simple: whatever you want to say, you can find passages in the old scriptures that will seem to support it. And that goes for rape, murder, brutality, incest – you name it – as well as spiritual insights.

Core of Eighth Problem: Messianic Prophecies, used to "prove" Jesus' Messiah status or emphasize the validity of supposedly prognosticated events, **are often misconstrued, overly general and falsely applied.** Ultimately, scriptural references *don't prove anything at all.*

Poetic Distortion

As if this compilation of problems weren't enough to expose the unreliability of the NT, I must add yet another caveat to the mix. It is entirely possible – and frequently done in the Bible and elsewhere – to compose poetic passages that are compelling and inspiring, yet have *no basis in reality*. That is, you can dress up a noncept or fallacious claim in mighty fancy adornment – but that doesn't make it valid.

The 23rd Psalm is a great example of this root tradition. "The Lord is my shepherd, I shall not want ... He guides me in paths of righteousness ... Yea, though I walk through the Valley of the Shadow of Death, I fear no evil ... My cup runneth over ... Surely goodness and mercy will follow me..." Even though shifting from third-person reference to the Lord to second-person midstream, this is touching, moving poetry.

However, the referenced "Lord", the all-powerful Yahweh-god of David's time, doesn't exist and never did. So the beauty of the poetry deceives the unwary listener – as I was during childhood when I believed that sort of thing.

The NT is much less poetic in style, but its passages can carry poetic power through their fine wording – and a long tradition in which quoted Biblical passages are commonly taken as unques-tioned truths.

John 3:16 stands out in poetic form: "For God so loved the world that he gave his only begotten son, that whosoever believes in him shall not perish, but have everlasting life." Wonderful that the deity is so feeling, so caring, eh? But why, then, did he make us so flawed that we need to be judged *at all*? Why did he have to conjure up a Son to send to try to save the mess he'd created? Stirring words those were from the evangelist – but based on fallacy.

Actually, I have to concur with the second half of that passage. If you believe in Jesus, your consciousness won't perish – it will continue after death. But *it will do that anyway*, even if you don't believe in Jesus or never even heard of him. Consciousness is the basis of our existence, the driving force to manifestation of a meaningful Reality. On death, you exit the body and find yourself still embedded in a reality – but the nature of being then as now has nothing to do with beliefs and gods.

Consider Paul's famous words in his letter 1 Corinthians 13:1-13 about love – "… Love is patient, love is kind. It does not envy, it does not boast … Love never fails. But where there are prophecies, they will cease … faith, hope and love – but the greatest of these is love." These expressions are full of meaning, articulated in fine words. But subtle negatives within them are masked by their stirring poetic construction.

Love is far more than fine words can depict. First, love is not a thing unto itself, to be described as though you can own or obtain it, but a fundamental quality of consciousness. It is the nucleus to being, the driving force, synonymous with the life experience. It can be distorted by conflict, fear and ignorance, thus twisting its positive intent into life issues, pains and failures. But it can't be destroyed, because in the bleakest of lives, love still flows as a river under a glacier – hidden but not hampered by the dense ice above.

Acceptance and deep appreciation, core components of love, drive the manifestation of your life and the direction of your being. Love underlies your rational nature. Yet you won't see it fully and clearly and experience it without compromise so long as you project being and power to external sources, as Paul strongly advocated. Can you love your neighbor when you fear him? Can you love or trust a god, any god, when you think he might punish you and believe he has the power and will to do so?

To Paul, god was mysterious, aloof, powerful – yet the source of all things, the provider to which each must bow and grovel. His impression of love had to fit within that image.

But Paul was wrong. No god makes your life; *you do.*

When you see that, in your attraction of specific patterns in life, you are the cause of qualities unfolding in your life's events and relationships and quit projecting that causality to gods and other people – only then can you love your neighbors and accept them as they are. Only then, consequently, will you engage people who accept you *as you are*. For love isn't a trait to be turned on by the intellect, just because Jesus or Paul tells you that you should love others – it's your core nature, compromised by beliefs in other powers, by fear, by self-doubt.

Paul considers faith and hope in conjunction with love, judging love as the greatest. He's right, of course, but the margin is so great that the three don't belong in the same sentence.

Faith in a phony god is very damaging, highly self-limiting, negating one's personal power and free will. Faith in oneself is better, but also not the goal. Seeing clearly that you, yourself, attract events and relationships reflective of your own nature and *that you can change your nature* – Clear Awareness, as I term it – eliminates the need for faith *at all*. Faith, thus, is a substitute psychic mechanism that is necessary only so long as synthetic credos and distorted understanding lead you to attribute life's encounters to false forces and sources.

Hope is even worse. Hope is powerlessness projected outward, innate lack of self-confidence that leads you to wish against personal conviction to the contrary, that your intent will endure over other perceived possibilities.

So, Paul's words were moving and emotional on the surface – true poetry that has affected the faithful for centuries. But his base understanding was flat-out wrong, his god nonexistent, and his vaunted Christ image completely in error. So the poetry masks with stirring words a flawed viewpoint – and helps to keep the flock huddled in seemingly secure ignorance.

My point here is that poetic expression can doctor falsities into attractive points, making fallacies seem wise and negatives appear positive. Until you see clearly, for yourself, your immersion in a life of meaning reflective of your own mindset, you may have difficulty discerning the negative in the nice sounds of poetic expression.

Reliability, Dependability, Veracity

If you grew up, learning that the Bible, particularly the New Testament, is holy and truthful, inspired by God, guided by the Holy Spirit – perhaps even perfect and flawless – and having accepted that "Truth" as a child, built it into belief and understanding of the world, you will likely see it that way. The mind readily adapts to accepted guidelines, filtering information and judging validity based on core definitions held as true.

But rational, critical examination of ancient writings that constitute the Bible reveals many factors, both in a literary sense of compositional elements and in a reasoned evaluation of stated meaning that shed overwhelming doubt on the whole work as a reliable source for information on Jesus – who he was and what he meant.

With such a thorough critique of veracity as presented here – with much more detail on each caveat that *could* be reviewed – it might seem like I hold the New Testament in very low esteem. The case presented above diminishes virtually every aspect of NT reports that would deem it worth consideration.

While these ancient accounts are indeed flawed in the core message they purposely present, they do preserve one core attribute that supersedes their many flaws: a remarkable set of teachings.

To perceive the essence of Jesus' wisdom, however, and gain value from those insights, it is necessary to sweep away all the distortion generated by all the above factors. Nearly hidden among impossible reports, myth, meaningless scriptural references, conflictual conjecture are absolute gems. Nearly overwhelmed by embellished claims of divinity, flawed literary communication, forgery, archaic fables and lore are Jesus' simple, deep insights into consciousness and reality. These are embodied in Jesus' parables and aphorisms, his terse comebacks and *Kingdom* illustrations.

Scholars, in seeking the historical Jesus, have often noted these parables as unique to Jesus. They've stripped away much of the myth and fantasy, using clever analysis of text, writing style, word usage, historical comparison and other tools to evaluate the ancient manuscripts. They've stripped away common cultural phrases of the time and things attributed to Jesus that are inconsistent with his unique perspectives. Extensive research has gotten about as close as objective sleuthing can get to Jesus himself.

But in the end evaluation, scholars are limited to an ultimate interpretation whose conclusions rest on standard western thinking. They can determine that the parables offer a different message in a unique package. They can note that parables made it through many distorting influences *because* they were different, puzzling, catchy, often twisting reality in ways unconventional then and now. But they can't grasp the deep insights he expresses: logical analysis has limitations.

As mentioned, that sieve of belief and definition distorts the scholar's conclusions as thoroughly as the blinders of rampant religious convictions do the Christian devotee. Thus, scholars differ widely, finding Jesus to be anything from an apocalyptic doomsayer to a stand-up comedian, from a judicious teacher of Jewish traditions to a wise lecturer suggesting an alternative, mystical lifestyle, from a wandering preacher to an itinerant, charismatic healer. Some think he was God incarnated; others think he was a magician, still others that he didn't really exist.

But *all* opinions across that spectrum are formed by interpreting diverse, often contradicting information through the subtly limiting goggles of the modern mindset. No religionist nor scientist nor philosopher steeped in complex, rationalized views will ever discern the "real" Jesus who stands, smiling as subtly as the Mona Lisa, behind two millennia of distortion, fuss and fury – because his core message extends beyond the ken of standard thinking.

You won't recognize the real Yeshua until you can see what he was presenting in his *Kingdom of God* depiction, wrapped in parables and surprisingly simple, pert statements – comments that substantially survived oral transition, overzealous editing, wars, religious doctoring and repeated translation.

We have explored Jesus' first-century world and the mindset of his peers, embedded in gods and metaphysical causality. We've looked at modern thinking, its addition of real-world causality through science, its maintenance of old religious credence, while still adhering to luck, occult whims, fate and chance as driving mechanisms. And we've seen how, in reality, each individual attracts patterns consistent with his/her own mindset, making each person the real cause of resultant life's qualities.

In searching for Jesus, we've seen that no really reliable historical accounts exist – only the gospels and peripheral NT accounts shed *any* light on his life. And they are extremely unreliable in their overall picture for many reasons. But they do preserve the parables, and in them, Jesus' words and his level of awareness.

But before approaching the parables, I need to reconstruct Jesus' life trek: how he came to see the world as he did.

As all men of all ages, the real Jesus grew through life. He started with a standard Jewish mindset, steeped in observance of Law common to his culture, influenced by prophets stemming back nearly as far into his past as he to ours. But he encountered other ideas, experienced real events and relationship qualities that had him grow to see life differently. He didn't do that, sitting around Nazareth for 30 years making chairs and hearing local gossip and reiterated scriptures.

Understanding his viewpoint *and* requisite trek, I can reconstruct his character growth from start to finish. Because I traveled widely as a young man, hitchhiking on my own through foreign lands – eating, sleeping, engaging people, learning and growing with each adventure, I can recreate where he would have gone, where he *must have gone* to learn the lessons needed to gain his perspective. Because I had my own mystical experience, I can see his viewpoint clearly (it has precious little to do with the religion that grew out of his presence). And because I engaged a thorough *inner* journey, I can uniquely leverage modern knowledge of his world and times, his region and its influences to trace his path leading up to the final journey that is sketched in the gospels.

As you will see, his life path makes sense when extracted from myth, lore and gushy tradition – and injected with *life*.

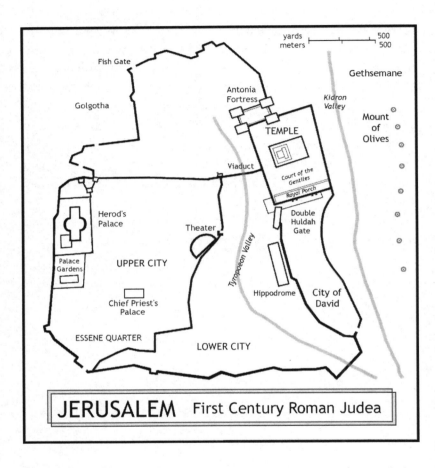

JERUSALEM First Century Roman Judea

Regional Maps: Maps of Jerusalem and three regions of the First-Century Roman Empire of the Eastern Mediterranean, c. 30 CE, provide reference for the following recreated life trek of Jesus of Nazareth. I emphasize the small scale of Palestine as a region vs. Asia Minor and Egypt.

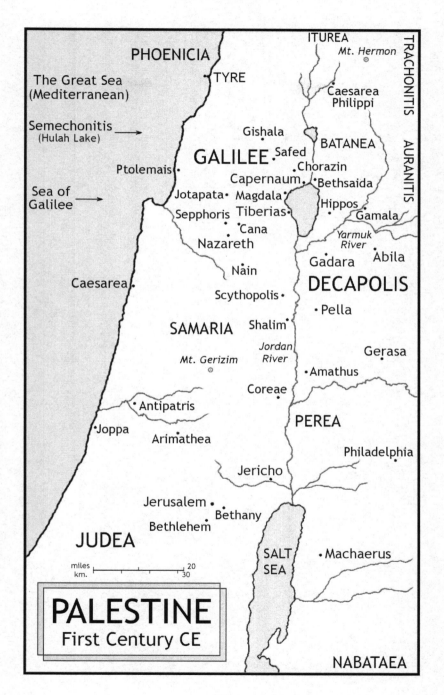

PHOENICIA

The Great Sea
(Mediterranean)

Semechonitis
(Hulah Lake)

Sea of
Galilee

ITUREA

Mt. Hermon

TRACHONITIS

AURANITIS

TYRE

Caesarea
Philippi

Gishala

BATANEA

GALILEE Safed

Chorazin

Ptolemais

Capernaum Bethsaida

Jotapata Magdala

Hippos

Sepphoris Tiberias

Gamala

Cana

Yarmuk
River

Nazareth

Gadara

Abila

Caesarea

Nain

DECAPOLIS

Scythopolis

Pella

SAMARIA

Shalim

Mt. Gerizim

Jordan
River

Gerasa

Coreae

Amathus

Antipatris

PEREA

Joppa

Arimathea

Philadelphia

Jericho

Jerusalem

Bethany

Bethlehem

JUDEA

miles
km.

20
30

SALT
SEA

Machaerus

PALESTINE
First Century CE

NABATAEA

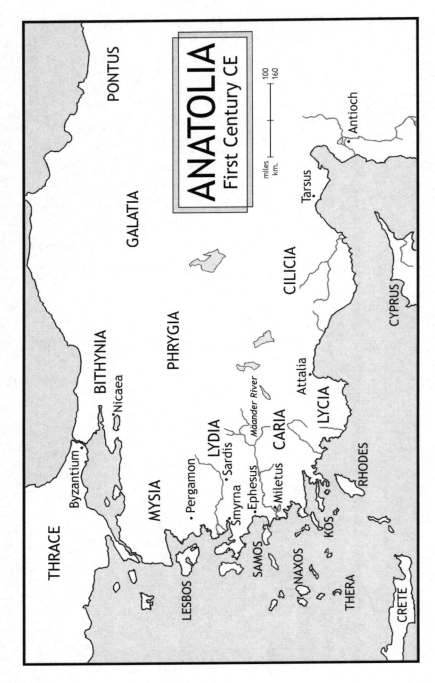

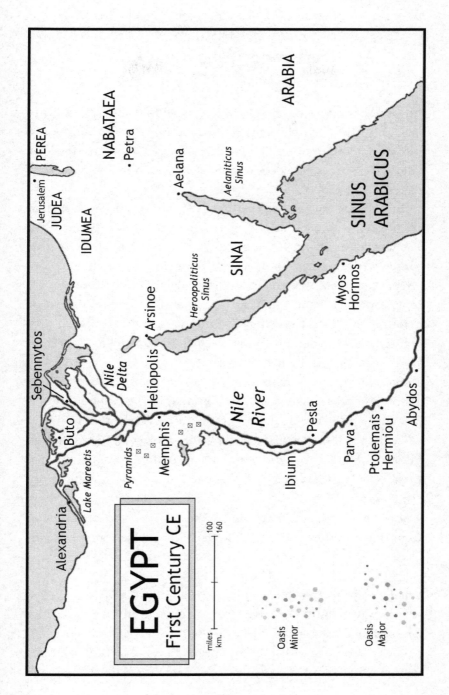

EGYPT
First Century CE

Alexandria
Lake Mareotis
Buto
Sebennytos
Pyramids
Memphis
Nile Delta
Heliopolis
Arsinoe
Ibium
Parva
Pesla
Ptolemais
Hermiou
Abydos
Nile River

Jerusalem
PEREA
JUDEA
IDUMEA
NABATAEA
Petra
Aelana
Heroopoliticus Sinus
Aelaniticus Sinus
SINAI
Myos Hormos
ARABIA
SINUS ARABICUS

Oasis Minor
Oasis Major

miles
km.
100
160

133

Straight:
Recreating Jesus' Real Life

So four canonical gospels plus the Gospel of Thomas constitute the only first-century written accounts that provide any substantial information – however removed in time, however flawed as sources, however unreliable based on rational criteria – on Jesus of Nazareth.

But the canonical gospels and Acts above all else promote specific viewpoints concerning Jesus, his life and its meaning. The Gospel of Thomas, compiled without narrative from oral or earlier written accounts of Jesus' comments, seems less a sales pitch. Were these works – or any writings that constitute the NT, replete with the many flaws just explored – guided, driven or determined by the Holy Spirit? Were they directly ordained by a deity? That's the default Christian position, one which – in their view – establishes them as authoritative.

Should such a powerful entity exist, though, wouldn't he simply make himself known? Couldn't he just announce his presence and need for attention with a big, booming, heavenly voice (like at Jesus' baptism), send Gabriel to give lectures (like he informed Mary of her forthcoming conception) – something like that? Why the mystery? Why this need to believe something not apparent?

Let's sort through a couple NT basics before reconstructing Jesus' life and times – en route to deciphering his core message.

The Holy Spirit

What exactly is the "Holy Spirit" supposed to be? This ethereal entity conveniently appears in gospels to spur mystical action or stimulate elevated insight. It is frequently enlisted to inspire and energize people to speak profoundly or rally to the task. And this nebulous being – deemed a "person" by early believers – ended up sharing the billing with two other "persons", the Father and the Son in a centuries-later invention called the Trinity. But what exactly is/was the Holy Spirit?

The Greek NT word, *"pneuma,"* translated as Holy Spirit, appears over a hundred times in the gospels alone, hundreds more in the Acts and various NT epistles (though, curiously, only once in Thomas). It implies a metaphysical agent at once *part of* God, yet *separate* – and that's an image that exceeds confusing and barges into the realm of impossible: can't be both!

For a moment, let's step back to basic, rational thinking and verbal communication reflecting those thoughts.

When you name something, you set boundaries around it. All languages feature names for things, called nouns. Nouns set boundaries between what a thing *is* and what it *isn't* (everything else). A tree or table, a cloud or car are easily differentiated, conceptually, from the space that surrounds them. They are bounded by surface level molecules that enclose their shapes. Using those nouns, one can communicate defined quantities to listeners who understand English. Here is a table (knock, knock as I rap on it); everything else in the universe is *not* "table" – at least not the stuff of *this particular* table. By so defining tangible objects, we can converse about them.

Intangible nouns are trickier. "Joy" and "expectation", "green" and "love" are less quantity than quality in nature – though such qualities can themselves be quantified in a sense (levels of joy, intensity of green). But, even qualitatively, *joy* can be easily differentiated from *sadness* (its opposite) and *boredom* (its absence), so boundaries are implied. *Expectation* proscribes a firm line separating it from *doubt* (its opposite) and *confusion* (its absence). *Green* in the light spectrum borders with blue to one side, yellow to the other with less determinate edges – but there comes a shaded boundary point in the spectrum where the eye stops recognizing green and sees cyan or chartreuse; that forms in effect, a boundary, however fuzzy. And *love* is clear, though graded perhaps in intensity and compromised by many other emotional variables, as bounded from *hate* and *indifference*. So even with intangibles, boundaries exist, if less firm than table surfaces.

Nouns, then, generally stipulate real-world objects or concepts, separating them from what they *aren't*. You'll notice that, for "noncepts", the noun defined at the outset of this book, boundaries are illusory: government, headaches, climate, fairies, ether – examples offered initially – *have no real boundaries*. They don't exist as separate entities unto themselves, but as collective attributes or imagined essences; as illusions, they can be imagined, but not quantified, not bounded.

So, what limits could delineate that *Holy Spirit* – what could separate it from everything else? To specify that, let's work down from the top: what constitutes the Christian "God", that all-purpose deity with the capital "G"? Let's start the Holy Spirit quest by considering what *God* might be, based on boundaries.

If a god, any god with any name, would be thought to permeate all things, as is sometimes claimed for the Christian deity – then it has no boundaries and consequently, *the name doesn't really apply!* As all-permeating, it simply **consists of** *all things!* Since you and I and all our possessions, the Sun and Moon, glaciers and rabbits are part of that same whole, the name is rendered useless: "God", quality or quantity, would be fully *unbounded*. Without boundaries to separate it from something, *anything*, that *isn't* God – because per this notion, nothing is excluded – the word is devoid of meaning. You might just as well say "All That Is" and leave it at that. Creating a word *generates* a conceptual boundary: it firmly conjures God as an entity unto itself with his own thoughts and agenda – expressly to the degree that the mind invariably assigns real qualities and real being to definitions like that.

This viewpoint, which many people actually hold, is called Monism or Pantheism: seeing reality as an all-inclusive whole, with all things contained within the overriding divine nature.

Were that the nature of Reality, the word "God" would be worse than meaningless. It would be deceiving, indicating a separate, functional, cognitive entity that isn't really there – but *seems to be* solely because it's named, leading the mind to imagine boundaries, as it does around named concepts and noncepts alike.

To the point: if all things are parts of the same entirety, **you don't need a word** (like Yahweh, God or Allah) **to describe** *the whole*. God (one thing) creating reality (a separate collection of things) is much different to that of God *being* reality.

If, though, as per another idiom, God is equated to *love*, then where does that leave suffering, inhumanity, environmental degradation and other heavy negatives within the scope of such a Creator? What kind of "love" indeed would inflict lifelong agony and deprivation on some people and pester wild animals with fleas, ticks and beasts that attack and devour them.

Basically, beyond those poetic generalities, the typical Christian God-notion presents an entity *separate* from the real, visible universe and from the believer's Self: a big, powerful being residing out there, suspended in dimensions unseen. Projected as unfathomable in scope and sense, believers deem this entity to hold exclusive creative power. And that elite, singular God has, it appears, used His innate power to generate the universe. From that point, depending on the conceptualized details, He (with a capital "H") has *either* let the physical cosmos ride, hands-off, to proceed as it might, riddled with flaws and pain, *or* He still fiddles, hands-on, with unfolding events. From creation onwards, Monotheism features many options – all imagined, none real – as to how its god might function.

So NT conjecture presents the deity as authoritative and powerful, capable of creating and energizing his universe. Early on, Yahweh was imagined as much more substantial: a material being occupying the heavenly region above that blue "firmament" canopy spanning the flat, four-cornered earth, holding up the waters above. We now recognize vast collections of galaxies out there billions of light-years across – such that God, somewhere along the last two millennia, got pushed into spiritual dimensions, where imagination can formulate any sort of far-fetched environment.

Pretending for a moment that this conceptualized deity actually exists – he not only doesn't, but couldn't possibly – what was the implied nature of the Holy Spirit, the *pneuma?* What did or does it consist of – if it exists at all or ever did? How does it work and function on a daily basis? Some such notion found its way from archaic Aramaic expressions and religious lore into Greek and on down through a hundred generations of society and a plethora of languages to modern times. Exploring the original sense might elucidate the current English phrase.

Aramaic for the expression is something like: Rukha d'Qudsha – with its Hebrew equivalent: Ruach HaKodesh. But Aramaic, as Jesus spoke it, apparently doesn't have a close equivalent to "Holy". The *Qudsha* part more literally means something like "set apart". "Rukha" means "Breath" or "Spirit" – as the thought back then related breath coming in and going out to *being alive*. With one's last exhale, the "spirit" aspect was gone (dearly departed, one might say). The word *Rukha* also meant "Wind" – and would be related to mind-images of the spirit realm interacting with the real world, swooshing about unseen but felt. Remember, *back then* people didn't understand an atmosphere covering a planet, oxygen and nitrogen molecules bouncing around, being inhaled and exhaled to maintain oxygenation of body tissues.

(They *did* understand cannabis and heroin, however, which may have influenced the qualitative experience of "breathing in" spiritual elevation – when it included pleasure-inducing smoke from either. How this artificial means at elevated spiritual status would factor in, though, would be difficult to trace.)

So the *Holy Spirit* proposition of Jesus' time must have featured some pervading spirit/breath force, pictured in light of an overarching god-figure that dominated one's own being. Breath – and focus on breathing – has often been incorporated into mystical practices, spanning a range from basic relaxation to a meditative state meant to lead, ultimately, when practiced, to heightened awareness. In looking for the *Holy Spirit* impression, it seems clear that traditions incorporated evolving notions of "spirit" as a god-related force and/or agent. References to Holy Spirit as an active force or agent are very common by the time of gospel composition, seen even earlier during Paul's promotion of proto-Christian communities, and likely stem back to and beyond Jesus' time. Yet, it wasn't universally featured: Acts 19:2 indicates that early Christians Paul encounters in Ephesus *had never heard* of the Holy Spirit.

So what does all that imply as to the Holy Spirit's nature, a notion that ultimately got rolled into the theological backbone of that most Christian doctrine, the Trinity?

Again, I must reference the illusion formed by creating a word or phrase. The Trinity is pictured as three "persons", at the same time separate in nature and "co-equal", but all united into one Trinity. In conjuring that image and holding it as true, one must necessarily create *boundaries* – conceptual ones, as a Spirit-thing can't have a surface like a table. If all three, the Father, Son and Holy Spirit are knit together, then *there isn't a boundary* in reality – only an apparent one, created by virtue of inventing the words. If, though, some quality separates them – such as if God made decisions, utilized a spirit-force to implement them and employed the Son-figure to help put things into order – then separate words would have some validity. But then the Trinity would be *three separate entities*, not united – and still make no sense: what does the Father's skin look like? Where does the Holy Spirit hang out while sin is rampantly breaking out? (Obviously not sitting watching daytime TV.)

In Reality, in this *real existence of life* we each find ourselves embedded within, none of those connoted entities actually exist

– except as *ideas*, or more accurately, *noncepts*. Various gods embody notions that have been formulized into thousands of shapes and mythical descriptions by mankind since humans long ago started conceptualizing and naming things – but none ever really existed *in Reality*.

The English phrase "Holy Spirit" stemmed conceptually from *pneuma* and, earlier, *Rukha*. These ancient words doubtless began equating the breath of life, the inhale-exhale cycle that keeps each of us animate with a Self-essence that survives death. As the impression grew, *breath* conjoined with the *spirit* image, highlighted by a mentality featuring an active, engaged spirit world. When you gave up your last breath, your spirit exited *with* it – or *was* it – to rejoin the spirit world, unseen yet known to persist.

But the notion *spirit* took on a reality of its own – as all ideas do when passed along to succeeding generations. The English word "spirit" stemmed from Middle English, rooted in Latin, *spiritus*, from *spirare* – meaning: *to breathe*. So the meaning of *Holy Spirit* in ancient times equated to something like, *Divine Breath* – as though the deity actually exhaled magnificent power in a mystical *Whoosh!* And that Holy Spirit could empower miracles, spur insight, invigorate healing, etc.

Why was that necessary? Because in the ancient mindset, the mundane reality we live in as flesh was impure, low and corrupt, even evil, whereas God was great, wonderful and perfect. Power, goodness, righteousness – all positive things *had to come from above*. Thus, Holy Spirit was a breath of the divine forcing goodness onto tainted reality. Lowly humans couldn't manage good things on their own.

In actuality, what exists is *Consciousness*, always with an individual, customized viewpoint. That essence, Consciousness, as a noun, is *qualitative*: it is the *nature of conscious existence*, not an isolated thing unto itself, but a quality-essence that always involves an entity sensing a Reality surrounding itself – just like you and I do.

Consciousness per se is unbounded, finding no "boundary" or definitive division – neither inward within the psyche nor outward in physical space. Consciousness, as used here (having to employ a word that *implies* boundaries), permeates the Real, infusing experienced events and relationships of real life with meaning drawn from its own inner store. And Reality is not a collection of isolated items, but a single, inter-related field whose elements interact in specific, meaningful ways.

So I refer to *Consciousness* as the quality of the self-aware *Self*, the perception all reasoning humans have of existence within a multi-dimensional framework: a real world during waking state, a dream environment during sleep. Consciousness manifests – that is, *we each,* as conscious entities, manifest – a reality about it/us at all times. But that Reality can take an illusory appearance of almost any nature and seem real – with its attributed nature depending on *the beliefs and definitions held by the individual holding them.*

And therein lies the problem in conceptualizing, naming and communicating.

The Trinity consists of ideas and definitions *only* – not elements of this encountered universe. As structured thought, it exists in the mind realm – in imagination. Thus, the Holy Spirit doesn't exist now any more than *pneuma* did to the Greek, or Ruach to the Hebrew. Rukha and pneuma seemed real to the ancient mindset already rife with deities and demons – because *and only because* they believed divine force was needed to instigate good things into an otherwise flawed, mundane world.

When evangelists or Paul depicted the Holy Spirit coming down on someone to trigger an elevated state or communicate something special, they imagined a celestial agent that would supercharge low-level, impotent humans with divine power. And that's because they deemed the material world and lowly humans inhabiting it to be inferior to the wondrous spiritual realm: great powers *could only come* from above, from that enormously greater realm.

So what is/was the Holy Spirit? The Divine Breath of a magnificent Creator God impelling goodness on His Creation? No. That's an illusion formed by believing in it: a noncept. The Holy Spirit, like its other Trinity buddies, doesn't exist and *never did*, save in the fervent imagination of those who "believe in" it.

Drawing Conclusions from Flawed Pretext

New Testament authors, writing decades afterwards based on reports long removed from original witnesses, concluded a nature for Jesus guaranteed from the outset to be errant. Where Jesus was illustrating a new, clearer view of life, they interpreted his words through the dark lens of old beliefs. Succeeding generations of Christian adherents, led by the blind, have fallen into the same pit: faulty conclusions based on flawed understanding riding invalid assumptions.

Scholars, despite extensive, thorough analysis and appreciable objectivity, face a similar fate. Neither religionist nor scholar, biased or objective, can perceive the real Jesus. No one can without realizing the simple, core Oneness with which reality functions. Deceived by their own belief systems, they will interpret Jesus consistent with expectations.

My approach is *fundamentally* different: *first* clear away deceiving precepts and definitions common to modern thinking – a long process requiring extensive inner reconstruction – *then* you will see clearly enough to understand Jesus' message. Basically, I first removed the plank from my own eye.

Reconstructing a Life Trek

Before approaching Jesus' parables to reveal their glowing insights, the task of reconstructing his life trek is imperative – a journey that provided him insight into life needed to create his parables.

The general thought is that it's impossible to regain the major gap in Jesus' life leading up to his appearance, aged 30, for baptism by John – no accounts exist for this period. For most, that's true – although it hasn't stopped many from speculating.

But actually, the task of recreating Jesus' life trek is rather straightforward. These elements are reliably known about Jesus' life, listed along with implications:

- Actions known: from age of about 30, he began to travel around to teach and heal.
  - This indicates he reached the requisite mindset and maturity only then, *not earlier*, that he was ready to present a well illustrated message people were ready to accept.
  - And *that* suggests a prior life journey involving years of exposure to greater lessons gleaned by personal encounter. He had to outgrow standard, first-century Jewish thinking to become aware of life's interactive, flowing qualities.
  - That inner growth couldn't have taken place in backwater Nazareth; he must have traveled to places where he could learn significant lessons while working to support himself.
- Capabilities known: Jesus' family occupation, as per Joseph, was, in Greek, *tekton*, that being craftsman, woodworker or builder.
  - The traditional reference that Jesus was a carpenter is doubtful. Building in Galilee was principally mud brick or stone. Wood supports were part of construction, but not prevalent in a dry region. Common people had sparse furniture, so cabinetry would not have provided a career.
  - Given obvious intellectual capability, Jesus would have learned various building techniques from early exposure, based on natural curiosity.

- ○ Sepphoris, a major regional city just an hour's walk from Nazareth, was being rebuilt during Jesus early years owing to its destruction about when he was born. Likely, Joseph – then Jesus and his brothers – would have worked on construction projects there.
- ○ Traveling later, he would have found other building jobs in related applications – as versatile, resourceful construction people do.
- Character: he was clever, curious and intelligent – all evidenced by recorded comments. He *certainly* was open-minded, observant and exceptionally quick-witted.
  - Jesus would have been drawn to Tyre, old Phoenician city, and Asia Minor, with numerous exceptional cities. Guaranteed, Jesus couldn't have resisted Alexandria, Egypt's gem of knowledge and liberal attitudes. Decapolis, Judean and Galilean cities where he spoke during his mission, he likely would have already visited while younger.
  - He would have learned to read Hebrew during childhood, and received traditional teaching in Law and Prophets. But his liberal take on standard interpretations would have been unusual already during his youth.
- Philosophy: his recognition of life's integrated quality, evident throughout his "Kingdom within" illustrations, reveals exposure to Greek ideas – Heraclitus' *Logos* and Platonic ideals – and eastern precepts.
  - ○ With strong, regional Hellenistic influence and extensive east-west trade through Palestine and Tyre, etc., Jesus wouldn't have had to go to Athens for exposure to philosophy, nor to India for Hindu basics. He would have encountered travelers from those regions.
  - ○ Curious and vigorous, he would have sought out locations where stimulating discussion abounded – and would have engaged scholars as energetically as he'd countered Pharisees and scribes back home.

Trail, Trial and Consequence: The Life of Jesus of Nazareth

With those basics, and with considerable research into regional history and politics, Hellenistic influence and Roman domination, Jesus' life trek becomes rather obvious. To recreate Jesus' experience all that's needed is:

- Understanding elements necessary to expand one's mindset from standard thinking into open recognition of the Consciousness/Reality Oneness.
- Recognizing what features of eastern and western thinking available in Jesus' time would have helped lead him to this clarified viewpoint.
- Knowing how to travel on little money into strange cities, getting rides, avoiding trouble, communicating, finding cheap places to stay and getting enough to eat.

It just happens, having left my hometown of Tarentum, Pennsylvania while young to travel extensively on my own without much money, *and* having done my own spiritual journey through life – *plus* having extensive exposure to paradigms east and west – I'm uniquely equipped to reconstruct Jesus' life. Considerable research familiarized me with the region, the gospel accounts, peripheral traditions, etc.

Specifics of the following life scenario are recreated as viable "historical fiction" to illustrate the *real* Jesus. This approach is basically what gospel writers did – except the Gospels of Matthew, Mark, Luke and John are *just plain fiction*, not historical. My access to information on Jesus' historical and cultural setting, plus my own untainted perspective, provides me a vastly superior standpoint from which to recreate his life than that of primitive, anonymous authors of the late first century.

And, perhaps most important: I'm looking to reconstruct a scenario as close to reality, to how Jesus' life actually must have unfolded, as possible – *not to talk you into believing some mystical fantasy*.

So, here goes! Let's dub this, with tongue at least partly in cheek:

The Gospel According to Thomas of Tarentum

It has been some time, indeed, honored Theophilus, since you've been updated on previous information originated by eyewitnesses but handed down through others concerning our respected teacher. I've endeavored to assemble additional points of interest for you so that you can formulate a more reliable understanding than possible from earlier writings.

The days of Herod the Great were dwindling when, in Sepphoris of the Galilee, Mary, daughter of Joachim and Anne, came into puberty. Marriage arrangements had already been negotiated with Jacob concerning his son Joseph when Mary was 12. This looked to be a good match, for this family of nearby Nazareth, respectable and hard-working, stemmed from the house of David. Thus, the bonding was deemed to add prestige to Joachim's line – always critical to such arrangements.

But betrothal was delayed briefly as Joseph, some years older and already on his own, prepared his own small, mud-brick domicile connected to the family courtyard area in nearby Nazareth. Working as well to save up the requisite *mohar*, Mary's dowry or "purchase price" owed to Joachim's family for losing its daughter, Joseph was stretched somewhat. He hadn't much time to visit Mary, let alone get to know her well.

Political unrest was building locally, as radical voices were raised in Sepphoris anticipating Herod's imminent demise, further complicating plans. Still, the betrothal took place there as Mary turned 13, making the tie official, though it would be some time before the actual wedding, when the bride would ceremoniously walk to Joseph's domicile.

But yet another snag surfaced, threatening to halt proceedings altogether. Mary, naïve, had been sexually "compromised" just before parental arrangements had been finalized, succumbing to the wiles – and youthful exuberance – of her earlier, personally-desired mate, who had since fled the scene (rumor has, he joined the Roman army).

Mary came to realize the stark implications: she might follow through on wedding festivities – the three mile procession from Joachim's home to Nazareth would finalize the bond – without issue. Perhaps Joseph would consummate the marriage without detecting her lost virginity, though even keeping that scandalous encounter secret would strain her honesty and sincerity – as well as risk death by stoning. But pregnancy? Well, that was another thing. Mary, distraught and confused, her dreams filled with emotional symbology about her coming child, had no choice but to tell.

Joseph faced a quandary: male dominance of his culture dictated that a *real* man take his wife's virginity. Implications of impurity, coupled with dishonor, intensified by this pre-marital affair – after all, *everybody* heard the gossip – these were difficult to accept. Joseph could drop the whole arrangement and move on with no damage to his honor or shame to *his* family – though it would devastate Joachim's.

But...

Still single and approaching twenty, Joseph was expected by tradition and cultural pressure to marry and father children. And fewer opportunities would present themselves now – for most girls were promised by age 12, whereas widows and divorcees were no better by social measure, as things were, than a bride pregnant to another.

Working through these cultural conflicts, both Mary and Joseph reconciled the situation, assuaging doubts and emotional twists through vivid dreams and rationalized hopes: Joseph would go through with the ceremony and accept the situation;

he could always take a second bride, he reasoned, if the situation presented itself (and if he could afford it). Mary would make up for it, she reckoned, with many other children and personal devotion.

Not long after Jesus' birth, conflict broke out. Herod, having executed his two principal heirs, sons by Mariamne (herself executed years before), and his oldest son Antipater, finally died himself. While his will was being contested in Rome, dissident Galileans attacked the royal palace in Sepphoris, made off with weapons and began to terrorize the surrounding countryside.

That particular strategy, as history would bear out, never worked, for Rome was the power behind local nobility: Roman forces, issued from Syria, ended the insurgence and leveled Sepphoris. When the dust had settled, Herod Antipas, yet another son of Herod the Great, had been installed as tetrarch of Galilee and Perea, a portion of his father's realm – with Archelaus, Antipas' older brother, named ethnarch of Judea, Samaria and Idumea. The latter proved so cruel and unpopular the Romans deposed him and assumed direct control through an appointed Roman Prefect or, later, Procurator.

The consequence of all that for Joseph and his budding family – after Jesus' birth about 4 BCE, Mary proceeded to bear several other children in subsequent years – was fortuitous: lots of construction work available. Sepphoris was rebuilt on a grand scale as centerpiece of Antipas' realm. An hour's walk from Nazareth, this principal district city (renamed Autocratis – though locals disliked that name as much as they hated Antipas himself) was to become the cultural center of Galilee.

Joseph worked for years on several Sepphoris projects – rebuilding the palace, fortifying walls, creating Romanesque baths and Hellenized features to accommodate the region's ever more urbane, multi-ethnic population. As Jesus grew through childhood, he soon enough had to give up adolescent games, makeshift swords made from sticks and fighting imaginary enemies – be they Assyrians, Canaanites or Romans. Age 10, he started to accompany Joseph to work sites, learning construction skills as *tekton*, all purpose builder – or laborer if need be.

So, while Jesus absorbed cultural traditions and practices at home and at the synagogue, duly learning prayer, fasting, purification and other necessary modes of living, he also gained early exposure to diverse viewpoints from different cultures prevalent in the big city – while earning a few sesterces to add to the family kitty.

Jesus, intelligent and witty by nature, picked up street-wise cleverness from various ethnic co-workers in Sepphoris. As he matured, he would ever more frequently overnight there with other youths, finding city attitudes – and females – more liberal and stimulating than back home. "Think of the sandal leather I save by not trudging home every night," he would tell his mother. Always curious, he would compare concepts encountered in the city with those absorbed from Hebrew traditions – the defined practices of the greater and lesser prophets, the Law as practiced. He found Zeus and the mythical stories of Greek traditions to be shallow – lacking meaning compared to his own views, founded in practice and cultural truths. Notions held by Syrians and others to the north weren't much better – resting on papyrus-like gods with simplistic purposes. Armed with a greater perspective afforded by exposure to these varied views, he debated with the men on Sabbath get-togethers in the village.

But *his* take on things, unlike strict viewpoints of rural Galileans – and even Judeans – encountered in synagogues and meeting places, was ordered by the world he observed around him, tempered by alternate views from a liberal city environment. This often opened space between his personal understanding, resting on the reality he engaged, and the time-honored convictions of others that relied solely on scriptural support.

"The prophets had unique connections to the divine – they

must be followed, along with prescribed practices," elders taught him.

But the thought occurred to Jesus as scribes read out various scriptures: *well then why do they say different things?* Jesus would retort, "Did Yahweh change his mind between Moses and Isaiah – or did they hear different messages?" His questions often received stern looks rather than answers. "Why are there no more prophets anymore? Priests never add to the scriptures – they only read words and echo their meaning."

Still, he prayed often enough, as he'd been taught, but came to wonder if Yahweh didn't already know his thoughts *before* he thought them – and if the answers he heard in his mind came from heavenly realms or from his own expectations.

On the early death of his adoptive father, Jesus, by now well into teen years, was still unmarried. With Jesus having spent much time in Sepphoris, exposed to diverse cultural viewpoints via late-night debates over wine in city taverns – instead of Nazareth's gossipy social circles – his matrimonial match hadn't materialized: no early teen arrangement in small-town Nazareth seemed suitable to Jesus' broad interests and eccentricities, despite parental inquiries. And, while the town was hush-hush on gossip about the handsome and personable character everybody knew, Jesus' illegitimate status limited his possibilities – was he really of the house of David if those old rumors are true?

With the chief breadwinner gone, Jesus had to provide for his mother and siblings. Well connected to projects in the growing city, he had started to bring along his younger brothers as they came of age – James, then Joses – to city worksites. James soon married and moved into the adjoining unit Joseph's parents had occupied years before; he commuted to Nazareth daily. Joses, per arrangement, had become betrothed to a local girl, though he preferred to stay in the city with his big brother whenever he could.

Eventually, though, nearing twenty and feeling restless, the free-spirited Jesus appeared at home late one afternoon. Mary was working cut figs into cakes of coarse meal ground from emmer and barley by James' wife. She was pleasantly surprised to see her eldest; he mostly came around only just before the Sabbath if at all.

After hugs and greetings – and mandatory chasing of his two young sisters around the mud-brick house – Jesus waved across the small courtyard to James' young wife. Mary brushed the mill clean, oiled the cakes and placed them in a plain crockery vessel near the fire to bake. "So, what brings you back to Nazareth at this time of week, Yeshua? Home cooking?"

Jesus sampled a fig, then wandered over to the family till, hidden behind a wall panel near two small courtyard windows. Lifting the wooden cover and drapes, he dropped a few denarii into the concealed bin. "I've been offered a new job, mother," he explained, hesitant to break the news. "They're surveying for some new building projects over by the sea. They want me to help with preliminary layouts."

Mary was rather jolted from her comfort level with the family unit, its daily routine and stability. "Girls, take jugs and fetch some water. And don't dally at the well – we'll be eating soon," she said. Salome and Mary – the youngest, dubbed "Babe" – scurried out with two jugs, giggling as they closed the door.

James, not yet home from his daily commute to city construction sites, was living in their small complex with his daughter and wife, now expecting again. Joses, working labor in Sepphoris, looked to bring his bride home soon; the younger siblings were growing rapidly. True, with the family about to expand, things were getting a bit cramped. Whenever Jesus stayed over, Simon and Jude, the youngest brothers, and some of the sheep had to sleep over in James' section. But Jesus was the principal breadwinner – though he wasn't home all that much and had a bachelor lifestyle to fund, his contribution helped. That looked to end.

"By the, ah, sea – the Great Sea?" Mary, referring to the Mediterranean, was confused – and scarcely could cover her motherly twinges at her eldest son moving off. While Nazareth was scarcely 20 miles inland, Galilee had no coastal outlet. Neither Caesarea in Samaria nor Tyre and Sidon to the north in Phoenicia were known for recruiting Galileans.

"No, the Sea of Galilee, of course," he replied, referring to freshwater Lake Genneseret to the east, that fishing and agricultural area lying well below sea level at the head of the Jordan Valley. "They say Antipas is planning a new city there – near the hot springs. Should be a big project. They've made me an offer…"

Mary shuddered as she interrupted. "But isn't there a pagan cemetery there? Aren't the gentiles…"

"Relax, mother – you know I pray often and follow the Law," Jesus smiled as he silently added the word *mostly* to that declaration. "Look, I'll purify myself before I come home. Good enough?"

"I can't imagine our people working near a gentile cemetery." Mary was troubled – defilement was a great concern and her son often took such things too lightly.

Jesus continued jokingly, not wanting to fully expose his more Hellenized, open-minded reputation in the city, "That's probably why they want *me* – Greeks can't communicate with most natives there. Besides, isn't it written: 'dust you are and to dust you will return'? I don't see buried corpses nearby as a major threat to my purity."

In truth, the city subculture of Sepphoris was brewing with conflict again, prompting Jesus to look for alternatives. Zealots were spreading anti-Herod, anti-Rome sentiments and Jesus didn't want to be involved – even though cafes and taverns he frequented were meeting grounds for such underground activity. This offer provided a way out. But how to explain that to his mother? *Some things*, he concluded, *you just don't*. He simply added with his touch of sarcasm, "I'll wade in the lake if my feet get overly defiled."

Jesus already had plans for his two youngest brothers, Simon and Jude, "Yaakov and I can line up a job for Shimon in Sepphoris. He's already working around here; he'll do better there and he can ride into town with Yaakov. Yehudah will be working soon, too. He's ten; I was already working at his age. You'll be OK, mother – and I'll bring you some money when I come home."

Mary nodded silently, then muttered, "the wind will pick them up and a gale will blow them away." Obvious was, he wouldn't be home much if he lived so far away – over 20 miles! For Mary it might as well have been Jerusalem – or Alexandria! But it was time for the young man to move on, to make his own life – a clear reality obvious to each.

Jesus had already traveled with the family, of course. As a youth, his clan group or a contingency from town had made the long journey to Jerusalem for several festivals – complete with donkeys and carts to haul the children. He remembered that even the "direct" route through Samaria, some 70 miles, seemed to take forever using that newly paved Roman roadway. On the last trip, he and Joseph had actually climbed Mt. Gerizim to view ruins of the Samaritan Temple, finding people friendly there, unlike their reputation.

Oh, and that *other* pathway, that hot, arduous trek down through Scythopolis, then along local paths and marshy foot trails through the Jordan River Valley. That endless, bumpy trudge along the meandering river to Jericho, the flies, the marshes, the ancient dusty trail, all those stories told by elders along the way about Jericho's long history – what a long journey, he'd thought, marveling as they passed first the aqueduct, then the huge hippodrome in that ancient city. Oh, and that hike up to Jerusalem: hot and dry, up, up, up, always climbing, the whole way.

He could vividly recall the grandeur of Herod's Temple and the walled, timeless city, endless rows of houses and markets, the haggling and trading, the din, dust and ever-needed caution. He'd listened at Pesach, fascinated at the endless debate over interpretive points about Passover and all other things, argued by priests and scribes, engaged with vociferous bystanders – each with his own stanch opinion, each supported by *facts* as drawn from scripture. On occasion, when he and cousins hadn't skipped out to explore the old town, Jesus joined in. But his logic and reason, hard to question, stunned the listeners, often to silence. His recall of testament proofs from Isaiah or Micah, tinged by his unique application of established lore leading to *differing* conclusions – that unconventional twist, from what, *a mere kid(!)* – confused and sometimes angered participants used to standard conclusions and dogmatic utterances, a give-and-take that never convinced opponents, but showed off the scriptural prowess of each.

So the journey to the lake and a new situation was not intimidating for Jesus as he rode with six others in a large utility cart down to lakeside construction acreage. Rakkath, the only nearby town, a sleepy village, occupied an ancient, strategic spot overlooking the blue lake and surrounding hills. But housing for the expanding pre-construction teams was in tents spaced among dusty bushes, where the incoming crew joined dozens of other stonemasonry, excavation and support people. Workers began to mingle with planners and scribes from the government to clear space so the lay of the land could be determined and thereby shaped usefully into streets and building settings. Jesus soon learned that the project would be huge – a city to rival or surpass Autocratis as Herod Antipas' principal glory. Rumor soon emerged that it would be named after the new Roman Emperor, Tiberius.

Work was mostly physical for several months, with various crews clearing shrubs and making preliminary excavations to allow planners a better view. As space opened up, some building could begin – the layout of streets and dimensioning of structures – but changes were frequent, with time-consuming revisions coming down frequently from Antipas himself. The tetrarch would appear on site occasionally, accompanied by extensive security and overdone fanfare. As workers were cleared away, he would ride a coach or chariot around the layout, pointing and questioning.

Over time cornerstones were placed to demarcate boundaries. But procurement quickly became a problem: construction materials, the proper stone for various building components and facings, were not available locally. Towns dotting the lakeshore were mostly built of hard, roughly-hewn basalt whose darkness was undesirable for large buildings intended to be ornate, appropriately spectacular in Herod Antipas' style. But importing white meleke limestone from Judea was as politically problematic as shipping from quarries in Mesopotamia was expensive.

Thus, two crews, including several supervisors, stoneworkers and one scribe each – Greeks and more Hellenized Jews – were selected to tour neighboring areas, seeking to contract for needed building supplies. One would head north to Tyre, checking inland at Caesarea Philippi, the other to the Decapolis to the southeast. Jesus was added to the latter team, owing to his Aramaic and Hebrew language skills: some potential quarry operators or suppliers might not speak Greek.

The first stop, the fortified city, Hippos, to the east of the lake, proved fruitless – significant building hadn't gone on there for some time. Heading east towards the desert, they passed the "Camel's Hump" peak, stopping at Gamla to inquire about building materials. Quarries there weren't active, so they proceeded on eastwards, then south on the king's highway, diverting for stops at Abila and Irbid – both city-states with fine structures in their capitals. But those only yielded potential contacts with quarries to the east. Time-consuming trips out that way produced only stone samples seeming too soft and porous for large buildings. Much façade work even as far south as Irbid was done in dark basalt.

As they continued south, days turned into weeks. Repeatedly suggestions arose to use newer Roman building techniques such as opus incertum, rock fragments filled with lime-based concrete, instead of classic stone. Nobody, though, thought that Antipas' building supervisors would entertain anything but white stone – at least for the facing of visible portions, façades, etc.

So they continued south to Gerasa, a vibrant regional center east of Perea where building trades were active and well connected. There the crew – reduced slightly as two had returned to the lake to report progress – settled in to explore possibilities. Colonnades lined many city streets, sporting magnificent stonework of various styles, for much of the city well predated Roman expansion. Making connections, questioning sources outside the city and gathering information took weeks. During that time Jesus got to know his companions well. Off hours spent socializing with locals were easily as informative, businesswise, as days spent tracking down builders in dusty back-alley warehouses and outlying villages – and much more fun.

Diverse ethnicity of the Decapolis – the "Ten Cities", Hellenized in nature, established under Roman rule a century before as autonomous city-states – provided color and stimulation, not only for business purposes. Evenings at cafes and public houses featured the Greeks, when not dancing or singing, poking fun at their gods by twisting myths in satirical ways – and the occasional Hittite, making fun of the Greek – or both, poking jokes at rural, often naïve Galileans. To them, unlike conservative folk Jesus had encountered in Nazareth and even Sepphoris, life was to be enjoyed and religion shaped to that end – not the other way around. Games often took the focus of the young, unmarried, working sector of *goyim* that formed the local population – none so tied down to the daily grind as back home.

Some days were spent not "working" at all, but sprinting, hurling a discus or gaming with dice in a convenient wine garden. True, Egyptians kept mostly to themselves, Phoenicians loved only money and workers from the north seemed unengaged beyond labor, food and sleep. But Greeks, educated and interested, had migrated to Gerasa from many areas. And that group, fun-loving and open-minded, enjoying the local economic boom from trade and handwork, kept things lively.

Jesus, taller by a head than the average 5-foot male of the time, and quite vigorous, could sprint right along with the athletic Greeks – a robust activity they would engage in whenever down time had been declared. This was a far cry from nose-to-the-grindstone work he'd had in Sepphoris. Jesus found he *could* compete with his Hellenistic peers, be it running, late-night singing and partying in the pubs or – once he'd filled in some foreign background, debating Stoicism vs. Platonic realism. As Jesus' Greek skills improved and those wine-induced debates – spurred by youthful idealism and an expense account – wove many a philosophical thread, he could easily note how various schools of Hebrew traditions corresponded roughly with Greek schools of thought: Essenes seemed similar in thinking to Pythagoreans – with mystical orientation and propensity towards vegetarian lifestyles. Pharisees, "separatists" literally, an influential Jewish sect promoting strict adherence to laws and traditions – rarely seen in Galilee, Jesus had encountered some on Jerusalem trips – appeared more like the Stoics: their ideas and logical regard dominated their emotions.

"You know, Yeshua, you people take your Yahweh god far too seriously," said a Greek companion, Neophytos, one night at a Garasene tavern. The group sat relaxing following several days' journey eastward to hilltop quarries. "We keep our deities up on Olympus – far away – where they don't meddle in our affairs." He poured another round of the sweet local vintage as others dipped their bread in olive oil.

"Hadn't you better be calling Aphrodite down for some help?" Jesus replied to the laughter of their companions and neighboring tables. "*Your* affairs seem as remote as Greece these days."

"Don't blame the gods," said Lysandros, a local who was helping show the group around, "but the lack of females in this country. Too many are sequestered at home, then married off before you even see them! Eros himself would be challenged to find a woman in this desert of femininity on whose treasured behind he might loose his arrow."

Jesus smiled, "Have you considered, my friend, that perhaps you carry the dryness of the desert airs along with you? Birds land on olive trees far more willingly than cacti!"

They all howled again, but a disturbance across the lamp-lit room caught their attention. A drunken customer, clearly Judean, was pounding the table, yelling at a servant woman.

"Look there! That one's got a demon in him for sure!" Lysandros was ribbing Jesus with a play on words, as the Greek *daemon* didn't imply the evil spirit connotation of Semitic lore.

The girl was cringing in fear and embarrassment. Her status didn't allow any defense to the patron's bullying. Jesus ambled over to the scene as the crowded tavern, quieting, backed away. The drunk was cursing the girl, "Look what you've done, you whore! You spilled my drink – and you expect paid?"

Jesus placed himself between the girl and the rowdy, facing the servant, backside towards the man. "We would like another bottle of wine at our table, waitress. Can you fetch us one?" he said.

"Hey, you, there! I'm talking to that slut. Who are you to butt in here?" the man bellowed.

Jesus turned and stared down at the rotund, bearded Judean, "Strange! I see only this hard-working young lady here."

The man fumed, but didn't have room to stand up. "The stupid bitch! She spilled my drink and now she wants my money for it!" he yelled. "Why should I pay her anything?"

"If you pay her, she'll feed her family with that money. That's why. The real question is, will you do the same for *your* family with what you have left?" The man, shamed in front of the crowd – for they all knew he was frittering away his pay on wine – threw down two coins and stalked out of the tavern.

"You seemed to handle the demon as well as the idiot," commented Neophytos as Jesus returned to the table.

Jesus shook his head. "But they both left together. The man learned nothing. He'll be back when we're gone."

Having made useful connections and procured several interesting samples, the crew headed home. Venturing south to Philadelphia wouldn't have found any new suppliers, they heard, so they turned west at the Jabbok River and headed down into the deep Jordan River Valley passing the old fortress at Amathus before crossing the Jordan. The main road, rough – despite Roman improvements – but straight, led north, then bypassed another grand city, Pella, transiting through Scythopolis before crossing the Jordan again to enter Gadara on the eastern flank of hills surrounding the Jordan.

Gadara featured the darker basalt look again, but provided some insight into more localized supplies of aggregates needed for concrete usage. Newer Roman building techniques – cheaper and quicker than Jesus was used to from his experience in Sepphoris – would certainly play a role in the new city on the lake. The Greeks in the crew invariably derided cheaper Roman construction. But somehow, Jesus pointed out to them, they didn't complain about imported Roman wine.

Tired from months on the road, sleeping in dismal flophouses – with night pots emptied not all that frequently – or empty storage halls of potential business connections, they could enjoy the offerings of one last lively city before returning to primitive tent life back at the lake. In Gadara, they learned that the new city on the lake would officially be named "Tiberias". Their expense money was running low, but they had enough to spend a few coins to see a Greek tragedy at the theatre.

But the pub afterwards proved more enlightening than the show had been: recitation of older Greek epigrams from noted poets. A long evening of Attic Greek – not the Koine version Jesus was used to – was difficult for him to follow, particularly with flowery poetic meter. This led to Jesus' occasional dozing.

Neophytos felt obliged to give Jesus a hard time. "Galileans absorb their poetry better while asleep, it seems," he commented.

Another companion added, "Perhaps the short love poems of Meleager are less invigorating to Yeshua's ear than unending praise of Yahweh of the Psalms," to general laughter.

Jesus brushed them off, "If what I missed while sleeping was anything like what I heard while awake, I think sleep was more beneficial!" He shook his head... "How many different ways need a poet describe the same superficial attraction to women and boys? There was one good one, though. What was it? About a candle, a moth or something?"

"Oh, the Moth and Candle," answered Dexicos, a local who had joined them at the theater. "I know that one. You realize that Meleager, master of the epigram, was born here – that he was a Gadarene?" The young man sat up proudly.

"I thought he lived on Kos," said one of the travelers.

"Well, he moved to Tyre for a while, then Kos. But he came from here and we treasure his work."

Jesus responded, "You do now, apparently. But I guess not back then – when did he live?" A century ago, he was informed. "It seems like Gadara didn't prize Meleager until he was long dead."

"It goes like this, the epigram..." Dexicos, ignoring the comment, stood up and gestured dramatically. "It equates candles to love: 'If you would so often singe the soul that flutters around you, dear Love, she will fly away from you – for she also, Cruel One, has wings.' Doesn't that speak volumes?"

Jesus nodded, appreciating the point – although poetry picturing such things as love, as in physical attraction to a female, indeed wasn't common in his background. Marriages were arranged, looser women of pubs and cafes frowned upon. Life back home just didn't feature Greek-style romance woven into poetry. Still, the message had stuck with him even though he couldn't remember the words.

While the discussion went on into the night, looking west, out over the hill from the public house where they enjoyed the pleasant evening air, they could all see the calm lake in the moonlight. Each was reluctant to call it quits, knowing the next day's trek back to lakeside construction site would end the Decapolis venture. But as they talked, Jesus noted just how much could be said in short, catchy phrases – key points, poetically voiced, that would be lost on listeners if only stated.

Shortly after the Decapolis venture – already three years after leaving home – Jesus managed to return to Nazareth for a brief visit, catching delivery wagons to Sepphoris and back, with that well-known hike to and from home.

James' second child had died shortly after birth, but a third pregnancy resulted in a daughter. Joses was married, too, and living in a room added to the small courtyard complex. But his wife, much to their consternation, hadn't conceived – bringing stress to their relationship. Simon was working on a farm near Nazareth. He'd already fathered a son and lived with his in-laws on orchard grounds. Jude was spending harvest season as a picker to the north while staying with relatives.

Of the two sisters, Salome, the elder, was approaching betrothal age, but local boys seemed a bit intimidated by all her older brothers. Still, Mary, James and Joses were in discussions with eligible families. They'd already arranged a betrothal for Jude, but that was through a family connection in Jotapata, north beyond Sepphoris.

Mary, now taking in tailoring to help make ends meet, was visibly overjoyed to see her eldest. She missed Jesus and his lively sense of humor much more than she put on – James, the businessman, was ever serious, Joses too wild. She enjoyed Jesus' Decapolis tales and hearing about Tiberias building. Daily life kept her busy – helping prepare evening meals for James and Joses when they got home, looking after Salome and Babe, tending to James' young ones, visiting Simon – and making sure they all followed traditional cultural dictates.

As she watched him leave, Mary cried as much for the passage of time as for the separation she would face – not knowing when she would see him again. They'd caught up on things, seen to a couple of repair jobs and visited the family crypt. But Jesus' stay was fleeting, and the man who now exited the same threshold he left as a youth years before, while he had a destination, seemed not to know where he was headed.

Jesus was nearing 23, heavily involved with the huge project of laying out a city. He was making good money for a hand worker, as he'd gotten to know the scribe and supervisors during his Decapolis venture – and impressed them with his imagination and practical grounding. So he was often consulted for input on layout matters, earning extra pay, despite cultural limitations on his job level. While the resident tax collector was always keeping an eye on things, for this official state project some income wasn't taxed. All in all, with busy days and no night life to drain income, Jesus could accumulate some cash.

In time, though, Jesus' urge to move on was overcoming the attraction of savings. One day, the balance tipped.

The team had hammered spikes into a gently sloping area well off the shoreline, meant to demarcate corners of an official courtyard and adjoining stable area. Jesus had commented that the stable should better be set *behind* the courtyard so that animal waste could be removed through back alleys rather than through the courtyard – a practical feature not included by architects. A foreman, typically running base laborers and unfamiliar with Jesus' usual input, took issue.

"Keep your tongue, worker," he barked. He gestured toward the stable markers. "Go over there and help carve out that trench so we can see how it looks. We'll decide where it goes and don't need your opinion!"

Jesus was taken aback. Not knowing this foreman, he wasn't sure of his rank – but didn't really care, either. "I'm a builder, overseer, not a ditch digger. Your crew seems hearty enough."

The stocky, gruff Greek turned to Jesus and bellowed, "We don't need a building right now, we need a ditch – go build that. I'm running this crew – if I tell you to dig, you dig. Get at it, Galilean!" The foreman knew from his accent and look that he was a native – and he wasn't used to locals working his crews.

"Not only am I not a ditch digger," Jesus replied in subdued tones, firm but not wanting to stir up an incident, "I'm even less a slave." He was well aware of ethnic friction among many Greeks and Galileans. Often basic attitude differences led to conflict through a simple failure to communicate.

The Greek was steaming. His crew would never talk back like that and he'd had few Judeans working for him, never a Galilean. Precious few natives came around, given the nearby graveyard, and most of them worked on business aspects, not on construction. "For the praise of Alexander and Zeus, what do we have here, a peasant who would be boss?" He grabbed a shovel and threw it at Jesus – who caught it. "Take that shovel and..."

Jesus laid the shovel gently down on the ground, turned and walked over to the paymaster building. Taking his total back pay and picking up his travel bundle, he quickly left the construction site – before word could get around that he was traveling with a lot of cash. Supply boats frequently crossed the lake to retrieve salt fish, so he picked up a ride to the north rim for a couple of semis.

Capernaum and Bethsaida sat at the north shore – either would be worth the change of scenery. The boat landed first at Capernaum, so that would do for a while. Asking around, he found day's wages in short order with a foreman who repaired boats and carts, sometimes even reshaping grain mills and olive presses if wood-working business lagged. Workers were scarce as most able-bodied laborers headed down to the new construction site. So the foreman took Jesus on, provided he could do the work. While pay was low, it was mostly cash "under the table" – thus tough for tax collectors to notice. And the big bonus: not every day was there something to fix. Off days could be used to explore the countryside, wandering dusty trails leading out past olive and date palm groves to hills to the west and north. After the heavy workload with little free time and no social life in Tiberias, that sounded great.

Capernaum, a fishing village far less sophisticated than the grand city of Sepphoris, even looked different than villages back home. Houses, single story with ladders up to the roof for summer sleeping, were built of that chiseled, hard basalt stone seen in northern Decapolis rather than mud brick common to Lower Galilee. Filled in with stone-packed, dried mud, houses and walls concealed private courtyards. Dark in appearance, they seemed sturdy, better able to handle storms that might whip up across the lake.

The main street, running north-south dissected the small market place towards the center; otherwise it was bounded by houses and courtyards. The tent-draped open space and adjoining enclosure, not occupied by sellers on the Sabbath, would serve to house discussions of scripture. This gathering spot often featured itinerant preachers, anything from Zealots to Pharisees, oracles to apocalyptic doomsayers. The town offered but three eating places – little variety, but home-cooked food, fresh bread from courtyard ovens and local wines. Jesus soon found a place to sleep – the half-empty storage shed of a fisherman named Zebedee who lived in Bethsaida but docked his fishing boats near Capernaum.

Except for his height and unusual self-confident air, Jesus passed, hardly noticed, within the common exchange of fishing people – counting, butchering, salting and hauling daily catches off to larger towns – itinerant workers and work-seekers that came and went. Once he got used to frequent wafts of fish, he found Capernaum rather amenable.

In short order, he met Mary, one of the serving girls at the largest tavern. They soon became friends and began to see each other frequently – despite small-town rumors and gossip that churned up quickly. Mary had come from nearby Magdala, on her own now after leaving home on less than friendly terms. Far too spirited at age 12 for local boys, she resisted various suitors until her father began to abuse her. Possessed, they'd called her, as she often talked back when ordered about and rebelled at his suggested marital arrangements to dull-witted bumpkins. By her fifteenth year, she had left home for Jotapata, but retreated to Capernaum a couple years later when her status was questioned by conservative folk of that old city.

"Yesh'" as she called him, seemed different. Nobody had treated her as a person, valuing anything beyond her looks and what she could do for them. As she and Jesus walked the hills on free time – even on the Sabbath, when they had to sneak away – they could talk about many things. Jesus got right to the point, unlike all the others, who chattered in meaningless repetition of stock phrases, clumsy scriptural references and daily drivel. He joked about things and laughed – a freedom he'd nourished thanks to his old Greek friends. He kidded her and disarmed any sly criticism of their free lifestyle by local townspeople with his quick wit.

One leisurely day many months later, as they ambled up a trail overlooking the lake, Mary asked, "What do you want here? You're better than this little dust pit, Yesh'. What keeps you here?"

"There's nothing back home. Believe me, Miriam, if you think Capernaum is boring, Nazareth is worse yet. Nothing to do in Tiberias but work, take orders and slug down wine," Jesus paused in thought as they walked along. "I'm thinking to travel up to Tyre, maybe down along the coast," Jesus answered. "My Greek is pretty good – though it's getting a little stale now." He pondered briefly as they rounded a bend to a spectacular view of the lake below. It lay, blue and rippling, in a timeless calm, surrounded by hills browned by mid-summer dryness, yet dotted with dark green patches of orchard. Far to the south was a haze of dust surrounding Tiberias, visible from this vantage point. "What do I want? There's a lot I want to see, but I've got to save up a few more denarii.

"I do enjoy the quiet and our talks," he continued, breaking into a smile. "Down at the beach while I'm working, Zebedee's kids keep things going. And their buddy, Shimon – they call him *Kaipha* – comes around. I joke with them while they're helping, tell them things I've picked up in my travels. If they never hear anything but gossip and scripture, they'll end up just like all the others – stuck in old, dead ideas." The wind whisked past, shifting dust across the path as gulls called out and circled above. "Somehow children seem more aware than adults. I guess you have to learn to be stupid."

"You should be a Rabbi, Yesh'. You have a way for explaining things."

Jesus smiled. "That's what my mother used to say. She used to tell me about her dreams – thought I'd become a Pharisee. Imagine that! You were there a month ago or so, when that puffed up windbag from Jerusalem – claimed to be a Pharisee – started lecturing at the tent, eh?"

Now Mary was laughing out loud, "Yes."

"His nose, the blessed beak of a hawk, was buried so deep in the scrolls he couldn't see the world in front of him. I caught him every time he spouted off one of his stupid interpretations."

"Yes, you did – but you'd better watch what you say. Those people don't like to be shown up – and they don't forget anything."

"Donkeys remember, too. But they can only kick you if you follow along behind them," he laughed. "I won't be following any Pharisees!"

Mary added, "But, Yesh' – they can also bite you where it hurts if you try to get in front of them!"

Another month and more had passed with steady work. But Jesus was restless again, wearying once more of meaningless toil. So the next break in work, he ventured outward. He hitched a ride on a farmer's cart, traveling east past Bethsaida, then hiked the gentle slopes up into Gaulanitis – there he sought peace from his uneasiness. He'd tired of Capernaum and its rigid thinking, but had grown comfortable with Mary – should he settle down with her? Accept easy-going village life? Somehow, there must be more; his urge to travel, now that he'd saved some money was pressing. He was torn.

As the trail headed on up, he found a flat rock in the shade of some scraggly trees. *Good to stop here for a bite to eat*, he thought, and sat, leaning back to pull out his bread and dried fish. Seated for a moment, he gazed at the lake below circled by beige and green dabbed hills. As he cleared his mind, clouds thickened to darken the sky. Dust swirled in the distance as the wind kicked up.

Daydreaming, at ease, with nothing pressing and time dissolved into the present, a vision unfolded. He could see the dark sky part to brilliant blue, as if opening to a truth more than a place, and a dove descended to land softly in front of him. As he blinked, snapping out of his mind-image, he saw that indeed, a pair of pigeons, apparently sensing possible crumbs, landed nearby. He couldn't quite decipher the vision, but his feeling of peace was overwhelming and ebullient. A dove from the heavens, he quizzed himself for meaning, and pondered that vision much of the day as he made his way back.

Scarcely two weeks later, Jesus, working repair patches onto the inverted hull of a fishing vessel, noticed Mary approaching in earnest. "I'll be back in a minute," Jesus said to the workmen.

"Wow, take your time, man," said one of them, a grizzled fisherman, Jesus' age but looking ten years older, ogling the attractive female as he dabbed his sweat. Another added, "Har, better holes to fill than this leaky old tub," he cracked as they all laughed.

The sun glazed off the sand by the docks as a dry wind flittered at Mary's long hair. "Yesh', I had to find you – sorry to..."

"No problem. I'll catch up."

"Look, I..." Mary started, tears forming in her eyes. "A cousin just brought me news. My father is lying ill and wants to see me. I'll have to go back home for a bit. He's ... well, he's forgiven me and wants me to come back before he..." Her voice tailed off.

"Hmmm," said Jesus, aware of her situation, "amazing how forgiving people can be if they need you."

"I'll be leaving this afternoon. Don't know when I'll be back."

Jesus nodded, "Yeah, I guess you have to. Maybe it's best I leave, too. This looks like an omen."

Now Mary was dabbing her tears and sobbing. "Will I see you again, Yesh'? You're the only..."

"What do you think, Magdalene? Where can I go that the trail does not lead back here?" he said quietly, embracing her – but unsure just where that trail did lead.

Shortly, Jesus returned to the inverted hull. The inevitable kidding of the small work crew was interrupted by some boys approaching.

"Yeshua, tell us some stories," said James, elder son of the family whose shed he had called home for the better part of a year.

"You' better learn to patch," said Jesus. "Here, see how these slats fit into place. Secure them, then seal them with pitch."

"What did that woman want?" said another, the one called Rocky. "Man, was she ... I hope my family finds me one like that! I think..."

"Don't be confused by looks," Jesus interrupted. "The taste of a fig doesn't come from its shape or color."

As the boys observed Jesus' technique for patching the vessel, Simon lost interest. He wandered towards the water, chucking stones and getting them to skip. A younger boy, unknown to Jesus, yelled at him, "Dad said not to do that, Shimon! You'll fill up the lake!"

"Now don't you tattle on me!"

Jesus interrupted, "Hey, guys, take it easy."

Simon protested, "Dad's always bossing me around. Now I've got to put up with Andrew, and he'll tattle on me everything I do."

"He's your brother, kid," Jesus said, pulling the boys all aside away from the boat and work crew. "You know, you boys are all on the same side. You'd better stick up for each other – you'll have plenty of strangers in life to deal with without fighting each other."

"Yeshua, tell us about the Decapolis and the Greeks!" said James, "or Jeru..."

"Listen up, guys," interrupted Jesus, sitting down in the sand and herding the boys in closer. "I'll be leaving soon. I've got to be on my way."

"No," they all cried out. "What'll we do? Where..."

"I'm going to head up to Tyre first – don't know from there," Jesus said, tailing off. Life hadn't seemed to offer a clear direction – just places that eventually spurred him to leave. "I'm sure the path will open up."

"Hey, can we come?" asked Rocky. "I've never been so far away! We only go out on the boat and come right back."

Jesus chuckled. "No, Kaipha, I'm afraid not. But you'll be able to travel one day, when you're older."

"We'll just have to work. All dad does is work – every day but the Sabbath, then we sit around and talk *all day*. That's what you do when you're grown up – work and talk! *How boring!*" Simon stood up, grabbed a stone and hurled it into the water.

"Well, sure – you have to live, and to do that, you have to eat, and to do that, you have to earn money. But you can make your own lives – remember that. You don't have to do things just like you're taught, think like you're supposed to. Make your own way through life, each of you."

James, just nine but already helping with the fishing operation – when he couldn't sneak away to play – looked sad, "We'll miss you, Yeshua. You're not like other grown-ups. You say interesting stuff; you're fun! I want to be like you when I gr…"

"No, kid – don't do that!" Jesus cut him off. "Be yourself! Be who you are, not who I am. Got that? All of you, just be yourselves – not Moses, not Elijah, not me – or you'll never be free."

At a shout from the distance, the boys ran off. Jesus finished that project, but quit a week later. He took his pay and put together his few things – sewing some coins into seams of his tunic and more into his outer mantle. On his way through town, he bought a new pair of sandals with cloth side coverings for easier hiking. Heading out, he figured he would need them.

The 40-odd mile trip northwest to Tyre passed first through Chorazin – a well-traveled path to that nearby town – then up to Sepph, climbing from Capernaum well below sea level to over 2500 feet. From there a pass and various valley trails led west, down to the Mediterranean. An abandoned shed just before Chorazin provided cover for the cool night.

As Jesus entered town, early morning village life in Chorazin was busy, with vendors offering various spices, wares and produce. Jesus picked up some bread and bean curd for the journey. But as he walked out of town, a mule driver pulled up beside him.

"Ho, where're you headed, man?" the stern-looking driver called down from his wagon.

"Tyre." *Pretty well off, this guy,* Jesus thought – quickly assessing a wagon with two hitched mules to be beyond the average farmer's means. "Got room for a rider?"

"I'm headed for Gishala, but I can get you up over the hills," said the driver, seeming generous with his offer.

As Jesus settled into the rough-hewn seat beside the driver, he asked, "Do you usually pick up riders? What if I'm a robber?"

"I'm not afraid of you, fella'," he muttered. "I can handle one guy if I have to. Anyway, you look pretty straight." The older man prodded the mules and the cart lurched forward. "But having you sitting there might hold off any real highwaymen."

The driver liked to talk. Introducing himself as Raphael, son of Joses, merchant of Gishala, he told of his pottery operation, making lamps, cups and other wares. He'd just made the rounds of lakefront towns and was headed home with a load of dried clay. "I'll get you to a fork in the road, just past Sepph. You'll walk on to Meroth, then north to Tyre. I'm headed home, but have some stops to make. You're better to take the Meroth road."

The day was hot for late fall, and dust from hoofs and wheels seemed to encase the two riders. Occasionally they passed a donkey cart or pedestrian along the rough road. Raphael explained the potting trade, lamenting slow business, high taxes and the danger of thieves, as he'd rarely made this trip alone.

They'd passed Sepph, stopping only for a drink and a break for the mules, and came up over a crest when Raphael flinched and slowed the mule team. In the distance, near a split in the path, stood a group. "I don't see so good anymore," said Raphael. "Can you make out…"

"Robbers," said Jesus. "Four of 'em. Got horses. They've stopped an old couple and their donkey cart."

"Curse Herod, the swine," grunted the driver. "If they see us!" He pulled back on the reins.

"No," said Jesus. "Keep going. Do you have a dagger?"

"What good's a dagger against four thieves? Curse the Idumean swine, I can't outrun them – and they'll jump this wagon when they see we're a bigger prize."

"Just give me your dagger and keep riding – slow down when you get close."

Raphael handed Jesus his weapon. Jesus turned it and pressed it to the driver's throat. "What in Moses' name…"

"Quiet," said Jesus calmly. "Just look scared and keep going."

Raphael had no difficulty implementing that suggestion. As they approached, one man, mounted, turned to look, while two others on foot, accosting the old couple, looked up and started talking. A fourth held the horses.

As the wagon approached the scene, Jesus barked out in a gruff voice and crude Galilean hill dialect, "Hurry your business, brothers. But keep quiet! Roman patrol up over the hill, ten or so on foot, some mounted. They were resting, but I wouldn't hang around long." He turned to Raphael, "Move it, you!"

Raphael swatted the mules, working them into a rapid trot. He turned right at the fork and kept moving.

The thieves blew by in a gallop.

Raphael stopped the wagon and Jesus handed him his weapon as he hopped off. "I'd better check on those old folk."

"Don't hurt us," they said as Jesus approached. "We haven't got much."

"I don't want anything. Are you OK?" Jesus said as Raphael, having turned the wagon, drew near.

"Yes, they had just stopped us when you came into sight," said the old man, "But…"

"You take that other fork, Yeshua," Raphael yelled out. "I'm going back to the Romans. I don't want to catch up to those thugs."

"What Romans?"

"You said..."

"Your eyes *are* bad, man," Jesus smiled. "Look, just head home. Those crooks will disappear into the hills. If they see you without me, they'll assume I took your cash. Thieves like that aren't too bright. They won't care about your clay." Raphael wheeled about and headed north.

Jesus turned as the older woman climbed onto the cart. "Where are you headed?" he asked.

The old-timer was now smiling. "We live near Meroth. We'll carry your pack on the cart if you want to join us."

As they thanked Jesus, they headed off the left fork, Jesus walking alongside the donkey and the man. Brush was greener on the eastern slope towards the sea, with stands of trees frequenting the scenery.

"We dress flax canes," the old man explained as they walked. "We'd been in Sepph selling a small load of heckled fibers – don't have the water up here for much retting. The price was pretty good, so we were happy, but..."

"But if those thieves had taken our profits!" the wife exclaimed, shaking her head and beating her chest.

They explained that one of their sons and his older children worked along with them – indeed, he had taken over heavy work, along with hired help. When they learned Jesus was headed for Tyre, they mentioned that another son and a daughter lived there. "Gideon helps run a purple dye operation. He comes to visit sometimes. Rachel, too."

"Nice that your family comes by," said Jesus, wondering when he'd get back to Nazareth. Over two years had gone by.

The woman on the cart spoke up, "not Noam – he never comes. He's more like you. Got wanderlust." She shook her head and beat her chest again.

"Now, woman, don't get riled up," said the old man, limping slightly at the rocky section of the path. "Noam left a few years back. Last we heard, he'd moved on north from Sidon. Don't know where."

"But the Sibyl in Tyre – the good one, up north of the causeway – told Rachel that he's fine, that he's just traveling," the woman piped up. "And she's always right. It is written, 'Watch over this vine, the root your right hand has planted, the son you have raised up for yourself.' I'm sure the Lord watches over him."

As they turned the cart off the roadway, down a path towards home, the couple offered for Jesus to come in for a meal. He ate a bite, but declined to spend the night. "I'd better make a few more miles yet today," he said. "You know, I'm sure one day Noam will return. Don't worry."

"We'll welcome him with a great party," the old man said, bidding good-bye. "We love all our children and five grand-children now. But your heart is always with the one you don't see or know about."

As Jesus left them by the road, he hiked along as thoughts turned to home. *Going on three years,* he thought. When he came to a walkway off to the left that clearly turned south, he asked a couple of workers hoeing around trees in an olive orchard where that path led.

"Take you past Ramah to Cana, but it's a pretty rough trail," one said.

Cana was close to home. He'd know the way from there – Tyre could wait a few days.

A knock at that old, familiar door – one he'd helped Joseph set into place when he was seven or eight, he reckoned – got no answer. *Strange,* Jesus thought, *somebody should be around.* It hadn't been *that long* since he'd been by. Should be two brothers' families still here, plus Mary, Jude and the girls.

The door slowly swung open as an older man peered warily around it, leaning on the frame – hair shaggy and grey, looking unkempt. "What'd'ya want," said the man, his eyes a bit dazed, squinting in the bright sunlight.

"I'm looking for Miriam, my mother," Jesus replied, "or Yosev or Yehudah."

"Miriam? She ain't here," the man sputtered as he swung the door wider and moved into the opening. "Hey, you Yeshua?"

"Yes."

"Now don't you come here looking for no money! We don't have cash to give out to every…" He continued to blabber as he held the door, more or less blocking the doorway.

Jesus began to recognize the man as his uncle. "Are you Yoav? Uncle Yoav?" he asked, "Look, I don't want anything – just came to see my mother and family. Where is she? What are you doing here?"

"*I live here*, that's what I'm doing here. I bought into this house," said Yoav brusquely. "Miriam's not around, nor your aunt. Nobody's here but…"

"Look, will they be back? I've come quite a way. Can I come in and wait?"

"In here? Are you clean?" Yoav blustered. "I hear you been living with Gentiles, living near cemeteries – you'll not defile *my* house with your…"

Jesus cut off his rant, "Where is Miriam? Where are my brothers?"

"You expect to come back here, unclean, and bring the judgment o' Yahweh down on us? Last time you were here, Yaakov got punished!" Yoav shouted, referring to James. "Lost their second-born."

"Yaakov's baby died before I ever got here. Just tell me where I can find my mother or brothers."

Yoav leered at Jesus and backed down. "Far as I know, she's in Sepphoris visiting her son, one of them. She doesn't spend much time around here."

That's not surprising, thought Jesus. "Where does Yaakov live?" asked Jesus, hoping to find James.

"No idea. Somewhere in the city."

"How about Yosev?" he asked, wondering if Joses were still in the city.

"Don't know. Up there, too."

"Or Yehudah?"

"Farther up north I think." Yoav was backing into the doorway and starting to swing it shut. "Look, I'm kind of busy. Anything else I can help you with?"

Jesus smiled wryly – *wouldn't want to let that bottle of wine get lonely*, he thought. "No, guess not. Next time I want a fig, I won't look to a thistle plant." He turned and walked away.

The sights of Sepphoris, Antipas' grand gem, had changed in the years since he'd been there: new buildings, expanded residential quarters, different look and feel to the neighborhoods he knew and the projects he'd worked on. But in taverns he'd frequented back then, timelessness transfixed the scene, rendering ageless attributes where only faces change – either by aging or replacement – not the atmosphere. So it was at Harmocydes' Haven.

Jesus' weariness abated slightly as he sipped new wine. The bread and oil tasted like home – many a meal he'd had at the Haven.

Asking around, finally querying a couple older patrons, he quickly found what he needed.

"Yaakov, son of Yoseph? Yaakov of Nazareth? Who doesn't know Yaakov?" said a tanned and dusty Galilean worker sitting with some others who all nodded in agreement. "That would be Yaakov *the Just*, eh! Not a man here who wouldn't want to work for that man, eh, right?"

James seemed to have built quite a reputation. Finding his address, though, wasn't so easy. "Why do you want to know that at this hour?" the men demanded, turning dour – for the sun had long since set and most such queries in bars at nighttime weren't for magnanimous gestures.

"Yaakov is my brother."

"Now hold on! You aren't Yosev," said another. Most of them knew James' brother, Joses. "He was around earlier, but we don't know you."

"Show me the olive tree in Galilee that sprouts but two olives," Jesus replied. "Where can I find…"

He stopped when someone grabbed his shoulders and spun him around. "Yeshua! Brother! Can it really be you?" bellowed a lanky, clean-shaven Joses as he warmly embraced Jesus. He was taller, far more a man than that uncertain, moody teen Jesus had last seen before leaving home nearly six years before. His hair was clean and oiled, his tunic near Roman in style.

"Yosev! The kid of a goat – are you still butting heads with the world?" Jesus grinned and hugged his not-so-little brother. He recalled a spirited sibling, four years his junior, who only ever wanted to wrestle as a kid, rebelled as a teen and always resisted authority – especially after Joseph died.

The two quickly caught up on things: since Jesus had last been home, Joses had divorced his barren wife and moved to Sepphoris. He had taken up the bachelor lifestyle of his oldest brother and apparently enjoyed it. Coming to specialize in stone masonry, Joses did well for himself – though his carefree lifestyle demanded considerable revenue and relieved him of most of it.

"Come, brother, the house of Yaakov isn't far. Mother's staying there with our sister – they can't take too much of dear Uncle Yoav!!" Joses said as they headed out into the street, lit by occasional torches, towards James' abode. The near-full moon helped considerably, showing off the grand architecture of Sepphoris with a mystical tinge.

"Salome just got married. She's living in Nazareth, out a bit towards the farm that Shimon runs," Joses related, referring to Simon, the fourth oldest of the brothers. "You missed a mighty good feast, Yeshu'!"

Passing through the forum gleaming in the moonlight, Jesus pointed to the colonnaded public works building and its attached military station. "I worked on that complex, way back when. Your father and I used to hike into town each day," he reminisced. "You were still kicking dirt around the courtyard back then. I think we were still on that project when Yaakov started work, hauling water – and ... getting in the way, mostly."

"Seemed like you were always working, Yeshu'," said Joses. "When I was little, you weren't around much. I used to really look forward to you coming home. Then, after while..." He tailed off, pondering his fleeting childhood, "after while, you didn't come around so much."

Jesus explained, "Once I was on my own, after your father died and I had to support *your* appetite, it wasn't worth heading back to Nazareth every night. And, well, life was better in the city – as I guess you've discovered."

The two talked at length, filling in years that separation had left undefined. They had much in common, though Joses seemed content with his active bachelorhood as an achieved goal, whereas Jesus could never seem to escape his inner drive towards an unfixed destination, an undefined, intangible goal.

The family reunion at James' house was as tearful as it was joyful. Jesus was amazed how Mary, the youngest, the Babe, had grown – now 11, she was becoming a woman: searching for a mate had started. James' girls were seven and three now. An infant son – appropriately named "Yeshua" – added to the mix. James had been promoted to foreman, a station exceeding his attributed status – but his character and know-how greatly improved building capabilities of the project he worked on. He had judiciously leveraged Jesus' connections with the managerial elite before the elder brother left for the lake.

His house was roomy enough for comfortable accommodation: three separate quarters off the common, fairly spacious courtyard – plus the luxury of a separate stall for animals. After extensive greetings and breaking out bread and snacks, James' wife took the children off to bed; the Babe joined them shortly thereafter, while the three brothers and Mary talked into the night.

"Will you stay around here now, Yeshua?" asked Mary at length, having heard his Tiberias and Capernaum stories.

"Just passing through, mother," Jesus explained. "There's nothing here for me now. I have a connection or two in Tyre and, well, other places I want to check out." Jesus sipped at a tasty, imported Roman wine from an amphora James had been saving for a special occasion. "One isn't satiated by two bites off a lamb roast."

Mary protested, "But such travels are dangerous, Yeshua. You spoke of thieves along the road – such men could kill you! Yahweh may not watch over you if you travel to Phoenicia. And you can't properly keep the law and stay pure while traveling among gentiles. Yoav was right to not let you in! The Lord punishes sinfulness – and evil spirits lurk by those wells and springs you drink from while traveling."

James rescued his elder brother from Mary's onslaught, "No spirit could displace Yeshua's own, mother. There's no room in that man for any breath but his own.

"But, brother," he continued, turning to Jesus, "what is it you're looking for? You seem driven – by what? Towards what end? You only have so much time in life to work and collect, to build a family."

Mary broke in again, "You had a good job there in Tiberias – and maybe that Magdalene woman would be…"

Jesus laughed, "Everybody seems better at running my life than I am! The seagull lights and flies away again – from where and to what goal? He doesn't know when he takes off where he'll end up, but he always lands in the 'right' place. Would you tell him *here* is better than *there?*

"For many years I worked as seemed best, collecting pay, building other people's dreams. But each shekel earned came in exchange for a piece of my life. When, one day, I am gone, will a stack of silver denarii stand in my place? Will man live better – will I rest better – for a column raised or a slab laid in place in Autocratis or Tiberias?

"Mother, you stitch up a new sash or tunic – and you use a pattern to guide your cut and determine your seam. Yet, I've found no pattern to which I might hold up my life for sizing."

James looked his brother in the eye, "You may never find such a pattern, Yeshua – such a blueprint form may not exist. But if you only ever wander from place to place, your life will be measured neither by that stack of coins, *nor* by a clan of offspring to bear your blood."

Jesus smiled, enjoying his brief moments with his family – remembering that youthful, daily toil to feed and clothe them when he had to, remembering the guidance he could supply as father-substitute, when he could. But whatever his family thought of him then, they didn't understand him now. "I don't know what it is exactly that I seek. But I pray only that I will know it when I've found it. The Yahweh that really is, that I feel when I pray, isn't a Zeus or Marduk, sitting up there in the heavens guiding warfare and shaping history – he's watching out over me, guiding my journey.

"I have to follow that guide – taking life as I feel right, as it's presented.

"Mother, evil spirits don't lurk around swamps and outhouses. They don't invade with grit and slime. From what I've seen, they only come upon those who fear, those who feel weak and in danger. Don't worry about me. How and why the Lord punishes people, I don't know. It seems the sinful often find reward where the good-hearted find pain.

"As I travel about, it's not new flavors of wine I seek, nor grander buildings and more accomplished people – it's answers to those questions, to understand *why*. If and when I find that…"

Mary shook her head, "But the answers are in the scriptures! The prophets of old…"

"Were wrong as often as right," her eldest interrupted, drawing a laugh from his two brothers, a frown from his mother. "Did Moses know where he would end up when he left Egypt? No, or they wouldn't have wandered the Sinai for decades. Moses had to feel his way along – and so do I."

Growing weary, relaxed from wine more than conversation, the family, one by one, pulled up their sleeping straw and blankets. Jesus, having followed his whim, would leave the next day.

Heading north, he made a quick stop in Jotapata to find his youngest brother. His mother had expressed worry that Jude, married the previous year and living with in-laws on a flax farm, wasn't happy. The road led from there down to Ptolemais on the Mediterranean, where the main coastal way ran north to Tyre.

Jude was sweating, carrying bundles of flax from carts to the combing room, when Jesus approached. Barely 15, he was pleased to see his oldest brother again – but hadn't been as close to him as the older two had been. He'd rarely seen Jesus during his childhood, though it was always a treat when the eldest arrived from Sepphoris, often bringing a small treat from the big city.

Jesus scarcely recognized his kid brother, but greeted him warmly. They sat and talked for a while. Jude, taking a break, fetched some water and small fruit cakes from the main house near the fields and workrooms.

"I couldn't labor for that swine, Herod," Jude stated once Jesus had filled him in on his travels. "As it is, my in-laws here pay so much in taxes – and now my wife is pregnant, taxes will go up again. All so the pompous can feast and bathe in luxury! I started working with Yaakov and Yosev in Sepphoris and couldn't take it. All that work, for what? The glory of the tetrarch?"

"Hmmm. Your operation here does seem freer. City construction is confining," Jesus observed.

"Nobody's free – not here, not there. Only the swine royalty and their puppeteers, the Romans," Jude was getting fired up. "I hate them and all they stand for! Yeshua, did you ever have contact over at the lake with the resistance?"

Jude caught Jesus by surprise. The Zealots had a presence everywhere, not the least in Sepphoris. Their unrest was part of the reason Jesus moved on – they not only hated Romans, but lashed out at Judeans and fellow Galileans who cooperated with the authorities. But they, along with other resistance groups, had brought destruction to that city just two decades before. Jesus had avoided them in Tiberias, where only workers could pass security. Rebels recruited few cohorts in nearby fishing villages and rarely ventured into the Decapolis. Capernaum, too, by virtue of its size, remote location and general prosperity, was little affected by the resistance movement.

"Well, not so much there, but I've been around. I helped rebuild a city that their last uprising got destroyed," Jesus said.

Jude's eyes opened wide with excitement, "But Yeshua, you are free! You could become a leader of the Zealots – with your wits and cleverness, you could…"

"Get Galilee demolished again? The Romans have but one answer to rebellion. That answer is brought, not by Tiberius, nor by Antipas, but by the Centurion."

"But to *not* fight, Yeshu' – to cower in fear or hold back? That is to bring dishonor to our people, blasphemy to Yahweh! We must be free from foreign domination, as Yahweh promised, as David bequeathed," Jude proclaimed, now standing and waving his fist. "And that means…"

Jesus cut him off, "You'll be free alright – free to join generations of warriors in their crypts. No, actually, you'd join them in fields of unmarked graves, pecked at by ravens where you fell to Roman short swords, with anything of value on your shredded body having been picked over by the townspeople you fought to defend."

"Then so be it," declared Jude. "If Judeans are too soft to fight, too pampered with their Temple cult and Roman ways, then Galileans will stand alone against the oppressors."

"Standing is a position trees maintain only so long as they live," Jesus said. "Cut down, they make boards to trim Roman villas. It is soon forgotten that the wood was ever a tree to begin with." Jesus could see that the discussion was going nowhere – the fire in his brother's heart was not about to be quenched. He changed the subject, thinking to discuss family matters. It didn't help.

"Uncle Yoav is a buffoon, a fool," declared Jude. "He pestered Salome until she moved out. I told him if he ever bothered Miriam, I would cut him to pieces," he said, referring to the Babe. "As it is, mother can hardly live at home."

Jesus was stumped. Each line of discussion led to an aggressive response. He only hoped that Jude would mature, that hard work on the farm and the responsibility of children would channel his energy into building and away from conflict. It occurred to him that fighting *never* led to peace, only more conflict – until the clashing forces were both dead.

But he thought the better of planting that seed in the stone-hard mind of his youngest brother where it would only wither.

After a short meal with the family, Jesus filled his water bag. Jude walked him to the main road leading down to the sea. It was afternoon, hotter at this lower elevation; but he could feel the sea breeze already. He looked to make Ptolemais by evening, or find shelter down along the mild coastal area. As he hugged his brother, he had the fleeting thought that he would never see him again.

"Take care of yourself and your family, Yehudah," he said.

"Remember that every Roman you might kill will be replaced by five more."

Jude looked away, "Then I must keep my sword sharp and my feet nimble so I'm ready for those five."

And the 25 that will replace them? I doubt it, Jesus thought as he walked away. He waved several times as he walked down the road toward...

He knew not where.

Tyre proved even grander than Decapolis cities had been, dominating the broad end of a peninsula, jutting out into the Mediterranean. Approaching from the south, the grand city, with its walls, varied architecture and exposed harbors, looked intimidating – even to a traveler who had already encountered many proud, adorned cities.

Tyre proper, once an island perched secure directly off the Phoenician coast, was now a peninsula, owing to Alexander's siege from centuries before. The causeway his army constructed had led to the channel silting, so that the city was now accessible from the mainland.

Walking through busy, bustling streets, some narrow, most dirty, Jesus was amazed at the extent of building and the sheer activity – he'd gotten used to lazy old Capernaum. The large port was the hub of old, prosperous shipping routes, connecting distant lands to the east, from which goods would be transported via caravan, to ports across the Mediterranean. With this ancient Canaanite area now secure under the Roman umbrella as the province of Syria, trade was booming. As Jesus made his way across the connecting causeway, carts large and small traveled in both directions towards the northern harbor and the smaller southern docking area.

First thing for a traveler entering a city is finding a place to stay – inexpensive being good, free better. Making his way down to central Tyre, Jesus found and explored the agora – the "gathering place" – that held a cavalcade of activity, mounted or afoot, circulating around tables, tents, shops and stand-alone sellers. Merchants offered spices, fish, grains, meats, cheeses, bolts of cloth – coarse and fine – jewelry, fruits, sandals and other leather goods, and just about anything else imaginable. Prime merchants roosted in spots centered within the colonnade and cross streets, but everything from discount hucksters to potters, jugglers to freelance musicians, craftsmen and other artisans populated side streets all around, presenting a dazzling maze to the stranger.

Dickering, bargaining, offers of unmatchable deals, clatter of hooves, shouts, whinnies, braes and an occasional trumpet or scream filled the ear while a plethora of odors and fragrances confronted the nose. The wary eye, though, else captivated by the scene, had to keep alert for ever-present thieves camouflaged among buyers.

At length, picking up some tasty bread and fruit to quench an appetite, Jesus started to inquire for a flophouse or cheap hostel. But the Canaanite tongue was strange – nearer Hebrew, which Jesus understood from early training in traditions, than Aramaic. But dialects of the more common Aramaic seemed to stem from everywhere, some known to the Galilean, others not and scarcely understandable.

As Jesus made his way past the hippodrome, an arena seeming even grander than Jericho's, people were still wandering out from an earlier event. Building after building, some clearly ancient as remnants of Phoenician splendor, many added more recently and obviously Roman in style, dominated Jesus' view as he explored central streets. Wine, he soon found – and practically everything else – had been cheaper back on the mainland. A flophouse would be, too, unless he could spend the same money on wine and find a quiet spot down a secluded alley to doze until morning. His spending money, mostly of Roman issue, was accepted by all.

Work was scarce, though, it turned out. At the dock operations where crews repaired and refurbished large cargo vessels, foremen laughed at his experience mending fishing boats on the lake – and kept laughing at his hill dialect. Speaking broken Koine Greek didn't help much, either. But as he made the rounds inquiring about potential jobs, a very dark-skinned young man, standing nearby in one warehouse loading area, spoke up in broken Aramaic as he approached – though the region of his accent was impossible to pinpoint.

"Pardon me, sir," he said, smiling. "If you looking for the job, you try ... maybe you try to south docks. They have less business, not so big ships. Don't pay so well. So, they need often workers. They do."

"Thank you," Jesus answered in a clear Aramaic, trying to reduce his hill dialect. "I'm not looking to work the docks. I'm a builder. Thought maybe the harbor control or one of these warehouses might need carpenter, a builder."

"Still, sir, I think you better off on south side. I've slept here, ah, lived here, for a while now – I tell you, guys that work jobs here in north harbor, they don't leave." The speaker introduced himself as Devdas, coming from far to the east, his dark complexion accentuating his effervescent smile. He suggested to Jesus some possibilities: ships in port were sometimes short on carpenters for their voyages.

Devdas spent his days at the docks, hiring out as a translator. He'd picked up Latin as well as Greek during his time in Tyre, and could get by in Egyptian and Arabic. His native Hindu and a bit of Farsi were unique, however. As traders would load caravans from ships, Devdas helped negotiate prices and agreements. He'd hooked up with some scribes to help them write out contracts in the local Canaanite tongue, Aramaic or Greek.

As Jesus thanked him and turned to leave the storage yards – following another rejection – the Indian caught up with him. "If you like eastern food, me can you join for dinner – I be off work soon. Ships don't dock or leave, ah, depart this late in the day – and wagons, they like to pick up goods in the morning. I start with Sun come up."

The small canteen where they met was just north of the causeway on the mainland side. The food was strange to Jesus – very spicy and heavy on a whitish colored grain Jesus hadn't encountered – rice. Still, he'd ignored traditional Judean eating dictates for so long, the unique meal, mostly vegetables, wasn't an issue.

Devdas had recently moved into a warehouse ground-level storage area – with permission of the owner for whom he often did favors. He could offer Jesus some temporary housing for free – a price the latter could afford. Packing hay, laid on top of rough wooden slats, insulated the cold floor and made for comfortable sleeping. They had to get up and get out before workers arrived – and that was early.

In coming days, occasionally another itinerant or two would join them in the damp, dingy – but gratis – storage room confines. With lodging costing nil, board was the only expense. Jesus could pick up bread and things at markets, living much cheaper than were he eating at taverns. This allowed time to explore Tyre – its extensive shipping trade, its purple dye operations and job possibilities.

For ages, the Murex rock snail had been harvested from the eastern Mediterranean and processed into an intense purple dye – an early and longstanding contributor to Tyre prosperity, aided by Roman royalty preference for that color toga. Devdas' lodging on the peninsula, primitive as it was, was strategically upwind – mostly – from several mainland dye production sites: rotting snails put off a horrid odor.

Even with expenses low, Jesus couldn't manage for long, not wanting to dig into cash reserves. Jobs were indeed available at the south dock. Hard work there paid very little, but it covered food plus a little. And it was day labor – Jesus could take days off as he wished to walk out to the countryside and explore the province. He'd befriended Devdas and learned much from him. Late night discussions of Hindu precepts vs. Hebrew traditions exposed many contradictions as well as some similarities. And with some practice, the easterner's Aramaic improved rapidly.

"We have gods, indeed," related Devdas late one night after some shared wine that soothed Jesus' aches and pains from heavy labor, "but they are optional, more or less. You can acknowledge them or, you might call it, worship them – small sacrifices and specific rituals..." Indeed, often Devdas would imbibe a special ritual drink he called Soma – an extract from a mysterious plant he could get only from that mainland Indian café. He did this in front of a small oil lamp flame while sitting erect and chanting quietly. The easterner explained chanting – its purpose to free the mind, allowing it to transcend its fixation on the real. He described as best he could, sometimes relying on Greek, seeing the life experience as spiritual unity, a connectedness to the whole, the cosmos.

Such thinking was foreign to Judean understanding, which posited a creator god and his interactive intent for mankind – basically ignoring any context to existence or any significant status to individuals. Such discussions, with the need to illustrate ideas outside the scope of thinking in the Galilean/Judean culture, was impeded by the lack of Aramaic words – and even concepts – to allow easy communication. Jesus, to explain, could counter that his Hebrew traditions saw Yahweh-god as the supreme source, which might relate to Devdas' ideas, in that events encountered must manifest from the single god-source, as power was seen to reside in him.

"But gods must fit into the universe, not dance around outside, it seems to me," Devdas commented. "For us, *Dharma* is all inclusive. You can't sit on the outside and observe it. You can't create mind pictures and descriptions – you can only clear the mind in order to perceive it." As he continued to picture *Samsara*, the life cycle of birth, death and rebirth, and *Moksha*, ultimate release from that cycle, difficulties increased: Devdas' native Hindu expressions were complicated and had no equivalent in either Aramaic or Greek. To get his points across, he had to painstakingly explain each aspect of the Hindu world view. But conversations spanned evenings – though mostly they confused and irritated any others that might spend nights sleeping there.

Jesus had a feel for Devdas' meaning, though. He'd encountered Greek concepts of Logos and related it, in his own thinking, to a creative power agent, perhaps emanating from Yahweh, perhaps equivalent to the "Holy Spirit" aspect of divine breath, where an agent force actually implemented Yahweh's initiated will. This notion, difficult for Jesus himself to put into words, constituted a conceptual leap from the dictatorial, punishing war god normally pictured in Hebrew lore and prophetic poetry. Such conclusions he'd earlier tried to formulate only raised the ire of rabbis and traditional thinkers in Sabbath synagogue discussions wherever he'd been. Few of them, he'd noticed, ever liked to have their favorite ideas questioned.

But late-night talks with Devdas presented another eye-opening realization he hadn't picked up on earlier – though *it should have been apparent*, he thought. It didn't matter if you held and worshiped a god, be it Yahweh of the Judeans, El of the Canaanites, Zeus and his pantheon of the Greeks, Chemosh of the Moabites across the Dead Sea, or take-your-pick Hindu gods – life worked *anyway*, in all instances. It might incorporate goodness and evil, health or illness, prosperity or poverty, but it worked. Accepting Yahweh or gods Devdas pointed out, Shiva and Vishnu, and even sternly following divine dictates as revealed by prophets or rituals held by pagans had seemingly little effect on life's quality – people from any culture had good lives or bad regardless of ritual. These ideas impacted Jesus – from then on, as he prayed, he often would simply quiet his mind, not formulate his desires and queries for presentation to a god who, he concluded, *must have known them anyway.*

After some months, Jesus found construction repair work to alternate with heavy labor jobs. As those stretched out – bringing some money but no satisfaction – at some point, Jesus felt ready to move on. One option was hiring onto a ship, if they would take an inland-trained carpenter on a sea voyage. Devdas, always helpful, inquired around through his many connections. After several months more and a few dead ends, he found a ship owner, Anakletos, who needed a carpenter on board, provided he was willing to work otherwise – and accept low wages. His shallow draft cargo vessel, clearly not in the best of shape, was headed to Greece with bags of crushed lime, amphora of Samarian wine, hemp along with rope made from it and loads of grain.

Anakletos anticipated the standard, good weather route: proceed northwest out to Cyprus, sail west around the south shore, then head north for Lycia and pass by various islands on the way to Argos and Athens. Should bad weather kick up, they would veer north, then skim the coasts of Syria and Cilicia as needed.

"I take you on, Yeshua, once we are loaded" said Anakletos, "but you go first to Sibyl and tell me what she says."

Jesus agreed, not really knowing whom he meant. Devdas clarified it that night: no seaman would set out on a voyage without consulting an oracle to prognosticate the weather and success. The Indian laughed, "that Greek only wants to save his own money on the Sibyl. He'll have *you* pay for his divination!"

Devdas knew of the Sibyl – and only later did Jesus recall having heard of her. Three main fortune tellers worked the city – more, even, at bargain prices if you inquired in back alleys. But the best was the Sibyl. You needed connections to find her, as the authorities and sometimes the public would blame earthquakes, foul weather or other disasters on such oracles – seen to anger the gods through their inquiries.

After work one evening, just after dark, Jesus met Devdas at the mainland café. He thought it must be the Sabbath: as the two walked, many local Judeans were filling the streets in their quarter, talking rather than working. The Galilean mostly hadn't followed traditional precepts during his stay in Tyre – when working, he was expected there every day, customs or not. *Good,* he thought, *that mother doesn't know.*

As they wound their way through ever darker streets – poorer quarters weren't well lit – they had to watch their step, feces and urine, animal or human, being an ever present hazard adorning the rough hewn street blocks and gravelly dirt. Soon they headed up a hill; past a noisy tavern and closed shops, the street turned to sandy dust. Shortly Devdas turned into a dusky courtyard and stopped, motioning to Jesus to stand back. He knocked on a large gate with a measured rhythm – apparently a signal. The gate was opened by a hefty, remarkably light-skinned man, seemingly gray-haired in the dim twilight. As Devdas waved for Jesus to join him, it became apparent the man was blond – giving a strange effect in torch light inside the enclosed courtyard.

Entering a fragranced room, their eyes adjusted to colorful silken curtains covering most wall space. Baskets, wicker shelves and small tables sat along the walls; three oil lamps extended dim, moody lighting, animating flickering shadows around them. The blond man motioned for the two to sit on large pillows near the center. He spoke in broken Latin, which Devdas answered, then translated, "We should wait here. He says to relax and clear our minds – to think on whatever troubles us."

Fortune tellers were found everywhere. Jesus had seen many around the Decapolis; one actually frequented Tiberias even before people were living there. Capernaum had its seer, albeit an amateur – unless, that is, one wanted to pay. (Word had it that paying would elicit better readings and many thought that to be true.)

But this Sibyl, a title reserved for the best, for those who *communicated* with the gods, not just tapped into their realm as seers, was highly regarded. Hadn't that woman along the way said she was always right? Jesus had heard several stories about her at the docks and in taverns.

The blond man having left, the two sat and waited. "Should we ask her something?" whispered Jesus. "How does this work?"

"Don't know – never, ah, been here," said Devdas, cowering noticeably. "But I will ask Lakshmi to watch over us."

He stopped when the far door slowly opened. A fair skinned woman with long, silken sash, shimmering blue entered slowly and deliberately. Neither young nor old in appearance, she looked as one who, once reaching an early maturity of womanhood, never changed – or else, Jesus thought, amusing himself, *she dims the lighting accordingly as years pass.*

The Sibyl looked at him and smiled, as though she had heard and gotten the joke. Indeed, she looked younger as she approached, staring directly into Jesus' eyes as she sat on her own pillow across a small table from the pair – itself unusual, as women generally avoided eye contact.

Jesus started to speak, but her immediate hand gesture quieted him. "Tell me nothing," she spoke in Aramaic heavily tinged with some exotic accent. Pontus? Cholchis? Jesus couldn't tell the origin and could hardly ask Devdas for his thoughts. She had no cards or bones, no glass crystal. She sipped a small drink and closed her eyes, then gyrated slowly. She hummed, tipping now gently right then left, raising her hands in gestures, as though beckoning, resisting, denying, urging.

Devdas, sitting at first in meditation, slumped as he dozed off. Jesus sat in rapt attention, fixated on the softly rocking woman. At length, she stopped, then opened her eyes, now piercing, gazing directly into Jesus' eyes, but with a focus through them, as if to something beyond.

The Sibyl spoke, now in a guttural, distant tone, "You lead

your sheep to high mountain grasses, but when you sleep, they wander down to parched valleys."

Quiet filled the room as wine a goblet. Jesus sat transfixed as the woman closed her eyes again and resumed rocking, left to right, right to left, humming, sometimes mumbling.

At length, she stilled her motion, then glared again at the Nazarene. "I see a lioness surrounded by four bulls and two doves. One bull approaches you and lifts you on his horns. Two lie down and sleep. The fourth walks away." She closed her eyes momentarily. "The doves fly off, leaving the lioness. She is raised up on a throne, high on top of a pillar. But the column turns to straw and the throne to chaff."

Eyes closed again, the woman resumed rocking. Speaking now with eyes shut, she said, "Ships will take you to lofty places."

Huh? Lofty places? Jesus thought, *ships only ride the sea.*

Immediately, the Sibyl stopped rocking and opened her eyes, peering with intensity. "Cities you build on those hills will all crumble. But their foundations remain. Others erect buildings on those footers and call them yours – but they are not yours." She spoke now forcefully.

Her gaze drifted through Jesus again, as though to a horizon unseen. "You speak of the sunrise, but people hear only about the sunset." She paused. "You speak of orchards and green hills, but they hear only of the valley of the shadow of death." Another pause. "You hand them lambs, but they receive only bears."

The woman wilted, eyes shut again, as though faint, slumping like Devdas momentarily before reviving and speaking, "Generations unborn, will follow your name but *never know you*."

Eyes open and ablaze, she spoke firmly, "Those who try to be first will be last."

Jesus was trying to analyze these statements. *A lioness, ships, first and last,* he thought. *People often miss my meaning, but this is crazy.*

"You are about to continue your journey. Act when you must." Her stare now emphasized an immediacy, a focus on more timely things. "Follow as the scroll beckons. The journey will end only when the wooden post is fixed upright."

She closed her eyes again, rocked for a moment, then relaxed noticeably into a casual posture and opened her eyes. "That's all I get now. Do you have any specific questions?"

Jesus' mind was whirling. "Yes, about the lioness and the bulls…"

"I said nothing about animals," she said. "The realm of the gods swirls with images, with symbols. I can only report these. You must make sense of them according to your life and your understanding."

The thought occurred to Jesus that such divination was strongly forbidden by the priesthood, condemned as sinful and punishable. But how did this soothsaying, tapping into information in intangible realms differ from what the prophets did?

"So the lioness was…" Jesus started.

"Someone? Something? I don't know," came the answer. "You must know. That's all I was given."

Interesting, thought Jesus, then his pending voyage came to mind. But he wasn't sure if her comments about the journey and the wooden post – *the mast*, he thought – covered that. "Ah, how will my sea venture work out?"

The Sibyl took a drink and started to rock gently, eyes shut. Momentarily, she looked downwards, eyelids seeming heavy, and spoke, "Keep land always in view off the starboard. The ship will attain its destination, and you your destiny."

"I'm curious," Jesus said as he reached for his money pouch. "What are you drinking?"

"Water."

"Water? From the Tigris, maybe? The Jordan or…"

"No, from the local well."

"But most seers use…"

"Props? Tools? Potions?" The oracle smiled. "If you live far from the market, you must ride a mule or a wagon hitched to a donkey. If you live near the market, you can walk."

Jesus smiled and nodded. He turned to nudge Devdas.

"Huh," the Indian awoke.

"We're finished here, unless you have a question of the Sibyl," he said, then turned to face the woman as he shifted to stand. "What do I owe you?"

"I waive my fee," she said, to the surprise of both men. "Indeed, I've been told to give you these." She reached into her tunic and laid out five gold aurei on the small table between them.

Jesus was stunned. He picked up the coins and handled them. The gold glittered even in dim lamplight. He'd never seen an aureus, but knew the value of one to be at least 25 denarii – or 400 copper asses. With that cash, he could travel for some time, take a ship in comfort instead of working on one.

"Very nice of you," he said as he laid the coins back down. "But I feel more comfortable with money I've earned." He laid a sesterce and an as on the table, which he calculated to be quite generous – her information seemed valuable, however cryptic.

Devdas' eyes widened in surprise. The Sibyl took the coins and returned them to her pocket. She smiled, rose and quietly left the room.

Anakletos took Sibyl's prophecy as reported by Jesus to indicate fair sailing for his intended route, as Cyprus would always be off starboard when they rounded the southwest coast, then sailed north to Asia Minor. So the vessel, *Praise of Antigone*, heavily laden when Jesus arrived, set out for Kition, roughly central on Cyprus' southern coast, from which they could hug the coastline westwards. Taking on fair winds from the southwest, *Antigone* made good progress. The ship creaked steadily as wind drove the smallish sails smoothly on its northwest heading.

Scarcely glimpsing the white Cyprus town, they curved westward to proceed around the island, stopping at a village cove at twilight to take on fresh water and overnight. Pulling anchor next morning, they approached the Kourion promontory off Cyprus' south coast, navigating as close to shore as convention and experience allowed. Rounding that corner, they'd planned, the ship could proceed west-northwest around the island.

But winds picked up abruptly. Crewmen trimmed the sails, but began struggling to maintain balance and western heading – now having to tack, as their intended course headed straight into the wind. Bearing too far port would put them into deeper waters now rougher, kicking up in the wind. Their carpenter, already forced into numerous quick repairs on the aging ship, had been busy, learning rapidly on the job. But now he had to help with rudder maneuvering, correcting frequently as southward tacking attempted to clear the headland. Sailing out of its lee, stiff winds drove them eastwards – they couldn't tack to make the turn to northwest, and had to retreat to where they'd been. Hours passed as they tried repeatedly to clear Kourion's jutting shoreline, but the gusting wind scuttled each attempt.

Anakletos wanted to make yet another try, when Jesus intervened. He suggested to run south-southwest well clear of the promontory, then turn the ship with the stern to the wind, dropping the sails enough to not travel very far east, then continue the turn around and shoot northwest to clear the island. If they could just get around the edge, they could proceed, he reasoned. Mnesus, chief mate, questioned the plan. If they succeeded and a real storm kicked up – looking likely – westerly winds could drive them into Cyprus' west shore. They should head back east to dock somewhere, he advised, maybe circle the island that direction. Convinced of the Sibyl's warning to keep land off starboard Anakletos dismissed Mnesus' suggestion and was even wary about a jibe maneuver. But, faced with no alternatives, he decided to proceed. When the wind seemed to ease somewhat, he gave orders to go.

Mnesus barked commands to crew: they pulled in the foresail, whose mount, angled steeply to bow, groaned excessively, and trimmed the mainsail by half to maintain sail pressure and keep control. All the while, the shallow vessel began heaving in rhythm with the rougher waves out on deeper water, tempered only by the heavy ballast of full stores.

The south run worked. Clearing the outcrop by a safe margin, they could jibe around quickly, turning stern to the wind, while swiveling 270° to a NW heading. The ship caught the heavy wind and proceeded, though the sails took a shock during the jibe. Jesus, called to check mast supports, was sent back to the rudder: the crew's Attic Greek – differing in usage from the Koine dialect Jesus knew from eastern provinces – was difficult to follow when sailing got complicated. While *Antigone* passed Treta Promontory, then Paphos – midpoint on Cyprus' west coast – squalls churned up rapidly. Anakletos, now committed, doggedly pushed forward.

Storm clouds darkened the late afternoon sky. With land ominously close off starboard and surging gusts picking up, rain let loose. The ship's small crew quickly shifted into full emergency mode. Crude and rough when relaxed, the men intensified attention when conditions threatened not only the voyage, but, by now, the ship – and their lives.

Waves started to heave the ship first up, then sideways before dropping it in anticipation of the next roll. The crew tried to reposition the ship leeward to reduce roll, but gusts changed direction at a whim. Anakletos gripped the main mast in the stiff wind, reassuring then badgering crewmen with a slew of epithets – occasionally countering Mnesus' commands. The two started to argue, forced now to clear the island altogether – or end up dashed on its rocky Acamas outcrop. Meanwhile, waves splashed over the deck periodically and the skies darkened completely, leaving little visible from Jesus' angle at the stern, gripping the rudder hard with another crewman, reacting to surges and orders.

Having reduced sails and finally cleared Cyprus, the crew struggled into the night, hour after hour, with winds buffering and deep-water waves lashing *Antigone* relentlessly. Each lurch required corrective action to keep the ship at even keel. As skies lightened with morning, winds abated – but fog set in to dim visibility. Exhausted sailors could rest now, but not relax while drifting in thickening mist. At the bow, Mnesus began swinging the lead – sounding for depth – as the ship floated blind with the current. Tension escalated with low visibility and position unknown, *Antigone* relatively helpless in the calm: emergency oars on board were of limited effect with heavy cargo and no visibility.

Anakletos, soaked and frazzled, clambered up the stairs astern. "Poseidon has it in for us, Yeshua! – what in…" his next phrase wasn't clear to the Galilean, but had something to do with Venus' crotch, "did that devil female Sibyl tell you? I followed what you said! Look what you've gotten us into!"

Jesus, weary, cold and sore, didn't feel like taking any blame, "She said keep land off the starboard!"

"We did that!" bellowed the ship's owner. "We should have had fair sailing! The gods…"

"No we didn't!" Jesus shot back. "From Tyre out, we were in open seas! We would have had to hug the coast north."

Anakletos scowled and started, "You got us…"

"I didn't do anything!" Jesus cut him off, holding the rudder steady. "You heard what you wanted to hear, Anakletos. Crossing straight to Cyprus isn't keeping land off starboard. You're the seaman – you should have known that!" They both knew routing along the Mediterranean coast – though considerably longer and slower – would have been safer. They could have ducked into a port or protective shoal when bad weather hit.

The Greek fumed, "Hold your tongue, carpenter, or you'll be in big trouble!"

"Big trouble?" Jesus laughed out loud. "We could have died back there!"

Just as he spoke, sailors on the prow yelled, "*LAND AHEAD*," "*MAN THE POLES!*"

The ship lunged suddenly to the starboard as a loud crack rang out.

Anakletos turned. "We've run aground!" He flew down the stairs and clambered to port bow. Within seconds, he waved for Jesus to follow. At impact, Jesus had veered the ship starboard, sensing further danger off port bow; he now gave up the rudder to hurry forward.

The ship, at the mercy of wind and current, had traveled blindly an unknown distance northwards during the night. Approaching land somewhere along the rugged southern coastline of Cilicia, adrift in the fog, it had impacted an underwater boulder and reeled to the right as consequence. While crewmen pushed the vessel away from the rocks with long poles, Jesus scrambled below deck, pushing past cargo, feeling his way in the dark to the damaged area – with Mnesus right behind, cursing that he hadn't detected the reef. Water gushed in rhythmically as the ship lunged in the waves. The two, struggling against water pressure, managed to force broken hull slats back into the hole, reducing flow to periodic rushes during dips in the rocking.

"Hold this, Yeshua? I'll get help." Mnesus said. "If we founder, we'll have to abandon ship!"

"No," said Jesus, getting a feel for the situation, "damage is pretty high on the hull. Start somebody bailing. If we can move some heavier cargo to starboard and back to stern – we could lift this port side out of the water. The hole can be patched, I think – but it has to be out of water as much as possible. And somehow, I'll need some light."

Mnesus, grabbing a heavy wedge from under a carton, slammed it several times into the deck above, cracking two boards. He then twisted the wedge between the boards and broke out a hole to let in some light. "Yeah, we can trim to starboard – I'll shift some cargo – see if we can trim the hull to stern. That'll lift your hole out of the water."

The ship had cleared the rocks, as crewmen pushed it away from shore. Maneuvered about, however slowly with long oars, then having picked up a breeze, *Praise of Antigone* made the lee of an apparent headland. Waters were much calmer there, but the crew was spooked. Mnesus hustled back up on deck. He ordered available hands – against the owner's railing – to move some cargo to starboard stern, reducing pressure on the break.

With the damaged hull visible now, Jesus calculated provisional repairs. One crew member, sent below to help, held the broken boards roughly in place, Jesus smashed two large amphorae of wine – already cracked and leaking from the jostle – to provide pieces of crockery to reinforce shattered planks. He grabbed several boards from his small work area and nailed them into place, pressing large shards of crockery against the wood to hold it firmly.

It wouldn't push inward, but might get sucked out by wave action, he concluded. Thinking quickly – tar couldn't be melted to fill the cracks – he broke into a container of crushed limestone cement.

"How you gonna mix that down here?" yelled the crewman, as *Antigone* rocked and lunged. His back pressed against the patch and surge pressure.

"We'll let Poseidon do the mixing!" Jesus answered. He stuffed handfuls of dry cement into spaces behind and around amphorae shards and patching boards. As it rinsed out, he added more and pressed it into place with rags and straw packing material. Slowly the margins hardened and eventually quit rinsing out. "Hold that as best you can. I'll have Mnesus send down relief when you get tired."

The captain and mate were bellowing at each other as Jesus came up on deck. Imminent danger had abated, but their loud quarrel had the crew confused.

"If you two have a minute," Jesus stepped between them. "The hole is patched – it's holding. If we can keep the damaged area raised up like that, we should be able to sail on for now – but we'll need to find a harbor to replace that patch. And we'll need somebody down there to hold it – keep an eye on it."

Anakletos and his first mate eased up squabbling. As fog lifted, winds picked up appreciably. And correspondingly, tempers abated. Weary crewmen worked the vessel to resume full sailing posture. Blown northwards they'd caught rocky outcrops off Cilicia. With manageable winds now, they reset sails. Tacking first away from the coast, they turned northwest toward Attalia, then southward around Lycia.

"We might have just put in at Attalia, to the north," Jesus commented to Mnesus as the ship, resuming a southeast heading, rounded – and judiciously avoided – craggy outcrops off Sacrum Promontory and headed west. He didn't feel comfortable, after several heated encounters, approaching Anakletos. "Don't they have a port?"

"They cater to Romans," Mnesus explained. "They don't provide dock space to wayfaring merchant vessels – without a hefty price."

"Then we'll stop at Rhodes?" questioned Jesus as they sailed well clear of Myra parallel with the coastline, but well away from any potential hazards. "We shouldn't risk Athens with that patch."

Mnesus frowned. "They know Anakletos too well there. It's not where we want to be going. I think it's pushing Fortuna against Poseidon, but he'll likely press on to Kos. That harbor's reasonable."

In time, they cleared north of Rhodes and passed rugged Triopium Peninsula, jutting out westward from the mainland.

Headed north, approaching Kos, they learned from a passing merchant vessel that harbor repair facilities there were overcrowded and likely couldn't allot the *Antigone* any dock space for days. Pulling in briefly to replace tainted drinking water, though, they heard that Miletus might host them for repairs. "Yeah, they'll host us, alright," moaned Anakletos. "All they'll want in return is my profit for the whole Caesar-to-Hades voyage."

Still, whatever the cost, they needed a more secure hull repair before navigating the complex of rugged islands and treacherous rocks between the Anatolian coast and the Greek mainland. Once they rounded Halicarnassus with its treacherous offshore islands, the next major port was Miletus.

Two days spent docking at that ancient Carian city offered much-needed relief to the weary crew – and some solid land to recuperate those sea legs. But, as they negotiated to rent dock space, other problems arose. Part of Miletus' harbor was closed – permanently. Whole sections had lost depth due to excessive silting from river runoff: the whole bay from Mount Mycale was slowing filling in from Mäander River runoff. That limit to docking space impacted the ship repair business, which had dropped accordingly – so supplies of pitch and sturdy repair materials were hard to come by.

Anakletos heard of a Jewish merchant in town who had cornered the remaining ship supply market – even though having lost prime docking space to silt. The next morning he sent Jesus and a helper looking for one Samael Yacovian, whose main warehouse was supposedly located on the south edge of Miletus, inland through the city.

From the west harbor, the two passed the theater and the baths, stopping at the lion statues to ask directions. Communication was tricky – the commonly heard Greek dialect here was neither Koine nor Attic. And the local language was a Carian-Lydian dialect – sounding to Jesus something like the

Hittite he used to hear from imported Sepphoris construction workers. That exposure had provided Jesus communication skills that covered *yes, no, thank you, "two goblets of wine, please"*, *"I don't understand Hittite – do you do Greek?"* and a wide variety of curse words and body part descriptors. That helped little, as townspeople weren't familiar with businessmen from port operations.

Passing the Temple of Serapis and the South Agora, the two tried repeatedly to ask directions to the Yacovian household.

No one was particularly helpful or even friendly. Miletus, formerly a prosperous city – the greatest of Greek outposts at setting up subsequent colonies around the Mediterranean – had fallen from its past glory. Merchants were active, wares and foodstuffs readily available at the extensive markets. But Jesus couldn't help notice that Miletus lacked luster, that certain vibrancy that accompanies prosperity – façades were chipped, things needed paint. People who could converse in Koine Greek – and cared to talk – spoke of old times: the heyday of shipping, Thales and the natural philosophers, the colonies, how things had been *before* the Romans.

"Anaximander and Anaximenes, they started it all," said an old-timer seated at an outdoor café off the South Agora. "Without them, Plato would have been a cook and Pythagoras a second-rate scribe!" And no, he wasn't familiar with the Yacovian operation.

"I've heard of Aristotle," Jesus noted, thinking to strike up a conversation, "but..."

"Pah," huffed the old man, lightly inhaling some wispy smoke. "Thales started it all right here! All things are made of water – he knew that. Anaximenes thought it to be air – of course, in different degrees of density. They were the first to actually *think!*"

"Ah ... air?" Jesus looked puzzled. "I don't understand that word."

"*Air*, you know." He pursed his lips and blew towards Jesus. "Air, the stuff we breathe, what holds the clouds and the rains." He exhaled a puff of smoke. "You see what I breathe out? Without the smoke, it is only 'air'. But it's *something*. It's not nothing!"

Jesus was taken aback. He hadn't thought of breath as a substance, like a "thing" such as water or clouds. But surely the clouds must ride something – it seemed obvious, now that he thought of things that way. He just hadn't considered that before. Back home, *breath* had a word for it, "*rukha*", but that referred to an action or *part of* the breather, even a spiritual aspect. "Did Thales mean all things have a spiritual aspect, as the gods and demons?"

"You mean Anaximenes?" the man leaned forward with a puzzled look. "Air is real – you can feel it!" He fanned his hand at Jesus' face. "I don't know what you mean by 'spiritual'. Daemons don't blow in your face."

It was too difficult to explain, given the language barrier. And time was fleeting – they had to find repair materials.

Finally, they'd made their way out of town along the main road. It had to be out here somewhere, they reasoned: harbor supply houses aren't hidden in the mountains. They finally asked at a large Roman villa, figuring a prominent Roman – or his slave – might know.

"I am Sama'el, the elder – son of Jacob, merchant of Pontus," said a smallish, white-haired man after alerted by the slave who answered the door. "How can I be of assistance?" He started in Lydian, switched to local Greek dialect, then on to Hebrew when the others didn't work.

Samael led the pair through several large rooms en route to the warehouse. The first room had a huge table for feasts or meetings apparently; the next featured several fountains, while another had three prominent altars, shrines to Apollo, Hermes and Aphrodite.

"Sama'el, I'm curious," asked Jesus, never shy about such matters. "Have you abandoned the Torah and the covenant?"

The elder man was put on the spot, a rare occurrence for the wealthy, established businessman. "Well, I, ah, no, not at all," he muttered, avoiding eye contact. "This is just for show, you see. I practice our long traditions, but I've found it – let's say – conducive to business relations to display the Roman gods prominently. We entertain various business contacts and…"

"And you imagine that Yahweh approves – as long as it's business?"

"Well," Samael huffed, "I've become very prosperous here, a stalwart of the community and, of course, the Jewish community. I've been blessed with great abundance and I fund many activities."

Still, the house seemed empty as they walked through spacious rooms and hallways. "And your household?" Jesus queried, "Are *they* all well?"

"Ah, well, ahhh … my wife, she died years ago. We have only daughters, and…" Samael opened the door to the storage room and seemed relieved to be able to change the subject. He directed two workers to retrieve pitch, connectors and planks requested. As Jesus and his helper worked with the supply attendants, discussing the ship's needs and potential repairs, Samael bid them good-bye and turned to leave.

Jesus commented, though, "you were telling me about your daughters."

"See here!" Samael protested, "I don't have to explain my personal life." He stopped abruptly. "Come with me. Let your helper gather materials. I'll have a wagon return you to your ship."

They walked back through the villa to a veranda, overlooking a spectacular view of the bay to the east, an adjoining lake scarcely separated from the bay, but highlighted by hills and promontories. Samael had his slaves bring cakes, dates, grapes and some late-harvest wine.

"Wealth covers many a wound, young man," the elder spoke in earnest, having tipped a couple of glasses and loosened up.

"But a deep wound will fester under any bandage," Jesus observed.

Samael shook his head, lamenting... "Two of my three daughters married Phrygians. They follow the cult of Cybele – scoundrels and sorcerers, both. They teach my grandchildren all manner of strange activity.

"And my youngest – the sweetest of all as she grew in these very halls and fields, now empty of her voice and charm – my youngest fell to all evil. She haunts Athens' streets, plying her very flesh in that vilest trade of all time, harlotry. I ask, how am I to endure it all? I would give my fortune to return my lovely daughters to their pristine innocence of youth!"

Jesus sat, taken aback, sipping his sweet wine. "Is it possible that you have provoked the ire of our Lord? Did you raise your children with the Law and Mishna teachings?"

"I tell you, sir – and I feel I can trust you as one of our own, close to our customs and honoring our traditions, yet removed from our community." Samael was trembling and near tears. "I tell you I taught them the way as purely and unwaveringly as the sun crosses the firmament. We never deviated in those days from Sabbath practices, from food preparation, from all the sacred rituals.

"But it seemed the more I showed them the way, the more they rebelled! I believe the eldest sought out a mate – she defied my arranged betrothals – sought out mates of the oddest formulations of blasphemy! If her boyfriends were not following Isis, they were raving of Mithras. If they didn't practice ancient rites of mariners, they cast evil spells and hearkened to Beelzebub.

"What is a father to do? I forced them to review the words of the prophets! I had them schooled in all of the aged writs and practices – but to no avail."

Jesus could only listen. *Shouldn't the honored traditions have brought reason to these girls*, he wondered to himself. *How could the innocent go so far astray?*

"I think I post shrines to Apollo and these other silly western gods just to punish the Lord for pain *he's given me*. I hate to say it, but how can sincere action be so thoroughly punished? I tread these empty halls alone, the echoes of my feet a yoke of punishment for the fleeting joys of my lovely daughters as they grew."

A servant interrupted to inform that materials were ready, already loaded onto a cart to head to the harbor. Jesus realized how late it was and expressed his sympathies, but, puzzled and lacking proper words of encouragement to give Samael, could only wish him well.

Back at the harbor, Anakletos was livid when the cart approached. "Where have you been? Drinking at the pubs? Finding games to play? They're going to charge me an extra day in port, while you are enjoying the city!"

"Next time, skipper, hire a magician in place of a carpenter," Jesus had grown sincerely tired of this owner, his demands and his blame of all things on anybody available. "Do you want me to repair the patch or not?"

"No, not here, not now – unless you want an extra day's dock time charged to your pay ledger!" the Greek bellowed, implying responsibility for all ship's ills were caused by its latest caretaker. "We'll move on to Ephesus – that is, if your patchwork will keep us afloat that long." He stomped off to order the ship ready to sail.

Jesus looked at Mnesus, who had heard the tirade; both shrugged.

The short voyage north to Ephesus required westward navigation to circumvent Trogilium Promontory jutting out towards Samos Island. Normally routine, the maneuver was hindered by the patch. This provisional repair, done in near darkness under threat of sinking, having held for many days, was now cracking and leaking with each surge in the waves. With a point of sail nearly directly into the westerly wind, they had to angle a close reach to the south and beat windward several times to clear the cape. This was nearly impossible to do while favoring the patched area with starboard and stern hull trim. With progress slow, it neared dusk when they finally could tack north to catch the lee of Samos, then ease into a downwind run. By then, not risking a run in darkness through the channel, they had to find a protected spot to anchor for the night.

The next day, with the patch barely holding with two crewmen pressing it firmly, they limped into the channel leading to Ephesus' port. Once *Antigone* was secured, Anakletos, looking grim, approached Jesus before he could begin repairing the patch.

"You're finished on this ship, Galilean," he barked. "See the paymaster at the table on the dock. We don't need you anymore. Shouldn't have hired an amateur ... hah! Fishing boats on the Sea of Galilee!" He muttered with derision as he walked away.

Jesus felt more than relieved at his fortune – the hull was so bad that little firm wood remained to patch to. Affixing a new patch to old material seemed idiotic. *The only thing likely to make the Greek mainland would have been my patch*, he chuckled to himself, picturing cemented planks and amphorae shards floating up onto a Greek beach. He retrieved his pack, two turban scarves and mantle from his cramped quarters – under the work bench – and his store of cash from behind the inconspicuous slab of wood where he'd nailed it. His extra tunic was too sticky from salt water, too old and dirty to bother with. *The next carpenter can at least start with a good rag*, he thought, tucking his money sack into his leather girdle while checking seams of his mantle for the rest.

Several sailors were approaching the paymaster's small table, where stacks of coins sat neatly in order of value: denarii, sesterces, asses, semis and quadrans. It was apparent Jesus wasn't the only crew member being let go. *Looks like Anakletos is saving some money on the short voyage to mainland Greece*, thought Jesus as his turn came up.

Counting the money he was given, he looked up at the paymaster and protested, "Hey, this isn't what I was promised!"

Anakletos and a gruff-looking crew member approached quickly as voices and intensity escalated. "Still causing trouble, Yeshua! Take your pay and get out of here."

"I'll be happy to if this gentleman will provide it. This isn't half what I was promised."

"We're only halfway to our destination," smirked the owner.

"Your destination would have been Poseidon's anteroom if I hadn't saved your ship. I should get a bonus! Besides, we're three quarters of the way to…"

"Give him a bonus," said Anakletos with mocking tones to the paymaster. "And make it three quarters – but deduct two amphorae of wine he broke and floorboards we need to replace!" He looked up, turning dour and threatening, "that makes us just about even. Now get…"

"Ah, yes," Jesus said, nodding. "But captain, if I'm buying the wine, you'll need a tip, too, eh?" Jesus tossed two quadrans gingerly towards the stacked money. Both the paymaster and Anakletos lunged for the table, sending coins flying in every direction. The sailors, anticipating getting cheated, too, dove for the bouncing coins in a melee of shouts and elbowing.

Jesus walked off the deck, heading down the road into Ephesus.

From the city gate, along a dredged access waterway, a wide, stone-paved path led gently upwards past the baths then directly eastwards towards the theater, sitting prominent, carved into the hillside. It appeared to be full. The walkway was busy, people hustling to and from the agora, stopping at stalls and tables all along the way. Jesus pondered finding a river to rinse off the salt, grit and general stickiness from the voyage, but thought the better of it when he realized how large a city Ephesus was – and just how filthy its river would be. He knew harbor baths would be water piped in from elsewhere – *something, if one of a very few obvious things, Romans were good for*, he thought.

A leisurely bath and rinse of all his clothes at the old harbor bath house – they would dry quickly in the hot sun – was well worth it, although the facility was well worn. Clean and feeling great, his long, black hair hanging out from the fresh turban, beard trimmed shorter from its scraggly, sea-farer look, Jesus headed into the throng. First stop was a café for a decent meal – the first in days.

He learned that the throng was in town for the upcoming festival at the Temple of Artemis – the famed shrine to the Greek goddess of something-or-other, Jesus couldn't remember. Next stop was the public toilets – fifteen or so holes cut into a long slab of stone, rinsed continuously underneath by a stream of water. Most were occupied with but a small gap between a large variety of cheeks.

Jesus wasn't used to group defecation, but *anything* beat facilities on the ship – hanging one's behind out over the railing, with guarantees to be laughed at if you took too long. He disrobed as best he could, given tight quarters, and sat down.

"Jewish, eh?" the next occupant noted. Conversation was lively in such facilities, and Jesus' origins were obvious, given the longstanding Jewish tradition of circumcision. "What brings you to a festival for the daughter of Zeus?"

"One or the other," joked Jesus, "Tyche or Yahweh." The seated crowd laughed heartily.

"Maybe the Moirai have spun a snag into his thread," blurted out another to more laughter.

The assemblage of seated men explained to Jesus that housing would be very difficult to find if he just arrived. The city population had swelled considerably for the annual festival at Ephesus' world-renowned Temple. Travelers arrived from all over, as evinced by the various skin shades and accents found even in that public facility. There would be celebrations in tents, entertainment in the theater and large gatherings at the huge Temple, just on the north edge of town. He might find the perfect match for a lifetime, Jesus was advised, or a good one-night stand, and certainly would find mead, wine or harder beverages – whatever in life he might be looking for. Except for, as one man sporting a Latin accent noted to more laughter, enlightenment.

Having attended to various physical needs, Jesus began to consider his next move. He had thought to land somewhere near Athens and perhaps explore that venerable home of philosophy. Why did he end up in Ephesus – near one of the great pagan shrines? What should he do here? Go look for another job on a ship to Greece or even Rome? Find the Jewish community and look for a place to stay, maybe work?

He wandered through the huge swarm. Clearly these partiers and celebrants would be up to all hours – he could join in and just sleep somewhere, though with considerable cash on him, that might not be wise.

Jesus shuffled along with the crowd. The main street ran north around the high hill dominating Ephesus' eastern edge and on eastwards to the Artemiseon, that great Temple. Heading south, it passed through more of the city, past an agora into a housing area. From there the broad walkway led eastwards and skimmed the hill past many more houses and other buildings.

Hmm, he thought, *big city … Might as well explore it.*

Heading past the agora then eastwards, he heard music from within a building to the left. Venturing in, he noted it was clearly Greek in nature, highlighting music and performance along with education and training. He saw much less emphasis on music back home, even in the Decapolis, though his traditional training did involve vocalization. He could recall chant and singing from childhood trips to the Temple, but not much at meeting places in Nazareth or Sepphoris.

Continuing on, he came to a Gymnasium. He wandered in through sports facilities – training rooms, baths and changing rooms – then into the inner court, an athletic field surrounded with columned walkways. The whole sports atmosphere reminded him of the Greeks he'd worked out with while touring the Decapolis: they loved their games and social engagement, one blending with the other, both lubricated by wine.

"Hey, big man," called out a blond, young runner from a group sitting in the shade by the track, clearly sweating. The athlete jogged over, smiling, passing along the colonnaded portico. The red roofing tile and clean, white columns set off the area from the hill behind. "Are you a runner? Ah … do you speak Greek?"

Jesus smiled. "Not usually both at the same time," he answered in his best approximation of Attic Greek. He wondered what he was getting himself into. He had competed well back then with his construction team, *but these young guys look pretty agile*, he thought. Stuck in Tyre doing heavy labor, he had bulked up somewhat – and was older now. He wasn't in shape for sprinting, and he expected these guys took running seriously. Adding in time spent in Capernaum and back at Tiberias, it had been years since he'd done that gaming. Now nearing 26, he wondered if he still had his legs about him. *Anyway*, he thought, *it's just great to be on dry land*. He rapidly concluded his sailing days were over.

"My name is Praxilaus, son of Melas of Sardis – well, originally of Sardis," the blond said, offering a handshake. He led Jesus over to his group. "We're looking for some competition – thought maybe you were in town for the games."

"I'm just passing through, I guess," Jesus answered. "Ah, what do you mean 'originally'?"

Praxilaus introduced his friends, four of them, then responded, "my parents moved to Pergamon after the last earthquake five or six years ago. Sardis was a mess – still is actually. But I like things better here. It's not always busy like this, but it's mostly fun. We work out, study – you know, business studies, philosophy."

Jesus quickly realized these were all young men from wealthy families, likely studying, maybe training for official games – certainly not working. He thought it fun to run a bit, so he joined the next round of competition.

"Oh, you're Jewish," Kerkyon noticed as Jesus removed his inner garment and girdle – Greeks always competed naked. "You'll have the girls all rooting for you if you compete in the games!" he joked.

Jesus kidded him back, "when you light a candle, do you put it under a shade?" The youths howled at his unexpected joke – Greek humor being more ribald and liberal than that of traditional Jews. He'd caught them by surprise.

After a few sprints and discus hurls, the group headed in for baths and refreshments. Jesus had competed well, but could neither keep up with Praxilaus nor out-throw Kerkyon. But he joined them as guest for the bath session – complete with food and rubdowns. The large pool and multiple hot baths were fairly busy, but not like the huge throng swarming about in the streets.

"So, outside of the Temple and festival, what goes on in Ephesus?" Jesus asked.

"Outside of the Artemiseon, there *isn't* any Ephesus!" came the answer from one stretched out on a massage table as others lounged in a spa. "This town lives off travelers, selling them food and cheap junk, kitsch associated with Artemis – oh, or Diana, as they call her now to suck in Roman travelers."

"Yeah," added Praxilaus, "but that makes it a good party

town. And the wine is good. You asked what goes on? That's about all you need, isn't it?"

Jesus smiled. *These kids must be 18, maybe 20,* he thought. *Life is a party for them and always will be.* Still, after months of works in Tyre and that miserable voyage, the waters sure felt good. *Two baths in one day,* Jesus pondered – *a couple more and I might shed this sea crud I've built up.*

Another man, older, approaching with a towel draped around his neck, spoke up. "Ephesus is an old and very cultured city," he said. "Don't confuse this madhouse with daily life here."

"You're Ephesian?" Jesus asked.

"Yes, my family has lived here for at least thirteen generations, probably more." The man spoke with a sophisticated air, accentuated by graying hair and beard. "Ephesus is the gem of Asia – third in the world for population, first in culture.

"Artemis is core to the city – but nobody honors the gods anymore, not like they used to. They go through the motions, yes, pay lip service. But stone statues surrounded by columns and old stories – these are only of meaning to the simple-minded. More important to Ephesus – far more, no doubt, as the future unfolds – is the heritage of Heraclitus."

Praxilaus interjected, "Yes, we've studied him – are you a teacher, sir?"

"Yes, Macharenes is my name, family Diophantine. I teach metaphysics and logic – you young gentlemen would do well to study onward."

"I might do so," said Kerkyon, "but these guys are more interested in studying female anatomy." The others laughed.

Macharenes smiled, "Truth is useful, and I suspect there is truth in your observation. But one must not exclude exploration because of infatuation. The two are aligned, not opposed. Though, I suppose," he added with a demonstrative sigh, "the latter may well eclipse the former in focus during your time of life."

"Heraclitus," Jesus reiterated, "was from Ephesus, then?"

"Oh, most absolutely – in former times when Cyrus of Persia ruled, some five centuries ago," the elder spoke while easing himself into the water. "But his message lives today in these halls – and throughout the world in gymnasia where clear thought is prized. He understood the flow as few others. The flame seems to be a thing, yet is always changing, always in a state of flux. He saw life like that. 'No two men ever step into the same river,' he said, 'for it is always changing.' We look at things and desire stability, fixed conditions and reliable situations our minds can deal with.

"*Hērákleitos*," Macharenes continued, emphasizing the philosopher's name in local pronunciation, "looked at this same realm we all see, but saw it differently. We see things engaged by the gods through men's actions and believe we derive meaning from it. He saw movement as the basis, unfolding in its own meaningful way – whether or not influenced by or even *noticed* by the truculent participant."

Jesus, relaxing, eased himself waist deep into the spa. "But how would this change, this flow, affect life? What difference does it make *how* you see the world – what meaning you apply – if what you experience is the same anyway?"

"Aha, but who can detect a difference? You only walk down one path – and that path seems fixed ahead of you. But if you change your evaluation of the path, might not that revise the coming course – somewhere up ahead, around the bend and out of sight?" Macharenes leaned back, settling deeper into the warm pool. "If I believe the world is static and fixed, as per Fate, I might not try to change it. Why should I? What difference does it make if I'm sitting in this basin or standing to the side? Worse, if I believe some god – Artemis or Tyche on a whim, or even Yahweh for his own purpose – is decreeing all events to their own rationale, *their* intended ends, why should I try to accomplish anything? But if I see the world in flux, flowing, changing, might I be able to divert that stream's flow to my own purpose, my own ends?"

"Good point," Jesus noted. "You could – and I think many people do, so far as I've seen – just sit back and take things as they come. Divine what their favored gods have in mind and concede their lives to that. Heraclitus must have thought that, detecting the *source* of the flow – if not from the gods – one could divert it from the source!"

"Yeah, I can see that," Kerkyon added. "If you think things are frozen – or even predestined, why try to do anything?"

"You got it, friend," chimed in Praxilaus, "better to drink wine and chase girls!"

Kerkyon ignored the frivolity. "But what about *Logos*, master, the *Word*? Is that the source? Didn't Heraclitus develop that idea of Plato and Aristotle?"

Macharenes interrupted quickly, "Let us line up our thinkers in order, young man! Heraclitus predated Plato and his student Aristotle by a century. Our townsman laid out an image of Logos as a principle *by which* reality is generated, one might say. The later thinkers had differing conceptions as to Logos, more limited.

"For Aristotle, *Logos* was a means of argument, a way of formulating thought into words that could make a point. But beyond straightforward 'logical' reasoning, *Logos* itself constitutes the very ability to express complex thoughts. It sets man apart from other animals. It allows the differentiation between good and evil, just and unjust. Hmm? Important points of argument, gentlemen, but not what Heraclitus meant.

"To Plato, *Logos* seemed to be an intermediary step between creative thought and real event – *The Word* doesn't *cause* the happening so much as shape it, formulate it. For Plato, the overall 'One' was the cause of the Form and the Form in turn was the cause of the material."

Jesus, sitting fascinated, had to interrupt. He had a general notion of Plato's ideas from long discussions late into the night in Tyre and Greeks from the Decapolis. But those, he thought, weren't all that accurate, nor certainly detailed enough to grasp Macharenes' meaning. "I don't quite follow. Sorry, my Greek isn't equipped with some of those terms. As I recall, a '*Form*' is Plato's indication that behind each *real* object is an *ideal* one, a perfect example whereas real things are just flawed variations. Every block of stone, say, is but an example of an ideal block, an imperfect instance of a perfect stone-Form that exists somewhere, maybe in Yahweh's mind."

"Yes, indeed," Macharenes cut in. "But you must understand that Plato's deepest insights were never written down. Plato, unlike Pythagoras before him who rendered *nothing* to writing, composed many dialogues. But he was adamant that his most significant metaphysical vision *never be recorded*. However, his so-called 'unwritten doctrines' were passed to his most trusted students. I don't know the wisdom of not writing things down – it's difficult enough to comprehend things when written. Oral accounts or notes taken by others must be less accurate than words expressed by the originator. So I'm not sure."

"No, Macharenes, not necessarily," argued Jesus, raising his hand to emphasize the point. "I think, had Plato tried to be specific in all things, particularly the deepest truths, he could only have *failed* to pass along his ideas. Don't you see? Lesser minds would only argue over words and not see the real essence. Even I have encountered such resistance to argument – from people who don't really listen to better ideas, but only formulate their own viewpoints into rebuttals.

"On the other hand, those *open* to new perspectives and *capable of understanding them* would only be misled by the written words. They have to arrive at truths by themselves.

"Yes, it's clear." Jesus leaned forward, hand outstretched in emphasis. "For Plato, he would *have had to leave* his greatest insights unstated! It's the only way he could do it. He could hint and illustrate – but never state directly!"

Macharenes sat back, "I suppose you have a point there. I hadn't looked at it that way."

The Galilean went on, "For him, perhaps, *Logos* was a means, a … a sort of agent that transmitted meaning from a god – or wherever – into reality. It was a *Word* – that is, a meaningful utterance – whose sense became realized."

"Yes, yes," the elder continued, gaining excitement from a real discussion beyond his normal lecture points, "I think you have something there – concerning Plato. But Heraclitus *did* explain his deepest insights. We have lost some of his writing and some scrolls are aging now – it's always difficult to find funding to make copies – but we know his take on *Logos*."

"All the more reason to *not* write your thoughts down," Jesus noted. "Scrolls crumble and turn to dust. Ideas, if explained to intelligent listeners, persist."

"Well, perhaps," offered Macharenes, "perhaps. And I must admit that Heraclitus seemed to try to be cryptic rather than explicit. And at times his statements seem more to embody his point – in how they are phrased and illustrated – than simply explain the meaning.

"But beyond that – let me make this point – for Heraclitus, the idiom of *Logos* is much more significant than Aristotle's logical expression or Plato's agent of manifestation. *Logos* for the Ephesian Master was the *very process* of the 'One', the very progression of the *Word*, as meaning conceptualized in mind, becoming realized in events of life. His *Logos* was the link of the thought to the real – the *process* of manifestation, not the agent.

"He noted, perhaps with frustration, that humans seem inherently unable to comprehend that particular point – though it defines the flux, the flow of reality, thoroughly. I know how difficult it is in our modern day for people to see life as connected, self to all. It must have been worse in his primitive time. He noted that *all things* come to be in complete accord with the Logos. But people simply didn't get it when he explained it.

"Heraclitus wrote that most people simply follow common thinking. Even though he would explain the Logos, most of his contemporaries just lived as though they had their own private understanding – thinking that their view was valid *just because they held it!*"

Jesus stepped out of the spa and grabbed a towel. A servant had brought some breads and vegetables, so, still deep in thought, he helped himself. "My people, with long traditions of shared belief, see the world as the creation of a single god. But the *Logos*, as you picture Heraclitus' view, doesn't seem to feature a source – an initiator. How could you have an outcome, a result, without a source? Doesn't an effect need a cause?"

Kerkyon added, "Yeah, where is the *prime mover* in the Logos of Heraclitus?"

Macharenes sighed, "Alas, I am not Heraclitus! I can relate what I know of his philosophy, but I cannot answer queries as though I were he."

"Perhaps the cause isn't external, isn't a god off somewhere else," Jesus paused to chew while silence settled over the group, all awaiting the darker complexioned man to speak, "Perhaps…"

Jesus' mind traced his many experiences, his observation of how troubled people encountered trouble, with aggressive people only ever coming upon conflict, with some having only good happen to them and others only bad. He thought of his own prayers, of Yahweh seeming aloof and unattainable, but how things always worked well as he himself journeyed through life – while many others only encountered difficulties.

"Perhaps the cause is…" He finalized the thought, as much to himself as to the others. His face brightened, "One's … own … *self!*"

Praxilaus protested, "Huh? How can I make my own life? I would give me everything I wanted!"

Another started, "but the gods must…" But he was cut off

by Kerkyon.

"Nah! Too much in life just happens by chance," he said, at which point many conversations broke out, even from others who were sitting nearby and listening.

Yes, those are all good points, Jesus considered, but kept his original thought stream in mind.

Macharenes approached Jesus near the food as the youths sat in the pool arguing. "You have quite an astute mind for philosophy, young man. Are you a student here? I haven't seen you here before."

Jesus introduced himself. "I'm only traveling, passing through. I haven't studied, save for the scriptures back home. But I've been around – heard some of those ideas."

"I couldn't imagine you were here for the festival. Fawning after Artemis seemed well below your level. In any case, I must go now. If you stay in Ephesus, I should enjoy another such session. Heraclitus had much more to say – we could continue the discussion."

For Jesus, persistent talk over mere concepts was much less important than personal realization – like the one he'd just had. He'd been thinking for some time, noting how people consistently experienced similar situations and it all seemed to fit: the *Logos* – or whatever name one would put to the process – simply reissued meaning back into one's life, instilling events which one's own nature attracted. He was impressed that a man 500 years before had grasped that, as did Plato a century later. Had Moses also understood this? Had the prophets seen the connection, but failed to explain it adequately?

Leaving the bath, Kerkyon offered Jesus sleeping space for a couple nights, but no more, as he awaited cousins from Smyrna for the festival. The following day, as the group reassembled, Jesus told the others of his travels and work experience. Not attuned to such hordes of humanity, though, he made plans to set out the following day, perhaps to Sardis or Smyrna, and inquired about the two cities.

Praxilaus recommended Sardis. "There is plenty of construction going on there. The city crumbled down to its foundations not long ago. They're rebuilding everything, always looking for construction guys. But you might consider my father in Pergamon. He could use help. Father and Uncle Oliatos – along with two other families – decided to relocate to Pergamon after the earthquake. He had a small cottage there to live in while they built a villa on his land. The others are building, too. But it's going very slowly – local builders are not trustworthy, especially for outsiders. And they're too busy, so they cut corners. He and the others have said many times that they could use a consultant to watch over the projects. You might advise them."

Jesus considered his options through an evening's partying at a busy tavern, but decided to head off the sixty miles to Sardis. *More opportunities*, he reasoned.

Leaving Ephesus the next day, Jesus swung past the grand Temple of Artemis – truly a sight to the experienced builder, who had seen and worked on many a grand edifice. Some 450 feet long and half that wide, a roof the height of twelve men – held by 120 and more columns – it was spectacular. Although aged over 300 years, it was kept immaculate in accordance with its value to the city. Jesus didn't see it appropriate to pay to enter the central chamber, but could see the gilded adornments, paintings and sculptures between the columns.

With a long hike ahead, Jesus kept his eyes out for an approaching wagon to maybe catch a ride. But most traffic was headed into Ephesus, not away. He had passed through several adjoining towns, each diminishing in size as he left the city, when suddenly, he was grabbed from behind.

Pulled into a shadowy alleyway, two men pulled his arms back while a third pressed a dagger to his throat. The knife bearer uttered something incomprehensible, but the meaning was pretty clear. Jesus answered in Greek, "You would like my money, I guess."

"Good guess, Semite," said the one holding his right arm and pulling hard on his hair. His turban had already fallen off as he was pressed onto a bench. The alley was deserted and rather dark, though occasionally a horseback rider or wagon would pass by. "Call out, and those will be your last words."

"OK, let my arm loose and I'll give you my money. No problem." He reached into his girdle for his money bag.

"And your mantle." The thieves had felt coins sewed inside the seams. "We'll have that, too."

As the two held his arms behind the bench back, the first removed his sandals and wrapped them into the mantle. They left his small pack and water pouch. "Follow us and you'll die." They scurried off down the alley and disappeared into a side street.

Jesus rotated his arms, as his shoulders were sore, then walked back into the city.

"Prax," he said, having made his way back to the gymnasium to find his friends, "I've reconsidered the possibility about working for your father. Pergamon sounds like a good idea."

With spare coins sewn tightly inside the leather of his girdle, he'd purchased a new mantle, this one lighter and more local in style than his Galilean one, and sandals. He considered checking the marketplace the next day and simply repurchase his old one, but thought the better of it.

Before leaving Ephesus, Jesus acquired a long staff. This made hiking the roads more amenable, but also provided a useful deterrent to ward off mongrels and potential thieves. Villages on the way to Smyrna, rather clean compared to those back home, seemed heavily populated with children and unruly dogs – both roaming the streets, despite considerable traffic of horses, carts, mule-drawn wagons and an occasional chariot. Languages heard in village marketplaces were mixed, with most unintelligible, none noticeably Semitic. But Greek worked everywhere – though the accents were sometimes difficult to comprehend.

Smyrna lay on the coast, a prime and bustling port connected to a spectacular city. Its broad and colonnaded walkways, active scene and obvious prosperity made Jesus regret he had no time to spend here. So far, though, the cities of Asia Minor had impressed him in ways he hadn't anticipated. Walking through Smyrna, taking only time to purchase food for the next leg north to Pergamon, Jesus noticed just how active and lively these cities were – much more engagement of the present: business all around, but not to the exclusion of pleasure. He heard music as entertainment, saw billings for theater as art. Back home, by comparison, life was a daily grind for most, yet taxes here were at least the equal to those of Galilee – *except*, he reasoned, *for the Sadducee Temple tax and ongoing expense to cover ritual religious needs*. And he couldn't help but wonder what was gained by those expenses. Could Yahweh really care about temple activities and monotonously repeated rituals?

Rides Jesus managed to attract were short, as most traffic – at least farmers and villagers willing to take a rider, were local. Caravans of military supplies or merchant transports were clearly, from their attitude and armed guards, not inviting to even an inquiry. He laughed to himself, pondering asking a Centurion for a ride on his horse.

Jesus' generally clean look did help with the solo driver: the new mantle and trimmed beard presented a trustworthy look to private owners, who often simply wanted company during their journey.

From Smyrna northwards, though, roads led either over hills or around them – neither conducive to making good time, none well marked. Hiking through the hills provided some peaceful ambience and great scenery – much welcomed after the work of

Tyre and dangerous sea voyage. But sparse and poor villages, eking out existence, seemed universally suspicious of the tall Semite. Unable to get trustworthy information from locals, Jesus tried heading west towards the coast, reasoning that coastal ways should be straighter through lower regions – but that didn't work either. Hills and ridges jutted right out into the water.

Finally, trusting his sense of direction, Jesus simply headed north as much as possible and made corrections in towns where he could get a reasonably friendly, knowledgeable response.

Where Ephesus lay in the valley area surrounding a hill, much of Pergamon's splendor was perched pretty much atop one, visible from all around. The way there had been long and scenic – Jesus' first experience of countryside far removed from both Palestine and pure Hellenistic influence, as towns retained pre-Greek, pre-Roman character. One thing noted along the way – while his hike over many days took him nearly double the expected fifty miles – prosperity here, as back home, was held by a select few, while most worked hard with little to show for it.

Melas of Sardis was one of that select few. One of a long family line, well-connected and diversified in wealth, with agricultural holdings, fruit production and wagon manufacturing, as well as dye and textile production – most of which was manned by slaves – he and his brothers constituted one of a handful of families that controlled most financial resources in the region. Formerly centered in Sardis, he'd opted to expand to Pergamon when the most recent earthquake destroyed considerably portions of his holdings.

He first looked askance at this Galilean coming so boldly forward, offering to consult with his building projects. But he'd already heard from his son – a letter that arrived by sea carrier on a company shipping line – to expect this man. He didn't so much trust his son's good sense as want to promote his inclusion in decision-making. He interviewed Jesus for some time. The latter's knowledge of building technique and trustworthy demeanor were convincing in the end. Melas and his associates would provide sparse but comfortable quarters in his city holdings and Jesus would spend a day or two at a time at his villa construction site overseeing work there, then rotate to that of his brother, Oliatos. These adjoining plots on the opposite hillside to the west offered a spectacular view of Pergamon's theater, Altar of Zeus, upper Agora and all. Plus, if that worked out, Jesus would consult on two other nearby projects of friends and a city construction operation rebuilding and expanding some palace units behind Athena's Temple.

The job proved ideal in some ways, but demanding in others. Melas' need was an expert eye on building technique. Jesus had no work to perform, just oversee what was being done and report shoddy construction or faulty materials. And there was plenty of both, as neither slave nor low-wage laborer had much motivation to excel. But Jesus' many reports of short cuts and sloppy structural work hidden by plaster, a boon to his employers, was not welcomed by construction companies. With each report, he deepened his trust with Melas and Oliatos, but made enemies of people he dealt with daily who resented any skilled oversight.

But demands were minimal for excellent pay and free housing. With numerous sites to cover and various bosses to report to, he could make his own schedule. If he didn't show up for several days, each of his clients assumed he was tied up elsewhere. Rainy days and festival periods, he could do as he wished – though often he could inspect the work better on such days when no workers were on site.

The Pergamon arrangement quickly generated a comfortable lifestyle. With gymnasia and theaters, a vibrant social scene and many scenic, outlying areas to visit, Jesus was always active. He planned, inspected, gave reports, socialized, worked out, heard lectures and engaged in often deep, meaningful discussions with a wide range of scholars, students, itinerant speakers and philosophers. He connected to the Jewish community to keep his traditions in perspective – but increasingly argued with the rigid viewpoints of Sabbath lecturers and scribes, winning points, but often raising ire.

As weeks became months and even *they* passed quickly, Jesus made another discovery. He'd started out one day from his apartment – a room above palace maintenance operations behind Athena's Temple – when a heavy storm let loose. He ducked into the large library until it let up.

Curious, he approached the main counter clerk. With a glance at the many trimmed columns and marble accoutrements of the main hall, he made his way through quietly mumbling discussion groups and tables, half-filled with scholarly-types scrolling and perusing documents. The female clerk was pleasant and, he couldn't help but notice, quite attractive – darker in complexion than most he'd encountered in this more northerly region.

"Do you have scrolls in Aramaic?" he asked, thinking to try his eye at something unusual. He could read Hebrew well – as all fairly studious youths had learned back home. But Aramaic script differed. Jesus knew the characters, but hadn't ever read more than inventories and short accounts. It quickly occurred he might pick up the ability to write with a little practice – maybe expand to Greek as well – and enhance his role and other opportunities considerably.

"Yes, of course." As she looked up, the girl's dark eyes dazzled the tall Nazarene, who hadn't struck up a relationship of any depth since he'd watched Mary leave the beach in Capernaum. "We have over two thousand in Peshitta and other related Syriac. We have some ancient letters in eastern Mesopotamian. What subject matter are you looking for?"

"Ah," Jesus stumbled slightly, looking for a way to indicate he didn't read well while not revealing his shortcomings. "Well, something reasonably easy. I can read Hebrew and I know the

Aramaic script, but I just wanted something simple."

"Oh, yes," she responded cheerfully, "you want a short study guide. We have introductory scrolls in lower Syriac – you are from Palestine, then?"

"How did you know? I thought my Greek was pretty fluent."

She laughed, "Greeks don't speak Hebrew. I'll get you some scrolls – just be seated. Should I bring a Greek reader, too?"

"Hmmm." Jesus thought about that. He knew the Greek letters, too, and could read many words, but wasn't sure he could handle text.

"I'll bring them both. With that storm going on, you'll have enough time to peruse them." She disappeared through a door. In the great hall, few scrolls were stored. Most were retrieved on request from categorized storage rooms, built with air ducts to guard against dampness.

Aramaic, with some study over time as his work allowed, proved to be readable. But there was little variety in content in Aramaic scrolls held by the Great Library. For substance, Jesus needed to perfect his Greek reading skills – which he attempted in coming weeks.

At a café in the lower city, where he'd invited the library worker – Urshanabi was from Pontus to the east – they sat one afternoon over an early dinner. "Greek is very difficult for me to read," Jesus admitted. "I understand the words, but once I've read half a column, I don't know what it said."

"I know the problem, Yeshua," Urshanabi said. "I learned script as a child, both reading and writing and even I find long explanations difficult. Stick with things of most interest – they hold your attention.

"I enjoy reading about geography – I would love to travel – so that's easy for me to read. We have scrolls, new ones actually, from my region – they are wonderful! The author, Strabo – I think he's still alive – tells of people and places all over. Do you know how many lands there are?"

"Well, I never really thought..."

"Oh, there are people to the west, way beyond Rome, up through Gaul and to Britannica – as far west from Rome as Rome is from here! There are people from Spain on the endless ocean and Africa to the south."

"All the way past India in the east!" Jesus added.

"Oh, you know of the Hindus?"

Jesus told of his time in Tyre and his friend Devdas, the many discussions they'd had, and that easterner's different way of seeing things.

Urshanabi interrupted, "You know, if you are interested in such things, there are philosophy groups who meet at the library. You could chat with them and not have to dredge through long scrolls in Greek."

In coming months, Jesus engaged the philosophers' group and found more discussion sessions at the gymnasium he occasioned. He enjoyed the exchange of ideas, but had some problems on occasion with the participants.

One evening, after a long and detailed presentation on Aristotle's structured logic by a visiting scholar from Alexandria, the discussion turned to Plato vs. Aristotle on the nature of the universe. Several pro-Plato participants argued for his model that featured *forms* behind real objects, while others issued proofs – more rational than empiric – to back the Aristotelian model that *forms* are innate to the object itself, not properties separate and removed. The argument went back and forth. At length, Jesus interrupted.

"Much of the disagreement here," he pointed out, "rests on the *philosopher* more than the idea itself – its soundness, whether it's true or not. I've heard the implication over and over that some point is true *just because* Plato proposed it – or Aristotle, depending on who's saying it."

"Well, of course, Plato's works are the basis of..." one spoke up, only to be cut off.

"No, his pupil corrected many of Plato's errors…" interjected another.

"Errors? *Errors!?* Aristotle only posed conjecture," the first argued, "that questioned Plato's fine model."

"There you go – just what I mean," Jesus reiterated. "Something isn't true just because a great philosopher said so. It must stand on its merits."

"I beg your pardon," the evening's presenter broke in. "Who are you to question either of these two great thinkers?"

Jesus countered, "It doesn't matter who I am. That's my point. My identity, my authority, my reputation – none of these has anything to do with the validity of my ideas. They have to stand on their own rationale."

"Hah!" scoffed the Plato supporter who knew Jesus from earlier discussions. "Who has the mental acumen to even question these pioneers of thinking? Do you? Your people hold Moses and Isaiah with such esteem that no question is *ever* ventured."

"Many do, but not I – for that is just as blind," Jesus responded. "To me, what Moses said must always be questioned, doubted, explored until it is understood and verified. And that's the problem with these discussions. Many here exalt philosophers, holding them up as flawless authorities, never to be questioned."

"We are here to study what these brilliant masters taught, not to hold them up to exploration by lesser minds," countered another of the group.

Jesus spoke up: "We *should* be here to get at truth and understanding. If a past master is wrong, you'll never realize it if you *never question* his ideas. In any case, think of it this way: Plato and Aristotle proposed different models – you'll all agree to that, right?"

The group murmured in approval.

"So one of the two – or both – must be incorrect! To see which one, you have to question. If you hang on to either as the final expert, you'll never see his shortcomings."

Some of the group eventually caught Jesus' point and agreed. Others, while not relinquishing adherence to their favored source, could scarcely refute Jesus' point with a rational argument.

On other occasions, Jesus would take a Sabbath off to attend synagogue discussions in the Jewish quarter – a fair walk from his apartment on the hill. He enjoyed maintaining the connection to his people – it reminded him of home. But issues arose frequently that paralleled those of the philosophy group.

Once an itinerant speaker named Nachowr, claiming patrilineal connections to the Zadokite priesthood, spoke. He emphasized the need to conform in one's daily life to practices as specified in the Law and through tradition as promoted by the real experts in such matters, the Temple hierarchy. He reviewed the complex set of food preparation and asked if the local community was in line with these. Most in attendance were, but some looked away and didn't volunteer any comments. And not all were there.

Jesus spoke up, "Why should we follow those practices so routinely? Wouldn't the Lord be more interested in how we treat others – how we love our fellow man – than how we curdle milk?"

Following a stunned silence, quite a stir began to hum – just as Jesus had expected. Nachowr was jolted and immediately recited several passages of scripture to emphasize the need to conform.

Jesus shook his head, "But wasn't it written, 'For I desire mercy, not sacrifice'? Isn't it clear that one's actions are far more important than old rituals?" Jesus spoke calmly, while launching a boulder from his catapult of unusual perspectives.

"But, no, ah..." The visitor, visibly shaken, was searching through his memory of scriptures for a rebuttal. When nothing came to mind – he wasn't often challenged – he rationalized, "The Law can't be shoved aside, practiced *only* when convenient!"

Jesus shot right back, "What's the purpose of our detailed traditions of food preparation anyway? Isn't it to please the Lord so he will know our covenant is honored?"

"Why, yes, of course!" Others nodded.

"But for centuries now, no son of David has ruled the homeland. I come from there and can assure you that the house of Herod rules by *spilling* blood, not by holding a royal bloodline. Why is not that promise, as stated by the prophets, up for question?"

Jesus was cut off by an eruption of emotion. Nachowr's jaw dropped as the local principal bellowed, "Do you question the Lord?" The din rose.

"No, not at all," Jesus replied coolly. "I'm questioning Nachowr. He wants everybody to follow the rules. I'm just asking 'Why?' Simple question."

Nachowr raised a pointed finger towards the heavens, "Because the Lord punishes the unclean, the sons of Israel who don't abide by…"

Jesus stood, towering over the paunchy visitor, raising a hand to stop him. "I work with a lot of local natives here, with Greeks and Gauls and even Romans. You all know them, too," he continued, looking around the room. "You work with them and trade with them daily. *None* of them follow kosher rules. Not a one observes Purim, Pesach or the Sabbath. Most never heard of Yahweh and few give a hoot about Zeus or any other god. Yet they are healthy, free of poverty and live good lives.

"Back home in Galilee and Judea, our people live in poverty and often filth. They pay triple taxes – to the Romans, to Herod and to the Temple. Life is tough, a constant struggle. So I ask you again, why should we follow these practices when doing so seems to bring little by way of blessing?"

The crowd rose to their feet and several rushed at Jesus. Nachowr held his hands up to quell them, but one yelled out, "this man isn't one of us. He only comes sometimes – and he comes from the hill. Indeed, he must have walked very far today."

Nachowr took the lead, quickly falling back to a personal attack to undercut Jesus' critique, "So you, who would defile the Sabbath and question our Lord's commandments, want me to answer your blasphemous questions?"

"Well, yes, I thought you might at least try – rather than attacking me. So, you admit you don't have an answer to my question?"

The local authority, sensing growing difficulties amid swelling tumult, broke in to adjourn the meeting and herded his people out of the building. Nachowr avoided any further words with Jesus and hurried into the crowd to absorb adoration from people who had enjoyed his talk.

Jesus walked home, stopping at a tavern for dinner.

Having grown closer to Urshanabi during this time, he would often spend the night at her lower city apartment if they'd been socializing there. Urshanabi had been married, arranged in her youth with a Pontic tradesman. But her husband had been taken into the army and killed during a security action. Her father's family had settled in Pontus only after the Mithridatic Wars with Rome, so, not a native, she wasn't so tied into the culture there. When her husband died, her father brought her to Pergamon and, through connections, got her a position at the library. "You are very gentle, Yeshua," she confided one night in the quiet of her apartment. "Not like the men of Pontus. I didn't think men could be so considerate."

Jesus smiled as he gazed into her dark, trusting eyes. "You are a gem, Urshi," he said. "You would travel all of civilization if you could – yet you see much more in your scrolls than anyone could in a life of adventure.

"I tell you, travel isn't the carefree fun you think. Sure, if a festival party in Ephesus or a parade in Rome is your desire, that's gratifying. But for me, seeing the minds – hopes and dreams, interests and viewpoints – of the people, *that's* what is interesting.

"But the problem with even that, girl, is people's woes and pains. Some have so much – uncountable wealth, freedom and power beyond imagination. But others are so poor, diseased, troubled. How can that be changed?"

Urshanabi stared for long moments into Jesus' eyes. "I don't know. The asclepeions are built as healing operations. People come here from all around."

"The really ill and weak won't be coming to the baths of Pergamon. You should see the slums of Tyre outside the grand city, the poor villagers of Syria and Gaulanitis, plagued by taxes and thieves, the weak of spirit all over. They don't come out to celebrate wild festivals of Ephesus or healing spas of Allianoi. They sit in darkness and suffer; they rot as though dead, already looking forward to death as release."

"But the gods…"

"The gods, the gods, yes, the ever-loving gods!" Jesus sat up. "What good are they? Zeus? Show me the thunderbolt he ever hurled! Ba'al or Ra – what are they doing for their people now, right now?

"My people follow as sheep to the Lord Yahweh as shepherd. They mimic all the rituals of the great prophets, follow all manner of divine dictate – and what do they have to show for that devotion? Subservience to the likes of Herod Antipas. Slavery to the Roman Eagle! The priests at the temple in Ephesus – like priests everywhere – do mighty well for themselves and help nobody improve life, not a soul."

"Yeshua, what can be done? If gods are powerless, what can mere people do?" Urshanabi caressed Jesus' arm and held his hand. "Don't the philosophers have ideas? Can't understanding help?"

"You know, I meet with the philosophy group – intelligent folk, great discussions on thoughts from brilliant thinkers. But strangely, these ideas breathe in closed rooms, yet suffocate when let out into the open air. Offer Galilean workmen thoughts on Epicurean materialism and they'll rip your head off. Tell a Pharisee that Mosaic Law disintegrates in the face of Zeno's stoic approach and he'll explode like a boulder hurled against the Temple Mount.

"Much worse, tell a pauper that his own pessimism causes his depression and he'll damn you to whatever Hell he believes in.

"I don't know what can be done. Philosophers get caught up in their own precepts as much as priests and peasants. Often they deal with *much better ideas*; they yield understanding and confidence. But they are mere ideas nonetheless. When I pinpoint flaws in Plato's thinking advocated by the philosophy group – or Aristotelian – they only want to argue, not question the master to find a better understanding."

"Yeshua, I don't think we can solve the world's problems tonight." Urshanabi stroked Jesus' long, black hair, cuddling her head on his chest. "But we might enjoy some of its mysteries…"

Jesus' consultant work expanded as his reputation built. Within a year, connections yielded other opportunities. He expanded his work, traveling for short periods to Bithynia and Galatia, even across the straits to Thrace. For lack of time – and an unwillingness to spend every day working – he had to turn down requests from Cappadocia and Kos. He moved into a larger apartment and furnished it appropriately – not ostentatious, but tasteful. Still, back home, it would have been the height of luxury.

His wardrobe expanded somewhat as well. But avoiding the Roman style toga and traditional Mysian-Lydian robe with undergarment, he found well-cut mantles in the Jewish quarter of the city and elsewhere during his travels. Jesus smiled to himself on occasion at how his Aramaic accent in Greek and his plain traditional, coarse-thread Jewish mantle and turban projected an exotic quality that enhanced his business image. Back home – or in Tyre or Tiberias – he would still be working construction, even digging ditches if so ordered. Here, elevated by his relationship to Melas' family, plus subsequent connections he'd developed, he was looked upon as much higher in class, far more respectable than the *tekton* he'd started out as.

Local Jewish communities, those near Pergamon and in the other cities he frequented – surprising to Jesus just how many there were – varied in character: some prospered, others eked out a menial existence. But Jesus, coming from the homeland – a man who had been to the Temple and knew the scriptures – was always welcomed by Jewish communities. And, with his unique style, wit, straightforward attitude and trustworthiness, the small-town Galilean was invariably regarded as exotic and thus exceptional with his business connections. Consequently, his prominence – and self-confidence – grew along with his wealth, that owing to his moderate lifestyle.

As seasons wended, Jesus would take trips out to surrounding areas. On one occasion, he and Urshanabi ventured a two-day excursion out to Mytilene on Lesbos, off the coast west of Pergamon. The city was unpretentious, yet clean, the food pleasant. To walk around streets and roads where Aristotle had trod and Pittacus thrived was relaxing. Indeed, vendors and tavern-keepers alike recited that ancient motto of the Sage Pittacus: *Do not do to your neighbor what you would not receive willingly from him.* It reminded him of a quote he'd heard from Thales and common expressions from the scriptures.

As busy as Jesus had become, it was great to relax in the spring air. The pair had left an outdoor café near the sea for a late morning stroll up a gentle slope into the countryside.

"What are people in Pontus like, Urshi?" asked Jesus as they walked through dry autumn breezes toward a herd of sheep. "Do they hold religions, cults – what's popular there?"

"Well, there's quite a mix, as I recall. The Cult of Isis was active and growing last I was home. My husband had gotten into Mithraism. That was big in the army – though with its rituals and secrecy, it seemed pretty silly to me."

"Was there much of a Jewish community there?"

"I don't know," Urshanabi said. "Girls there don't get out much. When I was little, I would hear people down at the well, but my father had a slave teach me and my two sisters. I did have friends, but we didn't talk much about religion."

"For us, it dominated daily life."

"Not in Pontus. My father thought the gods silly and old-fashioned. He had no room for old stories."

"Did you read religious texts when you learned script?" Jesus wondered.

"No, ah, yes, sort of." Urshanabi stuttered slightly. "We read stories of all sorts – Greek gods, Mesopotamian, Egyptian. I guess those were religious – but they're only stories if you don't believe in them. And they were simple, easy to read. Reading primers often had such stories."

Jesus thought back on his childhood. "The only scrolls we had access to were Hebrew scriptures."

Urshanabi giggled, "Yes, I remember when you first came into the library."

"Oh, that reminds me..." Jesus paused as they rounded a bend to a great view of the mainland across the clear Aegean waters. Wind whistled through cedars and low brush up the hill as the bright sun peaked in the sky. "I'd heard several times that Antonius, the Roman general or whatever he was, gave Cleopatra all the scrolls from the Pergamon library. Pergamon's pretty famous, you know – I'd heard that story first back in Tyre.

"When I came into the library that first time, I wasn't sure if you had scrolls or not."

That brought a laugh. "Well, as I've heard, he did – but long before I got there. The authorities wanted us to send our whole inventory down to Alexandria to make up for a fire during Caesar's time – years before that even, I think. But you know: libraries aren't run by nitwits!

"What we did was have copies made of scrolls worth keeping – then send the copy if the original was in good shape, or keep the copy if not. When the shipment was finished, we had fewer scrolls, but only useful ones, scrolls in good condition. I think that was fifty or sixty years ago. Since then, we've built back up – they tell me we have over a hundred and fifty thousand scrolls.

"Scribes are starting to make what they call a codex – they cut the paper and stack it in pieces, then bind the edge. You can find things a lot easier like that."

Jesus had seen codices, but not read one. "Yes, makes sense... You can get right to the middle of a manuscript without having to scroll through everything. Pretty clever. I imagine they last longer, too – without all the flexing."

Urshanabi explained, "And, of course, in Pergamon they're written on parchment paper not papyrus. The Egyptians restrict export of papyrus, so we developed parchment – those are dried skins, not pulp from..."

"I know what parchment is. How backward do you think Galilee is?" Jesus joked.

"No, no, I didn't mean..." she protested.

"I know what you meant!"

As further months dissolved into a year then another, Jesus got ever more deeply embedded in his work. His services proved invaluable for businessmen contracting construction crews, giving them protection from dishonest construction crews and substandard work. Contracting on his own in addition to work for Melas' family, he increased his income considerably.

But his unwavering approach continued to aggravate builders, getting workers into trouble and whole crews punished for improper bracing and finishing work – generally shoddy practices. He resisted payoffs offered quietly in taverns and ignored veiled threats, shying away from reporting them on the rationale that these were *his* problems, not issues for Melas, Oliatos and his other contacts to have to deal with. But he kept his eyes open all the time, as he'd heard that several disgruntled operators were planning reprisals.

Amazing, Jesus thought repeatedly, *how I can simply hold people to their word as contracted and they get upset about it.*

One evening, Jesus returned from a leisurely hike into the hills to the north. He'd been in Pergamon for over three years now and was facing some changes. Projects were wrapping up and others were on the table, offering even greater sums. Yet the accumulation of money – and he'd saved plenty – was hollow and meaningless beyond the ability to eat well and do as one wished. He'd tired of the theater, the gymnasium and the social scene. Outside of Urshanabi, for whom he'd had little time in recent months, other women he'd seen, all much younger than his nearly thirty years, were plentiful and fun in this liberal environment, particularly for a man of means. In common, local values, he couldn't have it much better.

But there had to be more to life. The itch that drove him from Nazareth to Sepphoris, on to Tiberias and Capernaum and Tyre was tingling again. What had become of James and his brothers? Was his mother still alive? She would be 42 by now – fairly old and possibly, even likely, a great-grandmother.

He had just spent much of the day walking the hills, no goal, just a day off – meditating on occasion, looking inward, wondering what Yahweh wanted from him, that is, if his Lord *had* any such preference. Always, it had seemed, events directed his path. But now he seemed stuck. Life was comfortable and entertaining – was that Yahweh's intent? Pergamon offered interesting and rewarding challenges. But staying there would be a commitment. He may never return home, never see his family again. He was unsure.

Approaching his building in dusk, he could see from the distance two suspicious characters lurking near the door to his apartment and a third leaning against the building. In an area removed from much public traffic, this was unusual and immediately spurred his alarm. Jesus turned down a side street and made his way quickly down to the lower city. Knocking on Urshanabi's door, he got no response for some time. Exceptionally busy recently, he hadn't taken time to see her. *Was she away?* When she came to the door, she stepped outside and pulled the door closed behind her. Jesus explained the situation and asked if he could spend the night, not trusting to return home.

"Yeshua, I'm not alone," she said, looking down, not at him.

"Oh, I see," said Jesus, quickly realizing that he'd neglected her – and been somehow pulling away.

"I've always felt wonderful in your company, Yeshu'. I've loved you and wanted you," Urshanabi explained hesitatingly. "But you've never been mine to have. I had to…"

"I understand, Urshi," Jesus whispered, touching his fingers to her lips to quiet her explanation. "I don't think I'm even *mine* to *give*." They stood in silence for a time, peering into each other's eyes, then hugged. "I wish you my best, with all my heart. I will never see another scroll without thinking of you." He turned, with difficulty and not without a tear welling, and walked away down a dark street. An occasional torch flickered in Pergamon's dim glow as he spent hours wandering the lower city. He waited until late to head home.

Melas was indeed disappointed to hear that Jesus planned to leave. He offered him protection from thugs if he would stay – and quarters in a more secure setting. He offered more money and increased authority in some of his operations. But for Jesus, clearly the time had come to move on. But where to?

Back home? He had to laugh at the thought of returning to Nazareth – he could never fit in there again. What would he do there? Construction – when he just passed up the best opportunity he could ever hope for? In Galilee, he'd be laying mud bricks again for Antipas or some government official until his back gave out – spend his old age telling stories to James' and Simon's grandchildren. To Athens? That city, he'd heard, was well beyond days of splendor. With exposure to philosophy and theater in practically any city now, Athens had simply lost its appeal. Rome? No way. He'd heard of its swarming masses, looking to wild chariot races and gladiator fights for amusement, to government handouts and free grain for sustenance.

What was there left to see? As he completed projects and arranged for leaving his flat, he puzzled over his future. One night he dreamed of Moses. The venerable sage of his traditions beckoned him silently: but to Palestine? Or maybe to Egypt? Now that seems enticing – Alexandria!

Not needing to work cargo ships, he could travel in some comfort. No longer the young teen who'd moved to Sepphoris, the twenty-year-old striking out for Tiberias or even the 24-year-old hiking out of Capernaum, he was now a man. Years of learning, of exposure to other cultures and ways of life had changed him. He saw himself and the world much differently now. Egypt would be his destination. When he mentioned that, Oliatos asked him to carry along a letter to deliver to a business associate in Alexandria – the principal port there where Jesus was headed. Melas' brother assured Jesus that Rahotpe of Abydos would host him – and likely want to make use of his skills.

On inquiry at Elaea, Pergamon's nearby port, he found a merchant vessel, *Khutenptah's Fruitfulness*, bound for Egypt which took passengers. *That sounds interesting*, Jesus thought, secure in his decision. *Every man should see Egypt during his lifetime.*

That last morning, he picked up his substantial savings, packed them into an inconspicuous bundle with various other things, loaded everything onto a small cart he'd arranged for and headed for the docks. He was free again and could now, leaving an assortment of enemies behind, actually relax.

Sailing the Mediterranean carried the passenger through time as well as space. As the cargo craft left Elaea, it passed Lesbos, swung around Kos and headed south to Naxos. These islands, basking silent in warm sunlight, sat ageless, lapped by unending waves, immune to time. It was as though Odysseus might sail out from behind one on his way back to Ithaca or Octavian's Roman fleet might emerge to engage Antony's Egyptian vessels.

With time to relax and think – no deck duties anymore, no job, no commitments – Jesus could ponder life's peculiarities. *How odd*, he thought, passing tranquil islands with no feeling of time, *that people are so glued to the past. It seems like any argument, however concocted, that can be supported by scripture or by some great philosopher, will be accepted by most people – where the most obvious truth is rejected if people aren't used to seeing things that way.* Sea gulls, calling out in anticipation, swooped towards the ship from a clear sky as *Khutenptah's Fruitfulness* creaked and rolled southward. *Back home trying to explain Heraclitus or Plato to people*, he realized, *you would have to justify their points by quoting scripture.* Laughing to himself, he wondered if people would get the point at all, regardless of its truth or source – if not straight out of some prophet's words.

Brief commercial stops on Naxos – stories of Ariadne still abounded at the harbor tavern there – and Thera provided but a tantalizing taste of the islands. But difficulties on board led to a longer stay on Crete.

Headed southeast from Thera, as the ship rounded the east coast of Crete, heavy gusts snapped some starboard side rigging on the mainsail, causing excess tension on the mast – and a flurry of activity by the crew. The sail was reduced and temporary rigging hastily put into place, but the added pressure had cracked the sail's support structure, leaving the main mast cocked slightly and vulnerable. The captain decided to pull up the mainsail and put in on the south coast of Crete.

Docking for three days at Matala gave Jesus a chance to wander out into the countryside. He was told of the ancient Minoan civilization from ages past and saw some ruins that appeared to confirm the story. He wondered if people had lived in these buildings when Moses was leading the Exodus – or even back when Abraham first settled into Jesus' homeland.

Travel had taught Jesus great lessons. He realized now how extensive the land was – far greater than he'd imagined while growing up, making trips to Jerusalem and hearing tales of Mesopotamia and Rome. Stunning, too, was how long people had been around – things never imagined in Nazareth, never discussed during a childhood where time commenced with Adam. How could Adam have been the first human, when so many cultures spread across such vast space – and so many people, all looking different?

When the captain decided to cobble temporary support rigging and reduce sail, then fix the mast in Alexandria, Jesus thought of the Sibyl's words: proceed as "the scroll beckons", she'd said. Perhaps the famous Library of Alexandria – home of hundreds of thousands of scrolls – had some meaning, some things to learn there. Maybe his journey would indeed end, as the oracle had suggested, when the wooden mast would be fixed upright in Alexandria's port. Might he stay there? Would he fit in where people actually think?

At last, the huge Pharos lighthouse crept up over the horizon to announce approach to Alexandria, its flame burning brighter in the early evening twilight.

The Galilean could afford decent accommodation in Egypt's

major port city, the Empire's second largest after Rome – perhaps anywhere so far as was known. But his frugal upbringing led him to immediately seek out Rahotpe, Oliatos' associate. He'd long since learned that free lodging was the best – though overnight stays in warehouses or crude flophouses were in the past.

On one hand, he'd come to trust things to work out, as provided by Yahweh – though Greeks, he knew, would thank the Fates, Romans, Fortuna and Hindus, Lakshmi. His path always seemed to unfold in positive ways, leading him into beneficial encounters and interesting situations. On the other, he didn't have a distinct goal – no clear realization of what he wanted. At times he envied those many people he encountered who were content with a job, a family, food and sex every once in a while. Driving his every move, keeping him headed toward an elusive, hidden destination, was something – Yahweh? His own curiosity? His desire to help people?

Rahotpe's extensive grounds sat just inside Alexandria's Rhakotis section – originally, before Alexander three centuries prior, a city itself – well to the west of central city buildings. The concentration of the Gymnasium, Forum, Theater, Library and other monumental structures – glittering in evening lighting – outdid anything Jesus had seen previously. He'd heard of Alexandria's focus on learning, the assembly of scholars from all places, but the city itself was marvelous to behold. He fully intended to explore the setting and the learned community – and, too, investigate that large, long-settled Jewish quarter.

The way to Rahotpe's led Jesus and his hired porter down a very broad street past one massive structure after another – Temples and official buildings – all fronted by columns. *I wonder*, Jesus contemplated, *whether I've seen more people during my travels – or more columns.* He was directed towards the Serapeum, huge temple to Serapis – a sort of Hellenistic-Egyptian amalgamated god, deemed protector of Alexandria – situated in the southeast corner of the Greek section. It overlooked the broad, rather marshy Lake Mareotis to the south.

How strange, Jesus noted of the abrupt shift in character, as he left the Greek quarter for the Egyptian. He'd grown used to the Hellenistic style, helped build or oversaw construction of many variations of it, but had never seen Egyptian architecture – larger, heavier, more staid in traditions.

Rahotpe was not home, but his main servant, Djutmose, let Jesus in, having examined his letter of introduction. Djut knew Oliatos and concluded this man worthy to occupy a prime guest room until return of his master, anticipated in several days. With a bath and refreshment offered, Jesus released the porter and settled in, relaxing in comfort after several days' journey.

His host's absence gave Jesus time to explore Alexandria – and time was needed. For starters, a lengthy walk to the Jewish quarter the next day – it being the Sabbath – gave Jesus an altogether new perspective on his own people.

First, the city was huge – heavily populated by the three ethnic groups, but with visitors of all complexions, sporting diverse styles. Jesus had heard of friction among native ethnicities, but found only friendly responses from everyone he approached for information. In the bustling crowd of an unknown city, needing directions happened frequently. But swarming traffic eased considerably as Jesus crossed into the Jewish Quarter, quieted by its Sabbath.

At the large synagogue, surprises emerged from the outset. Scripture, he noted immediately as he quietly slipped in among attendees – was read in Greek. Communities in Asia Minor, true to Judean roots, still used cherished Hebrew texts. Not so here in this cosmopolitan setting. It wasn't long before Jesus, well schooled in traditions and quite fluent in Greek now, noted subtle differences even in content.

Scripture reading and subsequent discussion centered around

anticipation of the arrival of an Anointed One – a great leader to restore glory to his people's status. Jesus awaited – indeed, expected – the standard phrasing he'd heard repeated back home *so many times* over: that a charismatic leader would be sent by Yahweh to usher in a golden age, throw off Judea's oppressors and establish a heavenly kingdom. All lands would bow in acquiescence to the great god, Yahweh, now in direct control, and his new rules of justice would prevail. The elements of the story were almost rote in order – the scheme of discussions he'd heard wherever he'd been.

But it didn't happen. The words of Isaiah and Micah, read aloud, stirred up a conversation about local affairs and community concerns. That led to business discussions – barely connected to any scripture *at all*. Only occasionally did talk connect with scripture, and that was to quote passages that attested – or seemed to refer – to current affairs.

Jesus spoke up, wondering if the local community – quite extensive, witnessed by this large assemblage – had abandoned Messianic hopes. He was simply curious, but his question cued murmurs from the whole crowd. His Aramaic accent in Greek gave away his foreign status, so immediately local leaders, caught off guard, emphasized assurances that their hopes and dreams were tied in with traditions. Clearly, they thought Jesus to be Judean, coming surreptitiously to test their Torah basics.

"Well, sir," one Rabbi replied, "we certainly share in all of our people's customs. But we try to find meaning in the teachings for life today."

Jesus nodded. "I believe that is critical – what other value would words have? They would be dead tones of a dead people. In my travels, I haven't seen such useful applications of our traditions. I applaud your approach."

The group leaders seemed to collectively sigh in relief. Obviously they'd encountered many a visiting scribe or Pharisee, unannounced, coming to dispute – i.e., nitpick – any divergence from strict protocol or standard conclusions. "You see," another principal continued, "we adhere to our own practices as laid out by wonderful, learned scholars of our Alexandrian traditions. Of course, we bow to the school of Hillel as we have received it. But our scholars, including Philo, have tried to draw meaning from our Law to help us live *today* – not in the past of the prophets, nor in the future of promised Messiahs."

"That makes sense to *me*, but I can imagine Sanhedrin and Temple elite don't share your viewpoint," Jesus commented. He knew that the Hillel school of practice was less strict than that advocated by Shammai of a recent generation. But this local approach seemed considerably more liberal than even that.

"We welcome you among us," the Rabbi tailed off, inducing an introduction.

"Yeshua," Jesus filled in, "of Nazareth – son of…" he thought for a second, then reiterated, "Yeshua of Nazareth."

"Nazareth?"

"Um, the Galilee – just south of Sepphoris, well, Autocratis?" he said, not sure what name they might be familiar with. "Anyway, lower Galilee."

The group was generally surprised. Galileans were known as fighters and workers, not well-spoken travelers. "Yes, Yeshua of, ah…" The Rabbi had already forgotten the name, "of Galilee. Since you are new to us, I would point out that we hold, consistent with the obvious and revealed by Philo most recently, that many scriptural passages can be interpreted as allegorical – not literal. We find deep and rich application of these stories, when taken as wisdom, to our lives. Conversely, it's far less useful to reiterate generalities ever again, just to please our Lord. We hope you will join us often in this pursuit." He then went on with the topic of the day.

Sharing a meal afterwards, Jesus learned that Philo was an elder at a different synagogue. Later, in a more private discussion with synagogue principals, he learned of Philo's descriptions of the *Logos* – sounding not far from the agent-type contemplation of Greek thinkers. Indeed, he was told, he should meet Philo, who excelled at relating scriptures to the teachings of Plato and the Stoics. It was that living orientation to meaning that had deeply influenced local traditions. Yes, exactly that liberal inter-pretation, Jesus replied, was conducive to having religion *improve* life, not provide shelter from it.

Jesus could see the connection there, between religious attitudes and quality of life, but couldn't quite quantify it. He determined to work through this relationship, perhaps seek out the synagogue this Philo attended. Somehow, a realization evaded his view.

Subsequent days found Jesus absorbing the academic scene; he explored the renowned Library and other Musaeum facilities. He had stopped by the Gymnasium – often the place to meet people and exchange ideas, as he'd learned in Ephesus and Pergamon – but found it rather exclusive. Many men lounged and interacted there, but they weren't open and inviting. Clearly the scene for intellectual stimulation in Alexandria was the Musaeum, with its Library and extensive intellectual facilities associated with it. The expansive building – under protective auspices of the Muses and fully supported by governmental funding – housed not only the most expansive collection of scrolls and codices in the Empire, but study rooms, lecture halls, theaters, research facil-ities and living quarters for hundreds of international scholars.

Jesus first reviewed the Library's entry level scrolls. But he still found reading Greek tedious – and the content of Aramaic scrolls totally without interest: contracts, restrictions on trade, regulations on merchants, taxes, etc. But lectures and conversa-tions were open to all.

He first attended a talk on anatomy – a rather specialized discussion of principles long established in Alexandria by Erasistratus and Herophilus. Three resident scholars talked about the long-established procedure of dissecting cadavers – a new concept for Jesus, for whom bodies were to be entombed quickly. They honed in on arteries, their nature in carrying, initiating or delivering *pneuma*, or the spirit quality of life, to the body – lamenting the use of cadavers from which the *pneuma* had since fled. Jesus caught their attention with a light-hearted question posed with a straight face.

"Do you propose seeking volunteers for dissection from this more spirited audience?" The audience broke into laughter, while only one of the three speakers enjoyed the joke.

Heading back to Rahotpe's after the lecture and subsequent conversation, Jesus deliberated *pneuma*, the essence of spirit. *Is spirit a thing or a quality*, wondered the foreigner – *does it actually flow through the veins, then leave the body at death, or is the whole of the person, the quality-measure that actually moves on after death to a heavenly realm?* These things were puzzling, but he didn't think scholars had the answers, either. He needed to know more, to meditate on these things, to query the Lord for insight – whatever would elicit deeper understanding.

Days later, with suitable fanfare from an extensive staff of slaves as cooks, housekeepers, security, etc., Rahotpe returned home in late afternoon, just as Jesus arrived from another day of exposure to the Library – this time, its store of geographical information. The old Egyptian was pleased to meet his house guest and greeted him warmly.

"These old bones are weary," he lamented with exaggerated sighs and a natural smile. "I've just returned from Samannud – that's Sebennytos – to look after our papyrus operation. But I couldn't resist a stop at Per-Wadjet – you would call it Buto – on the way home to enjoy the festival. But it tires me out anymore." He perused the letter of introduction.

"So my old friend, Oliatos, and his family have sent you to me?"

"Yes, Rahotpe," Jesus nodded. "I was headed to Egypt and had done considerable work for Melas, his brother. Oliatos wanted me to bring that note."

"Ah, my Anatolian friends always look out for me! I've known that family since before those brothers were born. In his letter, Oliatos praises you highly. He suggests I have you oversee construction of our new papyrus facility on the east Delta."

Jesus was surprised. He didn't realize the letter was about him.

"We do need help. Since Roman regulations have changed everything, we have great trouble getting reliable construction crews. Romans treat their slaves differently, and ours believe they should be given the same privileges, too. You can't get good work done now – the gods will punish them! Those with eyes must see that!"

"I can never quite adjust to slavery. We don't have much of that, Rahotpe."

"No, not when workers are paid less than slaves – you don't need them!" the old man exclaimed. His faced turned red, highlighting his white hair. "My slaves live better than most freedmen in Rome and most native Galileans in your district."

"I do understand customs and know the traditions. But still, as I wouldn't want to *be* a slave, so I wouldn't own one," Jesus said without air of accusation.

The old man nodded, "Yes, yes, I know. I see the short-comings in the system. But how does one change the world? If all slaves went free, none of us would eat, Rome would starve, business would halt, war would break out. The gods would punish us! Slavery is a part of life. It has been for 4000 years I believe – probably more – and always will be.

"Yushu, listen..." said Rahotpe with his Egyptian twang. "Whatever else, I *could* use your help. We expand old facilities in the Delta, yes? Demand for papyrus increases yearly – greatly so. We have abundant papyrus growth in our low lying areas and plenty of manpower to harvest and transport it. But we can't process it quickly enough – stripping, layout and cross-lay, pressing and drying – they all take space, yes? We have to expand, but have difficulty building in the east Delta where our papyrus banks are.

"I will pay you well. Accompany me in about two weeks – I need some time to rest – first up the Nile to Ptolemais Hermiou, then we'll make several stops on the way down. We will end up back where I just came from, on the east Delta in Buto, city of goddess Wadjet. Our interest is not the temple – but rather a processing site."

Jesus was not in a position to decline – besides the trip seemed quite interesting. And he still had two weeks to take in more of the Library.

The Nazarene soaked up knowledge like a camel would water in an oasis. Daily, he found stimulating discussion groups, lectures or simply conversations with individuals over diverse topics. Rahotpe had connections at the Library, so he sent Djutmose along as guide and to introduce Jesus to staff members – some scholarly activities were not open to public attendance.

"You are quite literate, Djutmose," Jesus commented as they walked to the cafeteria for a bite to eat. "Did you learn to read growing up?"

Djut seemed reluctant to talk about himself. "Master Rahotpe had me educated from childhood, sire."

"You can talk. Really. I'm just interested in how things work here. To me, you are a person like any other. Where are you from?"

The principal house slave relaxed, "I was born to the household. You've seen my mother, Ipip – from upper Nile. She still works, repairing linens and clothing."

"And your father?"

"I cannot say."

Jesus nodded. "I can relate to that. My father was not my mother's husband."

Djutmose seemed stunned, "Oh, and you would tell me?" Such secrets were generally guarded, most men not wanting to reveal this diminishment to status. "I don't..."

His timidity brought a laugh to Jesus. "I am who I am. Who my father was or what my mother did makes no difference to what I am. People who judge others on such old conventions will miss much value in life."

The two had gotten plates covered with appetizing morsels: flatbreads of barley with a yellowish tinge from millet, thin-sliced ox meat grilled with coriander and mustard – alongside onions and garlic, with radishes cut artistically. "Great food they serve here," noted Jesus.

"Yes, indeed. We use the Julian calendar now, so weeks are seven days long, not ten as in earlier times – even though," Djut laughed, "Caesar built his year on Egyptian understanding!

"Three of the days here, the cafeteria provides Egyptian fare, the other four Greek – although there are Jewish items daily. I'm surprised you didn't choose according to your customs."

"I don't always tend to such things just because other people deem them proper," Jesus smiled, then joked. "When traveling, I've found that I need to eat everywhere I go. Yahweh has never indicated a problem with exactly what that consisted of."

Djutmose, once they were seated, opened up: while never admitted or legally registered, people widely suspected that Rahotpe was his father. He'd had favored status in the house since childhood and always been treated well by the Master, particularly when that man's seven legitimate children, born to two different wives, left the household to pursue other interests.

While Djutmose returned home, Jesus thought to attend an afternoon lecture in one of twenty-five presentation halls. He found the room scheduled for a talk on Zeno of Citium and his Stoic philosophy, but that had been canceled. The next room's talk seemed crowded, though, so he entered, not knowing the topic, and found a seat.

Three rows of banked benches, laid out in a U-form, easily accommodated sixty attendees. For this lecture, though, seats were filled with several having to stand near the entrance. Some squatted in the open area in front of the seats.

The speaker, Teukros of Rhodes, was the Astronomy unit's ranking official, tasked with correlating existing knowledge with new information revealed by various current observation projects. His was a public lecture, providing a clear overview of cosmological understanding to general attendees – not a technical workshop. Jesus wasn't so sure he wanted to sit through this particular subject – everybody knew the flat earth surface was surrounded by water. The land, resting on columns, sat above and surrounded by waters; it lay *below* waters held up above by the firmament, a huge dome with gates that opened for rain. Jesus had never thought much about that, but it was common, background knowledge in Palestine.

Using a complex armillary sphere with a globe-shaped "earth" at the center, Teukros first demonstrated the tilt of the earth axis. Then he explained how a series of some 50 concentric spheres rotated around the globe of earth, with several needed to support first the Moon – for it often passed in front of the others – and the Sun in their daily tracks. Planets occupied higher spheres, ordered outward.

He then "sketched" with a long pointing stick in a large, central square of sand the general motion of the planets, attached to those spheres, around the central earth. After dotting the fixed stars onto the outermost sphere – occasionally one would fall off and shoot through the night sky, he noted – and discussing the crystalline material of the spheres, three people stood up in various parts of the audience, indicating they had a question.

Teukros pointed to one, a darker skinned, slim character dressed in a fine, eastern-style robe. "Sir, is there not reference here to values? I understood the sky affixed by Thvarshtar to separate the heavens of purest realms from the lower regions of tarnished..."

The speaker cut him off quickly, "we try to model our universe on complex observations conducted nightly by keen-eyed astronomers. They make notes on positions and we draw conclusions on elevated discussion of their findings. We don't evaluate *who* created the heavens, much less *why*. Our purpose is to observe *what*, to make sense of movement of the celestial bodies." He turned to another.

This man, clearly Greek by dress, confirmed his appearance with Attic enunciation, "I have studied this Geocentric scheme for years, but don't see how the Sun, which must be much larger – perhaps very much larger – than Earth's globe, can orbit our world. Don't you find more fitting to planetary movement the Heliocentric model? Centuries ago, Aristarchus of Samos proposed the Sun at the center of a system with earth traveling around..."

Teukros, amid some muted laughter, cut him off, too, "We find too many obvious flaws in the proposition that Earth could orbit the Sun. That would require our globe to spin – but we feel no such movement, eh? That would create uncontrollable winds – and spin us right off the earth up onto the crystalline spheres, right with the Moon!

"You must only observe and follow your observations faithfully. The Earth is clearly at rest – *clearly*. You need only stand and look around you! When on a horse, you notice movement. When running or falling, you know you are moving. There is no such experience to the static earth."

Jesus' mind was a blur. The flat-earth default thinking he was so used to was crumbling. *For sure, even from the highest peak, you can't see indefinitely,* he thought, *and a firmament from Britannica to India would be impossibly huge.* As Teukros continued, he pointed out Eratosthenes' calculation of Earth's diameter as 252,000 stadia – some 25,000 miles – done already two centuries before; Jesus wondered why he had never heard of such a thing, then marveled at the unfathomably vast dimension. *It can't be more than seven or eight thousand stadia from here to Pergamon,* he calculated. *The earth must be truly huge!*

Then he expanded his thoughts: why had he never questioned this obviously flawed model – the firmament holding up water? He'd accepted that notion simply because everybody else in Galilee and the region saw things that way. And he stopped cold in thought: *how many other things do I hold as true that are simply common misperceptions – wrong but shared across the culture?*

Now several others rose amid increasing murmurs. One shouted out, "But where is the abode of the gods? Your model must already anger them!"

Another, an Egyptian, cut *him* short, "Aton must somehow be more prominent in fixture than a mere planet!"

And another yelled, quite forcefully, "So who moves these celestial spheres? Who drives your universe?" By this point many were standing and shouting to frantic efforts by Teukros to restore order.

Later, with the crowd gone, Jesus caught up with the lecturer. "I appreciated your talk today – it pulled some weeds where crops should grow."

Teukros sighed. "I abhor these public lectures. They let just anybody in there, and everybody, when it comes to the heavens, thinks their old myths elucidate everything."

When Jesus explained his Galilean view, which he now questioned, Teukros commented, "Yes, the common Babylonian model – gates opening let down the rain from waters above. Who would hang up there, clinging to the firmament, to open the gates – angels? Hah! Many share your view – but those are old myths. And the earth, actually spinning? Hah!"

"But, teacher, if the earth spins, wouldn't the air be traveling with it – and people, too? If a fly lands on a mule that's turning a grist mill – would the fly notice that the mule is moving?"

Teukros paused, "Well … hmm, perhaps not – but a spinning earth doesn't account for varied movement of the planets. You would still need celestial spheres to hold the Sun and planets – and the Moon moves differently, too. If there is anything we're sure of, it's a fixed Earth."

Jesus wasn't. *If the earth were rotating, the whole sky would seem to move with it*, he reasoned. He resolved to pay more attention to the sky. That "firmament" idea – a fixed dome that immense – to a builder, it just didn't seem possible.

A fine, though slightly worn, carriage transported Rahotpe and Jesus along with Djut, household slaves and baggage to the nearest Nile channel. They took a small boat upstream, then back down the easternmost Nile leg to the papyrus bogs. There, after two days, they switched to a sleek cargo vessel for the trip up the Nile. It held considerable stores of delta clay and needed 24 rowers to drive it upstream. Its small sail gained some boost during favorable winds, but hardly a breeze stirred the heavy air – uncomfortably damp in the low-lying delta. As they pulled upstream, though, slowly gaining elevation as they headed south, the wind did pick up to boost velocity.

The three men stood astride the elevated prow railing as the ship channeled along, green fields a distance to both sides, dry sand on parched cliffs and mesas extending out of sight beyond that. So timeless and relaxing was the setting, they could cover many themes: Jesus reviewed the lectures he'd heard at the Library and his take on them, Rahotpe and Djut alternately listening or questioning. The old man contemplated life, its value and meaning, ever more frequently in his later years, he admitted. Djut as well, having studied with private tutors along with Rahotpe's "official" offspring, found such discussion stimulating – particularly Jesus' unique take on things. They put in briefly near Memphis so Jesus could gain a vantage point to see the pyramids five miles to the west.

"How many times have you made this trip, Rahotpe?" asked Jesus, adjusting his turban to keep the brilliant sun off his face.

Rahotpe laughed. "I often accompanied my father and my grandfather when they tended to up-Nile operations, Yushu, already by age 7 or 8, yes? My family has done pottery for many generations. It was only my grandfather who started our papyrus operation, back at the time of Cleopatra and Ptolemy Twelve, and, of course, Caesar."

"Augustus?" questioned Jesus. History, outside of Judea, wasn't his strong suit. But Augustus had been emperor for most of his youth.

"No, no, Caius Julius, of course," the old man shivered demonstrably. "Augustus was no friend of Cleopatra! My grandfather advised Cleopatra – though she rarely took his counsel – but wisely retreated when Marc Antony took up with her. I have done my best, like my father before me, to stay two arms' length away from royalty – even with bags of money to bribe them. Far too volatile – Ra can smile at you upon birth in the morning and frown before he dies that night!"

Jesus contemplated the time frame, "But Caesar, he lived long ago."

"The seasons and constellations have shifted by 20 days since I was born," said the elder, referring to the 365 day calendar, whose months, lacking leap-day every four years, marched slowly backwards in comparison to natural seasons. "I am over eighty now, yes? I met Cleopatra twice – she respected the well-fixed, but only loved the powerful. Ra smiled upon me that I was only wealthy! Those she loved and those she married – rarely the same men – are all long gone, as she herself. Wicks that draw strongly on the oil will flame brightly, but soon burn out."

Jesus, looking out over the quiet west bank of the Nile as planted fields eased by – for ships upstream hugged the shore line as much as possible to avoid heavier, mid-stream currents –

pondered out loud, "Few reach your age in Galilee. I was starting to feel old approaching thirty."

"Yushu, I have been boating this river so long now, to crocodiles I am part of the scenery. The crew who comes one day to mummify me will have precious little work to do!"

The Nile boomed with trade: many cargo vessels, traveling light upstream, picked up grain for distribution across the Mediterranean, often to Rome itself. But shallow river barges, having loaded at docks all along agricultural stretches lining the Nile shores, would transfer cargoes at various delta ports to larger sea-going transports.

At Ptolemais Hermiou, business pushed philosophy aside; Jesus was quickly pressed into duty. The wily old Egyptian explained to the construction foreman expanding the pottery works and kiln that his crew's work was so good, he wanted to show it off to his new project manager – so that he could hold builders down in the delta papyrus facility to those same standards. The management team proceeded to show off all of their work, suggesting that perhaps Rahotpe could use them at the other site, too.

Jesus, though, was busy examining stone joints and plaster work, subtly scraping away sand covering footers to inspect particulars. With the full cooperation of workers, as commanded by the foreman, he could check many details. He found many shortcomings, some critical. He made diagrams on papyrus sheets and reviewed that with Djut, Rahotpe and his local overseer following several days.

When it was clear that Rahotpe's local manager had let many flaws slide – either through incompetence or bribes – he fired him and left Djutmose on site with two other loyal slaves to enforce needed corrections. Predictably, the foreman was incensed at being duped, but could say nothing while grilled on specific evidence. His fuming stare had little effect as Jesus pointed out, one after the other, substandard masonry and structural support.

Having reviewed contractual requirements, Rahotpe whisked Jesus quickly to a partially loaded barge before any repercussions could unfold. He knew full well that local power brokers in Ptolemais Hermiou, a conservative region isolated from liberal city attitudes, might inflict retribution on Jesus, blaming him for their extra work, despite Rahotpe's authority. Before leaving, he hired several bodyguards for Djut, just to be safe.

They docked in Parva to pick up a small load of barley, then crossed the Nile to Pesla to load ceramic figurines before a rest-over in Ibium, back on the west shore. Once there, Rahotpe suggested they take some days to relax – that heated pottery facility confrontation back had tired him noticeably. He arranged for carriages and supplies for an overland venture out to the Oasis Minor, some 120 miles into the Western Desert. He knew of a comfortable place there to shed any stress.

Jesus had experienced desert country from his ventures into the Decapolis east of Irbid and Gerasa in search of reliable quarries, where only dry hills and bluffs interrupted extensive wasteland. But out there were occasional bushes and cacti. This trek featured only mile after mile of sand, interrupted solely by dry washes and occasional dunes, eventually odd, black topped mesas. Jesus wondered what he was doing here amid this desolation. This was Egypt?

Sekhemkare, short, stout, dark and bald, lit up with a smile upon recognizing Rahotpe – he ran out to greet.

His oasis inn, the *"Two Mirage"*, brilliant white stucco glaring pink in evening rays, seemed to Jesus unexpectedly large for such an isolated setting. Surrounded by trees and bushes, it was a welcome site. Three days of blistering sun and unpleasant drinking water had them all – no less mules and horses – ready for a break.

The moist area, while surrounded by the driest desert, was far from deserted. An abundance of beasts of burden fenced among palms and heavy-leaved bushes tipped off social activity – the eating hall, spa and gaming areas were filled with people. Having bathed, refreshed themselves and settled into their separate rooms, Jesus and Rahotpe met for dinner, highlighted by musicians and dancers. Sekhemkare joined them in lush ambiance – greenery, heavy wooden beams, sturdy tables – most occupied by mature men, well dressed, many socializing with notably younger women.

"Please, Mr. Yeshua – you call me 'Kemka', eh? Haha, you like it here, you do, eh? Haha," said the owner in clumsy Greek. The three chatted for some time, covering the history of the oasis and the *Two Mirage Inn*. Kemka, ever smiling – Jesus had to wonder why his mouth didn't desiccate, or *maybe it had and thus remained stuck, mummified, in that position* – had to explain, "Two Mirage – haha – you think it's a mirage when you see it – haha – but when you leave, you wish rest of the world was mirage!"

Jesus smiled at the pleasure Kemka took at telling his story for, who knows, the thousandth time?

"Whatever you want, you get! We have it – you get it – haha," said the man. "We don't have it, we find it, you get it – haha!"

Rahotpe, smiling at his old friend, added "and he'll be happy to bill me for it, too."

"Rahoot', what you want tonight? I have a new girl from upper Nile – she dark and sweet, like a Medjool date. I have light skins, too – new Celts from Britannica, two of 'em!"

"Now Kemka, what am I supposed to do with two females?"

"So, what? Your memory don't work no more or – haha – that thing down there don't work?"

Food was plentiful, and drink as well: wines from everywhere, imported mead, Nile valley beer – goat milk in the morning, pomegranate and date wines. Dancing girls – exotic and enticing – along with various music provided entertainment.

After a couple days of such luxury, Jesus was fidgety, feeling out of his element. He'd hiked out into the desert in all directions, but never far: the barren surroundings, blistering heat and annoying insects weren't conducive to meditation. Kemka explained that, west and south, a man could hike 2000 miles and see nothing but sand and dry hills. Pondering his old flat earth model, Jesus thought, *why would any creator make such a stretch of useless ground? Earth must be a colossal sphere considering the vastness of this desert.* As Eratosthenes had calculated, even that vast desert span wasn't ten percent of the way around.

Days of feasting and relaxing had grown boring. Conversations with Egyptian patrons, Greeks or barmaids, ranged from superficial chatter to business, pleasure or politics, none of which stimulated Jesus' intellect. The collection of lovely – and appropriately loose – females populating the Two Mirage simply didn't entice the Galilean as they once would have: he couldn't connect on a purely physical level anymore as in younger days.

For a man not sure of his next step, he was ready to take it – so long as it led out of this wasteland.

The return trip scorched no less incinerating than the venture out. After several hours, talk again shifted esoteric – with Jesus questioning the luxury they'd just encountered versus the struggle and tribulations of everyday peasants. After speculating on gods and the Logos, Jesus inquired about Rahotpe's understanding, based on the latter's long life.

The elder replied as to the Egyptian pantheon, "Min has been good to me, blessing me with several healthy children. But it was I who fathered them, yes? Had I waited for Neith to bring down an antelope while hunting or Ma'at to bring order to the world for my business to prosper, I would have neither trophy nor profit. Amun and Bes stand frozen on monuments, Yushu – I had to make my life."

"Still," replied Jesus, "you acted not alone. In the desert, you would have found no target for your arrow nor customer for your pots. Your fortitude and character led to success, but *only* when other things, outside your control, provided opportunity."

Rahotpe nodded, conceding the point.

Dusty wafts whipping up off hooves and creaking wheels make speaking difficult. But the oasis water tasted amazingly sweet and refreshing. Jesus sipped frequently. "But it seems that exactly a determination like *yours*, that disposition of assurance, elicits success from the gods – whoever and whatever they may be..."

As the coaches lurched through parched wasteland across gravel and sand towards Ibium, Rahotpe shifted focus, "Yushu, your insight at times dazzles me. You express your concern for people – *your* people and all others – their well-being and future. Why don't you help them? You explain things to Djut, to me even, yes? I thought I'd heard it all in my life, but you have opened my eyes to other visions, my ears to philosophies, my spirit to great humor.

"How long can you keep that to yourself?"

"My people don't listen. Prophets all died centuries ago – and took thinking with them, it seems. People can't imagine that somebody living can actually come up with better ideas than dead ones did! To the Judean mind, all has been spoken, long ago – by prophets as mummified as your kings.

"Now, instead of prophets, we have scribes, but they not only *read* scripture for the illiterate masses, they interpret it, too. Back home, scribes are unquestioned experts," Jesus explained, adding to himself, *unless I'm around.* "Oh, and Pharisees: self-appointed, self-promoting, wandering buffoons of bygone ideas who don't understand life and do their best to keep others ignorant, too. For them rules are to be followed with no recognition of *why.* And Sadducees? A joke – elite and pampered, they bluster and feign, live like kings in their quarters, while people scrape to survive and pay Temple taxes."

"But that's what I mean, Yushu. If *their* views are the only ones voiced, scribes and rabbis, no single man will ever hear anything different, nor change."

Jesus well knew that to be true.

Clomping hooves and rumbling wagons became mesmerizing. No single bird called. Only desert flies braved the late morning heat. Jesus, swooshing them away incessantly, wondered what the insects did for recreation before he appeared for them to pester.

Rahotpe persisted, "You don't need the prophet's mantle or Moses' staff. Tell them what you tell me, yes? People with ears will hear you. Those with heads of ebony wood won't. But does it matter if half the people benefit, or one of ten – or one out of a hundred?"

"That's what Plato must have thought," Jesus nodded. "For the greatest truths, you can only hint around, touch and sketch – never grip and paint." But, Jesus considered, what indeed would he say? *What would I tell my people – if somehow I could get them to listen?*

He continued, "You know, I see Greeks, pursuing fun and intellectual truth – and they find it. Their cities reflect their intent. And the Romans... They pursue domination and control – and achieve it. Look at their armies and navies, their catapults and engineers. They make what they want to – they may ask Mars or query bones for the gods' intent. But in the end, the *Roman* will is what happens, not Jupiter's.

"And your people, Rahotpe – did they build grand buildings, huge pyramids by waiting for Amun to lay blocks on one another? When, one day, they got too attached to Horus, suddenly, they lost their freedom.

"My people are like that. They look to Yahweh – follow all the rules of old to please him. They've become submissive to their god – and that's what he gives them: subservience." Jesus took another sip and brushed his hand across his lips. "But what can I do, Rahotpe? What can I do if they won't listen?"

"Judeans *can't* listen if you don't tell them, yes? They won't hear your voice from across the Egyptian desert."

The downstream trip to Samannud on the eastern delta would have been routine, but Rahotpe, feeling ill, put in at Letopolis, below Memphis. "Yeshua, you go on to the papyrus works without me. Take two slaves. I'll have a letter written to announce you – you know what you have to do, and you'll have full authority to do it. I must return home." The elder, having trouble breathing, felt dizzy. He would take the west fork and canal home, while Jesus would return to Alexandria only after reviewing construction at the papyrus works.

Three months later, Jesus returned to Rahotpe's palace, not knowing what to expect. He'd heard the senior was now practically bed-ridden, but hoped he would still be lucid and not in pain. Finding him weak and frail, but in good spirits, Jesus could fill him in on details of his oversight project to the east.

Rahotpe listened, but with far less engagement than he'd undertaken that last business trip. Now, three of his seven children had returned to the large house and two more were expected. From their looks and comments, it was obvious Rahotpe's days were dwindling.

Djutmose returned soon thereafter, and the two, Jesus and he, reviewed eventualities from both sites – considerable improvement had been accomplished in both projects. But authority was already shifting to Rahotpe's sons, who were clearly vying for control. Still Djut was in his father's thoughts when the dying man called Jesus in alone.

"My young friend," he whispered weakly, though his eyes were clear and intense. "I have had Djutmose transfer your savings and pay from me – with bonuses – to the financial overseer at the Serapeum. You can withdraw it at any time. I ask only…" his voice tailed off as he cleared his throat and Jesus helped him sip some pomegranate juice. "Please stay here long enough to assure that my children don't relegate Djutmose to servile stature, yes? He knows the businesses better than any of them – and is ... is more responsible.

"My sons, of course, will inherit the various works – but if they don't keep Djut to run them, all I've done will be lost..."

Jesus nodded and reached for the old man's hand. "I'll do what I can, but..."

"You can do *everything*, Yushu – you will be executor! Follow all I've laid out. The tribunal and city offices know this and will respect your word to follow my will. Don't let them fight and above all," he coughed to clear moisture from his throat, "protect Djut's interests.

"When all is settled, Yushu, you return home, yes? All of your wisdom is of no value if you don't share it, and forcefully!" He thought for a moment. "Would you put a torch under a barrel, or out in the open? You are a torch, young man – you won't shine any brighter among other fires at the library. Take your message home – only you can do that. Promise me you'll return to Galilee when everything is settled."

Rahotpe's words struck Jesus suddenly with the cold realization he had to make this ultimate decision. Would he spend more time gathering knowledge and debating irrelevant details on insubstantial ideas? Could he pursue any longer the meaningless acquisition of money or status? Or would he return and somehow convey to his own people insights he'd gained? *One can pull back the bowstring ever tauter,* he thought, *but until the arrow is released, the energy is wasted and the target empty.* "I'll go, Rahotpe. Somebody needs to counter the falsehoods, the dogma that stands for hope and brings only drudgery. I'll go. And somehow I'll make my message heard above all the prattle posing as truth."

Rahotpe looked up with a smile and released Jesus' hand as the tall Galilean nodded his promise. The elder's expression eased and he looked away, indicating that would be all he had to say.

Death came easily four days later. But settling the estate, complex business issues and fraternal bickering took three scribes and Jesus months to rectify. His only real escape from the complexities of legalities and added travel to construction and production sites was the library. Despite continual squabbling, Jesus assured that each sibling received the appointed share in business concerns that most suited their abilities. And he convinced them that Djut would benefit them all by managing each concern.

Retrieving his money from the Serapeum, he left over half of it in an account at the Musaeum – thinking that, should he ever wish to, he could retire to Alexandria – but should he never return, they would best use the money. Carrying so much while traveling home would be foolish. For one last review of the papyrus works, he accompanied Djut and the eldest of Rahotpe's sons to Sebennytos. The project there had gone very well – production was raised by thirty percent. The family was at peace, Djut was well placed and Jesus' work there was now finished, save for one favor.

Jesus first thought to take a ship back to Judea – perhaps to Jaffa – or directly to Caesarea in Samaria, a short trip to Megiddo and home. But while indeed yearning to see his family again after nearly eight years, he was anything but clear on what to do once back there. He must take the initiative to reach his people – but how? It troubled him.

As if to gain time to think – Jesus could be home in days by ship – he had Djut arrange travel by caravan to Aqaba and on to Petra. From there, he could negotiate a ride north towards the Dead Sea – and home. But the overland trek across the Sinai to Nabataea would allow time to grapple with possible plans – and, after all, hadn't Moses beckoned in his dream? *It won't take 40 years to reach the Promised Land*, Jesus reasoned, *but 40 days might help get my own promise in order.*

Caravans loaded near Heliopolis, a short trip back up the Nile.

Nabataean merchant, Garm'alba'al, regularly led east-west camel caravans, bringing myrrh, nard, cassia and other incenses and spices, raw and processed, from the east, then returning with Egyptian and western items – such as papyrus and pottery. Traveling well beyond Jesus' destination, Garm'alba'al, long time associate of Rahotpe – saddened by his death – agreed to include Jesus with four other passengers – among 9 files of loaded camels, running between 12 and 15 per file. Jesus would ride – and, half the time, walk – with the second file, but would have to share more time walking if any of the camels died along the way. Cargo, after all, couldn't hike.

The scorching Egyptian solar disk had passed half its transit before Tissaphernes, Persian caravan master, could activate the first file – having gotten the nod, finally, from all nine camel-pullers. Aimed east for Arsinoe at the north tip of the Heroopolite Gulf, 80 miles distant, the first leg of the trek would scarcely cover fifteen this day due to a late start. Three overnights would be needed – the second at a small oasis just south of the trail. No caravansary would be available until the second leg – the much more rugged stretch to Aelana.

Two days' trekking through relatively featureless desert, had Jesus doubting caravanning as the way to travel. While he rode, the tight, broad saddle inflicted constant discomfort during uninterrupted rocking, making walking seem attractive. However, hiking through blistering sand in sandals with impro-vised rags to protect the feet made riding seem better – until the next switch. *Alternating miseries*, he concluded. Camping that third night – outside Arsinoe – with more relaxed eating and fresher water to drink – was a pleasure.

But two days out into the rugged hills, ravines and desert washes of the central Sinai promoted a certain nostalgia for the flats between Heliopolis and Arsinoe. The way across Sinai was never straight, rarely level, mostly uphill – or seemed so to sore feet strongly competing with a raw undercarriage for attention. Then a sandstorm interrupted.

Tissaphernes had seen it coming; he broke down the caravan quickly. The camel-puller directly in front of Jesus' mount eased up. He had all five riders in his group of 13 dismount, drop their camels and take positions right near them, mantles raised for protection, before the sand arrived. Amid the bray of ornery beasts and the dry howl of sand-laced winds, Jesus, seated, leaned back against his camel and closed his eyes. Having dozed off, he startled awake when jostled.

"Hey, ho," yelled a voice outside his mantle. "Don't fall sleepy, mon," the man shouted in broken Greek. The wind and sand picked up again from a lull. "Wake you, hey!"

Jesus opened his mantle a crack to see the strange foreigner from several camels back. He was amazingly yellow in complexion with the inner corners of his eyes tightly skinned at the nose. He'd never seen such features in all his travels. Jesus, drowsy, answered spontaneously in Aramaic, "thanks – I guess it's better to keep alert."

The Asian replied in fluent Aramaic, but with a strange accent, "Very much better. Unless you like eat and breathe sand!"

That night at the first caravansary they encountered – an extensive shelter built alongside a small oasis – Jesus got to know his neighbor. Settled in, camels watered and fed and most of the men huddled by three camp fires, Jesus and Ping-Houn Soufan wandered off into the surrounding desert to escape the chatter. Both had grabbed handfuls of raisins, figs, dates, almonds, dried meat and breads laid out by the cooks.

From a crystal clear sky, the three-quarter Moon brightly lit surrounding sand, still quite warm. Both, weary from walking, made their way up a short ridge and found comfortable positions, leaning against a crusty ledge with feet elevated.

"Yes, very far from here," Ping-Ho answered Jesus' query as

to his homeland. "But caravans cover the whole route – every day. I start running one camel from Han home – my father official, he travel around – to Xinjiang and Tarim Basin. Go 'round. I pick up, drop off – you know?

"Then find loose camel – I think owner leave for dead, but she only lame. I help her – now have two camel. Make more money, buy more camel.

"I ran camel down to Peshawar and Khyber for a while – too much fighting. I start to run to Parthia – Persia, you know? Safer, easy. Now I go to Nabataea, sometime Egypt. Always something to pick up, drop off. Take to Basra and Persia, or Gerrha – even Saba in south. Now ships go there, to Saba. Not so much business."

Jesus gazed at the stars, wondering about the Milky Way, "You've sure been around, Ping-Ho. Will you ever go home?"

"I *am* home, Yesha," he replied. "My father say, 'Home is where you make it.' My camels and the sand – that's home. I have no other, now."

Conversation had quieted back at the fires – men had settled into sleeping spots near, but not too near, the camels. Crackling embers occasionally launched glowing sparks skyward.

"But don't you get lonely, want to settle down – find a woman?" Jesus squirmed around to make the sand conform to his own contours.

Ping-Ho laughed. "You make money, you have a woman. You like? You stay two nights, maybe three. Stay longer, she sounds like… You know bray sound camel makes when you load him? He bellow and bellow every time you load another sack, he bellow. When he stop blare, you know he has enough; you don't give him anymore. That beast tell you. Woman? Once she start, she never stop bellow.

"I live with camel. Him, I understand. I find woman when I need one – two nights, maybe three."

Jesus was laughing at the Asian's words, "Wouldn't you want

children one day?"

"I buy young camel!"

Tired and sore, Jesus thought he should go back and make a bed of sorts. But he wasn't sleepy.

"You from Galilee, eh?" Ping-Ho asked. "I know where people come from just from looks. People walk different, look different. You go east – or back home?"

"I've been away for near eight years. Lived up at the head of the Jordan, then Tyre – on to Anatolia, some travel, Egypt a bit, Alexandria."

"Oh, cities. Don't like them so much. Too many people. Too many crooks. Better to stay in the country – small towns. You put 50 camels together in a bunch, you can't do anything with them. String them out, you do what you want. City people are like camels in a bunch.

"Yesha, you must be Jew, eh?"

Jesus thought about that for a second. He'd never fully realized that the word meant not only his ethnic and cultural heritage, but his world view. "Well, yes. But, I'm … I guess I'm a little different – let's say, I think a bit different from most of my kinsmen."

"Uh-huh," Ping-Ho seemed unsure what that meant.

"Do your people have gods, Ping-Ho?"

"Oh, yes – many. But they're like royalty. They don't do nothing."

Jesus laughed again.

Ping continued, "I grew up with honorable ideas. My family, my father, he *help* me see – he didn't *make* me see. You know? You tell a child red, he see red. You tell him to look, maybe he see blue or purple. Maybe plaid."

"That's for sure. If you learn only about Zeus, you'll think for sure Zeus exists. If you only ever heard of Enlil, you're likely to bow to Enlil. A child hasn't been taught all that yet; he sees what he sees without judgment."

"Father read to me from Old Philosopher about the Tao. It's nothing itself, but the Way, the Way of things – don't know how to say in Aramaic. How things flow in life, you know? But I travel down, south of the big mountains. Hear of Enlightened One – you know, Gautama?"

"No that name isn't familiar."

"He lived long ago."

Didn't they all, Jesus thought as Ping-Ho spoke.

"In north India."

Jesus remembered Devdas, his old friend in Tyre, "Aren't they Hindu there? Was he a mystic?"

"He change things, see same things different – you know? Hindu think life come from karma – bad things you did in other lives, they happen to you now. Buddha said, karma, you carry *now* – like pack on the camel, not pack from last year's caravan."

"Hmmm … Interesting. Of course, you exchange packs everywhere you go – pick up, drop off equivalent weights…"

"Buddha think like Lao Tzu, Old Chinese Philosopher – he know life all tied together." Ping-Ho sat up and made a circular shape with his hands. "All things are connected, depend on each other – nothing just happen!"

Jesus nodded, "Kind of like the camels here – like each camel in file, a rope through his nose is tied to the saddle of the one in front, right up to the camel-puller. They all follow right along."

"Yes, yes, life split in ways, you know? Yin need yang, you see?"

"Huh?" Jesus hadn't heard those words.

The Asian explained how things had complementary attributes, pairing off as male/female, dark/light, cold/hot. But those were really yin/yang tied together in a cooperative Oneness. All things connect – *up* only seems *up* relative to *down*. "All things work together," he concluded.

"But then, Ping, the question becomes – doesn't it? – who is the camel-puller? Who determines where that file goes – where and how your life unfolds?"

Ping-Ho sat in silence for some time. A shooting star flashed across the sky as Orion crept slowly upwards as if chasing the setting Moon. "The caravan master tells the camel-puller."

"Yes, but who tells the master?"

"Well, the organizer?"

"And who tells him? Customers? Shippers? Kings? If all of life is tied together, who gives the orders?"

Ping-Ho thought about what Lao-Tzu or the Buddha would have said. "We'd better get to sleep, Yesha. We've got a long trek tomorrow."

Typical delays, two sand storms, a sickly camel that had to be left behind, additional hiking and numerous rifts among caravan riders all combined to slow progress. Once in Aelana, the port at the eastern Sinai gulf's northern tip, two files plus some others of the caravan – including Ping-Ho – joined with other camel drivers assembled to head south to Makkah, while three new files were added for the next leg north.

But as Tissaphernes tended to each file, readying to leave, another problem came up. A smaller southbound caravan pulled into their camp near Aelana. Word was quickly passed with excitement, raising a din among the drivers.

Jesus, not yet mounted, approached the caravan chief. "What's the issue, Garm'alba'al?"

"Ooo, big problem, Galilean – big for me, bigger for you," he said, looking glum. "They come down from Sea of Death, stop by Petra, get news. Antipas Herod, tetrarch of your land – eh, Yeshua? – he cause troubles, big ones. He divorce Phasaelis, wife many years. He marry other woman – what he say?" Garm'alba'al yelled over to the other caravan's master.

"Yeah, he marry Herodias – she wife of his brother, Philip."

Jesus didn't recognize the name *Herodias*, but he'd heard of Phasaelis, Antipas' wife of many years. And he knew of Philip,

Antipas' half-brother, Tetrarch of Iturea and Batanea – the area west of Galilee and Decapolis. *But his wife had a different name,* he thought. Then he remembered another half-brother, also named Philip, who lived in Rome, last he'd heard. "They're always doing that sort of thing."

"Hah, but Phasaelis is daughter of Aretas IV!"

"Who is that?"

"*WHO IS THAT*, you ask?!?!" roared Garm'alba'al. "Who is *Aretas Philopatris* – friend of his People!? He's King of Nabataeans! He sent army after Antipas, the swine – beat him, took territory!"

"When did that happen? How will that affect our journey?"

"That's the point, man! I don't know. They say Romans will come down from Syria – poor Antipas went crying to papa Tiberius. Past Petra, might run into a retreating army, Roman, Aretas' – Don't want nothing like that!"

Jesus quickly calculated that problems for Garm'alba'al could be multiplied for a Galilean. Passing through Nabataea at the moment wouldn't be wise. He walked over to the smaller caravan heading south and found Ping-Ho.

"Do you know if this caravan takes passengers?"

"Hey, Yesha – must be! I just bought two camels and picked up small pack of papyrus. I can take you – we clear it with Pharnazathres. He caravan master here."

So he started south with the smaller caravan. But after a day's travel, Jesus had second thoughts. He'd heard from other camel drivers about customs in the lower desert: they worshipped Hubal, an offshoot of the Canaanite Ba'al, idolized rocks and engaged in what seemed very primitive cultish practices. The landscape was desolate, with hundreds of miles of dry mountains and desert washes to cross, Jesus concluded, *no, this isn't right. What am I running away from? Moses had no choice – I do.*

He wasn't far from a small, oasis-based village and could walk back to Aelana. From there, he could make his way north, by foot if necessary. The way was arid, but water could be found in villages and oases, the route straight.

He hadn't feared Antipas while living in Galilee nor foreign rulers anywhere. He was ready to go home and leave this bleak desert for greener hills of Galilee. Three days' hike northward, he passed Garm'alba'al's caravan – being detained and searched by a detachment of Nabataean soldiers. Jesus walked quietly by unnoticed.

When Jesus reached the rift down into the Dead Sea basin, it almost felt like home. He continued on, then turned west for the long climb up to Jerusalem. He would rest there a few days before proceeding to Nazareth.

Save for a more obvious Roman presence – highlighted by the Antonia Fortress, a large, recently finished military stronghold off the northwest corner of the Temple – little had changed in and around the Temple Mount since Jesus' youth half his lifetime ago, that last family venture while Joseph still lived. After his long trek, he yearned for a thorough bath, but many such Greco-Roman customs of cities he'd visited hadn't found their way into Judea, lest they offend native sensitivities. A clean-up at the Inn would have to do.

Though already dusk, with minimal searching he found the Inn, Pinchas' Hostel, where his family used to stay – conveniently situated in Bethany, east of the city, across Hebron Valley near the Mount of Olives. To the west it overlooked the Temple Mount opposite. With no festival going on, rooms were available – but the old family who hosted his clan years ago had shifted generations. One daughter, now grown, ran the Inn.

It took a week to rest up – and hydrate – from the grueling journey. At the market near the western wall, he purchased sandals and a quality mantle – something approximating Egyptian styles he'd been seeing – amazed at lower prices here compared to Alexandria and Pergamon. *Pleasant surprise, but shows lower living standards,* it occurred to him.

Grand as the buildings were, in general, he noted how small things looked – compared to memories of his youth when the wondrous big buildings had him in awe. Herod the Great had rebuilt the city, expanding the Temple and his own quarters, refurbishing luxury homes of the elite and priesthood, upgrading the market and theater. But that was 40 years ago. Stone and columns lose their luster in time – and Jesus had now seen many grand cities, each kept pristine by teams of slaves. Neither Jerusalem nor Judeans intimidated him as they used to in his youth.

The Sabbath found Jesus entering the Temple. At the courts, it took no time to engage blustery expert-types who hung out there.

In one informal group, an over-dressed scribe had just recited all the key laws he deemed most important – never to be violated.

"What's the point?" Jesus asked.

"What?!?," came his retort, with feigned offense. "The point is inherent to the law – we must obey our prescribed dictates in complete accord with the scriptures, 'I will praise you, O Lord, among the nations.'"

"But is it not also said, 'Trust in the Lord and do good; dwell in the land and enjoy safe pasture'?" Jesus replied, coolly. "Reciting such laws, are you trying to help this crowd or impress them? Did not Isaiah say, 'All your pomp as been brought down to the grave, along with the noise of your harps.' Isn't it more important to treat people with love than to follow all the rules of the prophets?"

The official was shocked at unexpected, blatant criticism. The crowd cowered noticeably, murmuring, as the scribe bristled, his face turning red. "Who are you to question such scripture at the very Temple of our souls? Why, my words come directly from the Psalms of our David!"

Jesus spoke up, "More so should you speak directly from the heart."

The man stepped back, breathing deeply, raising his hand to his forehead as though hurt to core. "I have not to face these words of Satan!"

"Come again?" interrupted Jesus. "Would Satan suggest you speak from the heart of trust and love? Would Satan quote David's Psalms or Isaiah?"

The Temple functionary turned and left. Jesus wandered off, ambling around the crowd, as some started to follow him. Shortly the scribe returned with two additional priest-types, easily recognizable from their fine garments and overly contrite attitude.

"We've been informed, sir, that you have questions of the, ah, Temple operatives," said the heavier one, dressed in official robes. The three spread around in front of Jesus.

"You have?" Jesus said, standing erect, looking down at them each straight in the eye, saying nothing more. It was most common for people to drop their eyes in subordinate posture when confronting officials.

After a pause, during which men started to gather around. "Yes, well, if you have any questions..."

"Now, I wouldn't want to detain you from slaughtering animals. You've got your job to do, eh? Earn your money?" Jesus spoke with innocence, but his words rattled like a sword, as priests were the only ones allowed to actually slaughter animals for sacrifice.

The heavy priest cleared his throat demonstrably, then spoke up with an obvious counterthrust at his critic, "What brings a ... Galilean to the big city?"

Jesus took up the challenge, "I seek out wisdom and truth. Can you direct me to where I might find either?" His implication, not lost on the crowd, was clear: such insight would not be forthcoming from these officials.

All three were stunned. They could neither say yes or no, neither provide it nor point it out. They stood, motionless, unable to answer.

"Tell you what. Let me – and these people – know if you do."
He turned and walked away.

Over the years things had changed; Jesus felt it immediately.
As a youth in Nazareth and a young man in Capernaum, he
would toy with scribes and Pharisees – catch them in their rigid,
yet empty, logic. He knew they were wrong without perceiving
exactly why. But now, as a man experienced in the world, he'd
absorbed other ideas outside the restrictive confines of traditional Jewish notions. So now, in his mind, he directly related the
woes of his people with exactly that rigid thinking. He still wasn't
sure how to undercut it, whether he even could – but he knew it
was for him to make exactly that gesture. Who else would – or
could?

Invigorated from the exchange and recognition that these
small-minded priests and functionaries were not to be feared, he
had lots to ponder, to pray and meditate over, on his journey
home.

As small as Jerusalem had seemed, replete with its huge Temple
and other buildings, Nazareth seemed like a rabbit beside a
camel. Old, familiar streets – nothing changed here – alleys and
adjoining fields where he'd played with other children, the road
to Sepphoris he'd walked so many times, the well, the tiny market
place, open two days a week.

Twilight eased as he approached that doorway again, where
he'd been rudely turned away by his uncle some eight years ago.
In that time, to a culture attuned to death as a daily feature, many
of his family – particularly his mother – could be gone by now.

What a journey! He'd gotten rides across Samaria, but walked
through Galilee – so he could take in the scenery, beloved to his
eyes after so long. Now, walking the old main street of Nazareth,
he passed the well and headed home amid a flood of memories.

When the door swung open and an aging, yet deeply familiar

face peeked around, both stood in silence for a moment. First was that blinking moment of not recognizing the tall, confident man Mary's son had become. Then came just drinking in the moment as a sip of aged, but sweet, late-growth wine.

"Got a bite to eat for your boy, mother?" Jesus smiled.

The hug lasted until tears ceased. Mary ran out the back to get Simon, now living with wife and four children in the add-on James had built years ago. They sent Simon's oldest to get Salome and her three, and expected Joses home before too long. He'd have to wait to see James in the city.

The bad news was difficult to share, but Babe had died in child-birth three years prior. And Jude was missing now for months – feared captured by the Romans, perhaps hiding in the hills.

Once updated and thoroughly reacquainted, Jesus started to tell his tales, burning the midnight oil and then some, as children fell asleep one after the other. Room was made for Jesus, and he slept very well.

Some things were difficult, indeed, to relate to Mary, quite the traditionalist still. But even though many concepts Jesus covered in the next few days – things encountered and absorbed – were often complex, she reveled in the depth of her grown son's knowledge and his maturity and clarity in expressing them. They spent hours together in succeeding days, walking around the old town and out to the tombs, running into old friends, passing by Salome's house – and just sitting in the garden, chatting and getting to know each other again.

No, Jesus probably wouldn't be staying – nor would he be going so far away again. He'd had enough travel, long distance anyway. No, he wouldn't be looking for a job – he had enough money to last a while. No, he wasn't in a hurry to make any decisions. He had some distinct thoughts about what he would do, but wanted to discuss them with James before making any plans.

James was thrilled to see his brother again and impressed at his business acumen abroad. With limited communications in a world more unsettled under Tiberius than during decades of Pax Augusta, there was never assurance that Jesus was still alive, much less healthy and thriving. James himself, now successful with several building projects, had purchased a spread east of Autocratis, acreage with fruit trees and grazing fields for his horses, but with a house modest in structure. Jesus was invited to stay as long as he liked – plenty of room, now that James' older daughter had married. His wife had died during childbirth with a fourth baby, so he had two housemaids, a gardener and a cook caring for the second daughter, now 11, and Jesus' namesake, eight – and vegetable gardens.

Days later, James – quite active with business concerns – left his construction headquarters early to pick Jesus up for dinner away from home. Riding James' horses, they crossed the ridge to the north and down to a valley inn on the road to Cana.

Riding through the hills on a cloudy afternoon, James explained about their youngest brother, Jude, "I tried to get Yehudah beyond his angry streak. He had a run-in with Uncle Yoav, two, three years after you left. Hastened the old man's decline. Then he fell in with a rough crowd – the Zealots – and his father-in-law didn't approve. Tough all around." James explained Jude had disappeared nearly a year before and neither his in-laws nor James himself could find out where he was. "I don't have connections with that type – they see me as part of the estab-lishment."

Over wine while waiting to order supper Jesus spun tales of his travels.

"So, what's your plan *now*, Yeshua?" asked the younger, always the organizer. "I agree, absolutely, that our people need a different voice. You have some great points to share – but how do you plan to do that?"

"Well, the only way to communicate is visit villages and speak on the Sabbath. I figure some will hear and..."

James interrupted, "Lots of voices out there now. More Pharisees these days – they travel around to synagogues, spinning off their scriptures. They make money off it, as villages commonly pay them fees – mostly, country people are impressed by that type. How would you be different?"

"Different message, deeper look," answered Jesus.

"This isn't Alexandria, Yeshua. People are simple – farmers, peasants. A lot of those people *like* the same old message – there's comfort in that," James said, referring to the current scene. "But you know, there *is* one novel approach you might not know about. There's this teacher, the charismatic sort, baptizing people down along the Jordan – name's Yochanan, son of Zechariah. Mother says he's our second cousin, actually. Says we used to get together with them at festivals. I don't remember..."

But Jesus remembered John immediately. "Oh, yeah, he's about my age! Mother's cousin, Elisheva, married into that priestly line, *Abijah* – they do Temple service periodically," Jesus related, smiling. "We used to sneak out of the Temple, Yochanan and I, while grown-ups were babbling for endless hours. We found lots of adventures, exploring the lower city, down past the hippodrome. We even got to ... did you know there was a perfume factory down there?"

"No," laughed James heartily. "So that's where you went! Off sniffing perfume while I used to have to sit there listening while mother and dad argued about where you made off to!"

"You couldn't get into the new city – they always checked at the gate. And the upper city past the theater was too, I don't know, intimidating – big walls, big buildings, horses, guards. The lower city was fun, narrow streets, local markets. Sometimes Yochanan and I would just argue with Pharisees and scribes – but they didn't like it when we showed them up."

James continued, "Anyway, Yochanan has been attracting quite a following, catching people's attention. He started in Perea baptizing people in the Jordan down near the Dead Sea, and sort of worked his way up through Samaria. A bit of a recluse, he and his followers live in the desert. Now he's just south of Scythopolis, around Shalim, I hear."

"I'd like to see him again. He was different."

"People are saying he's Elijah come back. He's built quite a following," James thought for a minute. "We could take a ride down that way, if you want. It's less than thirty miles. Give us a day trip together."

Three days later, they took off. James had deposited Jesus' current funds with his business' banking connections in Autocratis. This, James assured Jesus, would safeguard his money even during current difficult times: Tiberius had tightened up finances in Rome, which affected all business operations by reducing access to capital. James' deposit alleviated Jesus carrying cash, yet he could withdraw funds whenever needed.

After all his travels – carts, camels, ships, hiking – Jesus enjoyed the comfort and speed of a good horse. A comfortable trot allowed time to relax, talk and enjoy the Galilean countryside. After stops to eat along the Jezreel Valley at Esdraelon and ask directions at Scythopolis, it was early afternoon when the two arrived at the Jordan. The crowd swarmed amid flies and mosquitoes in the warm valley, people arriving down paths in steady flux, taking a rope ferry across to the east shore. Mantle styles indicated Galileans, Samarians and Judeans – even Greeks, for the east bank, in Perea, was surrounded by Decapolis territory.

John presented quite a sight – not the gawky kid Jesus remembered. Tall and full-bodied, his camel-hair vest on top of a linen shirt projected an air of ruggedness yet unpretentious simplicity – in great contrast to fine, priestly robes or stylish, tight-threaded weaves worn by Pharisees. Jesus approached close enough to listen from the back of the throng. John spoke out continually while immersing one supplicant after the other.

"Repent," he bellowed above the river rush, gulls and continual murmur of the horde. "Our Lord's Kingdom approaches! The time is nigh! Repent now for the Lord's mercy!" People emerged from the waters muddy, but smiling and refreshed – for ritual cleansing was positive, but to have an up-and-coming prophet baptize you was a rare experience.

Jesus thought to talk to John, but the scene was far too chaotic. He crossed back over to James, who tended the horses. "I won't be able to talk to Yochanan for quite a while. Maybe you should take the horses and head back. I'll get back to your place in a few days."

"That's a long hike, Yeshua. I can leave you your mount so you…"

"Thanks, Yaakov, but the horse would just be a bother. I'll be fine."

"Good. See you when you get back. I'd stick around, but this repent stuff is a bit too much for me – and I'm busy tomorrow."

It was hours before the crowd dispersed. But people had to leave for home well before dark. John and his disciples were heading towards their makeshift campsite nearby when Jesus caught up.

"Cousin Yochanan – is your flock this frisky every day?" Jesus called out.

The Baptist turned and quickly recognized his clansman. "Yeshua, the son of god if I've ever had a vision!" He embraced his tall cousin and invited him to join along. "We'll have supper back at our resting place. We harvest wild edibles and honey – people bring us cakes from the towns. Not a Herodian feast, but it always suffices."

The two caught up on intervening decades and reminisced over oil lamps as night set in. Jesus held back on much of his unconventional viewpoint, wanting first to draw John out – see what his intent was, his purpose. "Yochanan, why didn't you just take up your father's priesthood succession rather than operating in this wilderness? You would have had a powerful platform in the Temple."

"The priests slither around the Temple like a brood of snakes feeding off mice. They echo words of prophets while knowing nothing. They live in wealth and above all else protect themselves. Pah! They would cut down any that might challenge them." John elaborated, "That must change – in our time, too! But no priest can do it from the inside!

"Our Lord must bring down his judgment on Israel and send a leader to us. I can feel it, I know it. The oppression from Rome and Herod are the signs. It must come soon – so people must be alert, repent to set themselves up for God's appraisal."

Jesus nibbled on the hard crackers and watercress, sipped a drink that reminded him of mead. "But how long have our people been waiting, how many centuries? What makes you think the time has come now?"

"Why it must, Yeshua! It must come soon!"

Jesus provided a different view – as he'd done often for John years ago during childhood. He first spoke of his travels, of new perspectives he'd encountered. "It's really obvious that the kingdom has *already arrived* for some, as they get blessings already while others suffer."

John had listened intently. "Do you think, then, could it come slowly, setting in as the Lord bestows his blessings on some then others?" asked John who hadn't considered such realities. "Perhaps the Lord is acting *even as we speak* – already setting some into positions of power to bring about His Kingdom." He came aglow thinking of that possibility.

Jesus recognized how some always did well in life, others suffered – as though they attracted blessings through their expectations and confidence, not their humble entreaties. John had only imagined the onset of a power from the heavens, wreaking retribution on sinners and non-believers. He was thrilled by a more realistic possibility

"As I've traveled, I've always been blessed," Jesus empha-sized. "Health, good fortune – the right connections when I've needed them, help when necessary. I want, personally, to communicate those things to our people." Jesus elaborated that all people were capable of attaining this positive state where life went well. John, interpreting Jesus' words through his idealistic bent, heard that Jesus intended to be Yahweh's voice to his people.

John recalled youthful Temple arguments with scribes and functionaries, "Yeshua, you have always had the right words. You must speak to our brothers. Then you must travel the roads of Galilee and Judea and tell the people. I can only help them cleanse, set them on the path. But I don't have your words. You must show them the way!"

They talked long that evening, covering many points. But set no specific plans. Jesus thought he would still have to devise a way to reach people. John thought he had one.

The next day, by late morning, people started to show up at the Jordan, some walking up the river path from Amathus in Perea or down from Pella in the Decapolis. Others took the small, swing-line ferry across the river by Aenon and Salim, having approached from Coreae in Samaria in the south or Scythopolis. They gathered around the clearing by a large bend in the river, tended to by John's followers, who explained what would happen. Jesus stood at the back of the crowd, wondering if he should volunteer to go through baptism as a fitting gesture to support John.

As the crowd hushed, their view was directed to a secluded spot on the hillside. The Baptist appeared dramatically; he walked slowly down to the crowd, raising his arms to the heavens. "Praise and behold," he projected as he approached. People murmured and gasped in anticipation; some cried out.

He quickly started the process, taking one or two at a time, walking them into the river and immersing them in ablution. "Be cleansed and prepare for the Lord, for the Lord's kingdom is soon at hand," he repeated in some variation, taking time for each person. This went on for two hours in a warm breeze as the sky clouded over, with people sharing food and sitting nearby to drink in the scene. With a few still trickling in by early afternoon, suddenly John, helping a last couple out of the Jordan, raised his hands. The crowd silenced.

"Body cleansing cannot reach the soul," his voice boomed out. "You must repent, for the Kingdom approaches – the axe nears, where it will strike down evil at the roots!"

A man, overcome, cried out and bowed before John, "But, master, what should we do?"

"Be fair and generous – don't cheat others out of money, take joy in your pay and use it wisely."

Another fell to his knees, "Are you the one Anointed to lead us into the Lord's Kingdom?" Others couldn't contain their emotions, calling out, cheering. John silenced them with his hands.

"I've told you all before, I'm here to make way for a greater one. I baptize you in water to cleanse your body; he will cleanse your spirit! Behold, today **he has come among us**!"

The crowd gasped as John motioned to Jesus to come forward, catching him by surprise – this hadn't been discussed the night before. Not wanting to embarrass his cousin – nor upstage him – he stepped forward. Tall and confident, appearing exotic dressed in a crisp Egyptian mantle, he presented a stunning image to the large crowd. With the focus on John and supplicants, nobody had noticed Jesus. He walked toward John almost as though he had appeared out of nowhere.

"Indeed, I should have you baptize me, Yeshua!"

"No, no, not at all, Yochanan," said Jesus, highly conscious of the focus of hundreds of eyes on him, yet following through as the situation presented. "I've come to you, make it so." Dropping his mantle and turban, he walked into the water. As John accompanied him into the river and, with his hand on Jesus' shoulder, eased him down into the flow, the clouds parted briefly to flood the valley in bright sunlight. All were mystified.

As Jesus emerged from the water, overcome by the coolness, the scene, years of travel and questioning, his cousin's sudden focus and his own uncertainty, the scene faded in his view, as though he were whisked back to that hilltop north of Capernaum in his younger days: he saw again the dove descend to flutter and light before him.

And he knew with great clarity, the meaning that had escaped him since that time: *the Lord presents peace to those who have it within*. He himself was at peace. Not needing money or praise, not bowing to anybody, nor fearing sickness or authority, he was fully at peace – *surely goodness and mercy will follow me*.

The crowd gasped as piercing sunlight broke through to blanket the scene; Jesus raised his hands. Some would claim later that they heard voices, others that the heavens split open. But for Jesus, it was another pointed epiphany: he had to share his insights with his fellow man, for no one else could – though he knew many would try, however lacking anything approaching awareness of the inner roots of peace.

Taking his mantle, he embraced John sincerely, spoke briefly of love and caring, then walked on up the hill where John had made his dramatic entrance. But Jesus kept on going, figuring that to be equally dramatic – and the only way out of John's scene.

East from the Jordan the terrain becomes hilly, on the eastern slope often forested and green – with deer trails to follow, if not paths. Jesus knew that, heading east, he would have to come to the Pella-Gerasa road. He could make it to Gerasa by the next day and go on from there. At this point he just needed to think, to get his churning emotions in order.

Knowing Gerasa well from his Decapolis trip, he spent a couple nights there. Picking up a water bladder and some food to carry along, he made his way out the road north – a camel trail that would lead to Auranitis, ultimately through Trachonitis to Damascus, though he had no intent to go that far. Coming to the Yarmuk River, he found a caravansary where he could overnight safely in seclusion with access to water – not too far from a small town and food.

He spent days in that semi-desert area, hiking and meditating, often walking along the top ridge of the deep Yarmuk canyon, stopping to enjoy the stunning scene.

Jesus knew now he had the creative power in his life – that he, *himself*, was the source of meaning. Yahweh would empower his intent, so fully as he trusted that – for trust itself was the key to fulfillment. Meditating, praying, simply peering out over the dramatic chasm below, he no longer felt at all separated from his deity, but connected – not judged by adherence to rituals, not regulated by divine expectations, but free to be himself.

So, while the problem had always plagued him of what to do, how to communicate his intense perception of connectedness, it became, he now knew, *how do I focus my intent, for I can accomplish exactly what I set out to do.*

One evening, in the quiet of brilliant stars and a crescent Moon, he imagined he could turn a stone into a loaf of bread – *why not*, he pondered, *if indeed I have the power*. Then he looked over the vast sky – the mysterious Milky Way amid known constellations – and thought about the enormous globe of earth he now perceived. *How silly*, he thought, *to perform such tricks when real bread – the harvesting of wheat, grinding meal, baking – these are all part of life, part of the splendor of existence. Why would I want to bypass that with silly tricks?*

One day, pondering a way forward, he thought he might tender an uprising – he would certainly have charisma and smarts enough to foment a revolution, maybe lead the Zealots as Jude had suggested. He could certainly overthrow that klutz Antipas, outsmarting him and the thuggish Romans. It was tempting. But, as he thought through it, Jesus ultimately realized, *revolution would accomplish nothing – so long as people still cling to conflict and mistrust, they will just realize their misery in other ways.*

He thought about wondrous tricks to show people, laughing to imagine climbing to the Temple roof and jumping off, imagined angels catching him, floating down amid money-changers and lamb salesmen in their den of merchandising that shamed the Temple grounds. He had to laugh to himself – *nothing, even that, would convince the hard-headed, hard-hearted priesthood and know-it-all scribes.*

At length, having come to peace with his true intent – to better mankind – he would simply speak, respond to events as they played out, unvaryingly trust in himself for wisdom and in his Lord to fulfill his intent, as was *always* his experience.

Having washed at the caravansary's spring, Jesus made his way south to the east-west road, where he got a ride through Abila to just outside Gadara on a farmer's wagon. As he walked through the city, bearing west on the Decumanus Maximus, the long, colonnaded main street, he was recognized.

"Master, I was there with Yochanan and saw you! Are you come to teach us?" he said, motioning to his friends. He turned excitedly to them, "This is the man I spoke of! Here he is!"

"Speak to us! We need you," they all began to shout, "for Yochanan has been thrown into prison!"

Jesus was stunned to learn that Antipas' agents had appre-hended John; people explained he'd been taken to Machaerus, a fortress east of the Dead Sea. But, taking that in stride, he said, "Let us find a place, for I have much to explain."

The basilica nearby provided an area beyond the markets to speak. But as Jesus talked, the crowd grew rapidly. Someone shouted, "Nobody can hear. The Theater is empty – let's go there." Just next to the basilica, the smaller city theater was open and provided much better acoustics. As word spread, more and more people entered.

Jesus, in his calm but penetrating manner, spoke to the crowd, mostly in Aramaic, as this crowd was primarily Jewish. But he filled in some things in Greek – making sure each point was clear: "The Kingdom of Heaven John spoke of *is* at hand, even as we speak. It will not come down from the sky, imposed by divine forces – but it is rooted within.

"The meek will enjoy its benefits, for they will be blessed with the peace they hold. Those who seek to find it will do so – and they will be amazed." Jesus spoke for some time, relying on thoughts that came to mind – he joked and chatted with the crowd as it filled the Theater.

One man limped in and sat off to one side in the front row. As Jesus spoke of love and acceptance, the man began to cry.

"Is it something I said," Jesus joked as he looked at him.

The man cried out, "I have never known love. My parents beat me; people reject me!"

Jesus approached him, "Come on up." The man stood, tears in his eyes. Jesus put his hand on the man's shoulder and pulled him closer, then turned him around and put his arm around him while speaking to the crowd. "Here is a handsome man, sincere and caring. What's not to like?" He turned, facing the man, "Your parents are gone now. Release the spirit of fear and pain – for that will only bring you more suffering!" The crowd cheered and the man's face brightened.

"You see," Jesus continued, "here are your friends – your new family. I call on you all, each of you here who can hear my words, to love your neighbor – for that love can only sow seeds in the world that will sprout nourishing fruit for you yourselves, as for others."

The man walked back to his seat, smiling – and without the

limp. The crowd murmured that he'd been healed. Jesus spoke for some time, then promised to return. He told the crowd to turn to strangers and greet one another, to make new friends and retain the attitude of brotherhood. As they did that, he left and walked through town – with many following, spreading the word of the man who was healed.

With John's imprisonment, Jesus determined he himself should pick up the slack until John was released – but with his own message, not the old apocalyptic line that John furthered.

The scene repeated itself several times in villages on the way back to James' house: each time, someone who had been at the Jordan recognized Jesus. Each time, as he spoke, visibly ill people came forth and, with Jesus' reassurance and warm manner, would find symptoms apparently alleviated. Jesus said each time, "Your trust has made you whole." But mostly people looked at these events as divine – as though the evil demons they blamed for illness were responding to Jesus' authority.

At James' place, Jesus explained what had transpired, including John's imprisonment.

"Yes, he was continually berating Herod for his illegal marriage of Herodias," James related. "Yochanan must have known that could only go on so long before some reprisal."

Jesus was deeply concerned about John's fate. While he recognized the empty hope reinforced by the Baptist's traditional apocalyptic expectation of heavenly intervention to overthrow Roman rule, he appreciated his cousin's vigor and effort to make change for the better. And he despised the uncaring attitude of royalty in light of widespread poverty.

Following a short trip home to visit his mother, Jesus picked up some of his savings from James' financial institution, explaining he needed a headquarters and knew the area north of Galilee's "Sea". Capernaum's living expenses were notably low, so he made his way back there – a good place, relatively central, to settle while traveling around to speak. His reputation was spreading rapidly: even James in Autocratis and Mary back in Nazareth were already hearing of John's revelation about him and stories of his healing and teaching.

Passing through Magdala, Jesus tried to find Mary – but found only more prominence. Recognized immediately, he was pressed into speaking – but didn't see Mary in the crowd. But it had been eight years – so likely her father was dead. *She may not be there anymore*, he reasoned, *maybe married, maybe even dead* – and in any case seeking someone with a common name would be tough. He went on to Capernaum.

People recognized him there, too – but not from the old boat-repair days: the younger generation in town hadn't known him then. Word had spread, so he was expected to address a crowd gathering near the market. After speaking of the Kingdom – he'd settled on *"Malkutha D'Alaha"*, Kingdom of Yahweh-god, as a phrase to illustrate the state of being where life works well by fully trusting Yahweh to manifest goodness – Jesus reinforced *health* among the people in lieu of their old "evil spirit" agent. He knew health to emerge from inner roots, from the same trust within as all other blessings. But, knowing popular lore attributed illness to impurity and evil spirits, he had to play the game. So long as people saw him with power over their demons, he could easily effect healing – and perhaps get the uninitiated to recognize their own power, thereby spurring improvement.

At the same time, Jesus also realized that *his* own trust would only lead him to encounter people who *could* be healed. Those stuck in rigid self-defeat wouldn't show up or couldn't get to him. Such was his own immersion in the "Kingdom".

Privately, after dismissing the crowd, he asked for a place to spend the night, the hour being late. Several offers ensued. When he mentioned looking for property outside of town, several townspeople excitedly offered to show him available places they knew of the next day.

In short order, he'd arranged to lease a vacant homestead, agreeing to renovate the buildings – four attached rooms, plus a larger storage building, all enclosed within a courtyard by a wall – in exchange for one year's free usage. He didn't anticipate getting any animals, but could clean out the rooms for guests. Here he could set up a home base, travel to speak, but have a central place to return to.

A quick trip to the north, covering Cadasa, Gishala – where the olive oil and silk operations shut down briefly so workers could come and hear him – and Sepph indicated that Jesus needed some help. Crowds were growing too large to handle and now that Jesus had a residence, towns were sending emissaries to request his visit.

Home for a few days, he took a break from house repair to head down to the fishing docks. Not far from where he'd left them years ago, Simon and Andrew were pulling nets across the shore and folding them after a day's catch had been sorted. Grown into their late teens, they were robust young men.

"Ready for some travel now?" Jesus called out. "Come! I'll make you fishers of men."

The brothers dropped their net and ran over. "Yeshua!" Simon yelled. "We've heard all about *you* – heard your talk in town. But we didn't know if you remembered us!"

"Of course, I remember, Kaipha – I had to come back to check on you. But you've sure grown!"

James and John, sons of Zebedee, heard the noise and joined in – *Sons of Thunder*, Jesus remembered calling them, when they used to make such ruckus on the beach as boys.

"You all wanted to travel, as I recall. I'll be spreading the word all around – could use some help with it. Get your boats in order and come on up – I'm laying out plans for a trip south."

When he got home, he found his messy bachelor décor rearranged: he had a visitor. "Miriam!" he yelled and ran to embrace her. Now in her middle twenties, she'd grown to full womanhood. It took hours to catch up.

Mary had stayed two years in Magdala before her father died. Her mother passed a year later. With no siblings, Mary inherited the house and some money. In time, she sold the house and returned to Capernaum, where she bought out the Inn where she'd worked. That kept her busy enough – but she'd hoped through the years that Jesus would return.

But she hadn't expected a celebrity to come back.

Jesus laughed. "I need a means to get my message out. Fame isn't something I've ever wanted, but people buy into a big show – so I'll give them the show if it can get the points across." As it was late, Mary stayed the night – and got her things the next day to move in. She could hold up the home front while, Jesus traveled.

During coming weeks, as Jesus visited towns to the west and in Lower Galilee, he assembled other men attuned to his message. These would act as "apostles", that is, men he could "send out" as messengers to set up appearances – even as ambassadors to teach and carry his message onwards, ultimately, once they each fully comprehended life's function as illustrated in the Kingdom metaphor.

He also honed that message, building up phrases and simple stories that worked to communicate his viewpoint, helping his unsophisticated audience to move beyond ancient thinking. The *Kingdom*, the word "*Malkutha*" he came to use, meant the power or authority, not a physical, geographical space as in a worldly domain. So his phrase, *Malkutha D'Alaha*, would indicate a state of authority one could attain by complete trust, wherein desired or beneficial effects would manifest – for one's desire, Jesus realized, was not always consistent with one's best interest. He used the Greek equivalent, *Basileia tou Theou*, when needed.

And he accommodated unusual, spontaneous things happening. His appearances became so emotionally charged, that attendees interpreted any sort of twist as miraculous. When people suddenly felt better in the exhilaration of his personal charisma and inspired message of love – it seemed a mystical healing in their eyes, and grew to even greater proportions as the story spread. When he woke on a boat during a storm and told his companions to relax and have trust, they were amazed when the storm subsided soon thereafter – and called it miraculous, attributing weather control to Jesus.

At all appearances, Jesus emphasized trust, faith in one's own connection to the divine – that the *very nature of trust itself* brought positive effects. But as often as he repeated, "Your faith has made you whole," or "Your trust has healed you," they wanted to champion *him* as the agent channeling Yahweh's power into healing. Most, he realized, with their simple Yahweh-centric view, didn't get his message of personal power. *But some will*, he thought, *and others will at least see their lives improve.*

With initial focus on Galilee, Jesus' close-knit followers were exposed to key perspectives during many appearances. But when Nisan arrived and Passover would have many villages empty for travel to Jerusalem, Jesus took the time to thoroughly train his disciples in frequent sessions at the Capernaum homestead. Following that, they were sent out to organize talks. Jesus would travel around on schedule, appearing to ever larger crowds energized in anticipation. During these talks, much more organized on preset dates arranged beforehand by disciples, Jesus would teach and interact, bringing laughter and levity to people's lives – showing the Kingdom's power through his deeds and caring.

Knowing that *recognizing* the connection between personal confidence – i.e., trust – and life itself was "key" to the Kingdom, he worked up, or spontaneously cited, new parables that conveyed this understanding. That simple recognition, he likened to a Mustard Seed, the smallest of seeds that would grow into a great bush – as would the Kingdom come to dominate personal life when nurtured within.

This simple act – recognizing one's *own* determinative role in unfolding life – he likened to yeast when applied to dough: it came to permeate and affect the whole, i.e., dominate life for the one who understood. Seeing the Kingdom work in life was like a treasure a man found in a field, Jesus illustrated: once knowing it was there, wise men would buy the whole field.

Through much of the summer, touring Samaria, northern Perea, Decapolis' cities Pella and Hippos, then north to Raphana, he frequently encountered people who tried to fit his new perspective into older prophetic accounts. Occasionally he would relate his points to scripture, because that was expected. But he explained that they couldn't attach his greater ideas to old teachings like a new patch to old clothing – it would only tear way. They should discard worn-out ideas like the old garment and accept a whole new one. Likewise, they wouldn't put new wine into old wine sacks – they would burst from pressure. They needed a new sack as with his new teachings.

Some, so used they were to their old garments – their traditional way of seeing things – couldn't get it. Others at least looked beyond standard thinking.

Knowing that all of life is connected – he had to think back on Heraclitus and Gautama, who long ago recognized that – and that its qualities reflect the inner self, he pointed out that whoever *has* wealth will be given more. For those with little, even what they have will be taken away – unless they change and begin trusting.

Between trips – and when not repairing his Capernaum headquarters as a welcome diversion to travel and speaking – Jesus would bring his followers in for long "training" sessions. He tried to pass along his awareness of the *Kingdom*: how life manifested blessings, fulfilling events, when recognized and

trusted in, but often yielded pain and suffering when not understood. Instead of the parables given to the public, he could teach
these insiders directly – wisdom, knowledge, things he'd learned
and personal insights. He knew that one day these men would
have to carry on the message if man were to outgrow obeisance
to old, dictatorial gods and fear of threatening demons.

Sometimes they seemed to understand, more often not. When
having to speak on their own, disciples mostly reiterated Jesus'
stock phrases, parables and witticisms. Not really grasping the
simple understanding that life's quality was initiated personally,
not a single disciple could illustrate the Kingdom from his own
enlightened stance.

"If the Kingdom were in the sky, the birds would get there
first," Jesus would explain. "If it were in the sea, then fish would
beat you to it. But the Kingdom is *within you* – and it's all around
you." He didn't know how much clearer he could put it. And he
added his colloquial kicker: "Those with ears had better listen!"
How often he got frustrated when even his own inside crew
didn't get the message but heard in his message apocalyptic
warnings and advice on living. *In time, perhaps,* he thought, *they
will get it, for life is exceedingly simple.*

As summer passed and the month of Tishri approached, James
rode down to Capernaum to invite Jesus to join Simon, Joses,
their mother and himself for a trip to Jerusalem to celebrate the
Feast of the Tabernacles. Jesus was curious if his reputation had
yet made it to Judea, but was rather busy and a bit wary to take
on a big stage as yet. He declined, but later reconsidered. He
picked up a mantle and turban tailored in Mesopotamian style.
Taking a boat to Tiberias, he got a coach to Jerusalem. Once there,
he found a small, commercial Booth to live in – the point of the
Sukkoth festival in honor of booths lived in when Israelites left
Egypt. Before circulating, he pinned his hair in Assyrian style
and trimmed back his beard, wearing his Mesopotamian garb to

avoid being noticed.

Mulling about the crowd, he heard his name often. Many proclaimed him the superior of the Baptist, most spoke highly of him, saying they'd heard him in Galilee or the Jordan River basin. Some, to Jesus' amusement, called him a phony, a cheap magician. He dared not speak, for his voice could give him away to any who had heard him – and he avoided his family in the throng.

Halfway through *Sukkoth*, though, Jesus couldn't resist shedding his costume and joining the debate at the Temple.

When teachers of the law emphasized eating and preparation practices as vitally necessary to avoid defilement and began to detail accepted practices, Jesus slammed them aggressively as hypocrites. "Isaiah foretold of you, 'They honor me with lip service but their hearts are far from me,'." Attracting a large crowd, he continued, "Listen and get the point: what goes into a man's mouth does not make him unclean – but rather, what comes out is what defiles him!"

He addressed growing crowds as officials cowered away, "Ignore them! They are blind guides – if a blind man steers a blind man, they will both fall into the ditch." Word of the incident spread through the crowd and went not unnoticed by the Temple hierarchy.

Through autumn, talks on the road got so crowded, Jesus and accompanying disciples couldn't even eat while people demanded more and pushed in. At one point, concerned at all the celebrity Jesus had built, his mother brought James and Simon to restrain him, thinking he'd gone mad.

Jesus pulled them aside once the crowd abated and explained, "You don't light a lamp and hide it under a barrel, right? I have a powerful message and have to present it. If our people don't change, they'll continue under the same yoke they've endured for centuries. To grow, they need to hear a clearer message. That's what I'm giving them."

James, able to ignore exaggerated accounts going around, grasped it before his mother and Simon. "Yeshu', I've got to get to know what you are saying – all I hear are inflated stories and crazy reports of miracles. I have more time now. If I can get involved, perhaps I can help you on the business end."

Jesus gladly welcomed that: James' level-headed intelligence would benefit the effort operationally and financially. "I have Yehudas caring for our kitty. We receive donations from several sources and don't spend much. Some of the disciples still work at their trades part time."

James had heard of Judas, and was immediately wary, "Isn't that the one they call 'Dagger-Man'? You want him to handle your finances?"

Jesus smiled, "He *was* one of the Dagger Men, the Sicarii – that group of rebels. We still call him *Iscariot*. But Yehudas sees now that only peaceful change will work. I think rebellion is out of his blood."

Pressure built daily on Jesus. Entreaties to speak everywhere, including Judea and even Jerusalem, kept Mary Magdalene and volunteers busy coordinating commitments. Word of ramped up operations had spread even to the Temple elite – and, clearly, they didn't like it. Increasingly often, Jesus encountered Pharisees and hypercritical scribes sent north to trap and embarrass. That proved difficult to do, but still Jesus developed wariness of establishment power sources.

"Prince of Demons!" A group of blustering Temple functionaries heckled at a talk near Dora. "You must be healing from the power of Satan!"

Jesus had to chuckle at their stupid suggestion, "Would Satan drive out his own minions? If a house is split against its own structure, it all falls in. If Satan drives out Satan, how could his kingdom stand?" He had listeners laughing at them.

Other scribes and officials asked him for a miraculous sign to prove his status.

Jesus blasted them, "What corrupt and warped fool would ask for magic tricks to prove anything? Do as I say – you will see for yourselves what the Kingdom is all about. Until then, I'll not be performing magic like cheap theater for a simpleton audience."

Yet again, when a Pharisee later criticized Jesus for associating with tax collectors and "sinners" – one of his disciples was a prominent supervisor of tax receipts – he commented, "A physician tends to sick people, not healthy ones, right? So I try to bring improvement where it's needed. Go study Hosea: 'For I desire mercy, not sacrifice.' You might get some insight on real living."

Eventually, when he deemed his disciples ready to go out on their own – *might as well get their feet wet*, he thought – Jesus sent his twelve out to different areas. "Travel light – you have to trust in yourselves, so don't take extra baggage, mantles, cash or bread. When you enter a town, tell them who you are and speak in a public place – they'll know you by now. If they offer hospitality, accept it. If not, just move on: not all ears are ready to hear."

While they were gone, Jesus could relax at home and spend some time with Mary. As he repaired courtyard walls and cleaned out the shed, Mary asked him, "Do you think your followers could take over for you one day? I don't see how long you can keep this up. You've been on the road for months – and those crowds overwhelm you."

Jesus mulled that thought as he cleaned out flaky plaster and prepared a hole for patching. "They don't really get it, Miriam – not nearly as well as you do. Some of them still look for heavenly host to come gliding down out of the clouds offering invitations to enter the Kingdom. Until they see for themselves, they can only repeat my words. That has some value, if they get them right. But if they see for themselves, they could weave their own parables."

"But where can this end, Yesh'? What can you accomplish

long term – change our Jewish traditions? Create another sect, like the Essenes? What's the goal?" Mary was concerned. She'd seen Jesus put so much into his efforts it had become his whole life; she wondered what lay ahead.

"My goal, Miriam, is to lay out a greater vision for all to see. Exactly how that will play out, I don't know. But I trust myself and Yahweh fully, so I just do what seems right. Everything will work out."

The disciples reported back after some time: they'd done well in most places, healing people, speaking to enthusiastic groups – but seemed happy to be back in support roles. Taking a break themselves, some resumed fishing and other jobs to pick up some cash, others went off to *Pesach*, wanting to check the scene in Jerusalem.

Before his next trip out in early summer, Jesus received a request to speak locally in Bethsaida, just east of Capernaum – yet, even on short notice, hundreds turned out. Overcrowding the town's market area, they had to move up the hill to high ground overlooking the lake – with its silvery blue, fishing boats, gulls and surrounding hills enchanting the scene.

The disciples eventually quieted the group and had them sit on an embankment where all had a view. Jesus, in simple terms, illustrated the connection between inner characteristics and the positive outcome they would elicit:

"Good must come to non-materialists – theirs is the Kingdom
   now…
Good must come to those with sincere empathy – they will
   find compassion from others…
Good must come to the unaggressive – in peace will they take
   over the world…
Good will unfold for those who hunger for honesty – they
   will have their fill…

Good will unfold for the merciful – for they will receive it in
kind…

Good shall flow to the genuine – for they will understand the
One…

Good shall return to peacemakers – for they will be revered…"

Jesus spoke for some time, the crowd listing in rapt fixation, as
gentle breezes blew through Jesus' long, dark hair, his hands
gesturing gently but effectively, his eyes connecting with each
listener.

"I tell you to love your enemies – do good to those who hate
you. Return kindness to those who mistreat you. None of those
you deem to be adversaries really is the cause of your ills, but that
the Lord allows it based on *your own* hate and ill will. The chief
priests of our traditions would have you purify your body – as
though washing only the outside of a cup. But I tell you, the
inside must be cleaned even more so – for it is from there that the
wine of your life flows."

As noon passed and questions began, the disciples mentioned
that people would be getting hungry. But, not anticipating such a
crowd, they hadn't arranged for bread or staples. Removed from
the village, they thought the group should be released so they
could make their way home.

But Jesus had noted many women in the crowd. Indeed his
message, much more inclusive than strict traditional views
depicting women as mere property – inherently tainted at that –
was always attractive to wives and young women. That parents
now brought unmarried daughters to his talks – effectively
showing them off to potential mates of like mind who attended –
wasn't lost on Jesus' perceptive view. But he also knew that the
women would be prepared.

Jesus turned to the crowd and quieted them. "We're all
working up an appetite in the open air here. I see that some have
brought provisions along. Others, though, perhaps expecting

manna to appear." Jesus paused as the crowd started laughing, "Well, sorry, we didn't have enough time to make those arrangements!" More laughter. "So perhaps we can all share. We are all mothers and brothers here – and, of course, we are all certainly our brother's keepers, right?

"We have just a few loaves and some fish along." Jesus stopped when he noticed some older children, already dispatched by listeners into Bethsaida, were returning with added loaves and dates. Coming up the trail on a cart were Simon Peter and John, son of Zebedee. They had anticipated the situation earlier and hustled into town, where they loaded the day's excess from fish salting/drying operations and were bringing it up on carts. All had plenty to eat, with lots left over.

Before a subsequent trip through Galilee that summer, Jesus decided to simplify his apparel. Removing his turban as per custom while speaking on sacred topics – and worrying about it during the mayhem of crowd pressure – had become too troublesome. Still needing protection from the intense sun, he began to wear a simple hood; easily folded back while he spoke, it required no further attention.

Followers of John the Baptist caught up with the itinerants near Cana. "Why is it that you and your followers don't fast as we and the Pharisees do?"

Jesus was never one for decreed rituals from olden times. Still, he didn't want to degrade the Law, as that would put his whole message in question. He responded, "During a wedding feast, while the party is going on, you don't hold back on food. So long as the bridegroom is here, the party is still going strong. People can fast when he's gone." He'd found that, putting an answer into a cryptic image – one which the recipient probably couldn't catch quickly, was always a disarming reply. It carried the answer, but didn't allow further argument: people wouldn't admit they didn't get it.

Traveling through his hometown, Nazareth, Jesus visited his mother overnight. On the Sabbath, he went to the synagogue and began to teach with the same parables and insights that moved crowd after crowd – far deeper insights than he ever could point out there as a youth. He read scriptural passages that indicated his own ministry. But people argued his points, insisting on further proofs from scripture. They demanded healings, as they'd heard stories from other towns. And they questioned, "What do you think, who are you? Aren't you the builder? Don't we know your brothers and mother?"

Jesus countered strongly, annoyed at their attitude, "I tell you there was more pain in the time of Elijah than follows in my wake. More skin disease abounded around Elisha than I ever see – with none of them in those times cleansed!"

The natives were furious at the implication Jesus – this hometown boy – was the equal of these vaunted prophets. Some rubes in the crowd grabbed Jesus and the whole group rushed to the top of the ridge overlooking Nazareth and meant to chuck him off. Knowing the ruffians and others by name, he looked them in the eye and they let him go. In silence, he walked right through the crowd back to his mother's house.

Amid such doubt, no healings happened and little wisdom shared with ears not ready to hear. *Only in his hometown is a prophet without honor*, he thought – and never returned to Nazareth.

During his subsequent talk at Nain, Jesus was again questioned by John's devotees asking on his account. "Are you really the one come to save the people, or should we expect another?"

Jesus answered, "Just tell John what you see and hear. People experience healing; they hear a clearer message and their lives are improved," then turned to the gathering of Nain towns-people.

"Did you go to the Jordan to watch reeds blow in the desert

wind? No? To see finely adorned Temple officials? No? Then what? A prophet – and *more than* a prophet.

"It was said, 'I will send a messenger who will prepare the way before me' – so Yochanan has done. If you believe so, he was the Elijah – as that prophet opposed the preachers of Ba'al, so Yochanan has exposed the Temple elite. Yochanan came neither feasting nor drinking, doing only good, yet they said he was possessed! But this *Son of Adam*," Jesus said, using a common phrase to refer to himself, "eats, drinks and befriends tax collectors – so they call me a drunk and a glutton. But regardless of their shallow condemnation, since Yochanan, the Kingdom has been advancing forcefully by men who grasp it with vigor!"

When they'd left, he spoke with his disciples about the Baptist. "You know, from the beginning through the greatest prophets, none born of a woman has been greater than Yochanan. But whoever of you becomes as a child so that you can see the Kingdom in front of you – you will be greater than he."

"But, Master," Simon said, reflecting the group's viewpoint, "we don't really understand that. How can we become children again? Should we go back and play on the beach – throw rocks into the water like we used to?"

With unending patience, Jesus explained, "You must clear your mind of all the rules and all the teachings. As the child each of us was, before hearing of all man's woes, before learning of the Law and how to be, to eat, to behave, to think, you were free and naïve, surrounded by the Kingdom. But as you learned seven, then seventy, then seven times seventy rules for living, being and seeing the world, the Kingdom faded from view.

"You learned to classify up from down, in from out; you learned to separate male from female – to think of a hand or an eye instead of just using them. When you bring *each of those pairs into One*, so that male and female are seen united, up and down as two parts of a whole, *then* you will understand the Kingdom.

"For this reason, I tell you: one who is *whole* will be filled with light. But one divided is filled only with darkness."

Thomas – known as the "Twin", for he looked much like Jesus – questioned further, "Why do you not speak of these things to the people?"

"They just won't get it. And they will argue and fret and walk away with no seeds planted, no sprouts to grow, no crop to harvest. I speak to them in parables because stories plant ideas in their minds – yet don't allow for argument. If you don't quite get the point, how can you argue? Yet it will have an effect within."

Upon return to Capernaum, Jesus expressed frustration that cities where people's lives had noticeably improved, where healing and brotherhood were experienced, hadn't totally embraced his new message. Chorazin and Bethsaida had declined subsequent offers to speak – likely pressured by local synagogue officials fearing a huge turnout from other places. Even Capernaum had rebuffed his gesture to hold regular talks there.

Then word came around that John had been beheaded – an offense beyond any reason, but infinitely more so as it had been a reward, so rumored, for a dance performed by Herodias' daughter. Jesus resolved to aggressively confront the religious authorities, but steer clear of Antipas, given his total lack of ethics and morals. He would provide no excuse for Galilean or Roman authorities to curtail his ministry. At that point, he started to conceptualize a comprehensive tour of Judea with pointed speaking at the Temple itself. He would go there at the next Passover, he thought, keeping a supportive crowd around at all times so authorities would be afraid to arrest him, lest they kick off rioting.

The disciples had set up a trip north, along the Mediterranean: James decided to come along at least to Tyre, so Jesus took Mary of Magdala, too. Jesus hadn't yet returned there since his labor stint at the south docks, so he looked forward to his three talks set for Tyre's Jewish communities.

Illustrating life through parables at the first Tyre appearance, he emphasized the nature of personal experience in terms of perceiving the Kingdom, "Many stand grouped at the door, but only one alone can enter the bridal suite." When Andrew later questioned that image, Jesus explained simply that it was a personal journey for each toward enlightenment – no groups could get through the door. This, of course, even Andrew realized, was a strong indictment against organized religions.

At the second talk, Jesus noticed, quietly seated at the back with a hood over her head, the Sibyl he'd consulted years ago. His talk there was particularly vigorous – for he'd figured out her divination imagery about the lioness – his mother – and doves, his two sisters. The bulls were clearly his brothers: James had approached, while Jude walked away.

And Sibyl's sheep prophecy: his disciples. He led them towards high ideals, pristine realizations, yet they invariably ended up back in the valley of old thinking.

His eyes met the Sibyl's several times. But, he thought, he must address the whole crowd and keep his message broad. But he used his best sayings and tied them all together – but would the sunrise he so eloquently depicted be only sunset for his listeners?

"Look, a farmer out in his field scattered seeds. Some flew onto the road where birds ate them. Some landed on rocks and dried out, while others were pecked by birds or consumed by worms. But the ones landing on good soil sprouted and yielded a great harvest." The Sibyl smiled as she looked into his eyes and for a moment the room briefly disappeared. Jesus smiled and nodded. Then she left. When the disciples later reported excitedly five gold aurei donated to the kitty, Jesus wasn't surprised.

Afterwards, as usual, the disciples argued over the meaning

of his *scattered seeds* parable. Jesus stopped the debate, "Many hear my message, but most don't get the point. But for those who do, life provides prosperity – and *they* will pass along not only their abundance, but the viewpoint necessary to achieve it."

After the third talk, many clambered forward to be touched and healed – which had become typical. But Jesus emphasized that, following his directions – had listeners functional ears to hear it – would *eliminate the need* for such healing. But in their misery, loneliness and hopelessness, what they wanted was immediate alleviation of pain and the stimulation of meaning added to seemingly trivial lives. In the energy state of these repeated scenes, both of those often happened. But Jesus wondered about those who proclaimed being healed during his appearance – how they fared subsequently if they didn't look inward to change.

James, not having heard Jesus in such a setting was exceedingly impressed. Privately, he assured Jesus he would help in any way possible, for this message had to get out. After the third talk, Jesus sent the disciples off to Sidon and Caesarea Philippi to put off scheduled talks there temporarily, claiming he needed a break. He arranged passage for three to Alexandria, then met James and Mary Magdalene at the docks.

After a brief, pleasant voyage, he showed his two closest confidants the grandest city he'd seen. They toured around for several days, exploring the Library and Serapeum – and the Musaeum, where Jesus retrieved his remaining money. Funds were being depleted and he didn't like asking for money. Though many followers were donating generously to cover disciples' living expenses, Jesus didn't use those donations personally.

Jesus thoroughly enjoyed the break in constant touring and pressure from hordes of people who always wanted something. He realized how hemmed in he'd gotten, to where he couldn't sit in a tavern and drink a goblet of wine without people approaching him. James and Mary relished the fabulous city with a noticeably more relaxed Jesus. But soon enough, those days passed. He returned to Sidon for talks there while James accompanied Mary back to their respective homes.

On their way, they could discuss the situation. Mary was deeply concerned that Jesus was overextending himself, knowing that he didn't want to build a new religion, just turn Judaism in the "right" direction. But James knew well that the priestly hierarchy would never concede that, so entrenched and bureaucratic it had become – its answers frozen in messages of old. Marble-lined halls of the Temple allowed no room for new prophets. Neither could calculate where Jesus' powerful message would take him, as an irresistible force one day must approach an immovable object.

Jesus, during days covering villages of the Syrian countryside inland from Sidon, spoke in parable of a feast: the host had prepared a great banquet, but found that, one after the other, his invitees had other commitments and gave excuses. Eventually, the host invited anybody off the streets to join him. After the third use of this story, disciple Bartholomew questioned its meaning.

"Think a second before you ask, Bar Talmai," Jesus said. "We offer many delectable items for thought here. But who amongst the experts in law – scribes, Pharisees and such – comes to the feast? They all have excuses – other ideas that preoccupy their attention. So what do we do?"

Bartholomew nodded his head, "We offer the message to anybody who will partake of it!"

From there south, passing through several villages in Iturea and eventually Gaulanitis and home, Jesus never mentioned the venture to Alexandria.

Shortly thereafter, with winter approaching, Jesus took the

disciples through Bethsaida back north to the high villages around Caesarea – missed previously – which had sent requests.

Caesarea Philippi had been founded by Philip the Tetrarch, half-brother to Antipas, as *Paneas* some years earlier – then renamed in honor of the emperor and himself. As administrative capital of Philip's holdings inherited from his father, Herod the Great, it was a prominent city – and scenic, sitting at the base of lofty Mt. Hermon. Philip still ruled his Tetrarchy, including Gaulanitis and its Lake Huleh, the upstream source of the Sea of Galilee.

Following a robust talk at Caesarea – likening the Kingdom to a pearl found in a consignment, which the merchant bought while selling off the rest – Jesus spoke with several disciples who were there preparing to head home. "What are people saying? Who do they think this Son of Adam is?" It was difficult to gauge people's impressions, so exaggerated the effect had become.

The sons of Zebedee said they'd heard people call him John the Baptist come back. James the Less, son of Aphaeus, said "Elijah is what I've heard." Others mentioned Jeremiah and older prophets. None of these surprised Jesus, as most people couldn't accept a new teacher whose message exceeded old boundaries.

"What about you all – who do you say I am?"

Simon, the "Rock", said, "You are the Anointed One who will lead us to the Kingdom!" Always animated and dedicated, Simon had seen his hero only in superlative terms since first meeting him on the beach.

"Good for you, Kaipha. I hereby award you the keys to the Kingdom – but what you do with them depends entirely on you: whatever is locked here, in life, will be locked also *within*. But what you wish to unlock here must first be freed in the inner realm.

"But listen, all of you: *do not* call me Anointed – the Messiah – out there in front of others. They will draw wrong conclusions." Jesus didn't want diversions to his message. But the disciples took that to mean he acknowledged being the awaited leader, anointed as prophets of old with the spirit of Yahweh upon him. Who else could attract such response wherever he goes? Where Jesus sought to empower people over their own lives, most, with ears not hearing, projected Yahweh's power onto Jesus himself.

Before leaving Caesarea, he pulled together some enthusiastic listeners and his disciples for a heart to heart talk. He explained challenges ahead, but felt that many were finally getting his Kingdom message and could realize its innate personal power: "Some standing here will not taste death before they see the Kingdom arrive, bringing its power." That would be needed, he felt, for any to be able to carry on his message. *All men must pass away in time,* he mused to himself, *and I will too.*

Jesus dispatched for home all but his most trusted three, Simon, John and John's brother, James. Those he equipped with extra tunics, mantles and special sandals enclosed with extra leather and papyrus padding. He'd had a great idea for a get-away up Mt. Hermon, a rare treat for those three who'd grown up in the constant heat below sea level. Having arranged for a mule cart out to the near base of the ridge that peaked over 9000 feet, he planned a rugged hike up as far as they could get – reminding them more than once that the way back down would be easier. Jesus knew that none of the fishermen had ever been so high to see such views – and he himself was curious.

Carrying along wine and food, they could relax for the day – quite unusual anymore. Climbing for hours, stopping to catch their breath in thinning air, they drank with gusto in the parching, cool air. They could freely reminisce about the old days, the future – plans to expand and take the message throughout Asia Minor, Egypt and elsewhere once Jerusalem was in line. They joked and bathed in awe at the view – the Mediterranean spanning the horizon, 35 miles west, and Tiberias, misty, barely in view hugging the far tip of the lake, easily 40 miles distant.

Fresh and exuberant, they hiked up to a first crest, then continued north down across a saddle, and up again, approaching the main peak. But wine and altitude were taking their toll – at a rest stop, the disciples got very sleepy and dozed off. Jesus noted clouds moving in rapidly, though, and yelled to wake them – exposed as they were on the ridge with no shelter. As suddenly as mountain weather changes, a blizzard struck from the north, with abrupt winds whipping, swirling up off the western slope, bathing the area in pure white as the afternoon sun cut under billowing clouds. Jesus, seeing the clouds were isolated, raised his arms in the fluffy snow – a phenomenon he'd only seen rarely near Pergamon and in Thrace, but never around Capernaum.

The disciples, slightly drunk, woozy from altitude and half frozen in the chilly wind, wakened to a strange, white-out scene with Jesus at the center. Lightning flashed with thunder in the distance, startling the men. Simon began to babble out of his daze – something about putting up shelters for Moses and Elijah. Clearly, he didn't know what he was saying. The cloud then wrapped the mountain peak in bright fog as the wind howled up the canyon. The disciples, fearing the wrath of Yahweh, covered themselves with their extra mantles.

In minutes, winds and clouds were gone and the warm sun returned. Jesus nudged his companions, prodding them to come out. Frozen, fearful and confused, the three hustled down the path just as Jesus had predicted: *much* faster than they'd come up. Only long afterwards did they recall the strange event and discuss their near psychedelic impressions.

Meanwhile, word of Jesus and his popularity had spread to higher quarters. Antipas, relieved now of John's constant criticism of his marriage to Herodias as illegal and immoral, wondered whether John had reincarnated or yet another charismatic lunatic was spreading falsehoods among the paupers.

Having sent out agents to secretly spy on Jesus' appearances, though, he had yet to sense any dangerous political incitement.

But operatives sent by Temple officials in Jerusalem detected heavy criticism in the overtones – words that, in their minds, blasphemed the scriptures and indicted the chief priests for incompetence and corruption. Reports to the Sanhedrin indicated widespread healing, even revival of the dead. Caiaphas, Chief Priest at that time, spread the word that so long as this man, this blaspheming magician, remained outside Judea, he would have to be tolerated. But if he brought his traveling circus to the Temple, trying to undermine all they'd worked for – including tolerance from Roman authorities – he would have to be dealt with decisively.

As for the Romans, their current Prefect, Pilatus, an equestrian level official of the Pontii family, had replaced Valerius Gratus long enough hence to have *already* violently put down Galilean fervor. But rumors he heard from clandestine sources were not yet alarming – so long as this Jesus character remained up north. Syria, the Decapolis and Philip's territory weren't Pilate's problem – but he had put Judea on notice: tolerance level was zero. He dealt quickly and decisively with any outbreaks of rebellious zeal.

Having decided to expand his assembly of insiders, Jesus took on six groups of 12, intending to train them to send out on missions as he'd done the twelve – perhaps streamlining public appearances and accomplishing things at each location more efficiently. These were all young men from different areas who had followed Jesus' teaching for some time. But sharing deep insights with such numbers was time-consuming, inhibiting for a while any extended travel.

Jesus did, however, make a short trip, on invitation, to Jotapata. Speaking just off the market square of the hilltop town surrounded by a panorama of scenic valleys and ridges, Jesus thought he caught glimpse of his youngest brother Jude in the crowd, hooded and standing behind some others. As he looked again, though, he'd disappeared.

Speaking at length, including many of his usual quotes, Jesus noted many in the crowd he'd seen before, "Why do you call me 'Master' and 'Lord', yet don't do what I tell you? The man who hears and changes himself so that his life can change is like the builder who digs deep to rest his foundation on bedrock – when storms and winds sweep, the house stands solid. But you who listen and nod, who leave just as you came in, are like the foolish builder who poured a slab on sand and built a house on it. Outwardly, it looked the same as that with the foundation, but when the torrent came, the house collapsed and flowed away."

He knew that many in attendance were more like the fool – but what else could he say? It was frustrating: people wouldn't take the personal initiative. They wanted *him* to be and do everything, heal them all, make everything OK. No words seemed to sink in with the message that each was responsible for quality of life encountered.

Back home, working with his expanded group, he would emphasize, "No student is above his teacher, but when fully trained, you should be at a level of your teacher. My purpose is not to polish your role as followers, but to make you leaders of men."

But even when it seemed to Jesus that they were coming to see the Kingdom and its impact on each *in the moment*, one would come and ask something like, "Master, when will the new world come?"

And Jesus could only answer again and again, "What you anticipate for the future is already here – you just don't know it."

Even Zebedee's sons, principal among the apostles in vigor and determination, gave indications that they really didn't comprehend the personal nature of the Kingdom. Back in Capernaum, they approached him, asking that they be given honored spots to his right hand and left in Jesus' Kingdom.

"You don't understand what you're asking," he said. "Can you drink from my cup? Can you go through all I've experienced and make the same commitment to spread the word?"

"We surely can," they agreed.

"OK, then," he answered, "*do so*. But your status is not for me to determine. "

The others were indignant when they heard about James and John seeking favoritism. Jesus had to address the point at their next planning session. "Kings and governors of surrounding lands'exercise authority over their people. But here, no such pecking order exists. This son of Adam didn't come to be served, but to serve others. Whoever would want to be first needs to serve his fellow man, not sit back, proud, in elevated status."

With spring coming soon, Jesus finally decided an issue facing him since the outset: he would conduct an extensive tour of Judean towns, ending with a major appearance at the Temple for this year's Passover Feast. He broached the subject first with Mary privately, then at James' house with his brother and mother. Not one was enthralled, whereas the disciples welcomed the move with excitement.

During a quiet, intimate evening, he revealed his plan to the Magdalene. She didn't want to hear anything about Jerusalem: "I'm deeply worried about such a venture, Yesh'. You know the attitude of Pharisees and those law teachers they send out to trick you, to sabotage your talks. They'll not welcome you at the Temple stairs with palm fronds and chorus, not with your reputation," Mary said, near tears.

Jesus looked at her, knowing himself that from Sadducee and chief priest down to janitor, the establishment wasn't about to welcome him personally any more than his message. He knew that his accomplishments were distorted in accounts reaching the Sanhedrin, that his message was stripped of insight and his sincere questioning turned to blasphemy by the time it reached

the ingrained "keepers of the faith." And he had always anticipated Mary's resistance when the time came to face Temple
bureaucrats and functionaries.

Jesus lay his head back on the tunic covering his bedding and
pulled Mary close. "It must come to this one day, Miriam. We
both know that. Should I spend another five or ten years circulating the hinterlands of our people? How many trips to
Chorazin or Sepph will I have to make before they will tire of my
message?

"No, the only choice is when – now? Next year? At this point,
my following is solid. I will send groups to cover Judea and
spread the word through the towns and at the Temple. Most
towns have already requested me."

Mary interrupted, "Towns won't be a problem – we both know
that, too."

"Yes, but until the Temple gang can out-argue my many
points, if I can approach them face to face, they will *have to*
acknowledge my message, condone my status and revise their
encrusted viewpoint."

"Maybe I'm missing something, Yesh'. I haven't traveled like
you, only twice to the Temple – years ago. But I don't think *they
have to acknowledge anything* or anybody. If you rode down from
the firmament on a blazing chariot, they would accuse you of
magic tricks."

Jesus laughed, but couldn't relieve the tension. She was right.
But so was he. He had to go – and the time felt right. *And anyway,*
he thought, *my intent always gets realized – things always work out.*

Later as Jesus – along with their mother – was visiting, James the
Just expressed his brotherly concern more forcefully and bluntly,
"Are you crazy? They'll do you in – somehow they'll get you out
of the picture. You're a thorn in their collective sides, and you
know it!"

Mary was beyond shocked.

Jesus smiled, taking some pride in that status, sloughing off the concern. "They won't do a thing. We'll have many of our people on the scene. Temple guards won't risk confrontations – so long as we're peaceful. I plan to do this yearly until we've gathered so many followers that the system must change."

James thought for a while. "I see your strategy, Yeshua," he nodded. "Somehow, I guess you're right."

Mary, hardly condoning many of Jesus' bold moves since his return, spoke up, "Yeshua, you have to respect the priesthood! They regulate the sacrifices and interpret the scripture. Without them as an anchor, we would be lost: 'See, my servant will act wisely', said Isaiah."

"Mother, really – they serve neither Yahweh nor the people. Look at widespread hardship – what do the priests do to alleviate that? Respect them? Illness, pain – they have no power, no sympathy, no use. As per Isaiah, 'Surely as I have planned, so it will be'."

At length James agreed, "Yeshua is right, mother. He can't be the grand savior of Galilee and points north as a final accomplishment. As prophets of old, he has to take on the system if his message is to survive. But don't forget," James said, turning to Jesus and clamping his shoulder. He looked straight into his older brother's eyes, "the Sadducees have the Romans to whine to if any trouble breaks out – any trouble at all, regardless of who starts it! Make sure your disciples keep things orderly."

Six weeks before the Festival, plans were laid and training completed. Hand picking the best among new groups, Jesus sent out disciples to Judea to organize pre-Passover talks, laying out a timeframe to travel from Jericho, up through Antipatris, Lydda, perhaps as far south as Hebron before circling back to Bethany to enter the city for Passover. As things were arranged, several would meet in Jerusalem – they already had lodging and meeting space there, offered by followers – to lay out the schedule. Then some would return to Capernaum with planned logistics for the tour, at which time Jesus would head south. All would converge at Jerusalem to work the crowds. Most would camp east of the city, while Jesus and core disciples would lodge in Jerusalem at a secret location.

Two each were sent to Joppa and Caesarea on the sea to arrange for talks following Passover. Jesus intended to lay a firm basis in Judea for subsequent focus and the Pesach "coming out" would be leveraged for added support at the Judean coast.

Reporting back from the coordinated mission, Andrew and James the Less explained finalized plans to Jesus. Only two stops could be arranged from Jericho up to Jerusalem as towns were all too busy to host events, preferring rather to hear Jesus at the Temple.

Mary Magdalene decided to travel on the mule wagons with Jesus to Jericho, then go directly to Jerusalem with the wagons while Jesus and several disciples stopped for talks en route. Tents would have to be set up and cooking facilities sorted out for the entourage. Mary and some of the disciples' wives would supervise that complex task. James, Salome, their sister who had brought her family along, and Mary, their mother, would join everybody, going directly to the camp site east of the Mount of Olives prior to Pesach.

Stopping only briefly for a moment of silent contemplation at the Jordan where John reputedly had started baptizing, Jesus vigorously followed the plan. People thronged from surrounding areas – Perea and Samaria, even Nabataea – to both Judean talks, taking them in before proceeding to Jerusalem. Long awaiting this miracle worker from the north, Judeans were energized and many proclaimed being healed.

Jesus and his contingent arrived late – as usual – from their previous event, but were informed that people had awaited his appearance for hours. "You'd better go ahead into the city, Yeshua," suggested James. "The men have people lined up out past the Damascus Gate. Take one of my horses. The others can follow in a wagon, then walk once you get there."

So the group headed to Bethphage, where they would leave the wagon to go on foot behind the mounted Jesus. But that seemed too regal, so Jesus stopped and told the men to find a donkey for him – that would better reflect his more common-man image. Simon galloped ahead on horseback to activate the disciples to spread the word.

As the group passed Bethany, wound up the hill and around to the north entrance, pilgrims from all regions, there for the festival, began to pour out of the city, waving and spreading palm leaves in his path. Even local city dwellers, not so familiar with this northern phenomenon, got caught up in the festive parade atmosphere – cheering him all the way into the city. The entry exceeded expectations: everybody knew the phenomenon from Galilee had arrived – even the chief priests.

At the Temple, though, things were closing down for the evening. Most returned to the campsite, while James, Jesus and key disciples stayed in Bethany – at their undisclosed location.

Next morning, Jerusalem throbbed with activity – visitors packed the streets. Events at the Theater by the upper city and the Hippodrome to the south across from the Temple literally buzzed with activity, as did lively markets and shops all around. At the Temple, the scene swirled: vendors offered lambs and doves – for those who couldn't afford lambs – for slaughter, along with trinkets and souvenirs. Of course, ever present money-changers offered Tyrian shekels to use in official rituals in exchange for common Roman coinage.

Pontius Pilate and his troops, normally garrisoned on the Mediterranean in Caesarea, were also in town – on high alert and dedicated to preventing any demonstrations or outbursts. They kept out of view in the Antonia Fortress, which, abutting the northwest corner of the Temple, gave lookouts a commanding view. But Pilate and his support contingent quartered at Herod's Palace when stationed locally.

As Jesus and disciples filtered through the throng, the tall Galilean was frequently recognized and stopped by people who had seen him speak across the region. The south Stairs of Ascent led up to the Double Huldah Gate entering the Temple and, adjacent, were other gates generally used as exits. Jesus' group, augmented by others from the seventy-two – some keeping a distance to appear detached – entered the gate, passing by vendors and groups of people talking.

They climbed the interior steps directly into the outer court, a broad space open to all who were ritually pure – non-Jews and women included, unless menstruating. Northwards, beyond the Court of Gentiles was space restricted to only Jews and a third court for Jewish *men* only. And centered in the roughly quadrangle expanse, colonnaded around the perimeter was the Inner Court, central to which was the Holy of Holies. Only priests, appropriately dressed, could enter there.

Filling the area were rows and groupings of vendors principally supplying animals for purchase. Most travelers, unable to bring their own livestock from home, had to buy them there: unflawed animals, properly raised for ritual slaughter, prepared according to all rules.

This complex sacrifice custom, stemmed from ancient times. While meant to reconnect each man with his Lord Yahweh, atoning for sins and emphasizing dedication, it had become highly commercialized – many merchants depended on the business; all visitors needed the service. However, Jesus, judging the scene as well beyond anything remotely spiritual, found it offensive. Above the din, he began to speak of Temple sanctity and its desecration by such practices.

Priests and other officials, already anticipating Jesus' presence, were ready with guards and plain-clothes security people. As Jesus bewailed the over-commercialization of slaughter rituals, officials closed in. One started to warn him about his slanderous remarks, at which Jesus quoted passages that emphasized mercy and forgiveness – all of which had nothing to do with the meat market Temple operation. Numbers grew around the standoff, as teachers of the law and other guards filled in, but were blocked and inhibited by Jesus' followers – well trained and alert to such possibilities – and those simply curious.

As people packed the area ever denser, tempers rose – both sides feeling justifiably indignant. Two guards pushed Jesus back towards the south basilica, where vendors' displays crammed even closer together under the roof of the Royal Portico. Simon and John, strong and physical, intervened between Jesus and the guards; others, sensing trouble, pushed Temple officials from the back into the midst of the crowd. Tables got bumped and knocked over, setting off a melee. As merchants began to yell at Jesus, he returned the favor complaining at their total commercial interest in what should be the holy temple. Pushed by the growing crowd, he launched off down a long row, spilling trading tables and money-changers' booths, while several disciples followed to inhibit guards coming up from the rear.

The crowd erupted in bedlam, as pushing and shoving spread up and down rows – pick-pockets and other shady characters made the most of the clash, spilling tables, scrambling after cash and merchandise. Animals bleated and some broke loose, as people skirmished, yelled, grouped and started punching and flailing.

Immediately, Roman trumpets blared. Soldiers swarmed quickly into the court from the Antonia Fortress. But the crowd, all of them, regardless of interest, hated Roman troops – so people inhibited any movement of the red-clad, armored soldiers towards the action. Amid a rising din, Jesus and disciples worked their way deftly to the exits and left the scene.

The following day, not to repeat the fiasco and totally disrupt the holiday, Jesus blended into conversations in more open areas of the courts, teaching his viewpoint, illustrating the Kingdom. Many had heard him or heard of him, and crowded around.

The chief priests and ever-present elders, recognizing Jesus, feared confronting him lest another skirmish break out – not wanting Romans involved. So they pressed him, avoiding aggressive tones, as he taught. "By just what authority are you doing things here? And who gave you this authority?"

But Jesus quizzed them back about John: what authority had he to baptize? The officials, surrounded by the public who had treasured John, couldn't answer without either offending people or having to admit Jesus' authority. So they stuttered, "We don't really know."

Jesus likewise declined to answer them and went on with his talk.

Later, the entourage, having exited down the stairs, on the way around the Temple, Simon the Rock commented, "Wow, just look at these massive stones! What magnificent buildings!"

Jesus, thinking back to Crete and its ancient Minoan ruins, recalling the grand pyramids and ruins of ancient Egypt, recognized the temporal quality of things – all great civilizations pass, leaving their grand edifices crumbled to rubble. "Do you see all of these grand structures – the Temple, over there the Hippodrome, the fortress? Not one stone here will be left on another; every one will be thrown down."

The disciples, living in a day-to-day world, wondered when that might happen. Sometime soon? What divine force could move these blocks?

The next day, now the center of attention and subject of all gossip, Jesus kept things light, telling parables and touching people – energizing and refreshing them. His crowd came to dominate the scene over many would-be speakers.

Having planned a strategy, Sadducees tried to trap him with questions on resurrection, a philosophical point their Temple sect denied. Jesus put down their feeble attempt with firm answers that even official teachers agreed with.

Reports to Caiaphas and his Sanhedrin governing body were enraging. This back-country bumpkin had barged into their Temple, their sacred charge to defend and honor, and, inside of three days, took it over as his personal pedestal. Caiaphas assembled a subgroup from the council – leaving out those he knew appreciated Jesus' teaching. They decided to put this disruptive usurper out of commission before the Romans clamped down on the entire operation. This Jesus, in his pious fervor, they judged, just didn't recognize reality: the delicate balance of cooperation and order necessary to keep the Romans out of Jewish religious practices.

But all recognized they couldn't detain him in public, in front of his many supporters. He was already bringing up John the Baptist's name, rekindling that dangerous zeal. Arresting Jesus publically, amid fervent Passover emotions, could easily ignite a full-scale riot. They concluded they had to detain him at night, quietly, and deal with him quickly. But how? Evenings, he disappeared into the huge assembly of pilgrims from everywhere. Informers thought his supporters camped to the east, but reported he never came back there.

One priest, having encountered this Galilean in the courts, explained that his contingent – experienced, dedicated and effective – always followed, shielding him from the throng. But perhaps one of them could be persuaded to lead Temple agents to him some evening.

Caiaphas countered, "I doubt any of that type would betray him. But one might respond to a ruse." Plans evolved to isolate one of his insiders, asking him to lead a few officials to Jesus for private discussions – a simple meeting to size up his motives. If necessary, a bribe might even be offered to facilitate setting up the meeting. All agreed this might work, but must happen quickly. If he would escape Jerusalem after the Passover, they voiced, who knows what mischief he could cause as his operation built up?

Most assumed Caiaphas would reprimand or imprison Jesus. Speaking out against the priesthood was neither uncommon nor unlawful. Caiaphas' closest allies, however, recognized political reality: the troublemaker had to be eliminated, quickly and smoothly. And that could only be done by pressuring Pilate to wield the Imperial power of execution.

The next morning, Jesus was back at the Temple courts, inspiring his large crowd. When experts in the law tried to trap him, Jesus sprung their queries back on them – using pertinent scripture creatively to debunk their arguments. They withdrew and ceased to challenge him.

With the crowd swelling, Jesus unleashed a powerful series of indictments against the Temple elite – flailing them verbally as hypocrites who place on people burdens they wouldn't bear themselves, who dress pompously and carry fancy religious articles, yet fail at mercy and justice. He railed at their placing value in symbols, yet ignoring real things. "Blind guides – you strain out a gnat but swallow a camel.

"You clean the outside of the cup, but, full of greed and self-indulgence, you need first to clean the inside – only then will the outside also be clean."

As this went on, people were riled and invigorated – praising Jesus and criticizing the bureaucracy that had festered within their Temple elite. Jesus felt his plan was working. He went on to illustrate the Kingdom, its real effect in life beyond prophetic teachings.

But while Jesus spoke, officials had isolated Judas.

Judas Iscariot, the disciples' treasurer, had financial troubles. He had stopped farm working and fruit picking over a year before. He could live simply as the others did, but the little allotted for each of them from donations as food allowance was meager. He missed wine and a good meal now and again, some cash to do things with.

When a Temple official pulled him aside, the offer seemed too good to be true. The chief priests, he said, wanted to query Jesus privately: learn his point of view so they might help him merge his ideas into accepted doctrine. They would actually pay Judas to lead a small committee to Jesus one evening.

For Judas, constantly worried about money, that offer was ideal. He could arrange this on his own, make some money and look like a genius for getting Jesus in touch with officials. Hadn't the Master always said that life would work out well with trust? *This is great,* Judas thought, *perhaps I've finally entered the Kingdom!*

Judas said quietly, "Yes, I know where he goes evenings. I can take you to him – just for discussion, right?" When the official nodded and smiled, Judas asked, "But, uh, how much are you willing to pay?"

The priest's eyes opened wide – he didn't even have to take the next step of threatening. He offered twenty Tyrian tetradrachms – the coinage, popularly called "shekels" – taken in daily from pilgrims.

Judas thought a second, imagining his gain in prestige at making this simple arrangement on his own – and getting paid for it to boot, "Make it thirty." At several days' wages, a Tyrian shekel – thirty of them – was four months pay.

"It's a deal. When can you do that?"

"He's too busy mostly," Judas said, thinking when Jesus would be away from crowds. "But I can take your people to meet him, say, just after the Feast?"

The priest smiled, knowing he would be rewarded himself for his cleverness. They arranged a meeting place and time.

Passover, a major traditional festival, commemorated Moses leading his people, the Israelites, out of Egypt. Drawing hordes of faithful to Jerusalem's Temple for official sacrifices, it included many symbolic features honoring that Exodus. High point of the long festival was the feast, specially prepared to include symbolic food items. Jesus, not wishing to expose his presence by eating with the main contingent at the camp site, arranged for a room inside the city where the disciples could prepare their official meal in seclusion.

After days of travel and exhausting Temple activities, commuting from campgrounds or Bethany, hiking, walking, talking – the men, particularly Jesus, were weary. Wine went down easy and the food was refreshing. Jesus spoke of plans for talks after Passover and looked for suggestions from the disciples as to how to follow up on criticism of the Temple operatives – how to roll that into grassroots support of his message to update the stultified scriptures.

They talked for hours. Judas nearly let slip his arrangement to connect with the priesthood, but kept the surprise quiet.

Jesus relaxed for the first time in months. The next day, the festival would end and they would head back with just a handful of appearances on the way. He joked with his men, "One day, when I'm no longer here, you guys can drink your wine and eat your bread in memory of me, eh?"

The disciples protested. Jesus had become so dominant in their lives, they couldn't imagine their quest without him.

Jesus gazed off out the window, seeing a handful of stars in the clear sky. He thought of Moses and the prophets, Plato and Heraclitus, Gautama – all the great thinkers whose ideas he'd encountered: they came, said their piece, then passed to become part of the ages as all do. "Nobody lasts forever," he said, feeling a strange stillness to the group that had been laughing moments before. "I've been trying to share my insights, my understanding, to all of you. One day you'll have to carry on, train others to continue the effort." He laughed, "Otherwise, I'll have to come back to make it right."

He glanced off to his left. The Iscariot wasn't looking at him, but rather peering out the window. Jesus joked again, "Yehudas, you look tired. We've all been under a strain. You can leave if you want to – head back to the hostel. We're about done here."

Judas looked up and nodded, "Yeah, ah … hey, I'll see you later." He got up and left.

"Man," asked Bartholomew, shaking his head at the strange exchange and quick exit. "What's with the Dagger Man?"

Andrew joked, "Must have a girl lined up or something."

After a time, they broke up. Three headed back to the campground, two to the hostel in Bethany. Jesus and the others walked back through the Kidron Valley and up to Gethsemane, the Gardens of the "Olive Press" near their dwelling place where they often walked; there the quiet of surrounding olive groves provided tranquil grounds to relax and chat. A full Moon lit the trail brightly from a cloudless sky.

Simon the Rock and Zebedee's sons walked along with Jesus while the others headed back to their rooms, but the three were weary and sat down, chatting, as Jesus walked on alone.

Something isn't right, Jesus thought to himself. He sat, looking at the still scene above – the brightest star, one that moved, still hung visible on the horizon following the Sun where it had set; two other wanderers hung overhead near the Moon. *Crystal spheres?* Jesus mused – *they'd have to be mighty big – bigger than the "firmament" would be.* He assured himself that he'd planned everything out. They would all swing by the Temple briefly the next day, then be on their way west for scheduled talks. Those should go well, like everything so far. He'd gotten his message to so many Judeans and others – *how can I feel so … so wary? Must be letdown from all the activity, the festival ending and all.*

He returned to the three, who'd fallen asleep. *Just like on Mt.*

Hermon, he thought, smiling to himself. "Hey, you guys keeping watch?" he asked. They mumbled something incoherent. Jesus wandered off again. *Maybe we should get out of here*, thought Jesus. *Something just isn't right!*

Down the hill from there, Judas was slightly concerned. The two or three priests he expected at the meeting point turned out to be five with a contingent of fifteen guards. They explained that Temple officials couldn't travel at night without protection. The security detachment would allow them to chat with Jesus without fearing robbers or interference. Judas thought to himself, *it must be OK – just have to trust...*

Back with the disciples, Jesus thought to arouse them, but didn't have to. A clamor kicked up down the hill, with a large group approaching with torches and clattering armor.

John awoke, "Hey, we'd better get out of here!"

"No," Jesus said. "We don't run away. We trust ourselves and Yahweh."

The group approached with Judas at its front. He stepped towards Jesus. "Found some new friends, Yehudas?" Jesus asked.

Judas started to speak, "They just want to..."

The captain of the guards demanded, "Are you the trouble-maker?" They held the torches high for a view.

"Yes, that's him – the tall one," a priest confirmed.

Simon pulled his sword and John had a knife, but Jesus waved them back, speaking to the contingent. "You think we're rebels that you come out with weapons? You could have arrested us at the Temple – but, no, you have to come in the dark."

They grabbed Jesus while others fled in panic, then hustled him back across the city to the Chief Priest's manor near Herod's Palace.

Cold, damp stone, smelling of urine, surrounded a man in

turmoil, but unafraid. Jesus, trusting and confident, thought through the possibilities – and all of them looked positive. If released – and he'd done nothing illegal or demonstrably rebellious – he would gain recognition as having overcome the establishment. If imprisoned for a time, the effect would be multiplied. He relaxed, despite the squalor of conditions, and meditated – at length falling asleep in the dim light and dank air.

At daybreak, he was brought, hands bound, before a partial council assembled in a lavish hall. Jesus was astounded at the opulence of the building – he'd never really seen the Upper City. A neatly dressed functionary quickly accused him of sedition against the state. Jesus shook his head, "Sedition – for teaching in the courts? Half the city speaks and debates..."

"No," Caiaphas cut him off, then read from a papyrus: "You purposely disrupted slaughter operations and have continuously violated religious values and cleanliness codes.

"We have several witnesses as to your claims for establishing a new Kingdom in this time. We know of your expanded gang and efforts to recruit followers throughout the region. *And* you were overheard threatening to bring down the whole Temple."

Caiaphas looked up from his list, "Another Samson, I suppose?" He stood and held the list up high, raising his voice, "So, we are hypocrites, are we? We, who are charged with promoting the people's good in the eye of Yahweh? We are hypocrites? Indeed *you* are the hypocrite!"

Jesus broke in: "Your principal charge is to serve yourselves. You live like Herods while the people you tax – the people you live off like parasites – have to grovel..."

The guard elbowed him harshly, "Don't talk to Temple royalty like that!"

A priest, dressed in full uniform, said, "Our responsibility is keeping religious traditions and the sanctity of Temple courts away from Roman interference. You have endangered that by bringing..."

"Sanctity?" Jesus countered. "You've turned the courts from a house of prayer into a den of thieves..."

The guard grabbed his shoulder and pulled back.

Jesus jerked free, "Can you call off your goon here? It's difficult to talk!"

Caiaphas raised his hand, "No need! This hearing is finished. You'll be taken to civil court under Pilate for trial." He waved to the guards to remove Jesus.

Jesus was now concerned. He'd purposely avoided any action that could bring involvement with the Romans – anything. But the priesthood was apparently even more corrupt and self-serving than he'd imagined.

Back at the camp, pandemonium had set in. Disciples had reported the arrest – Jesus was now in custody. Would they imprison him like John? Warn him and let him go? Judas had said they only wanted to question him – but the guards' attitude was very aggressive. Should they arouse people at night, or go to the Temple in the morning and rally people – no, either might stir up a riot and endanger Jesus. Why did the disciples leave Jesus so exposed? Why did Judas lead the guards to Jesus?

Hustled through Upper City streets lined with lavish mansions, Jesus was stunned at the dominating expanse of Herod's Palace – originally the residence of Herod the Great. There, in an official annex, a praetorium, abutting the gardens of the south section, Pilate held court. As early as it was on a holiday morning, Jesus felt apprehension that any legal proceedings would be conducted at such a suspicious time.

Pilate sat on a raised platform while accusers stood to his side, all opposite Jesus, leveling charges against him: treason, seeking to impose a new Kingdom, colluding to spread dissension throughout several Roman provinces. They went on at length.

Pilate leaned forward, clearly agitated and slightly ruffled, as though he'd had to hurry to get to the hearing. "We have no tolerance for rebels here," he said in Latin with an air of disdain. A translator put those words into Aramaic. Pilate was about to go on.

Jesus responded in Attic Greek, "I rebel only against false ideas, procurator, not against governments."

Pilate looked up, slightly surprised, and responded in Greek, "Oh we are well spoken, are we?

"Well, ah, what is it … Yeshua of, ah, Nazareth? Nazareth? We are wary of Jewish radicals who acquire a large following. Even more so, Galileans."

Jesus voiced his basis, "I have no quarrel with the government. I speak only of life's deeper truth."

"Oh, 'Truth'?" questioned Pilate, "and what exactly might that be? Dealing with rebellious brutes is difficult enough. Religious zealots? In Palestine, that's worse! I have no intention of letting Judean emotions escalate to where I need reinforcements from Syria. I intend to succeed in this region, keep the peace. My success is predicated on that."

Jesus spoke again, "I pose no threat to anyone. My message is one of peace."

"Yes, so I've heard. Once the Temple hierarchy is overthrown and you become chief priest, everything will be peaceful, eh? No, any threat to the status quo is dangerous.

"Still," Pilate continued, turning to his legal advisor, then to the accusers, "I don't see this man's accusations rising to a capital level. Antipas is in town for the holiday. He should have jurisdiction over Galileans. Send this man over there – we'll close this hearing for now."

Jesus was removed to a cramped waiting room for well over an hour. He could close his eyes and look for inner guidance, wary now, based on the turn of events – he had to rely on Antipas for judgment? Unsure as to the outcome of all this, he remained confident it would work out somehow for the best.

Brought back before Pilate, he could see more characters whispering among themselves, standing with the accusers.

Pilate, grim, spoke deliberately but not without sarcasm, "His *highness*, Herod Antipas, Tetrarch of Galilee and Perea, declined to sit in judgment – based on jurisdiction. Your accusers and your crimes are Iudaean, so he says, Yeshun ... ah, what is it? Yeshua." Pilate looked down at his papyrus forms, mumbling audibly, "Good excuse." He was made to know, though, that Antipas wished to be rid of Jesus for good. Added to political pressure from the Sanhedrin, with whom Pilate had to relate daily despite his personal contempt of them, pressure was overwhelming for the Roman Prefect to act.

Pilate looked up at Jesus, "Word has it that your brother is wanted for rebellious activity in the Galilean hills. Your manner and your personage impress me, Yeshua – but it is exactly that kind of charismatic personality that is so dangerous." He turned to his Centurion. "Flog him and hang him. Two crucifixions set this morning, eh? Add him. Do this quickly before the crowds assemble." He glanced at Jesus with little expression, waving his hand. "Take him away."

Hundreds of rebels, thieves, scoundrels and murderers had been crucified, but Jesus had only heard tell of its cruel, painful, disparaging effects. He was shaken beyond words, assuming release or imprisonment awaited.

But events transpired rapidly – prompted by the holiday, with interest in showing off yet another political dissident eliminated in disgrace, writhing naked, in pain and embarrassment in full view of the crowd. This would be another lesson to potential rebels in the throng: what happens when you challenge authorities.

Guards chained Jesus into an enclosed wagon and carted him hurriedly eastwards along the elevated wall and across the

Viaduct spanning the valley – right into the Temple's bowels. Following dark, enclosed passages, the contingent brought him into a dismal, musty room in the westernmost tower of the Antonia Fortress. As per routine procedure, a crew of torturers immediately and brutally scourged Jesus.

The whip, its multiple tassels wrapping pieces of bone, tore Jesus' back, legs and feet raw to the muscle; pain surged throughout his being. Two stout Roman soldiers bound him, strapping his waist between them. They hustled him along the street, forcing him to carry the heavy crossbeam, his back and arms crusted in blood, oozing pus – in plain sight of stunned viewers along the sides and pilgrims making their way into the Damascus Gate – in a grim, but rapid procession along several streets to the Place of the Skull. Murmurs and whispers accompanied the procession. Practically all recognized Jesus' forceful, impressive presence, highlight of this festival season – stunned glances and teary eyes lined the streets as other onlookers pressed in from side streets, now echoing with shouts and wailing.

Others, though, prompted by the establishment, taunted and shouted epithets loudly and derisively.

Passing through the Fish Gate, the city wall's north exit, they left the Damascus Road to circle around to Golgotha, the rounded hill shaped ominously as a skull cap. On that small knoll just outside the city's north entryway, hung two convicted criminals already mounted on high crossbars forming Ts on top of vertical supports. A third empty upright stood between them.

The small entourage – Jesus with a crossbeam recycled from ready inventory and several palace guards – followed by ten Roman soldiers, quickly approached the hill. Experienced executioners on site pulled the empty mast from its mounting hole, they lowered it to the ground and mounted the crossbeam onto two pins. Jesus was stripped and forced down onto the T-shaped crucifix where the executioners secured his limbs. His raw, bloody flesh pulsated pain against the hot upright and splintery crossbar. Executioners drove iron spikes first through small wooden retaining slats, then into each forearm, far enough from the hand so that bleeding wrists wouldn't precipitate death. Then they pounded one spike each through each of his feet, cracking bones and snapping tendons, hammering each into a two-piece wedge angled to allow some support of body weight. Unbearable ache now added to blistering, seething pain from the flogging. Jesus writhed in excruciating pain, severe beyond comprehension; tears gushed from the agony. Every flinch, every movement against pinned arms brought renewed surges of searing, throbbing pain.

Once mounted, Jesus and the cross were hoisted upright and wedged solid in the mounting slot, his feet a man's height and more above the ground. His weight now fixed on shattered foot bone and pulling at pierced wrists, new levels of pain ripped into his consciousness.

That task complete, the crew departed, speaking casually about breakfast plans, leaving soldiers to guard against any interference. For them, too, Roman recruits from elsewhere in the vast empire, this was routine – yet another boring duty assignment in the heat of this forsaken desert land.

To the east, disciples had assembled. Disorganized at first, they started packing wagons to depart. If Jesus were released, a hasty exit would be in order. But two youths, sent into town to anonymously keep an eye on things, arrived out of breath. Jesus was being led to Skull Hill for – they were hardly able to speak – crucifixion.

The camp was devastated. Cries and wailing broke out – this was unthinkable! The cruelest, most demeaning torture possible – meant for slaves and murderers – was issued for a man of peace and love? Disciples gathered and set out quickly for the city's north gate. Some women came, too, leaving others to care for children and fold up tents; they all should be ready to leave for home as soon as possible.

Jesus could gaze hazily out over the surrounding, surreal scene – gawkers lining up off in the distance. Even some disciples starting to arrive looked warily about lest they be identified.

Sensitivity accommodates intense pain after a time, blocking it out. Jesus, barely conscious, head spinning from the rapid, yet unfathomable, turn of events, held his body weight awkwardly from the small wedge supporting his feet. Still, he could ponder all things, assured now that death and reunion with his Yahweh – whatever his nature – would follow within hours.

The others hanging at his sides, occasionally mumbled incoherently. One, barely conscious, filthy and crusted with blood, his balding head already blistered from the relentless sun, urinated. In pain, facing death and imminent release from troubled lives of poverty, they had nothing to say, little breath to speak. Cared about by no one, each, but for the twist of events placing them near Jesus, would pass soon into anonymity.

For Jesus, a hardy, robust specimen, death wouldn't come so quickly. In his remaining time, he had to make some sense of it, some thought as to why his mission had suddenly been thwarted. Why, when all his efforts had yielded such success, such popularity, healing, and benefit – why would it end like this in disgrace, humbled by the very priesthood he justifiably disparaged? Why?

Having heard of Jesus' fate, Judas was traumatized, devastated beyond painful remorse that the priesthood had deceived him, that he himself had been so gullible as to open his beloved master to authorities' deception. He rushed past the guards at Caiaphas' manor and screamed at priests and functionaries meeting there, cursing them, accusing them of treachery. He hurled the coins he'd received, taunting them as they scrambled to fetch guards. Thrown out and warned to stay away, Judas returned to the hostel and hanged himself.

As the still-rising sun scorched his torn flesh, Jesus' thoughts began to parse his life memory, a rapid review of high points – quickly the Sibyl came to mind. Here at Golgotha, this, his mast, was finally fixed upright. Here the journey would end. And the cities he'd built, those ideas he'd planted in people's minds for better understanding life – would they simply crumble?

Time paced. The sun baked, ever hotter; the scarce breeze wafted ever drier. *The camels, the desert,* Jesus hallucinated as his head bobbed slowly. He could support his weight only briefly now, his legs giving out. Relaxing stretched his weight from his nailed forearms, collapsing his chest – both producing renewed surges of pain. *Why,* he thought, mumbling in near delirium, *has my Lord so deserted me to this end – did I bring this on?*

Too far back from the scene, James took their mother, Mary Magdalene and some other women forward to a closer viewpoint from the road where people cluttered. A Roman soldier came over to push them back, yelling something in Latin.

James spoke out, "Mater et frater!" And, using universal language, held out several shiny coins.

The soldier, glancing back to make sure he wasn't seen, took the coins, waved and hurriedly directed them to a specific spot, "Vado illac – ibi! *Velociter!!*"

They moved off to the side, as indicated, within about 30 feet of Jesus. They could reach out and gesture, call out words of love – at least be there.

Jesus noticed and could smile, looking as long as he could – for his eyes, crusted from tear, sweat and blood, were now drying out, his vision blurring as well from dropping blood pressure.

Time slipped inexorably. People in the distance milled about, passing, pitying, wondering – some cowering in fear as the crucifixion intended. To Jesus, the scene formed a surreal, wavering vista, frozen in the moment, dancing, stretching into timelessness, a dance, a parody of life.

Mouth parched, his strength waning, Jesus contemplated, pulling his waning focus within himself, *my intent had always been fulfilled – the dove had always descended. How could this heinous act interfere now ... with my plan ... block my intent?* He could feel his breath now, marking each shallow exhale as a slow, rhythmic pulse, thinking, *will my rukha, the next, be my last?* He strained for the next inhale.

But, as life ebbed and pain eased into the background, alone and exposed to the world, clarity returned; he realized in a burst of insight, *this IS my dove – my fulfillment – only this shocking end could make a statement.* It became clear: an unexpected, abhorred finality to such a temporal, fleeting mission would leave a unique impact. More talks, more healing, more trips to ever more towns – same faces, same problems. His mission could end in no other way possible that could realize his dream to have an impact – to reach people.

But will they get my message? He wondered that, focusing on that alone, with a pang of regret that he'd not recorded his core ideas. He thought about the people, his closest friends: the disciples, Mary, some dedicated listeners – *will they understand the moment to be the Kingdom, not the future, not some mystical intervention by heavenly forces.* His mind raced, bobbing into and out of shaded dream state. *The Kingdom stems from within,* he thought again and again as if to reinforce it, *it happens now. Did they get it? Will they pass that message along?*

He'd had a fascinating life, Jesus reckoned as a final, settling conclusion, the scene before him misting in his near detached view. His deity, whatever his nature, would welcome him, he thought, *I've done all I could, traveled, learned, shared my understanding with my people, had fun...* Jesus, shedding the pain and failing body, dropped back into peace. He knew that supporting his weight prolonged the agony. He smiled, exhaled deeply and willingly relaxed, his weight drooping to stifle breathing –

resisting the urge to stand. His relaxation overcame that urge, and he departed his broken body with its pain and travail to hover for a moment, tranquil, above the scene that would register in infamy.

Content in the moment with the unique statement his life had made, he passed through the dark tunnel – as all will do – toward the bright light.

Diagonal:
Clarifying the Kingdom

In the overland drive of human endeavor, no individual's death presents a stop sign to those left behind so much as a shift of gears to accelerate – or decelerate – around upcoming bends. Jesus' demise by no means ended his message to mankind, but it did present a parking garage for one aspect: his delivery. Crucifixion abruptly silenced a voice uniquely able to illustrate penetrating perspectives on *how life works*.

With that moment folded abruptly into the past, all that remained of Jesus' remarkable insights were illustrations of the "Kingdom of God", that state to be found *within*. And those parables, aphorisms and witty comebacks lodged precariously in the volatile memories of eleven disciples and a handful of others who'd heard him often. Illiterate, they were incapable of preserving their memories on papyrus. Worse yet: they didn't comprehend what Jesus meant. At best, they could recall verbatim what he'd said.

What ensued in the days, years, decades and centuries after Jesus' premature death will be examined shortly – with the same candor and strict orientation to *reality* as Jesus' life has been. Clearly, though, following Jesus' death, *not a single element was* – or ***could have been*** – added to Jesus' message that introduced greater insight or perspective. Followers of Jesus and succeeding generations, all people of lesser vision, could *only* distort his words through faulty recall and altered retelling, never improve on them.

Generally, convinced of Jesus' special status, followers told their stories to others, who repeated them, adding gloss and exaggeration sometimes inadvertently, often on purpose to emphasize the point. Ultimately, a generation or two – and many word of mouth exchanges – later, several anonymous writers snatched stories from, by then, passed-along oral traditions and rendered them to papyrus. While their intent was to record a point of view for local, oral reading within their respective communities, their hand-scripted renderings endured. Centuries later, these simple accounts were incorporated by long-succeeding generations into their Bible.

These "good news" (gospel) accounts recorded for posterity those *two key elements* regarding Jesus of Nazareth: his unique sayings and a rough sketch of his actions. Both, however, were laden from the outset with *other* statements: points of myth, rumor and lore accumulated during decades of oral passing. These sometimes reflected common wisdom of the time (e.g., Golden Rule), often directly contradicted Jesus' message (see Upright section) but invariably skewed the account to incorporate viewpoints in line with *the authors' personal understanding*.

That oral transmission phase, lasting from Jesus' death about 30 CE until the first gospel, Mark, written after 70 CE, was particularly prone to revision. You know how it works if you hear a good story or explanation: generally, you get the gist and can pass it on later – likely with some subtle revision based on interpretation. A good joke, though, you can likely repeat precisely – necessary to preserve the punch line.

So it went with Jesus lore: parables and witticisms, many of them catchy and unusual, passed along without appreciable distortion. Other stories retained elements of the original substance, but, when repeatedly retold, passing even across the Aramaic-Greek language and cultural divide, changed; they became distorted. The trick with gospel accounts finally recorded in writing is to distinguish reliable reports from *other* stories, from myth and exaggeration and to differentiate original parables from other statements put into Jesus' mouth. That action is possible, as I've noted, *only if* you perceive how life works.

Malkutha

How do you present to uneducated fishermen, farmers and

construction workers deep insights into the psyche and its interplay with real events and relationships? You don't. You can't. You tell them stories they can relate to life and hope some of them can generalize the meaning into their understanding.

Jesus underwent childhood indoctrination consistent with Jewish tradition, wherein he learned to perform various rituals – food preparation, animal sacrifice, prayer, etc. Per custom, these rituals attempted to appease the imagined Yahweh-god so that this deity would provide blessings: good events, not bad ones – health, freedom and prosperity, not illness, servitude and poverty.

As explained, Jesus outgrew early Jewish indoctrination to see the Oneness, the pattern-rendering nature of consciousness as it manifests health, freedom and prosperity only when it elicits those qualities through trust, inner peace and confidence. That spiritual growth required exposure to other cultures and ideas, based on his own brilliance and open-mindedness, plus – very likely – spontaneous mystical insights. He came to see that his Yahweh-god gave you *exactly what you elicited* – that life reflected one's expectations and intent, carrying both *good* from confidence and trust and *bad* from fear and perceived powerlessness.

Now, did Jesus make the next step – quite obvious once you see the inner-outer connection? Did he recognize that his supposed god, out there manifesting one's own nature into real life events, doesn't actually exist? That's difficult to distinguish from gospel evidence.

Jesus may have maintained belief in a "Heavenly Father" – his Aramaic expression would have been something like, "abon d-bash-maiya" (with "abon" an endearing term for "father") which in Greek is "pathr umwn" – but imagined that this deity manifested reality consistent with each individual's mindset. *Or* he *may* have realized that, within the metaphysical nature of Consciousness, each being stands alone in eliciting/attracting its life qualities – but couldn't present that advanced perception to unsophisticated peers without incorporating the deity projection, as they would have either not grasped it or not accepted it. In that case, he would have had to *invent* his Heavenly Father image – a loving provider deity – to displace the big, vindictive, judgmental Yahweh in the minds of listeners. It would at least get the gist across, such that the resultant trust engendered would improve lives.

Whether or not Jesus maintained belief in a deity is impossible to determine from scant gospel evidence, heavily distorted as it all passed through many people who *did* believe in one. But he clearly did construct a descriptive term to indicate the place – mentally, not physically – where one's life worked well, where one was blessed with good events.

The Greek-language gospels refer to Jesus' key phrase "Kingdom of God" as *Basileia tou Theou*. But in Aramaic, that phrase would have been *Malkutha YHWH* or *Malkutha Dismayya*, the latter referring to Heaven as the place above the waters (recalling ancient cosmology with heaven higher than the firmament, the imagined dome holding up waters above it). Jesus' sense of Kingdom, though, referred not to any physical location, but rather projected an analogy for a dominant status, wherein positive events manifested in life.

Clearly, he recognized the timeless metaphysical state of conscious being: what you hold within, specified in your complex mindset, manifests qualitatively into your life's features. Real problems and real successes in event and relationship are *all rooted within*. His parables reflect that awareness thoroughly.

Integrated Awareness (IA)

Mankind's current, standard state of mind can be labeled, "Self-Awareness". This status exhibits recognition by the Self of its own existence. Great Apes and dolphins, like man, viewing their reflected image in a mirror, perceive and recognize their own centered self.

Short of that, life forms from amoeba up through canines and pigs sense and perceive a world *out there* – in some ways, indeed, more intimately than we do via superior sensory attunement. From paramecia to lions, animals sense their prey within their surroundings and go after it. But *they don't recognize their own point of view*, their own role as part of the scene. Put a cardinal in front of a mirror and, at best, it will think it sees a rival. "Simple Awareness" features no recognition of *Self*, but only sensory detection and recognition of environment.

Self-Awareness is a quantum step beyond Simple Awareness. Only certain life forms on this planet have it.

The next level beyond that is a clear, intimate awareness of nature's connected quality: *Integrated Awareness* involves not only perceiving the Self as embedded in a vital environment, but also directly sensing the connection – how the apparent dichotomy, Self and Reality, are actually connected as a Oneness. (I call this *Clear Awareness* as seen from a *personal* perspective – being clearly aware of one's integrated nature with experienced Reality. The traditional phrase "Cosmic Consciousness" is avoided because it injects excessive mystical connotation into a straight-forward recognition. Here I employ the term *"Integrated"* in comparison to "Self-" and "Simple" Awareness, rather than *"Clear"* which describes the same thing, but from a personal reference point.)

The person with *Integrated Awareness* (henceforth: *IAP*) no longer interprets perceived reality as a collection of isolated objects interacting competitively, often conflictingly, in an objective, particle-based universe. The IAP realizes that *all things* are connected, that encountered reality is cohesive and coordi-nated in nature, fitting together in a framework of unfolding events and relationships that embody meaning. The advanced IAP recognizes that meaning intertwined in all encounters reflects precise value potentials held within – that the Self is integrated into a multi-dimensional projection of its own inner state.

Numerous individuals have achieved some degree of Integrated Awareness in their lives, Jesus included.

As with all who arrive at IAP status, Jesus' problem became communicating his understanding to those who didn't have it: people used to interpreting life through a veil of cherished convictions held as "Truth". Most of them were comfortable with their synthetic notions, invariably imagining them valid. Not only didn't they want to shed their favored fallacies, they likely *feared* doing so – even though fear itself is generated by artificial beliefs!

Before exploring the historic, logistic track of Christianity converting Jesus' insights into dogmatic tenets, let's trim the fillet away from this steak's bones and fat. Let's explore the most valuable elements presented in the *entire collection of ancient Biblical writings*: Jesus' parables and other indicative quotes. I've isolated nine categories of statement that indicate Jesus' awareness of the inner-outer connection (IA or CA here as per perspective), illustrating the functional Oneness of Consciousness-Reality by *his* phrase, Kingdom of God (KG):

First Indicator of Jesus' IA: Small Thing of Great Value that Comes to Dominate

One characteristic of intimately perceiving reality as inter-related is that it *takes over* one's point of view. The IAP no longer misinterprets external agents as causal.

Where the Self-Aware Person (SAP) affixes causality and thus blame onto various forces and sources "out there," perceived to be separate and apart from the Self, persons with Integrated Awareness (IAP) will understand that they attracted those external effects into life issues. The SAP will manifest inner conflict into, say, relationships – then blame inevitable problems on the other person. The SAP will experience health issues, then use chemicals and procedures to try to manipulate the seemingly stupid body back into a functional state.

The IAP doesn't attribute causality to others or to the body. The IAP, facing a situation of conflict, will delve within to expose inner elements of conflict – then eliminate them. Once eliminated within the psyche, conflict will abate outwardly: relationships improve, the body heals.

This connection, abundantly obvious to the IAP, is ludicrous to the SAP. The latter will blame gods, luck, fate or some element of reality – government, parents, weakness, spouse, bacteria, etc. – and try to solve the problem via planned action. Not seeing the inner-outer connection, the SAP will not recognize any connection, once a problem is solved, to the *next* problem that arises out of his or her own inner mindset.

Jesus clearly perceived the inner-outer connection, recognizing that the Kingdom of God began within. For him, if you reached that level of trust (a better English word, functionally, than "faith" in carrying his meaning), the Heavenly Father would provide for you. He would fulfill your intent for you *RIGHT NOW* – not after death in some fantasy heaven (a precept stemming from Zoroastrianism) nor later in an apocalyptic god-dictated state on earth (the traditional expectation of Judaism). For Jesus, the *Kingdom* was a state of mind attainable *now*, right *NOW*.

(I must add that life is much more complex – *trust* is vital, but more inner elements are involved in the complex manifestation that constitutes life. But Jesus hadn't the terminology in psychology or a sophisticated audience to get much deeper.)

In illustrating his *Kingdom*, he likened that basic recognition to small elements that dominate the whole – which personal *Clear Awareness* does: once you see the inner-outer connection, it takes over from the more primitive Self-Awareness state of projecting blame.

Various parables involve that small thing dominating – how they apply to Integrated Awareness as governing the IAP's point of view:

- **The Mustard Seed.** (Mt 13:31-32, Mk 4:31-32, Lk 13:19, Ts 20) KG is like the smallest of seeds that, once sprouted, becomes a large bush the birds of the sky can rest on. IA is a small realization that, once understood, all elements of life rest on.
- **Yeast/Leaven in Flour.** (Mt 13:33, Lk 13:20-21, Ts 96) Put a little yeast into a large vat of flour and water, and it permeates the whole – just like IA permeates the mindset once you have it.
- **Hidden Treasure.** (Mt 13:44, Ts 109) KG is like a treasure in the field. The wise man buys the whole field just to get that treasured awareness.
- **Pearl.** (Mt 13:45-46, Ts 76) Merchant finding a pearl of great value (IA) sold all he had just to buy it.
- **Sensible Fisherman** (Ts 8) Fisherman finds large fish (IA) among catch – throws the rest back.

Core of First Indicator: Clear Awareness of one's "integrated" nature (the *Kingdom*) is a **small thing** unto itself, but **is of greatest value to have. It takes over** cognition, displacing lesser awareness.

Second IA Indicator: Clear Away Old Notions

To the innate diminution of religion and science as paradigms, beliefs and definitions never clarify how life works – they only mask life's real functionality. The mind invariably confirms held beliefs, whatever they are, because it is *those beliefs* that underlie its comparative analysis.

So the path into Jesus' Kingdom involved (and still does) *getting rid* of old impressions, not layering on new ones. He likened this to being born again – to seeing life through the untainted eyes of a child:

- Mk 10:14-15 – "Anyone who will not receive the Kingdom like a little child will never enter it."

- Mt 18:3-4 – "Unless you change and become like little children, you will never enter the Kingdom."
- Mt 19:14 – "Little children … The Kingdom of Heaven belongs to such as these." (Matthew's author, Jewish, used the phrase Kingdom of Heaven rather than "of God" because by tradition, he avoided using the word for Yahweh.)
- Lk 18:16-17 – similar to above.
- Jn 3:3 – albeit framed by John's verbose, distorted elaboration: "Unless a man is born again, he cannot see the Kingdom of God."
- Ts 15 – "When you see one who was not born of woman … worship him. That one is your Father." Here "not born of woman" means reborn with a fresh, clear mindset.
- Ts 46 – Referencing John the Baptist as an advanced, but firmly Self-Aware Person, "Whoever among you becomes little will know the Kingdom and will surpass John."

Christianity distorts this notion all to Hell (literally). In fundamentalist jargon, being "born again" means *accepting* a definition (that Jesus was somehow superman) – not shedding such convictions to see clearly. "Born-again" Christians seem to have reincarnated, not with clear vision, pristine and untainted as a child, but rubber-stamped with the same fantasy-laced mindset they already had.

By the way, Heaven and Hell aren't some after-death change of address whose redirection is based on divine judgment – that's old lore straight out of Zoroastrianism and archaic Middle Eastern lore. Heaven is right here, *right now* if your life works well, if your intent is fulfilled with health, pleasing events and rewarding relationships. Hell is when conflict and struggle, held within, realize into your life: no matter what you try to do, you meet with opposition and resistance. Elements of each manifest directly from your own mindset: you do the judging, nobody else.

Core of Second Indicator: Jesus clearly recognized that seeing the Kingdom required **eliminating** old ideas – **to regain the innocent, uncontaminated outlook of a child**, as per CA.

Third IA Indicator: New Awareness Doesn't Fit into Old Thinking

SAPs, Self-Aware People, resting their world view on accepted definitions and paradigms, can sometimes absorb new beliefs into their philosophy. Pagans in Europe, for example, holding numerous gods from old pantheons, ultimately overcame heavy resistance to accept Christianity's single deity. And Christians somewhat later, over centuries, cottoned up to science, despite inherent differences in their core content. (Old propositions, however, never fully disappeared – fate, luck and astrology are pagan holdovers that, passed on to succeeding generations, persist in common thinking despite Christian tenets.) All such change, though, only redirects the SAP's projected causality from one set of imagined sources to another.

SAPs, except the most open-minded, invariably have trouble even understanding illustrations issued from an IAP's perspective, so fundamentally different is its nature.

The SAP attributes creative power to forces and sources external to self and has many complex conceptualizations in mind that illustrate how these work – how reality must be manipulated to overcome those external powers. Many of these notions were absorbed during childhood as core attributes defining life and physical reality – tied into parental lessons, woven into language and attached to culturally shared values. Presented with an alternate concept (one engenders *one's own* reality), the SAP, filtering that notion through honored definitions, generally balks emotionally as well as intellectually. It flies in the face of all the SAP understands, confronting not only definitions, but psychological underpinnings used continuously throughout life.

So, Clear Awareness, the view integrating Consciousness with Reality in a causal stream, is so fundamentally different – requiring elimination of the very convictions that delineate the SAP's understanding – it simply won't fit into a belief structure that assigns causality outward.

Jesus recognized this inexpedience: his Kingdom required *elimination* of old ideas, not the buildup of new ones attached to and depending on the old:

- Mk 2:21 – "No one sews a patch of unshrunk cloth on an old garment, for the patch will pull away from the garment..." Mt 9:16 and Lk 5:36, derived from Mark, are similar.
- Mk 2:22 – "No one pours new wine into old wineskins ... the wine will burst the skins..." Mt 9:17 and Lk 5:37, also copied from Mark, are equivalent.
- The Gospel of Thomas, #47, provides several similar analogies:
    - "Impossible for a person to mount two horses or stretch two bows."
    - "Slave cannot serve two masters."
    - "No one drinks old wine and immediately desires to drink new wine."
    - Plus those wine and patch metaphors.

Core of Third Indicator: Awareness of the Kingdom can't fit into old beliefs of gods and judgment. Old ideas can't accommodate greater understanding.

Fourth IA Indicator: Patterns Form in Life

Traditionally, even in the minds of great philosophers, Consciousness and Reality have seemed *absolutely* separate. Reality consists of objects, particles, fluids, people, planets and such: tangible things *out there*. One can sense them, touch them, engage them – indeed we all *have to* do that continually throughout daily life.

But this conscious I-Self, constituting the mind that perceives those things, the psyche that makes sense of them, deals with them, names them, etc., seems altogether different from the objects themselves. Even the body seems separate from self: an object needing external manipulation – fed, scratched, cleaned, etc. – as well as prompted through mind-cued muscle contraction in order to carry out that manipulation.

Apart from those, the mind/self, the memories and intent, plans formulated to realize that intent, the humor and creativity, thinking and hoping – all of that seems fully *intangible*, disconnected from the realm of objects it encounters.

But it isn't.

Even the SAP will note a certain inner connection: moving muscles by simply wanting to, sexual arousal purely via thinking sexy things, stirring hunger and salivation by just imagining a sizzling steak or Swiss chocolate, hearing music in the imagination and responding emotionally and physically. So the "inner" is surely connected at least to the body.

But the connection is *much more than that* – although that direct mind-body link is certainly part of the show. This overall connection comes in propensities: the tendency of each of us to create patterns in life. We all attract particular types of relationships through our lifetimes – people come and go, but types are consistent, evolving only as we change through life's stages. And we create patterns in health, experiencing various ailments that impact us in specific ways. And we succeed or fail in life's ventures, also in repeated patterns.

Those outer patterns *reflect* inner propensities: real issues in relationships always reflect specific inner mechanisms and can be changed outwardly by revising the inner – a connection clear to the IAP who has shed beliefs to the contrary.

Jesus recognized this pattern-forming proclivity.

Each gospel features a variation on the point in Mark 4:25, "Whoever has will be given more; whoever does not have, even what he has will be taken away." (Mt 13:12 and Mt 25:29 both voice this to conclude two different parables; likewise, Lk 8:18 and Lk 19:26. Ts 41 is the equivalent.)

Mark's pattern depiction and those in Matthew and Luke are immediately preceded by the *Lamp on a Stand* story (Mk 4:21, Mt 5:15, Lk 11:33 – Thomas' *Lamp* occurs somewhat earlier in Ts 33). These encourage shining a light everywhere – looking open-mindedly at all explanations of life – in order to see clearly: don't put the lamp under a clay jar or under a bed, as in accepting only one explanation, i.e., one religion. This is a slightly different connection, but only with that Lamp shining light freely will you notice the patterns you attract in life.

(Traditionally, Christianity presents the Lamp story as shining a beacon, undimmed, in promoting its Christ hypothesis. But that's not what Jesus meant: in his world a lamp was needed to see your way through the night. This parable indicates shedding light on life's functionality.)

Core of Fourth Indicator: Jesus recognized patterns created in life as Reality manifesting in response to inner nature.

Fifth IA Indicator: Where and When the Kingdom Will Come

Old Israelite lore anticipated direct intervention from Yahweh to restore David's lineage to govern a free Jewish state. That longing grew as centuries passed and Babylonian, Seleucid, Ptolemaic, Parthian and eventually Roman empires dominated the region – with the only respite being brief Hasmonean control, 110 – 63 BCE, a self-rule which was just as bad.

Deemed to lead this charge to divinely directed self-rule was an expected "Messiah" – one great leader, stemming from the House of David, anointed (with oil or fragrance as a symbolic gesture, one of great importance to primitive peoples) as either ruler or spiritual leader.

In gospel accounts, as Jesus began to be recognized as this Messiah, looked on as ushering in the new Imperial State of Yahweh, the question naturally arose as to just when this would happen, the new state free of external suppression.

Of course, *that isn't what Jesus was talking about **at all***. For him, the Kingdom of God was right here and now *for those who recognized it* – not a future state imposed on everybody by a big, tough dictator god and battalions of angels. He tried to communicate that in various ways:

- Luke 17:20-21 is most explicit when Jesus speaks, "The Kingdom of God does not come visibly, nor will people say, 'Here it is,' or "There it is,' because the Kingdom of God is within you."
- Thomas 3 elaborates a bit, concluding that, "The Kingdom is inside of you and outside of you." This indicates that what you hold within is qualitatively reflected in real world events you encounter.
- Ts 51: disciples ask, "When will the new world come?" Jesus said, "That which you are awaiting has come, but you don't recognize it." The SAP is oblivious to any personal role in attracting specific happenings.
- Mk 9:1 has Jesus saying, "Some who are standing here will not taste death before they see that the Kingdom of God has come with power." Of course, KG, to those who realize it, brings personal power. Mt 16:28 and Lk 9:27 distort Mark's statement slightly. That's not surprising, as neither author comprehended the Kingdom perspective; each tried to impart his own interpretation on it.
- Ts 113: disciples ask on what day the Kingdom will come. Jesus: "It won't come by watching for it. It won't be said, 'Look, here!' or 'Look, there!' Rather the Kingdom is spread out upon the earth and people don't see it."

Traditionally, many interpreted these as meaning that Jesus expected Yahweh's direct intervention to come any day – within the lifetimes of the listeners in that setting. But actually, Jesus expected some of his listeners, before they died, to simply grasp *what he was talking about:* the Kingdom within being reflected in the real world. He knew that inner-outer manifestation was and is how life works – whether the individual perceives it or not. He presumed that some of his followers would "get it" during their lifetimes. There is, however, no indication that any of the disciples actually *did* get it – indeed, all accounts show that they didn't.

This key pointer *alone* indicates that the Kingdom isn't a Yahweh-from-Heaven intervention, nor is it a post-death state. It's here and now. You need only *see that process*.

Core of Fifth Indicator: Jesus hoped his explanations could help others see life clearly within their current lifetimes.

Sixth IA Indicator: Reality is a Oneness – not a Duality

The Gospel of Thomas preserves a gem of Jesus' illustrations in Ts 22. He likens suckling infants to those entering the Kingdom (see second point above), then illustrates, "When you make the two into one ... the inside like the outside ... above like below ... male and female into a single one, so that the male will not be male and female will not be female, (etc.) ... then you will enter the Kingdom." Ts 106 reiterates the *two into one* meaning.

We invariably tend to draw lines and create boundaries in the reality we encounter: rather than a flowing, interconnected Singularity, we see a collection of objects bounded by surfaces and edges. But Jesus recognized, as Heraclitus, Lao Tzu and Gautama had a half millennium prior, that reality comprises an interwoven Oneness in which all seemingly separate objects function together. And they operate reflective of an individual's life, in response to that person's inner state.

Perceiving this connected quality of life requires a recognition that firm boundaries are artificial – not seeing the world as collected objects, but beginning to see it as a collage, reflecting, i.e., manifesting meaning.

Jesus was pointing out that various opposites must be understood as united – that they only appear to exist when defined as independent elements.

Core of Sixth Indicator: Reality constitutes a *Oneness*, not a collection of isolated objects.

Seventh IA Indicator: Love your Neighbor and your Enemies

One cornerstone of the Synoptic Gospels is Jesus profusely recommending that his listeners love their neighbors: Mt 5:43, Mt 19:19, Mt 22:39, Mk 12:31-33, Lk 10:27. This is consistent with traditional teaching (Leviticus 19:18). But Jesus extends this entreaty, rather surprisingly, beyond neighbors. Mt 5:44, Lk 6:27 and 6:35 carry this appeal into "enemy" territory, so to speak.

Why would you love your enemy? Or even your neighbor: you can get along, maybe like him/her a lot – but love? Remember, commandments already ruled out adultery!

Your enemy wants to do you harm, maybe kill you! Your neighbor may make noise, let his dog poop on your lawn, throw his debris onto your acreage – who knows? Why should you love these people?

Should you love enemies just because Jesus says to? Because, if everybody buys into Jesus' command, the world will be better? (That was Immanuel Kant's point – the great German philosopher. He didn't see a reality that rewarded or demanded such an attitude, thus encouraging it, but thought it advisable and preferable because it was intellectually satisfying.)

Actually, no, neither of those is correct.

First, you can't love your neighbor, your enemy or *anybody else* just because somebody suggests you should. Love is a feeling, an emotional response of natural tendency that lies much, much deeper within the psyche than a rational conclusion to do something based on advice. You can fool others and possibly even fool yourself into thinking you really love somebody who gives you trouble – a neighbor or an enemy. But that's a sham. It isn't anything remotely similar to love, to *sincere acceptance* – which is the basis of love. (If you don't accept somebody *exactly as they are*, wanting to change this or that, or else picking various aspects you do love and overcoming others which you don't – then you don't love them. Love = Acceptance plus.)

So, why should you love your enemy? Why would Jesus even say that? The standard answer introduces trite notions like: because we're all God's children, all the same in the sight of God.

Bullshit.

That fantasy, goody-goody God doesn't exist.

Jesus promoted loving your neighbor – and your neighbor is every other human on the face of this planet, friend, enemy or unknown – because he recognized that *no one else is causal to your life*. Your neighbor and your enemy are playing those roles because **you attracted** the relationship into your sphere of encounter.

When you become clearly aware of your innate tie to the unfolding events and relationships that constitute your life, and aware they stem from your own complex nature, you quit blaming others for issues you encounter. In the process, you come to see that others hold the same good nature you yourself constitute, the same hopes and fears, similar desires and disappointments – however much that inner goodness is compromised by fear and powerlessness. Recognizing that, you appreciate their being as much as your own.

Of course, faced with threatening enemies and annoying neighbors, it pays to search your own inner realm to see what combination of conflict and fear, of discontentment and prejudice might still populate your own nature. That is, referring to another Jesus classic, you might chip away at the plank in your own eye before you try to remove the speck in another's.

The benefit inherent to Jesus' entreaty to love others is that positive inner orientation promotes manifestation of affirmative elements in your own life. But that comes in the process of eliminating fear and conflict – and in all cases, reveals the inner-outer correlation with which life functions.

Core of Seventh Indicator: Love all others because they are high quality conscious entities – just like you. Accept them as they are, for they never cause your problems. You yourself attract the pattern, making you the prime cause of all effects in your life. (This doesn't mean you have to *like* or associate with everybody you encounter – just accept them as they are. Any conflict or control that they represent reflects your own inner turmoil or insecurity.)

Eighth IA Indicator: Seek and Ye Shall Find

In Mt 7:7-8 and Lk 11:9-10, Jesus implores his listeners to seek in order to find – knock and the door will be opened for you.

But he doesn't indicate what to seek – or where to knock. Indeed, if you only seek in a Christian church, you'll only find stock answers. If you only knock on the elaborate front door thereof, you'll only find yourself in its nave of ancient illusions.

What Jesus meant was to seek the Kingdom, to pursue *understanding* – not cookie-cutter, dogmatic answers. He spent his life decrying the religious establishment of his time and culture. He provided insights well beyond Judaism's encrusted prophetic "Truths". He would be stunned to realize that exactly that same encrustation ultimately formed around his *own* teachings – or distortions of them – in centuries following his death.

If you proceed with an open mind, relating real life encountered to tenets proposed by any religion or philosophy – and don't get entrapped within any particular set of ideas – you'll ultimately come to see your connection to a flowing Oneness that constitutes life.

Core of Eighth Indicator: Seek understanding, sincere and open-minded – not archaic belief structures – **and you will find enlightenment.**

Ninth IA Indicator: The Mind Directly Impacts the Body

In the original Greek, two words are typically translated into English as "faith" or "belief" in the Synoptic Gospels:

- *Pisteuo* in ancient Greek generally means, "to think something to be true, place confidence in, be persuaded of."
- *Pistis*, closely related, means "conviction of truth of anything, belief."

Neither of these sounds to me like they should be translated into English as "faith", in the religious sense of believing in some god or teachings with no rational grounds to support the notion.

Both sound more like the English word, "belief" in their common usage where Jesus describes the source of healing to somebody who just experienced it.

Pisteuo occurs in instances of Jesus' healing in Mt 8:13, 9:28, and 21:22, in Mk 9:23-24 and 11:23-24, and in Lk 8:50. In the original Greek text, *Pistis* is found in Mt 8:10, 9:22, 9:29 and 15:28, in Mk 5:34 and 10:52, and in Lk 7:9, 7:50, Lk 8:48, Lk 17:19 and 18:42. All of these are instances centered on Jesus healing somebody and stating that, translated into English, "your belief has made you whole," "according to your faith will it be done to you," or something similar.

Never, not one single time, does Jesus say, "God made you whole," or "I healed you." Not ever. He always pointed out that the individual's belief was the driving force behind healing.

Yet somehow, core to Christian tradition, Jesus is imagined to tap some deity's power or have it himself. Obviously *neither* was the case when he couldn't heal anybody back home. In Nazareth people saw him as a local guy, not a special power. Without trust or belief in him, locals lacked that psycho-somatic impetus toward healing which impelled peasants' abatement of symptoms elsewhere. If he'd had some kind of divine power, it wouldn't have mattered what others thought.

Core of Ninth Indicator: Jesus realized the mind-body connection and repeatedly explained to people that they personally, through their mind content, were the source of healing.

Deceptive Quotes to Sort Through

From these nine points, it's abundantly clear that Jesus was exceptionally aware of the functional Oneness of Consciousness/Reality. *None of these points* makes any sense if Jesus is regarded as a supernatural deity offspring, apocalyptic doomsayer, wise teacher on how to live, traditional Jewish rabbi or charismatic healer.

There are, of course, plenty of lines attributed to Jesus that would refute that status:

- Compare Mt 5:9, "Blessed are the peacemakers" and "Love your neighbor as yourself" with Lk 12:49-53, "I have come to bring fire on the earth … Do you think I came to bring peace? No, I tell you, but division."
  - Did Jesus regress from his recognition of inner calm as critical to outer peace, or just get confused sometimes?
  - No: other thoughts were put into his mouth by the evangelists or invented/inserted during the decades-long oral tradition phase.
- Compare Mt 5:3 "Blessed are the poor in spirit, for theirs is the Kingdom" with Lk 6:20, "Blessed are you who are poor" – different renderings of the same Beatitude. Ts 54 agrees with Luke.
  - Being *blessed* is a state where good things happen to you. It can have no other meaning: *damned* is the opposite, with bad things ensuing.
  - But the poor are anything but blessed – their lives are inherently difficult, full of struggle and difficulty. That version must have come later when Jesus became in some eyes a champion of the poor.

- ○ However, the Matthew version is brilliant and indicative again of Clear Awareness. "Poor in spirit," is an astute observation of the functional Kingdom. It doesn't mean "spiritually poor", or "psychologically downtrodden" – nothing like that at all.
- ○ "In spirit" implies a state you are in *imaginatively*. E.g., not home for the holidays, you are home "in spirit" if you feel connected to family. Likewise, *Poor in Spirit* means "by nature, not oriented to materialism" or "psychologically, not addicted to wealth". Regardless of current financial status – you may or may not be poor monetarily – you're *spiritually* detached from materialistic *desires*. Thus, that phrase means: ***non-materialistic***. And indeed, that's an indicator of Clear Awareness and life's inherent twist: not desiring things contributes to manifesting satisfaction. If you end the pursuit of money as though it would bring contentment, you'll engender a life wherein you live without stress, which carries abundance as a consequence.
- Compare, "Love your neighbor" and even your enemies with Ts 101, Ts 55 and Lk 14:26, all of which promote hating your father and mother. The latter grouping makes no sense at any level and was certainly twisted during the oral tradition phase.
- Compare statements featuring the rich getting more while the poor have their little taken away with notions of "The first will be last" and the last first. Huh? Something wrong there. What's missing is the desire part: those who want to be first will be last if they hold inner conflict and fear to negate their intent.

There is, of course, a great deal of gospel content that stems from a source far less aware of things than Jesus is indicated to be – as clearly evidenced above. Practically all of the Gospel of John falls under that category: Jesus' long, rambling discourses about the Father and his own status are pure invention by somebody, likely emerging long after Jesus' departure.

Two Clinchers

Two main points refute any thought that Jesus was principally an apocalyptic preacher, a mainline Jewish rabbi, an itinerant wonder-worker – or anything other than a highly aware teacher.

First: a visionary with Integrated Awareness, an *IAP* as illustrated above, *could* pass along points of wisdom he'd heard or agreed with from previous sources. The Golden Rule didn't originate with Jesus, but he could have expressed it along the way and been quoted so by others. (Of course, in unreliable reports, those words could have been simply inserted into Jesus' quotes.)

In any case, a true visionary wouldn't initiate clearly Self-Aware level, conflict-laced commentary – though, again, lower-level, more mundane views could have been assigned to him later.

But second, most importantly: no SAP ever uttered a phrase purely indicative of Clear Awareness – unless he/she quoted or repeated such phrases from a source of Integrated Awareness.

During the oral tradition phase lasting some 40 years beyond Jesus' death, his parables and other expressions indicating Clear Awareness were passed along, many intact – as shown above – some distorted. To them were added many expressions not consistent with advanced consciousness. But the many expressions revealing Integrated, Clear Awareness *must have originated* with the real Yeshua, substantiating beyond question his status of personal awareness.

Here are a few bonus notes from the Gospel of Thomas as kickers:

- Ts 56: "Whoever has come to know the world has found a corpse." Ts 80 substitutes the word, "body" for *corpse*.

Effectively, the Reality you experience is a *result*, with your inner state being the cause. In a very real way, the world you try to manipulate daily is thus an *outcome* – in effect, a corpse. You can only accomplish real change by delving inward to the source within your psyche. These two references indicate Jesus understood that.

- Ts 61 makes the point that, if one is whole, one is filled with light – if divided, filled with darkness. This emphasizes the Oneness of things.
- Ts 67: "Those who know all, but are lacking in themselves, are lacking everything." Knowledge about the outside world is useless if you don't fully understand the Self.
- Ts 74: "Many around the drinking trough, but there's nothing in the well." People, SAPs, flock to churches and organized belief vendors, but those sources offer no value – no understanding of Reality's pure function.
- Ts 77: "I am the light over all things. I am the All ... Split a piece of wood – I'm there. Lift a stone, and you'll find me there." This doesn't mean in any way, shape or form, what the Gospel of John is full of: that Jesus is one and the same with some god, son of him or anything remotely like that. It means that Jesus recognized that the entire realm he encountered was connected to him, a part of his essence – a reflection of and Oneness with his own being. That's the case *with everyone* – you included, of course.

But each individual has to recognize that connection, personally, clearly and intimately. Once that's done, that person has gained Clear Awareness, is "Integrated" – or, in Jesus' terminology, has entered the Kingdom.

Slant Out:
A Theology Off Course

Jesus, then, was presenting to his peers a crystalline view of reality: his Kingdom that anybody could enter *right now*, wherein life would go well. There (i.e., *here* when you realized it), they would heal from afflictions, not fear death and enjoy existence – because Yahweh-god would provide all of that if you fully trusted that it would be so. His Kingdom was *here and now*, energized from within based on trust.

Promoted within that framework was peace, forgiveness, love of others and trust:

- Peace, because having eliminated inner conflict, you don't manifest it in relationships.
- Forgiveness, because you don't blame others for problems you've attracted.
- Love, as you now appreciate others' qualities and don't find them in any way threatening.
- Trust, because by trusting yourself explicitly, you only attract patterns featuring reliable people.

Focused on personal aspects, Jesus' message highlighted disdain of traditional, organized religion and its bureaucratic, political, self-serving priesthood. It derided blustering experts spouting scriptures and pushing hard-line traditions – especially when they themselves, hypocrites, didn't follow their own dictates. He railed against the royalty and government of his time, championing the little guy and seeing women as equals. All had equal access to the Kingdom – *if they could only see how life worked right now!*

But the religion that grew up touting his name, asserting Jesus as exemplar of perfection, god-begotten or *God Himself*, consists of assorted priesthoods every bit as bureaucratic and self-serving as the old Temple crew. They glorify the *Christ*, turning a simple notation as Anointed One, Messiah, into some kind of other-worldly, perfected superman. They hype Jesus as "King", when he abhorred royalty. And they often institutionally suppress women's status.

Where Jesus promoted peace and forgiveness, Christianity has tortured and executed 40,000 or so in inquisitions, killed untold thousands during Crusades, launched and been the basis of countless wars and destroyed the lives of many native populations (e.g., Native Americans on both continents) when "Christian" civilizations came to conquer. Where Jesus spoke of self-trust to promote healing, his supposed followers focus all trust as faith in a god *who doesn't exist* and a Trinity that was fabricated on conjectural fantasy in the fourth century. Where he emphasized simple values of love and confidence, grand denominations have emerged in his name, riding wealth and political power, espousing uncaring "conservative" values while backing widespread gun ownership.

How could the plain, piercing insights of a visionary highlighting self-trust and love become so utterly distorted into the blind-leading-the-blind clergy and vast money-generating schemes sucking donations out of little old ladies that dominate Christianity? The Pope and his minions, donning silly robes and miters, living in luxury like Sadducee chief priests, promote fantasy-based symbols as significant. Evangelical buffoons dictate phony "Truth" to millions of brainwashed followers, and keep modern man awash in primitive world-views and archaic rituals.

How could Jesus' simple, personal insights get so thoroughly twisted into Christian fantasy and control-mongering?

Let's just take a look at that:

When we left Jesus, he had just exited one of the most memorable incarnations ever – certainly the most misunderstood (an issue currently being remedied).

Concluding the Gospel

Stunned beyond rational comprehension at Jesus' sudden execution, disgraced by crucifixion – nailed naked to a post like the lowest of criminals – the disciples were clueless as to how to proceed. They watched from a distance, fearing for their own lives, as James and some of the women approached closer. As hours waned and Jesus showed ever diminishing sign of life, they were lost. At length, his body slumped, lifeless.

One local follower, on the ruling Council but not able to counter the power sources, one Joseph of Arimathea, appealed to Pilate to manage Jesus' corpse once his ordeal ended. Given that permission, he arranged for a niche in his family tomb where Jesus' body could be prepared – washing, ritual purification and dressing. There, the corpse would desiccate for a year, then the bones would be placed in an ossuary – perhaps ultimately removed to a slot in his family crypt near Nazareth.

Mary Magdalene and Jesus' mother, devastated, went along to the tomb with Joseph's servants so they would know where to come later to prepare the body.

But James, Jesus' brother, livid with anger at the injustice, collected several followers who had made the trip. "My brother won't be left here to rot in the shadow of the priests' mansion," he declared. "Let us remove the body, prepare it quickly and return it home – I don't care about customs, Yeshua belongs in *our* crypt. We'll inform the others later. My wagons are ready."

Three joined him to heave away the stone covering the doorway. They'd finished their task, wrapped the stiffening, blood-encrusted corpse in a new shroud, then gently loaded it onto the wagon. Having returned the stone, they were riding northwards when they saw Roman soldiers headed towards the tomb. Relieved that they'd outsmarted the Romans, they decided – for safety – to ride immediately and hurriedly north through Samaria. They could inform the camping group and disciples later on.

Two days later, several women of the party went to the tomb with spices and perfumes – only to find the stone rolled away and the body gone. When they reported back, confusion and disbelief reigned. Disciples ran to the tomb to confirm the situation and all were left, not knowing what to do.

In ensuing days, the entourage made its way mournfully back to Galilee, with several disciples remaining in Jerusalem to pray and seek understanding. Many, deeply disturbed at the shocking turn of events and confused by the empty tomb, had vivid dreams of Jesus where he told them to keep the faith. Some, following long, late night discussions over wine, even had visions of their beloved leader and teacher and reported seeing him, offering his punctured limbs as proof of his ordeal. Those stories would grow over the years.

Birth and Incubation of Christianity
Within Two to Five Years

While some had initially returned to their occupations, the most devoted disciples ultimately settled in Jerusalem and continued to press other Jews to accept Jesus as Messiah, offering scripture as proof. They claimed that he would return or send another, as emissaries of Yahweh, to lead his people to their promised freedom from outside intervention. They shared amongst themselves Jesus' earlier Kingdom teachings, but couldn't press these as evidence to attract new people, for they were neither proof of his status in Jewish eyes nor clear points supported by traditional teaching.

Their message won occasional converts among Jews, but not many: the suffering, disgraced Messiah wasn't consistent with common expectations of a hallowed, Anointed One sent by Yahweh. Jesus supporters offered mystical features not common to traditional Judaism: miracle healings and other claimed signs, speaking, seemingly, in foreign tongues that visitors from abroad could amazingly understand and an energized *Holy Spirit* that brought divine attributes into inspired life. Reports even circulated as to Jesus' defeat of death, as he'd been seen alive by many devotees following execution.

And stories about Jesus, spread among the peasantry, began to grow in mystical content and continued that trajectory throughout the oral transmission phase. Simple encounters of snow on a mountaintop became glowing metaphysical displays of superimposed prophets and radiant light. Everyday feel-good exchanges with lonely, depressed people, where their symptoms temporarily abated, became glorified healings, powered by the divinity himself as channeled through his earthly agent. And that agent, Jesus, through time, grew to all-powerful – expanding from healer to Savior of Mankind, eventually to divinely connected Son of the deity himself, if not that god personally incarnated.

But emergence of super-Jesus took time and grew only slowly across cultures as the legend expanded. Early on, the movement promoting Jesus as Messiah to the Jews only took root with a central focus in Jerusalem. In short order, some converts and the most outspoken disciples caused dissension in the Temple, leading to arrests – and soon, the stoning of one follower, Stephen, whose blasphemy went too far. That and other threats led many local Jerusalem Jesus-believers to move out, taking the message elsewhere in the region.

Simon, the Rock (Kaipha in Aramaic, Peter in Greek), still young and unseasoned, yet inspired in devotion to his hero, claimed the Holy Spirit supplied his vigor in promoting Jesus as Messiah who would come back in judgment. His message at the Temple and elsewhere: repentance was needed – devotion to Yahweh and commitment to the Torah to push the traditions in this new direction. But soon a new player was to emerge onto the scene, one who'd been unrelenting in his opposition – one who had held the cloaks of those who'd stoned that first Christian martyr.

Going on Ten Years

With a stunning about-face in attitude, Saul of Tarsus became a leading advocate as to Jesus' survival of death and divine status. Headed to Damascus to round up Jews errantly succumbing to the spreading Jesus cult, he was shocked into contrition by a vision – more accurately, a hallucination – of Jesus hovering up there in the firmament upbraiding him for his opposition. From then on, now called Paul, convinced of the veracity of his phantasm, he took up the cause – traveling tirelessly to contact and nurture growing Christian communities from Palestine through Asia Minor and beyond.

But Paul's message differed significantly from the original disciples' variation off Judaism. While the others had known Jesus closely and followed him personally, revering his character and message – they at least heard and remembered, if not comprehended, his Kingdom of God metaphors – Paul cared little about the real man he'd never seen, even less about his message. His Jesus was the *Christ* – no longer an anointed Jewish champion aiming to free his people, but now a true Son of God in the heavens. The word "Christ," a simple Greek translation for "Messiah," had become for Paul a vaunted, super-hero designator. His focus was on death and resurrection of the *Christ*, one Paul knew from his personal encounter during his epiphany. That status would grow to mythical proportions as generations and centuries passed – the magical key to everything good.

Paul taught that Jesus' death was a benefit to all who would believe in him, a gesture meant to purge people's sins – previously accomplished within Judaism, so they imagined, through specified ritual – justifying the lowly sinners in God's eyes. When Jesus returned – an act imminent in Paul's conviction (except it never happened) – all proclaimed Christians would be saved as Yahweh exacted punishment on others.

The originals, principally Simon Peter, John and now James the

Just, Jesus' brother, who'd come to lead the group with his superior organizational acumen, maintained their focus on convincing Jews of Jesus' Messianic nature. Paul began to broaden his focus towards other ethnicities.

The Second Decade

With Paul's vigor and commitment – having suffered repeated threats, beatings, imprisonment, shipwrecks, hunger and thirst – along with eased entry requirements to the movement, the budding "Christian" proto-church spread more rapidly, drawing people of many ethnicities willing to give up pagan myth for an avowed single deity and big promises. Much of the growth spread by word of mouth, with uneducated peasants bringing friends and family into the fold, drawing common folk – and their now-indoctrinated offspring – in to a belief system that, however mystical and theoretical, at least featured love and caring. Still, most local groups in, by now, many regional cities, maintained connections with host Jewish centers in synagogues – with Gentile adherents tolerated to varying degrees, particularly if their tithes added to the kitty.

Other social issues sprang up, however. Roman authorities and most ethnic groups respected Judaism as an ancient and venerated religion. Generally, as the Empire spread, new religions absorbed had been welcomed and even incorporated. After all, most pantheons featured comparable fertility, war, and other specialized gods – easily identified equivalents to current deities. As long as the Emperor was accepted with proper allegiance – and taxes paid – all was fine. But those Christian Jews would balk at other gods, including the now deified Emperor. Increasingly separated in identity from traditionalists, adding ever more Gentiles to their numbers, they became irrepressibly staunch in their convictions. Consequently, authorities and neighbors took to persecuting them.

Even *that* fit into a growing expectation of suffering. Where

Jesus had personally promoted the *Kingdom*, a state that would lead to good things in life, later Christians began to prize martyrdom and self-sacrifice as gallant gesture of devotion – setting themselves up for bad things: certain pain and often death.

Through this period, stories about Jesus and collections of his sayings passed along, continued to accumulate lore in the retelling. But they began to be written down informally by peripheral anonymous adherents.

The Fifties

By now, while still an emerging sect attached to Judaism, proto-Christianity was spreading into many of the Empire's cities. Paul traveled extensively to meet with budding groups, considering himself the equal to original apostles by virtue of his encounter with the Christ-in-the-sky of his epiphany. Increasingly, he advocated loosening constraints on non-Jews for joining the movement, confronting the originals with his growing numbers of converts. Ultimately, the "elders" allowed that Greeks, Samaritans and other ethnic groups could join by simply following honorable standards – no need for circumcision or strict adherence to Jewish traditions.

Paul, through extensive writing, kept his various groups on track (or tried to) – and established a body of communication that survived. But Paul's message widened in differentiation from that of the disciples. Where they still preserved and repeated Jesus' unique insights, seeing the movement as a rational extension of Judaism, Paul vigorously promoted acceptance of Jesus as Christ, Son of God and Savior figure to all as "justification" in the eye of his God. Jesus' role *through dying* had been to provide atonement for sins, so Paul and his movement thought – those forbidden acts previously requiring prescribed gestures to make up for inflicted harm. Since God had provided this new way, his begotten and beloved son, adherence to old rules was no longer necessary. Indeed, as Paul's approach evolved, following the old Jewish Law came to be seen as counter to and even *damaging* one's efforts to please Yahweh.

Through the decade of the Fifties, Paul forged his approach onto vital, growing branches of this new sect, while the original movement, headed by James, Jesus' brother, and Simon Peter, retained dogged focus on convincing Jews to readjust their thinking and accept Jesus as Messiah. Paul's buy-in on relaxation of Jewish ritual was key to widespread growth among the Empire's many ethnic groups, but James, more conservative, never quite accepted this new variation on his brother's legacy.

Still, as the decade progressed, the other disciples, who had all been by character natural followers – not leaders – began to disappear from principal roles and ultimately memory. Paul came to dominate, aggravating Jewish authorities sufficiently as the decade ended to have to appeal for Roman protection to avoid an even earlier demise.

Paul did have to adapt his message to changes as the decade progressed. When Jesus didn't return in a short timeframe, as anticipated, Paul had to waylay expectations, revising his stance to suit: he'll be back whenever it's right – *don't worry about it*. As believers died off, he had to assuage others by claiming that the dead who were justified would be brought back – no problem. This established a pattern of shifting, murky theology – ready to change whenever expected consequences, unfulfilled, proved old claims flawed. *Reason* itself was not a means to arrive at accurate conclusions, but became entrenched as concocted, rationalized argument meant to justify preconceived ideas. This worked well with the naïve and gullible in most areas, with those only exposed to primitive pagan deities, but not so well in more sophisticated environs, such as Athens, where people would question Paul's fabricated tenets. Undeterred, Paul planted seeds wherever they would grow: early on, that was the illiterate peasantry.

Despite Paul's efforts at establishing a firm theology in line with his own staunch views, regional differences grew through the Fifties. Lacking communication and any sort of official organization, each local group, prompted by home-grown leaders and occasionally a self-ascribed visionary, would favor customized explanations and develop their own theological take. Paul spent considerable effort trying to keep the groups he knew in line. This pattern of local and regional differences based on varied interpretations would also persist within the budding religion, with certain common practices – baptism, belief in Jesus' divine status – as common themes.

The Volatile Sixties

Events ensued during the fourth decade following Jesus' death that rattled the religious structure fundamentally.

The disciples were aging and dying out. Paul, whose message had long eclipsed the originals, was in prison and would join Simon Peter in being executed in Rome, where the religion had spread prior to either of them arriving. Christians were increasingly in conflict with Jews from local situations up through the traditional hierarchy. But all such relationships, in Jerusalem and elsewhere, were about to change dramatically.

Jerusalem anti-tax protests built to attacks on Romans, then quickly escalated to rebels taking down the Roman military contingent; Agrippa II, last of the Herods, fled Jerusalem. Reinforcements from Syria were ambushed and defeated – a shock to the Romans. In 67, Vespasian and son, Titus, with four legions invaded Galilee (whose contingent was led by Josephus, later historian) and worked their way south. Following a lull owing to turmoil in Rome with the elimination of Nero, war resumed with the siege of Jerusalem.

In early stages of this major conflict, Jews and Christian-Jews with any sense fled Jerusalem, mostly to points north. Romans ultimately crushed rebels holed up in three sections of Jerusalem – while three factions actually were fighting each other.

Forty Years after Jesus – the Seventies

This huge upheaval produced several consequences that affected the course of early Christianity. For one, the Jewish Temple-centered culture evolved to a more local-centric approach around synagogues. It had to: the Temple, focal point of all intertwined cultural-religious activities, was basically destroyed.

The Jesus sect still adhered to its Jewish roots, although increasingly less so as strife built. Functional oddballs within both Judaism and pagan environments, proto-Christians garnered easy blame for maladies, natural disasters and wars alike, as divine wrath, whether Yahweh's or other gods' – making the martyr-prone, staunch believers easy scapegoats for punishment. Not only did that foster separation from traditional Judaism per se, but a new tax added pressure to the wedge: the Fiscus Judaicus was levied, payable to Rome by *all Jews* throughout the Empire, replacing the former Temple levy. Soon thereafter, the Christian sect lobbied for exemption from this tax, claiming separation. Ever more heavily populated by non-Jews, the sect, however diverse regionally, was sprouting its own nature.

At the decade's outset, while ancient infrastructure was crumbling in Jerusalem, somewhat to the north a dedicated Greek Christian was setting ideas into script. He'd accumulated copies of various Jesus sayings, passion stories and instructional scripts. He added various other points heard from traveling speakers and some old-timers who claimed to have heard Jesus give talks in their youth. He added a narrative based on general knowledge and recorded everything on a scroll. This unsigned work, centuries later, would be attributed to "Mark", a companion of Simon Peter.

Group meetings, increasingly in private dwellings rather than synagogues, had only scripture passages from the Septuagint, the Greek OT translation, to read at their meetings, with some having copies of letters Paul had written twenty years before. Local elders, though, thought it wise to collect Jesus stories to accompany such reference material. Thus, this first Jesus scroll proved popular, so copies were made for other assemblies in nearby cities of Iturea and Syria.

Into the Eighties

With older generations long gone – rumor had it that John, aging son of Zebedee still lived in Asia Minor – Christianity continued to spread through osmosis: some had taken it upon themselves to spread the word. A decent living could be made, it was found, by traveling about, speaking and healing in the name of Jesus. A certain personality type, from time immemorial, having learned it could live well by offering popular ideas back to the broad swath of ignorant mankind wanting to have its favored beliefs stroked and reinforced, conformed to sprouting Christian tenets as it had to others.

Ancient priesthoods of pagan gods, harbingers of Zoroastrian truths, cult officials of Greek and Roman gods and the Sadducee Temple elite of Judaism alike, all benefitted personally from public offerings, taxes, grain and prestige – a living far preferred to actually working the fields or carrying on trades. So it evolved with early Christianity: some became experts, learning standard phraseology from Paul's letters, stock scriptural quotes and took on pious-sounding tones to please listeners. A priesthood developed, specializing in Christianity. Over time, local leaders – deacons and elders – bubbled up to regional roles and began to organize, increasingly centered, as all things then, in Rome. The process was aided by increased friction with local Jewish groups, such that slowly Christian sub-groups, Jews along with Gentile converts, were ejected from synagogues who no longer tolerated their revolutionary ideas and unreasonable ideals.

By mid-decade, those original scrolls picturing Jesus and his mission, copied and dispersed, led to other enhancements. Within a more Jewish community, one writer expanded on that first scroll, adding material from manuscripts quoting Jesus' parables and witticisms. His work, long afterwards attributed to the disciple Matthew, corrected earlier errors and reformulated stories to coincide with his community's slant. Experiencing a late-century burgeoning of Pharisee expression in the post-Temple environment, he often pitted Jesus against that sect, planting his contemporary situation into Jesus' timeframe. Consistent with mystical lore that had accrued in the Jesus story and the rampant superstition of his community, his account reflected miraculous events, relaying them as factual happenings. Oriented to Jewish traditions in a society that still integrated the Christian adherents with Jewish traditionalists, he emphasized scriptural justification and Jesus' support of the Law.

Meanwhile, nearer Antioch to the north, an area that had absorbed considerable proto-Christian numbers, another writer composed a two-part story. This work, later called Luke and Acts, covered not only Jesus' life – with significant reference to that first manuscript and the same sayings compilation as his more Jewish-oriented contemporary – but added accounts of disciples and Paul *after* Jesus' execution.

Both writers liberally mixed in aggregated lore about Jesus' post-death appearances lacking in the original work. And both invented stories to pump up Jesus' miraculous birth and resurrection to impress potential converts.

Christianity, increasingly independent of its Jewish parent, was accumulating its own scripture.

By the End of the Century

Increasing in mythical qualities, the Jesus presented by such writing was growing through time, in part to conform to the superman-Christ image established decades before by Paul. The quietly suffering itinerant healer and teacher of that first document composed just after the fall of Jerusalem had become an offspring of the deity through a miraculously impregnated human mother who amazingly maintained her pristine virginity and implacable perfection through it all. The man who taught humility and simple acceptance was now glorified beyond recognition into a special savior sent directly by God himself.

And it mushroomed from there.

Yet another view of Jesus was assembled and redacted over time to promote Jesus yet higher on the cosmic scale – its final version ultimately attributed to disciple John. According to this latest work, Jesus had existed for all time, was thrust into incarnation by the very *Logos*, the *Word of God* made flesh – instilled from above into murky, ugly, materialistic existence to give lowly humans a shot at eternal redemption. Gone are the parables, spoken by a visionary and surviving for decades with their original flair. Gone is the healing, the caring, the touch of humanity. This elevated super-Jesus now lectures on end about his vaunted self and his Father. Gone is wisdom about life assembled cleverly into short images that could convey timeless understanding to simple listeners. Now the incarnated God knows all that will unfold and sees all that is coming, as though playing out a Hollywood script on a superficial set.

As the first century closes, a man, a living and breathing human with character, a sense of humor and a particularly clear view of consciousness, has been transposed into a Herculean Wonder. Christianity, in the process of severing itself from its suckling parent, had become a full-bore myth, every bit as inflated and conflated as the age-old pantheons of all surrounding cultures.

Onwards through Two Centuries

As the Apostolic Age ended, new leaders emerged. Gaining some structure of organization – the ultimate doom of any worthwhile idea – and suffering widespread persecution for believers' eccentric notions, Christianity was moved forward by emerging leaders. Ignatius of Antioch (c. 40 – c. 110), then

Polycarp of Smyrna (69-155), Clement of Rome (fl. 100), Justin Martyr (100 – c. 165) and Irenaeus (c. 130 – c. 200) defended growing conventions against offbeat interpretations, such as those of Marcion of Sinope (c. 85 – c. 160), Valentinus (c. 100 – c. 160) and Montanus (fl. 150). Whole movements opposing mainline thinking emerged into considerable popularity, prompting conflict over interpretation.

Clearly, by the commentary of Justin and Irenaeus, a principal theme had taken root that would persist as the Christian perspective moved onwards: God, who had created everything, sent his Son (Christ), who died (as sacrifice for man's sins) and who rose from the dead on the third day – after which he ascended into heaven (that real place up above the firmament) and would one day return in glory. The Old Testament was seen as predicting Christ's arrival and presaging the new one. Indeed, Irenaeus was the first to refer to this *"New* Testament". By mid-second century, gospels and letters were already assembled as accepted components, but not yet universally and exclusively agreed upon as an official canon.

As variations off that theme, the Gnostics clung to Greek philosophical argument to claim their own secretive truths revealing more mystical hierarchies. The Ebionites, "poor ones", kept Jewish rituals and didn't accept newcomers who wouldn't. Marcionism featured Jesus sent, not as a Jewish Messiah, but as a fully spiritual entity sent by the Monad – the absolute *One*, a deity way above the Jewish Yahweh level. Docetism, holding that Jesus was just a phantasm, not a real human, was fairly common at the time – and not much less plausible than other conjecture.

Valentinus, educated in Alexandria, launched his own movement when rebuffed for the bishop position in Rome. His tack, a variation on Gnosticism sporting selected elements from Platonic thinking, attracted widespread following. While Valentinus planted conceptions that later emerged as the Trinity, he was widely attacked – particularly by Irenaeus – and discredited, though his movement persisted for some time.

By the late second century, Montanism, while similar to general thinking, pushed reliance on the Holy Spirit and a strongly conservative view. To them and to other groups to a degree, when the Holy Spirit came down on somebody, it was God speaking through mortal lips. So had the various works of the NT been revealed: with God inspiring the writers, whoever they were, to reveal the "Truth" as it had been directly experienced and preserved by the apostles.

Beyond these and other movements, regional differences abounded. Theology, slowly debated among remote locations, had yet to be specified. In Antioch, the take on accepted manuscripts was very much literal. Alexandria's community interpreted scriptures and works about Jesus allegorically, finding hidden meaning to all stories.

Every region, every movement, every leading advocate, however, ***defined its/his own view as orthodox*** and considered others as heretical. No universal theology, during this time, had been established, beyond those core tenets of resurrection and God's wonderment. Rampant debate flourished on theological variations, because ***they were all only debating ideas,*** none of which had any significant relationship to reality and its simple function – nor any faint reflection of Jesus' Kingdom within. So interpretations varied based on assumptions and underlying definitions of each individual; differences unavoidably led to unremitting conflict.

That conflict was external as well. Christians, unwilling to give sacrifice to the traditional gods, were often persecuted – on a local scale through the second century, but by imperial decree occasionally through the third. As people attributed prosperity and all else to the gods, economic difficulties could easily be blamed on the Christians, who frequently accepted death rather than condone the old gods – though some gave in to offer sacrifices to pagan deities.

As the second century waned, Tertullian (c. 160 – c. 225) emerged, the first to write in Latin, speaking out against detractors, paganism, etc. Origen (185 – c. 254) taught in Alexandria and wrote prolifically – his views outside what became mainstream, but influential nonetheless. Tertullian first referenced (and thus invented) the Trinity – an idea that the single God consisted of three parts – Father, Son and Holy Spirit. All these are mentioned in the gospels, but never exactly linked. As such definitions are wont to grow in believers' imaginations, however, all these points seemed very real to pious thinkers of 200 CE: all three could be one and somehow maintain monotheism as valid.

Conflict over established theology concerning the Trinity boiled over by the late third century with the Arian controversy. Arius (c. 250 – 336), also of Alexandria, claimed that the *Son* – meaning Jesus, except that this doesn't reference the real person, but the vaunted fantasy of otherworldly *Christ*-ness he'd become – was subordinate to the *Father*. That viewpoint was logically drawn from Jesus' words in the Gospel of John (14:28) that the Father was greater. However, opposing views looked to John 10:30 ("I and the Father are one.") as indicating equality.

Huge conflict arose from this impasse. Again, such controversy is inevitable when debating ideas that have *no basis in reality*. Jesus, the real, visionary human, had referenced his "Father" to indicate a deity more loving and caring than the traditional aloof Yahweh – particularly in context of the *Kingdom*, that state of mind manifesting a life that worked well. Through oral traditions' unavoidable distortion and exaggeration through decades, that *Father* image took on its own meaning, along with the Holy Spirit (itself evolving from a state of heightened inspiration into being its own entity) and Jesus (by now, God's offspring), to become real "Persons".

Three persons, but all one. Who could argue with that? Uneducated peasants, roiling in superstition? Not likely. But other figures, themselves experts in their own minds, could and actually did. The Arian Controversy was settled like all other points of theology – not by rational argument, but by popularity and power.

That Fateful Fourth Century

As cultures evolve – nothing remains static – Christianity had changed considerably through the second and third centuries, growing in numbers and character. Distanced now from its parent Judaism, while it initially had appealed to poorer classes, for its general message gave hope to the downtrodden, it had slowly attracted wealthier and more sophisticated adherents. But the growing sect, with steadfast, uncompromising convictions, encountered growing resistance in conservative regions and via occasional traditionalist emperors. In 303, various emperors in the now regionalized Empire issued edicts that rescinded Christian rights, demanding that they comply with traditional practices.

Severe persecution continued until the ascendency of Constantine but reversed entirely as that single Caesar who had accumulated all power proceeded to downgrade all competitors. Constantine had won key triumphs under a banner of Christianity, interpreting that the Christian God helped the cause. Though he never fully rejected traditional gods, he ended persecution and made Christianity a favored religion in the Empire – quite an about-face.

Recognizing the array of regional versions of Christianity and consequent squabbling, Constantine convened a large gathering of regional representatives to iron out an agreeable doctrine. The Council of Nicea addressed the principal issue: Arianism – whether the "Son" had been around eternally or was brought into being by the "Father". Some 300 of the invited 1800 bishops from all regions – plus their contingencies – attended, as did Constantine, decked out in imperial finery.

Equipped with a reasoned argument – if a son is begotten, i.e., created, *there had to be a time when he didn't exist* – Arius lost. The alternate proposition: the Father, eternal, must have always been the Father, consequently always had the Son. They were thus deemed coequal, co-eternal and of the same substance.

That debate over existence and substance ironically epitomized the early church – for not a single component of their deemed Trinity really existed outside the fervent imaginations of those hearty yet archaic believers. Not only didn't the Trinity have substance, neither did their conclusion.

Such schisms are understandable in debates over noncepts. Primary proof of Arians and opponents alike consisted of excerpts from the Gospel of John, which itself was concocted – replete with internal conflict – by an anonymous set of writers that predated even Nicea by two murky centuries.

Yet another schism developed, Donatism, over whether officials who had given in to previous persecutions to offer sacrifices to pagan gods should be received again into communion. This echoed the Novatianist issue of a century prior. Again, disagreements develop easily over fanciful claims that have nothing to do with reality: conclusions will necessarily vary according to accepted beliefs and subtle assumptions – leading to conflict among parties who have drawn different conclusions.

The Result

The Catholic (meaning "universal") Church and its eastern sibling emerged from that first-century dispersion of loose-knit disciples and adherents into various regional components throughout the Empire. Followers grew in numbers early on, latching onto a diverse amalgam of conjecture all centered around the common theme of Christ as Savior – but incorporating many variations on emphasis, theology, dogma and ritual: was Jesus real or phantasm, subordinate to the Father or co-equal, of the same substance or different, created or always existed?

In time, one flavor of dogma came to dominate – with significant thanks to Constantine. Holders of that paradigm could then brand their newfangled religion as "orthodox", not because it was an accurate portrayal of reality, not because it was ordained by God or revealed through the Holy Spirit, not because Jesus had proclaimed it, but because it survived through popularity, wrangling and political force.

All other lines of interpretation became branded as heretical. The word "heresy," stemming from a Greek word meaning "to choose" (i.e., to choose a different interpretation from the standard) became loaded with negative implications that *any* reading outside accepted dogma was bad, evil and sinful – and highly frowned upon by the ever more powerful church hierarchy. Indeed, through early times as the church coagulated and gained power – awarded state religion status of the Roman Empire by 380 – it petrified (so to speak) a theology and pushed all varying ideas out. The *principal* argument for the version that ultimately became "orthodoxy" – self-defined by the holders as unquestionably correct – lay on a notion called *apostolic testimony*, leading to Apostolic Primacy.

The church asserted exclusive validity over and above other competing sects because, it claimed, it had received its traditions and writings directly from the apostles, who had gotten them from Jesus personally – been commissioned by him to carry the banner of "Truth".

Chief among the apostles had been Simon, the Rock – i.e., Peter. Via *Petrine Primacy*, then, wherein Simon Peter, held as the foremost disciple and first Pope in Rome, all popes would carry an ever more glorified mantle of inerrancy. That grew, ultimately, into *Papal Infallibility* – the impossibility of the current occupant of the position of ever being wrong (even when he clearly was). Stemming right back to the origins of budding Christianity, this level of claimed perfection rested on that Petrine supremacy.

Refuting that proclaimed notion, for starters: nobody bore the title of "Pope" until three centuries after Peter. This official designation, claimed to stem from Peter, is prime Church fabrication – typical revisionist history to concoct substance around pure fantasy.

But the unavoidable reality refuting the Catholic Church as valid based on Apostolic/Petrine Primacy is the *superficiality of the apostles as authorities on anything.* In the face of competition from other interpretations during those early centuries, Clement, Justin and other Apostolic Fathers argued that *their* view was valid, because they'd received it from highest authority. Polycarp held to Paul's letters and the gospels, not yet canonized, but already the ultimate in clout, as the core of their faith.

Thus, the whole, multifaceted declaration of unerring validity of orthodox Christianity ultimately rides *the original apostles' ability* to discern what Jesus meant and recognize what he was. If they misinterpreted his message and/or his nature, then what they passed along was not divine revelation, but inaccurate, insubstantial conjecture. And, if that's the case, then **the whole two-millennia-long, cornerstone influence on western development becomes baseless.**

The validity of Apostolic Authority, the rationale that undergirds Christianity, is easily gleaned *directly from the gospels themselves:* **the disciples to a man did not comprehend Jesus' message.** That's not only my evaluation – *that's what the gospel writers say!* Mark alone has at least 13 instances (Mk 4:13, 4:40, 5:31, 6:51-52, 7:18, 8:17-21, 8:32-33, 9:32, 9:38-39, 10:13-14, 10:24-26, 10:37-38, 14:4-6) where Jesus rebukes or criticizes his crew for missing the point, making wrong comments, dull interpretations, etc. Not a single situation is reported where any disciple actually demonstrates understanding of Jesus' Kingdom. No *single wise saying* or insightful expression ever comes from a disciple – not one! Not in the gospels, not in the Acts. NT Letters attributed to Peter, John and Jude, forgeries to begin with as those names were only later attached, are colloquial Christological ramblings with no recognition or reference to Jesus' inner Kingdom.

Writers of Matthew and Luke try to mitigate Mark's harsh critique by softening things they copied from that first gospel. But, despite that cover-up, the implication is overwhelming: *the disciples simply didn't grasp Jesus' meaning*. While he thought (Mk 9:1, Lk 9:27) that many of them would come to perceive his *Kingdom of God* before they died, clearly *none of them did*. After Jesus' execution, as reported in Acts, disciples focused on Judaic recognition of Jesus as Messiah, trying to impress them with miraculous signs like speaking in tongues – not *at all* referencing the Kingdom within.

So Apostolic Testimony is worthless – a farcical, insubstantial support for orthodox claims of authority.

Additionally, Christianity was principally *founded* **by Paul, not the disciples**. Paul took the message – *his own* message, *not that of Jesus* – to Greeks and other non-Jews, thus extracting Christianity from its Jewish incubation. And Paul wasn't a true apostle in the Apostolic Primacy sense: he'd never even encountered the real Jesus. He didn't know of Jesus' teachings, didn't care about his healing, his Kingdom *within* or any other facet of his life or message. Paul's Jesus was the booming hallucination in the sky, the resurrected Christ-figure stemming from his own superstitious imagination.

Thus, to claim ultimate church authority by holding Peter and the apostles up as witnesses to Jesus' direct message is phony. To perpetrate a message based on that multi-dimensional fallacy is akin to fraud.

When various gospels, letters and apocalyptic works were considered and confirmed for inclusion in what would become formalized as the official NT canon at the Second Council of Trullan in 692 – a process already underway in the fourth century – one key qualification was the *origin of the work*. (By the early third century, Origen already referenced the same 27 works; Irenaeus had embraced the gospels already by the late second; Marcion had proposed the canon circa 140.) To be seriously considered official and trusted, thus worthy of inclusion in the canon, the **work had to originate with or be closely connected to a disciple**. That was the key criterion: books, such as the *Didache* and *The Shepherd of Hermas* missed the cut because they lacked that connection.

But in reality, only seven or eight of the NT works – as earlier emphasized – *actually come from a known author*. And all those are letters of Paul. Unbeknownst to those early church fathers, who were duped by early and quite common forgery practices, *no single book* of the NT reliably stems from *any original, Aramaic-speaking, illiterate disciple*. Accepting traditions as valid and pseudepigraphic forgeries as authentic, church fathers assembled works for the NT which *didn't really have* the attributed apostolic authority.

So the church's entire paradigmatic foundation is based on **faulty reference** to apostles *who didn't comprehend Jesus' message anyway*.

The truly sad part of the Christian myth is that rampant New Testament flaws – all caveats I listed earlier – are well known to each denomination and to the Catholic hierarchy. When young students attend seminary at any but the most rigid evangelical fundamentalist schools, they study the gospels critically. They learn every point, every caveat, brought out earlier in connection to the gospels – the literary flaws, the errors, the forgeries, the conflicts and mutually exclusive claims – yet, when they're finished, they go preach the same old myth as "Truth".

Christian "Truth"

Christianity comprises theological and organizational attributes drawn from tradition, the gospels, etc. It includes, depending on the denomination, some variation off these points:

- A supreme, all-powerful creator God exists and one must profess faith in him, indeed *worship* him.

- He sent a Son, mystically conceived through a virgin by the Holy Spirit.
- That Son was crucified, died, buried and descended into Hell (that netherworld deep down from the archaic firmament model) and then rose again. He then ascended into heaven (that god-dwelling region above the firmament) and sits at the right hand of the Father (the other part of the three-part Godhead).
- Everybody will be judged upon death and absorbed into heaven or sent to Hell. (Catholicism features a waiting room called Purgatory – a feature dating from the late twelfth century, but rooted in truly ancient traditions, well pre-dating Christianity.)
- Various rites – rituals and sacraments – are performed to keep people on track and/or appease the God:
  - Baptism is performed, though its purpose is obscure. It likely simply dates back to John the Baptist as a purification ritual.
  - Confirmation might be done as an initiation rite, functioning as a means to impress ever new generations with Christianity as a brotherhood.
  - Eucharist, or Holy Communion, symbolizes consumption of Jesus' body and blood – extracted from gospel accounts and meaningful to the church, but a bit bizarre in nature.
  - Confession – Catholicism requires periodic confession of sins to allow repentance from them, presumably encouraging forgiveness by God.
  - Marriage, while the institution predates Christianity by millennia, is also considered a church-related function. (Direct church involvement was a relatively late development.)
  - Anointing and laying on of hands for healing purposes.

- Other factors and attitudes:
  - Privileged and pampered priesthoods: from popes to TV evangelists, religious leadership has often lived in high style off donations from church members.
  - Overt piety: priesthoods always put on a great show of godliness publicly while sometimes living excessively worldly lives privately.
  - Fear-mongering: Christianity has always kept its flocks in line through fear of divine retribution.

Now, in all those bullet points, did you notice any mention of an inner state of mind, wherein peace and success would be manifested? Was there any suggestion that trust and self-esteem were valued human qualities? *So, where did the Kingdom of God go?*

Given an overwhelming view that Jesus was the incarnated Son of God, virtually equal to the deity himself – at least on the same committee with him and the Holy Spirit – wouldn't it be of value to actually *pay attention* to what Jesus is quoted to have said? Love your neighbor, for example, doesn't have an asterisk next to it, allowing selective qualification – yet military chaplains regularly bless their troops to go out and kill others. Forgiving without limit doesn't imply judging and inflicting pain on others, including punishing children and people who disagree with you.

I could proceed to detail significant contributions of various visionaries who influenced the formulation of Christianity down through the ages:

- Augustine of Hippo (354 – 430) had insights into the body-mind connection and sincere concern for mankind.
- Pierre Abélard (1079 – 1142) brought a degree of scholastic approach to philosophizing about religion, introducing Aristotle and ethics to the mix.
- Thomas Aquinas (1225 – 1274) furthered the scholastic movement, bringing extensive philosophical thought,

including epistemology and ethics, into his theology – ultimately affecting official church stance and spurring revision. (Noteworthy observation: whenever the church historically revised its stated doctrine, it tacitly acknowledged that its earlier thinking was flawed – rendering all previous believers subject to that fallacy presented as truth. By accepting Aquinas' viewpoint, it admitted traditional teaching held as true prior to Thomas was erroneous.)

- Martin Luther (1483 – 1546), bristling at official sale of indulgences and other corruption, opened doors to reform.

But, there are far too many details, too many schisms, too many hypocrisies, too much corruption, too much banality – and too little relevance to the point here: *if you start with flawed ideas*, fallacious explanations about the reality each human faces daily, it doesn't matter how hallowed the scriptures become, how many millions have accepted the religion, how vaunted the church, how grand its buildings, how educated, erudite or wealthy the officials – *the resulting explanation can only be wrong*. Religion is supposed to explain how reality works. Christianity doesn't. It presents a synthetic explanation and indoctrinates adherents into believing it – at which point, to the gullible mind that's accepted it, it seems to be true.

I will close this exhaustive exploration of Christian "Truth" with an overview of where early efforts by those disciples, shocked at the sudden loss of their treasured leader, ultimately led:

The Outcome: Variations on a Theme by Paul

Many variations of Christianity existed before a single version won out as orthodoxy and eliminated the others. The schism of 1054 then split it into western (Roman Catholic) and eastern (Greek Orthodox) organizations. And many splintered off following that. Disagreements leading to these splits always boiled down to different conclusions based on differing doctrine by principal leaders and their flocks of followers.

Reality functions in a clear, reliable fashion: individual consciousness *always manifests its reality* in accord with its inner nature – Consciousness/Reality function as a Oneness. If you perceive that, having eliminated synthetic beliefs and definitions that distort the view, it's glowingly obvious.

But when beliefs cloud your view, leading to divergent philosophical conclusions, you easily disagree with others who perceive things similarly – but with differences based on subtle variations of held details. Christianity, by abandoning Jesus' insights – embodied in his parables – in favor of Paul's Jesus-in-the-sky superhero, rests its view on complex definitions and picturesque fantasies. Disagreements *have to* surface, as personal interpretation rides personal conviction.

Plus, *conflict itself* is a **direct consequence** of believing in any external god. Because the individual manifests personal reality, projecting causality out to another source imprints two divergent source patterns on the psyche – the real Self and a conceptualized other. Conflict invariably results, because one's intent and desire cannot be the same as that of the imagined deity.

So church groups and their leaders throughout time, invariably self-assured of their own righteous vision, are prone to argument, virtually guaranteed to disagree.

Were they to see life clearly – really perceive, personally, Jesus' *Kingdom* – there would be no disagreement. Of course, there would be no need for a church organization, either.

With Orthodoxy established theologically and politically, early Christians from the fourth through sixth centuries lashed out at their rival religions, pagan and other. They systematically destroyed priceless scrolls from earlier Greek and other sources, eliminating accounts from ancient Greek sources and many other origins containing any viewpoints that differed from mainline orthodox thinking. At their leaders' behest, they defaced and destroyed precious carvings and shrines from antiquity, as the superstitious early Christian couldn't tolerate ancient temples to pagan gods. Holding statues, images and reliefs from older religions from Britain to Egypt to be hosts of evil spirits and their genitalia to be perverse, they hacked at such carvings wherever found, defacing grand works of art from previous times on a widespread scale. They routinely hammered into rubble faces, breasts and genitalia – or chiseled them over with crosses.

Entire temples were bludgeoned into ruin. (Destroying other peoples' religious shrines is not uncommon. It recurred with the spread of Islam and continues to this day.)

Ultimately, the same fate awaited pagan believers themselves – heretics in the eyes of Christianity. In centuries following Constantine and adoption of Christianity as state religion, illegal acts punishable by torture and death – even by crucifixion – increased dramatically. Love your enemy? Love your neighbor? Organized Christianity from early on perfected love as theoretical and selective, something to be bandied about but not practiced in real life.

In the face of vigorous promotion of orthodoxy, early splinter groups diverging from standardized thinking died out: the Montanists barely made the sixth century, Novatians and Donatists not much longer. Gnosticism as a viable movement survived to perhaps 1400, but endures even today as a favored approach among some. A Gnostic sub-group, Manichaeism – followers of the prophet Mani from the mid-third century – held more complex views of Jesus and cosmogony. Once widespread, Manichaeism died out by about 1000.

Nestorians, early fifth-century followers of Nestorius, the Patriarch of Constantinople who tried to rationalize the incarnation of the divine Logos, survive to this day in Iran. Declared heretical in 431 over ideas concerning the nature of both Mary and Jesus (divine *plus* human), they simply created their own branch and have endured heavyweight competition of Islam and Buddhism.

The Paulicians emerged in Armenia around 650, spurred by – what else – a charismatic leader (Constantine of Mananalis) *who exclusively knew the right way*, focused on Paul's teaching. They died out slowly, surviving in isolated pockets into the nineteenth century.

After the Great Schism separated Roman Catholic from Greek Orthodox, the western church grew ever increasingly authoritarian and corrupt, spurring periodic rebellion regionally.

Catharism – hedging dualist/Gnostic ideals – emerged in southern France by 1150, influenced by Paulician ideas. When Pope Innocent III tried to bring them back into the fold, they killed his legate. So he sent a Crusading army to wipe them out. At a final massacre, with a mix of Catholics and Cathars holed up in St. Mary Magdalene church in Béziers, Arnaud-Amaury, an Abbot (the pope's commander), was reportedly – and famously – asked how to tell one from the other to avoid killing the Catholics. "Kill them all; the Lord will recognize His own," Arnaud replied in a timeless display of loving one's enemies. Some 20,000 of both sexes and all ages were mutilated, blinded, dragged by horses, used for target practice and otherwise slaughtered. (This pope was named "Innocent"?) When that didn't annihilate the sect, the Pope launched an Inquisition to rid the realm of anybody else who could think. Catharism died out by 1320 or so, with the last of them burned at the stake. Those recanting were, doubtless with holy pontifical grace, only tortured.

Of all the historic track of Catholicism, medieval Inquisitions (e.g., Episcopal Inquisition, some thirty years around 1200, and Papal in the 1230s) and later purges of dissenting heretics (Roman, sixteenth century onwards, Spanish and Portuguese Inquisitions) intimidated, tortured and executed untold thousands of people – all that in the name of a man who only ever preached love and forgiveness. The Catholic Church by the

Middle Ages, if not considerably sooner, was all about control and power.

North of Cathar territory, in Lyon, France, around 1170, people began to follow a man named Peter Waldo, who had criticized the excesses and intransigence of the church hierarchy. The Waldensians, rejecting the authority of the Catholic Church and its clergy, fared better than the Cathars. They survived to blend into the Protestant movement after 1500 – but just barely: in 1211, over 80 Waldensians were burned as heretics at Strasbourg. Avoiding the fate of the Cathars, they managed to go underground and survive.

When Martin Luther rebelled against the church's excesses – they were selling worthless indulgences, guaranteed to neutralize sin for ages, for large sums that allowed the clergy to live in posh style – he set off a chain reaction. Essentially by criticizing church-mandated interpretation of the Bible and by translating it into colloquial German, Luther emphasized that "Truth" lay in the scriptures, not in the mandated view of the church.

In short order, similar protests by John Calvin and others, building on earlier independence voiced by John Wycliffe against the church, had collectively launched the Protestant Reformation. Added to by King Henry VIII of England's eviction of Catholicism, which ultimately established Anglican and Episcopal lines and led to Methodism by the late eighteenth Century, the Reformation not only launched new denominations that later splintered even more, but set a trend of *being able* to branch off from an established sect.

The chart of offshoots gets complex. Anglicanism led to Puritans and Separatists; Anabaptists contributed to formation of Baptists; Calvinism begat Reformed Churches and Presbyterianism; Methodism contributed to establishing Adventists, the Holiness Movement and ultimately Pentecostalism. Tracking all these into modern times, with diverse variations of detail in belief and doctrine, would be prohibitively complicated – and fruitless.

The core notions underlying all these stem back to the same flawed conclusions, recycled Middle Eastern superstitions and supernatural inventions of the disciples and Paul – and ignore the highly insightful perspectives of Jesus of Nazareth, save for lip-service paid to gospel quotes not in the least understood. To compare how Presbyterians differ from Methodists in liturgy or core dogma can only yield an intricacy of favored beliefs.

And beliefs are only mind constructs. *Whatever* such mental fabrications an individual might hold, they seem to be true. All Christian deviations off original orthodox thinking, as well as that base line of deity worship *are only ideas*. Christian theology has *no substance:* it seems true to believers *because* and *only because* they believe it.

Religion is a substitute for understanding.

In no way does Christianity clarify how reality functions. It only distorts perception to confirm its synthetic notions. Christianity isn't a revealed truth, riding prophets' deep insights into God's mysteries; it is an invented "Truth", inflicting artificial proposals on gullible believers, mostly indoctrinated from early childhood into accepting conjecture – noncepts – as real.

Prime examples of blatant human gullibility are seen in two American-begotten religions: Mormonism and Jehovah's Witnesses.

Mormonism was fabricated in the dingy, early nineteenth-century recesses of the mind of Joseph Smith, principally as a means of lining up naïve females with whom to have sex. Huckster and treasure-digger, Smith concocted a series of yarns featuring golden plates delivered by angels with cryptic hiero-glyphics *only he* could translate with special glasses, wrote up a Biblical-sounding book by plagiarizing previous stories – including ones from the Bible – and rolled together a religion so totally beyond credibility that only pure country-rube suckers could buy into it. Many did, and with a freedom to marry multiple females and reproduce rampantly – then proselytize widely with new generations of deluded offspring – the religion has grown remarkably.

Mormonism's tenets, revision of history to suit its present fantasies and propaganda needs, closed society prone to shun apostates, cliquish business practices and secretive operation combine to assure stability among nearly 15 million highly brainwashed people.

The Jehovah's Witnesses revised its Bible to suit its bizarre beliefs, regularly revises its predictions – retroactively – when they fail to happen and dictates how and what to think to its seven million plus members. And it competes with Mormonism in door-to-door religion sales, seeking out the dull-witted to convert to its lunacy.

Without wasting space on details about either, I would mention them both – and the Amish, Mennonites, Unification Church and Scientologists in passing – as movements that glaringly demonstrate utter human gullibility: the propensity to absorb completely baseless, impossible ideas and have them appear valid and real.

Christianity: Unrelated to the Real Jesus

Considering the evolutionary track of ideas stemming from early disciple impressions concerning Jesus, the most remarkable factor is that the parables were noted and passed along *at all* – given the major bent of developing proto-Christianity to promote Paul's apocalyptic message and deification of Jesus.

Yeshua, a clear-thinking man of peasant roots two millennia ago, came to see life more clearly than his peers and more intimately than many a great philosopher. He explained the interactive workings of life, how you yourself manifest the qualities of your life – attracting good or bad based on trust and doubt. But his heavily indoctrinated Jewish peers didn't grasp his message. Nor did his dedicated followers. They turned his message on its head, founding a religious organization that very much replicated the elite Temple authorities that he had railed against in his day.

The real Jesus – seen only in the wit, humor and insight of his parables – would have been quite a humorous, personable, fun-loving guy. But the overly pious, mythical exaggeration created in archaic cultures and fomented by two thousand years of super-stition and political, power-grabbing intrigue of the church bears no resemblance to that real man.

Dot:
Good News

The word "gospel" derives from old Greek *euangélion* via Latin *evangelium*, which mean "good news." But being told, as per Christianity, you have no control over your fate, no freedom to act as your nature impels you without suffering eternal judgment based on prudish old mores, no personal value relative to some aloof, supreme deity and no creative power is *hardly* **good news** in any conceivable fashion. As false observations based on distorted perception, however, they aren't really news at all, but myth.

Here's good news: you are a free, fully powerful conscious entity currently engaged in an incarnation that you create. You do this partly because it's fun, challenging and interesting, partly because it provides a forum wherein you can grow – in character and in awareness of your unbounded nature.

Here's more good news: at death your consciousness exits your failing body, evaluates the life experience, encounters loved ones to ease the transition and eventually dives into another incarnation to further explore existence – and have a few laughs.

And more good news yet: problems you encounter *now* in health, relationships and success are all rooted within. You can change them for the better by delving into your own deeper mindset, finding the inner root and eliminating it there, at its core. You create, qualitatively, your experienced reality, just as you do your dreams. But you do so based on your total inner complex – fear and perceived powerlessness are integrated into ongoing events and relationships as much as your will is, producing negative events and flawed relationships along with desirable qualities.

You need only come *to see that clearly* to be able to eliminate inner conflict and struggle, discontent and fear – all of which, held within, contribute to manifesting that negative experience.

Exactly that journey into psychic value and meaning, connecting them to real experience, is the path Jesus, as all true mystics, traveled. The realm he found *within,* he tried to illustrate to his primitive peers. Frozen in traditional thinking, however, they couldn't understand. They scarcely were able to pass along his insightful perspectives clouded within common archaic notions and used his name to monger power and fear – counterfeiting fantasy and myth as "Truth" to a hundred subsequent generations.

I've clarified Jesus' path from holding traditional Jewish myth-based living restrictions and lore to an enlightened state which he attempted to communicate to his peers and mankind. I've illustrated the fearful, superstitious mindset of those peers: how, expecting a future Yahweh-dictated kingdom to be established by a Messiah, they twisted Jesus' inner Kingdom into an impending apocalyptic, cosmic event that never did happen – and never will.

I presented to you components of your own mindset: a determining *god,* capricious *luck, fate, chance* and the plethora of other seemingly causal – *yet illusory* – forces out there that appear to determine your life. *God* is the personified residue of ages of myth and fear, stemming from primitive, fearful, stone-knapping ancestors – the creative power you wield projected out to an imagined external force. *Luck,* like *fortune,* dangles as cultural residue of old, whimsical gods Lakshmi and Fortuna. *Chance* and all those external *forces* and *sources* man tries to manipulate roost on scientific tenets – definitions that acknowledge only an objective, outer reality, thus blinding holders to life's innate metaphysical connection to the consciousness that actually generates all effects.

The journey towards clarity involves perceiving those definitions and beliefs and all their projected power sources as mental constructs, not features of reality – and *eliminating them*. From the resultant "Clear Awareness", Jesus' *Kingdom of God* – a state to be found within – is obvious.

Parables as Illustrations

The only real value to the entire collection of 39 Old Testament works and 27 books in the New are Jesus' parables, preserved relatively intact, though muddled in a context otherwise lacking insight. All other teachings – repetitious rants from prophets, concocted entreaties from Yahweh, rules to follow, warnings of punishment, haphazard historicity – while culturally interesting, serve only to keep the devotee mired in archaic thinking and its resultant powerlessness.

But *gaining* a Clear Awareness of life's integrated nature solely by reading Jesus' parables and witticisms is all but impossible. They are too remote to modern understanding, too jumbled with traditional misinterpretation, too pastoral for a modern, techno-logical age. However, by scouring your mindset to eliminate its outmoded programming and rid it of inner negativity and struggle, so that you no longer blame external illusions for your own problems, you come to see the Oneness. Then – *and only then* – will you fully grasp Jesus' meaning, as I might weave it here into updated stories of our own time:

* * *

Clear Awareness is like getting into your car and realizing it will take you any place you want to go.

* * *

A businessman in the city developed sores on his skin, so he applied ointment prescribed by his physician – but they persisted. He tried acupuncture, but the ruptures didn't heal. He bought expensive vitamins and special herbs to try to cure the sores, but they got worse. Discouraged, thinking he didn't have long to live, he sold his operations and retired back to his hometown. The sores healed.

* * *

Clear Awareness is like an automatic sensor for your car's windshield wipers. When it begins to rain, hindering the view, the wipers come on with no effort.

* * *

Clear Awareness is like a golfer who kept hooking his drive, so he bought new clubs. He was so pleased at the improvement of his game that he entered a tournament. Walking in a winner following the last hole, he realized he had used his old clubs.

* * *

A colony of ants had built a complex set of hills and tunnels in a meadow. A boy came by and sat there to eat his sandwich. When he noticed ants getting on his bread, he threw it down and kicked the ant hills – then stomped on all the ants he could see. Shortly, grim-faced, he stalked off in a huff. The ants rebuilt their hills and slowly ate the leftover sandwich.

* * *

Clear Awareness is like a man who had a faulty refrigerator. Though it was new, looked great and featured an automatic ice-maker, external water tap, veggie crisper, self-defrosting and other fancy features, it froze the lettuce while the milk went sour.

He had the coolant replaced, then the controlling thermostat. When the lettuce still froze, he replaced the refrigerator with a simple model – no fancy frills. It worked right.

* * *

An avid veggie gardener regularly cursed the dandelions that sprouted continually and the purslane that spread throughout his garden. He spent years spraying them, pulling them up by the roots and hacking them angrily into shreds. Then he realized that they were not only edible, but tasted good and were very nutritious. Now guests remark at how crisp and tasty his salads are.

State of Mind: The Significance

You can't have a healthy forest full of blighted trees. Likewise, mankind will never achieve peace while its constituent humans are full of inner conflict.

But the path to peace is trod by *each individual alone*, because all roots to conflict lie within and can only be extracted by each human being personally. This path necessarily involves dispelling religious tenets – eliminating them, not finding a new set or refining the current batch.

It isn't so much that religion must die out for man to proceed to greater levels of awareness and accomplishment. It's that mankind must outgrow a mentality prone to substitute fanciful mind images – beliefs – for pure, direct recognition of reality. As that happens, religion will vanish.

Improvement in life for each individual, *you included*, comes, not when all of mankind improves, not even when the majority of humanity achieves inner peace – but when that individual achieves clarity in understanding and elimination of inner turmoil. For the specific experiential quality embodied in events and relationships encountered by *each and every person* depends not on any external factor, but on life values attracted, i.e., manifested, by each individual him- and herself.

You enter the Kingdom of Heaven when you see that innate correlation between Self and Reality – perceiving the Oneness clearly, that is, not just accepting that connection as a philo-sophical "Truth". For Truth is like a river that flows in a riverbed of its own making – eroding it ever deeper, the more you believe in it. Understanding requires seeing through the illusions presented by cultural "Truth" – and eradicating their fallacious roots.

Jesus recognized that. Obviously, I do, too. You must also.

The Final Account

Does Christianity, built on concocted ideas *about* Jesus rather than ideas promoted *by* him, have any positive aspects? I've pointed out much of the negative.

Actually Christianity, as a cultural movement, did nudge man beyond the pure myth and epic tales of archaic religions to a focus on human values and eternal existence. That was good – and appropriate for its early agricultural timeframe.

But the time comes when man must move on even farther, where proclamations and warnings to obey them no longer suffice.

Man lived for ages knapping stone and carving bones into tools by which he might accomplish his chores. But when bronze was developed, then iron, then steel, man put away, in turn, the older means. Knapped flints occupy museums as charming reminders of old ways.

Religion belongs there, too. Beside the Venus figurines, a huge relief of Amun-Ra and Zeus' grand statue should stand an empty platform with three hazy figures projected as holograms onto a misty cloud. *Behold!* The Trinity, forever bonded, on display as nebulous noncepts – monuments to man's fervent imagination, rampant fear and recycled ignorance.

But where stone was replaced by steel and plastic, gods and the religions that concoct them will be displaced by the simple recognition that creative power lies within the grasp of each person – not the manual grasp, but the conceptual. Jesus had that grasp – but vaunting him doesn't provide it for you or anybody. It takes it away.

Paul famously said in 1 Corinthians 13:11, "When I was a child, I talked like a child, I thought like a child, I reasoned like a child. When I became a man, I put childish ways behind me." Now it's time to pack Paul away, too, along with the religion he spawned – and return to Jesus' pristine recognition that the untarnished view of a child, clear and perceptive, undistorted by artificial beliefs and definitions, is far superior to a muddled view laden with complex, unsubstantial theology.

Man must outgrow religion – along with science and all such analytic philosophies that substitute *ideas* for direct perception of *what is*. The limited mind, clouded by its favorite illusions, will always, always, always confuse its synthetic "Truth" for Reality. Only the advanced psyche, freed of its ever-illusory beliefs, will perceive its innate connection to the Reality it encounters.

Select Bibliography

The Gospel According to Jesus – Stephen Mitchell, HarperCollins Publishers, New York, NY, 1991

Who on Earth was Jesus – David Boulton, O-Books, John Hunt Publishing, Ripley, UK, 2008

The Historical Jesus – John Dominic Crossan, HarperSanFrancisco, 1991

Jesus, Interrupted: Revealing the Hidden Contradictions in the Bible – Bart D. Ehrman, Harper Collins, 2009

The New Testament: A Historical Introduction to the Early Christian Writings, – Bart D. Ehrman, Oxford University Press, 2007

Jesus: Apocalyptic Prophet of the New Millennium – Bart D. Ehrman, Oxford University Press, 2001

Early Christian Doctrines – J. N. D. Kelly, Harper & Row, 1978

The Five Gospels: What Did Jesus Really Say? – Robert W. Funk, Roy W. Hoover and the Jesus Seminar, HarperSanFrancisco, 1993

A History of the Jews – Abram Leon Sachar, Ph.D., Alfred A. Knopf, Inc., 1967

The Jesus Dynasty – James D. Tabor, Simon & Schuster, New York, NY, 2006

The Changing Faces of Jesus – Geza Vermes, the Penguin Press, 2000

Tao Te Ching – Lao Tzu, translated by Gia-Fu Feng and Jane English, Vintage Books, 1997

A History of God – Karen Armstrong, Ballantine Books, New York, 1993

The Story of Civilization, Caesar and Christ – Will and Ariel Durant, Simon & Schuster, New York, NY, 1944

The Holy Bible, various authors, mostly anonymous, New York International Bible Society, 1973-1978

The Encyclopedia of Gods – Michael Jordan, R. R. Donnelley & Sons, 1993

The Ancient Gods – E. O. James, G. P. Putnam's Sons, New York 1960

The Oxford Guide to Philosophy, (edited by) Ted Honderich, Oxford University Press, 2005

The Ultimate Encyclopedia of Mythology – Arthur Cotterell and Rachel Storm, Hermes House 1999, 2007

The Parables of Jesus, Red Letter Edition – The Jesus Seminar, Robert W. Funk, Bernard Brandon Scott, James R. Butts, 1988

Various Online References, Principally...

Ancient Greek Names:

http://tekeli.li/onomastikon/Ancient-World/Greece/Male.html

Ancient Names in general:

http://tekeli.li/onomastikon/Ancient-World/index.html

Ancient Jewish Names:

http://www.20000-names.com/male_hebrew_names.htm

http://www.behindthename.com/names/usage/jewish/2

Various Online Maps of Ancient Middle East

Various Online Reconstructions of Ancient Cities

Various Wikipedia References for Overviews on many topics: Biblical and Early Christian Characters, Nabataean Trade Routes, Greek figures, Heliocentrism, Eratosthenes, Seleucus of Seleucia, Philolaus, Aristarchus of Samos

Original Cover Image: **Abraham M. Nehrer**

Grammar consultation and proofreading: thanks to **Sylvia Garzotto**

Proofreading: thanks to **Wally Mastropaolo**

Consultation on map creation: thanks to **Jack Kramer**

CHRISTIAN
ALTERNATIVE

Throughout the two thousand years of Christian tradition there
have been, and still are, groups and individuals that exist in the
margins and upon the edge of faith. But in Christianity's
contrapuntal history it has often been these outcasts and
pioneers that have forged contemporary orthodoxy out of
former radicalism as belief evolves to engage with and
encompass the ever-changing social and scientific realities. Real
faith lies not in the comfortable certainties of the Orthodox, but
somewhere in a half-glimpsed hinterland on the dirt track to
Emmaus, where the Death of God meets the Resurrection, where
the supernatural Christ meets the historical Jesus, and where the
revolution liberates both the oppressed and the oppressors.

Welcome to Christian Alternative... a space at the edge where
the light shines through.

Printed and bound by CPI Group (UK) Ltd, Croydon, CR0 4YY